THE LETTER COLLECTIONS
OF ANSELM OF CANTERBURY

INSTRVMENTA PATRISTICA ET MEDIAEVALIA

Research on the Inheritance of Early and Medieval Christianity

61

Samu Niskanen

THE LETTER COLLECTIONS
OF ANSELM OF CANTERBURY

BREPOLS

2011

INSTRVMENTA PATRISTICA ET MEDIAEVALIA

Research on the Inheritance of Early and Medieval Christianity

Founded by Dom Eligius Dekkers († 1998)

© 2011 BREPOLS ❧ PUBLISHERS (Turnhout – Belgium)
Printed in Belgium
D/2011/0095/205
ISBN 978-2-503-54075-7

Isän muistolle

Iustitia nostra superhabundare debet iustitie scribarum
Peter of Celle, *Ep. 33*

TABLE OF CONTENTS

VI. CONCLUSION

PLATES, FIGURES, TABLES

PLATES

Plates are reproduced by kind permission of the following:
1, 10: © British Library Board. All Rights Reserved
2, 3, 4, 5: Lambeth Palace Library
6, 9: The Master and Fellows of Corpus Christi College, Cambridge
7, 8: Bibliothèque nationale de France
11: The Dean and Chapter of Hereford Cathedral

FIGURES

TABLES

ACKNOWLEDGEMENTS

This book was written under the auspices of several institutions and individuals. My *laudes* begin with the latter. Notes and references will show how greatly I have benefitted from other scholars, in particular from Professor Richard Sharpe, Professor Rodney Thomson, and Dr Teresa Webber, who extensively commented on early versions of this study and provided subsequent advice, and in Professor Sharpe's case, also postdoctoral supervision. A heavy debt of gratitude is also owed to Michael Gullick, who has generously shared with me his extraordinary palaeographical and codicological erudition. I have likewise gained exceedingly from instruction by my postgraduate supervisors in Helsinki, Professors Tuomas Heikkilä, Outi Merisalo, and Erkki Kouri. Dr Hugh Doherty, Dr Elina Screen, who translated an early Finnish version into English, and Dr James Willoughby have made several crucial observations. There are indeed many more individuals to thank, but I name only a few: Markku Kekäläinen, Jesse Keskiaho, Anja-Inkeri Lehtinen, Dr Ian Logan, Martti Mela, Dr Teemu Roos, Professor Marc Smith, Jaakko Tahkokallio, and Dr David Woodman. Finally, I am very grateful to the anonymous peer-reviewers of the series for their prudent advice and to Luc Jocqué of the Corpus Christianorum for his tolerance and understanding to recurrent delays in my finishing the manuscript.

During the years this project has taken, I have been provided by several institutions and many foundations. Among the former were the History section in the University of Helsinki; the Academy of Finland in the project 'Books in Transition' (no. 121785); the Institutum Romanum Finlandiae; the History Faculty, University of Oxford, and Jesus College, Oxford. Among the latter were the Niilo Helander Foundation, the Emil Aaltonen Foundation, the Cultural Foundation (Päivi Priha Fund, and Alma and Unio Hiitonen Fund), the Jenny and Antti Wihuri Foundation, the Ella and Georg Ehrnrooth Foundation, and the Oskar Öflund Foundation, the British Academy / the Royal Society, and the Academy of Finland. My gratitude to all of these weighs heavy. Research has taken me to several libraries and I should especially like to thank the staff in the Biblioteca Apostolica Vaticana, the Bibliothèque

nationale de France, the Bodleian Library, the British Library, the Cambridge University Library, the Herzog-August-Bibliothek, the Lambeth Palace Library, the Merton College Library, the National Library, Helsinki, the Parker Library, the Troyes Médiathèque, and the Wren Library.

The final thanks belong to my wife. You made it all possible.

Oxford, February 2011

Samu Niskanen
Newton Fellow, Jesus College

ABBREVIATIONS

AEp.	Anselm, *Epistola(e)*
ASV	Archivio Segreto Vaticano
BAV	Biblioteca Apostolica Vaticana
BL	British Library
BM	Bibliothèque municipale
BMC	*Catalogue of Books printed in XVth century now in the British Museum*, 10 vols., London, 1908–1971.
BNF	Bibliothèque nationale de France
BRUO	A. B. Emden, *A Biographical Register of the University of Oxford* AD *1501–1540*, 3 vols., Oxford, 1957–1959.
CBMLC	*Corpus of British Medieval Library Catalogues*
CCCM	*Corpus Christianorum. Continuatio medieualis*, 1–, Turnhout, 1971–.
CCSL	*Corpus Christianorum. Series Latina*, 1–, Turnhout, 1954–.
CMDF	C. Samaran & R. Marichal, *Catalogue des manuscrits en écriture latine portant des indications de date, de lieu ou de copiste*, Paris, 1959–.
CMDNL	G. I. Lieftinck & J. P. Gumbert, *Manuscrits datés conservés dans les Pays-Bas. Catalogue paléographique des manuscrits en écriture latine portant des indications de date*, Amsterdam, 1964–1988.
CPL	E. Dekkers & E. Gaar, *Clauis patrum Latinorum*, 3rd edn., Turnhout, 1995.
EEA	*English Episcopal Acta*
EHR	*English Historical Review*
GW	*Gesamtkatalog der Wiegendrucke*, Leipzig, 1925–.
HC	W. A. Copinger, *Supplement to Hain's Repertorium bibliographicum*, London, 1895–1902.
LexMA	*Lexikon des Mittelalters*, 9 vols., Munich, 1980 1999.
Med.	*Meditatio(nes)*
Memorials	*Memorials of Saint Anselm*, eds. R. W. Southern & F. S. Schmitt, *Auctores Britannici Medii Aeui*, 1, London, 1969.
Mon.	*Monologion*
NMT	[*Nelson's*] *Medieval Texts*, Edinburgh, 1949–65.
OMT	*Oxford Medieval Texts*, Oxford, 1967–.
Or.	*Oratio(nes)*
PL	*Patrologia cursus completus. Series Latina*, 217 vols., Paris, 1844–55.

Prolegomena	F. S. Schmitt, *Prolegomena seu ratio editionis*, in *SAO²*, pp. 1–244.
Pros.	*Proslogion*
RS	*Rerum Britannicarum medii aeui scriptores*, 99 vols., London, 1858–1911, 1961.
SAO	*Sancti Anselmi Opera Omnia*, 6 vols., ed. F. S. Schmitt, Seckau, Rome, Edinburgh, 1938–61.
SAO²	*Sancti Anselmi Opera Omnia*, 2 vols., ed. F. S. Schmitt, Stuttgart – Bad Cannstatt, 1968 [repr. 1984].
Walther	Hans Walther, *Carmina medii aeui posterioris latina I. Alphabetisches Verzeichnis der Versanfänge mittellateinischer Dichtungen*, Göttingen, 1959.

SIGLA

Witnesses to the Major Collections

N	London, BL Cotton Nero A. VII
M	London, Lambeth Palace 224
D	Cambridge, Corpus Christi College 299
U	Cambridge, University Library Dd. 9. 5
L	London, Lambeth Palace 59
L^a	Anselmiana on fols. 160v–190r in L
P	Paris, BNF lat. 2478
E	Cambridge, Corpus Christi College 135
F	London, BL Royal 5 F. IX
J	London, BL Royal 8 D. VIII
C	London, BL Cotton Claudius A. XI
C^a	The first section of Canterbury letters in C (fols. 57r–81r)
C^b	The second section of Canterbury letters in C (fols. 81r–161v)
C^2	Oxford, Bodleian Library Add. C. 296
C^3	Cambridge, Trinity College O. 10. 16
C^4	Paris, BNF lat. 13415
C^5	London, BL Stowe 33
V	Paris, BNF lat. 14762, fols. 25r–204v
V^a	The first section of Canterbury letters in V (fols. 100r–125r)
V^b	The second section of Cantrbury letter in V (fols. 125r–204r)
V^2	Paris, BNF lat. 14762, fols. 1r–23v
V^3	Troyes, Médiathèque 836
O	Troyes, Médiathèque 1614
G	Trier, Stadtbibliothek 728/282
B	Brussels, Bibliothèque Royale de Belgique 8386–96

Witnesses to the Minor Collections

S	*Schmitt 15*
S^1	Cambridge, Trinity College B. 1. 37
S^2	London, BL Royal 5 E. xiv
W	*Wilmart 14*
W^1	London, BL Cotton Claudius E. I
W^2	Vatican City, BAV Ottob. lat. 173
W^3	Paris, BNF lat. 15694
W^4	Brussels, Bibliothèque Royale de Belgique 2004–10
W^5	Troyes, Médiathèque 513
W^6	Paris, BNF lat. 4878

W^7	Paris, Bibliothèque de l'Arsenal 984
W^8	Oxford, Bodleian Library Canon. Pat. Lat. 204
W^9	Cambridge, Peterhouse 246
W^{10}	Worcester, Cathedral Library F. 41
W^{11}	Worcester, Cathedral Library F. 132
R	*Sharpe 5*
R^1	London, BL Harley 203
R^2	Oxford, Merton College 19
R^3	Vatican City, BAV Vat. lat. 310
R^4	Vatican City, BAV Vat. lat. 10611
R^5	Paris, BNF lat. 14502
H	Hereford Cathedral P. I. 3

Other Manuscripts Including Anselmian Correspondence

A^1	London, BL Cotton Appendix 56 and Vespasian E. iv
A^2	London, BL Add. 32091
A^3	Oxford, Bodleian Library Laud. misc. 344
A^4	Durham Cathedral B. IV. 24
A^5	Paris, BNF lat. 17400
A^6	London, BL Stowe 31
Y^1	Paris, BNF lat. 2887
Y^2	Vienna, Nationalbibliothek 533
Z^1	Troyes, Médiathèque 513, fols. 45v–102v
Z^2	Vatican City, BAV Vat. lat. 6024

Hypothetical Collections, Compilations, and Manuscripts

α	the first major collection, Bec letters, *c.* 1086
β	the second major collection, Bec letters and a very few Canterbury ones, *c.* 1094
β^1	the first witness to the β collection, Christ Church, *c.* 1094, removed to Bec
β^2	Christ Church, *c.* 1094, copied from β^1
ω	the third major collection, Bec and Canterbury letters, apparently a register, Christ Church, not begun before 1101 but possibly *c.* 1106
γ	a compilation of Canterbury letters, derived from ω and L
δ	a great compilation of Bec and Canterbury letters from materials at Bec
δ^a	the first sequence of Canterbury letters in δ, derived from β^1 and Bec archives
δ^b	the second sequence of Canterbury letters in δ, derived from γ
$\varkappa$	an intermediary between M and DU

ε	a clutch of Bec and Canterbury letters deriving from β^I and Bec archives
ζ	an intermediary between ε and *Ga*, also including materials from Christ Church
φ	the archetype of *Wilmart 14*
χ	an intermediary between φ and W^3W^4
ψ	an intermediary between W^4 and W^5W^6, France
σ	an intermediary between R^I and $R^2R^3R^4R^5$
η	a source potentially behind the minor collections
θ	a source potentially behind *Wilmart 14* and *H*
ι	a source potentially behind *Schmitt 15* and *Wilmart 14*

Printed Editions

a	ed. Peter Danhauser, Nuremberg: Caspar Hochfeder, 27 March 1491 (*GW* 2032)
a^2	ed. Peter Danhauser, Strasbourg: Georg Husner, 1496×97 (*GW* 2034)
a^3	ed. Peter Danhauser, Basel: Johan Amerbach, 1496×97 (*GW* 2033)
a^4	ed. Anton Democharès, Paris, 1544 (the letters as in Danhauser)
b	ed. Jean Picard, Cologne, 1612
c	ed. Luc d'Achery, Paris, 1669
d	ed. Gabriel Gerberon, Paris, 1675 and 1721
e	ed. Étienne Baluze, Paris, 1683 and 1700

Note on sigla

Roman sigla refer both to entire physical witnesses of Anselm's correspondence — that is, entire manuscripts and early printed books — and to their witness to his letters. So far as possible I have retained those of Schmitt, which were also used in Southern's discussion. Where I occasionally replace one or add new ones for the witnesses unknown to his edition, the guiding principle is that the manuscripts that belong to the same sub-branch are referred to by the same letter, differentiated by a suprascript number.

Hypothetical witnesses are denoted by Greek sigla. Since the physical qualities of lost witnesses are often more or less imperceptible through the surviving evidence, Greek sigla have necessarily a less definite denotation than Roman ones. While most of the lost witnesses proposed in this study were, no doubt, books, some may have incorporated single-sheet letters, possibly representing Anselm's archive (this applies to α in particular), and some may have comprehended several separate units, such as folia, bifolia, and quires (this applies especially to hypothetical

sources behind the minor collections). In other words, a given Greek siglum may designate nothing more definite than a particular stemmatic
stage, with no implication for what this may have embodied physically.
Where possible, I naturally seek to observe the material realities of lost
witnesses through our surviving evidence. With regard to collection β,
two distinct manuscripts can be perceived, one derived from the other.
These two witnesses will be distinguished from the rest by way of a
suprascript number attached to their Greek siglum. In other words, the
modified sigla β^1 and β^2 are applied in a similar manner to the sigla for
surviving manuscripts, whereas the simple siglum β has a looser character, denoting the text to which β^1 and β^2 provided witness. But even
here there is a considerable measure of uncertainty, since it appears
that β^2 may have consisted of disconnected quires, one of which had
been lost before a subsequent collection was made at Christ Church.

As a reflection of the intrinsic complexity of some of the witnesses,
suprascript letters have also been used, for both surviving manuscripts
and lost witnesses. The members of one sub-branch include two stemmatically distinct sequences of Canterbury material, to which suprascript
letters [a] and [b] refer. Thus, V denotes the whole exemplar of Anselm's
letter collection in Paris, BNF lat. 14762, fols. 25–204, while V^b denotes
the second sequence of Canterbury letters in it. However, V^2 refers to a
booklet — originally a distinct manuscript — which includes a selection
of letters copied from V and which was bound to that manuscript at
some point (now fols. 1–23 in BNF lat. 14762). Finally, the application
of the siglum L^a — too well-established in previous research to be replaced here — differs fundamentally from the other sigla appended with a
suprascript letter. L^a denotes appendices on fols. 160v–190r in Lambeth
Palace 59.

I. INTRODUCTION

1. Context and Parameters

Anselm of Canterbury (1033–1109) was a prolific letter writer. The modern edition of his correspondence includes 475 pieces, mostly letters sent by him.[1] This makes up approximately half of his known literary output. No original letter survives, so we are entirely dependent on letter collections.[2] There was no single canonical version of the collection, and the extant manuscripts generally differ substantially: the largest medieval compilations include over four hundred letters, while the smallest contain only a handful. No authorial manuscript survives. Certain references in Anselm's letters reveal, however, that he collected his correspondence on more than one occasion.

In 1491 some letters were printed for the first time as part of Anselm's *opera omnia*. From then on, several generations of European printers have published his works, very often including letters as well.[3] F. S. Schmitt OSB prepared a critical edition, published in six volumes over the period 1938–61; this was reprinted in 1968 and again in 1984.[4] The modern textual criticism of the letter

---

[1] *Sancti Anselmi Opera Omnia* [*SAO*], vols 3–5, ed. F. S. Schmitt, Seckau, Rome, Edinburgh, 1946–51. The last three documents (473–475) are labelled 'cartae'.

[2] When referring to Anselmian letters, the formulation 'letter collection' is used to denote either the whole body of Anselm's surviving letters or a collection of letters that is *potentially* authorial. In connection with the group of 'the minor collections', however, the application of the term is slightly less precise, as will be explained in due course. Some surviving witnesses to the collections differ significantly from their potentially authorial (ur-)source in the arrangement and the selection of letters, of which a fine example is manuscript *M*. Such witnesses will be labelled compilations.

[3] *Cur Deus homo* had twice previously been published in print, in 1474 at the latest (*GW* 2035) and in around 1485 (*GW* 2036). Some early editions of Anselm's texts are listed in *International Bibliography: Anselm of Canterbury*, ed. K. Kienzler (with E. Brinacesco, W. Fröhlich, H. Kohlenberger, F. Van Fleteren, C. Viola), *Anselm Studies*, 4, Lewiston, Queenston, Lampeter, 1999, pp. 13–17.

[4] The original printing of the first volume (Seckau 1938) was destroyed by Nazis and this was replaced by the Edinburgh printing of 1946. The sixth volume includes appendices.

collection had begun in the mid 1920s, with the publication of a
long series of articles in *Revue Bénédictine*, intended to prepare the
ground for Schmitt's editorial work. Since the publication of the
edition, the subject has been touched on in many studies, including some recent monographs. At first glance, the situation appears
promising, but this impression is false. Schmitt never put together
a comprehensive and systematic survey of the textual tradition,
and furthermore the critical apparatus of his edition reveals that
at times his work was unsystematic and inaccurate. His *codices
collati* often lack important witnesses, and the apparatus does not
give all the significant textual variants of the collated manuscripts.
In short, it is impossible to understand the interrelationship of the
manuscripts from the edition. Last but not least, Schmitt's work
was influenced by his incomplete understanding of the tradition's
structure and its witnesses' quality. It is thus unsurprising that
subsequent research in the field has been marked by strident disputes.

This study, therefore, seeks to demonstrate how Anselm's letters
have come down to us and how our surviving witnesses relate to
one another. It also aims to define historical contexts within which
the foundations of the textual tradition were laid as well as those
in which our most important manuscripts were produced: where,
when, and at whose initiative were our key witnesses to Anselm's
correspondence made? All known manuscripts, as well as the
printed editions from the period of the incunabula up to the publication of the *Patrologia Latina* and beyond, will be examined in
the light of these questions, in so far as is relevant. Certain earlier
discussions of these issues must also be assessed in detail, because
the letter collection has attained an unusually significant position
in the field of biographically-oriented research on Anselm. In short,
this study seeks to establish a store and framework of information
essential to the execution of a critical edition.

2. The Sources

Defining the medieval letter (or indeed the letter of any period)
is problematic. According to Giles Constable, 'for most writers in
the Middle Ages a letter was any work which fitted the epistolary
situation, was furnished with a salutation and subscription and
paid at least lip-service to the requirements of the *modus episto-*

laris'.[5] I shall return to the structure of the medieval letter and the concept of the *modus* or *stylus epistolaris* in chapter II. Here it is sufficient to note that, though the problems of definition associated with the medieval letter apply to certain Anselmian texts too, the medieval collections and compilations of his correspondence help set relatively clear boundaries for my examination. His works that, despite taking an epistolary form, often circulated in conjunction with his other writings in the medieval period fall outside the remit of this study. *Epistola de incarnatione Verbi*[6] sent to pope Urban II; the correspondence between Anselm and Walram, the bishop of Naumburg (that is, *Epistola de sacrificio azymi et fermentati, Epistola Waleranni episcopi ad Anselmum*, and *Epistola de sacramentis ecclesiae*[7]); and the letter of dedication addressed to Lanfranc in conjunction with the *Monologion* belong to this group.[8] Schmitt excluded these texts from the letter volumes of his edition, though his letter numbering covers the exchange between Anselm and Walram by cross-referencing these three texts to the second volume.[9] Where these texts appear within Anselm's correspondence in our manuscripts, they are naturally material for this study. Letters misattributed to him fall outside its scope.[10]

Furthermore, only manuscripts including more than two Anselmian letters, clearly arranged in association with each other, have been studied. A preliminary list of manuscripts rejected for this reason is presented in appendix II. Collections that are clearly associated with another author, even when the correspondence between Anselm and that author is included as a consecutive section of letters, are studied only briefly in appendix I; this also applies to collections comprising letters by more than one author. Finally, this

---

[5] G. CONSTABLE, *Letters and Letter-Collections, Typologie des sources du moyen âge occidental*, 17, Turnhout, 1976, p. 25.

[6] *SAO*, vol. 2, pp. 3–35.

[7] Respectively *SAO*, vol 2, pp. 223–232; pp. 233–238; pp. 239–242.

[8] *SAO*, vol. 1, pp. 5–6.

[9] *AEp*. 415–417.

[10] See F. S. SCHMITT, 'Die echten und unechten Stücke der Korrespondenz des hl. Anselm von Canterbury', *Revue Bénédictine*, 65 (1955), *passim*. E.g. Wolfenbüttel, Herzog-August-Bibliothek 3181 (*olim* 19. 12. Aug.), fols. 1r–5r, 3199 (*olim* 19. 26. 2. Aug.), fols. 1r–4v (*Epistola s. Anselmi Cantuariensis ad coepiscopos Angliae de conceptione uirginis Marie*, i.e. Eadmer of Canterbury, *De conceptione sanctae Mariae*).

study includes only a preliminary consideration of Eadmer's *Historia nouorum in Anglia*, although it contains an extensive selection from Anselm's correspondence. *Historia nouorum* has been omitted on methodological and pragmatic grounds: the work represents a different genre, and it played only a relatively modest part in the tradition. It is naturally taken into account where it has transmitted letters, as in the case of Lambeth Palace 224.

The manuscript witnesses this study covers fall into two principal groups, which are independent of each other. The first group is made up of the manuscripts that descend from the great collections that were drawn up in Anselm's lifetime, or in the case of the last of these, possibly soon afterwards, at both Bec and Canterbury. Well before this study, it has been noted that on Anselm's own testimony, his letters were being collected on three different occasions in the course of his long career. I shall argue that our textual evidence corresponds to this scheme, that after textual criticism, three major collections do emerge.[11] I call the three collections α and β and ω. I have named this group the 'major collections'. Although some manuscripts in this branch have only a few letters, the majority of them, including all the most significant ones, are large and comprise tens or hundreds of letters. Our witnesses are generally very heterogeneous and it is common for them to represent more than just one of the three major collections.

The second group is composed of the 'minor collections'. The branch covers three distinct collections and one compilation, which are all independent of the previous group, but are related to one another. I refer to the three collections by the titles *Schmitt 15*, *Wilmart 14*, and *Sharpe 5*. The fourth sub-branch in this group, labelled as a compilation thanks to its characteristics and limited transmission, is represented by a single manuscript, Hereford Cathedral P. I. 3; this is manuscript *H*. The selection of letters in this branch is very limited: our largest witness, S^1, includes twenty-one letters (of which six are later additions) and the smallest, *H*, only three.

As the study focuses on the collections of Anselm's letters, the letters themselves are secondary to it. Individual letters will be

---

[11] Tripartite solutions have been proposed before me, but these remain, as I shall argue, slightly misleading and are therefore unhelpful.

treated with a view to illuminating aspects of the transmission of the correspondence.

3. METHODOLOGY

This study applies both the traditional, i.e. genealogical, methods of textual criticism, often associated with the names of Karl Lachmann and Paul Maas, and a new computer-based method to its central task of determining relationships between manuscripts. Since it is impossible to take every variant into account in a body of text as extensive as Anselm's correspondence, I established two different research corpora for detailed study.

(One.) I have collated thirteen letters, that is *AEp*. 1–5, 8, 13, 37, 41, 45, 65, 161, and 162. Appendix III lists the manuscripts used in or absent from these collations. Extensive coverage was the most important criterion in selecting the sample; the letters in question appear in both of the two groups of manuscripts presented above, the major and the minor collections. This accounts for the weighting of the selection towards Anselm's Bec correspondence (letters 1–147 in Schmitt's edition). My selection includes all the Bec letters found in *Wilmart 14* and *Sharpe 5*, and the greater part of those (10/15) included in *Schmitt 15*. In other words, the selection provides good, sometimes excellent, coverage of the letters in the minor collections. In addition, the letters selected are present in all the most central witnesses to the Bec branch of the group of the major collections, that is manuscripts *N* and *CV*, and (with the exception of *AEp*. 65) in the key witnesses to the Canterbury branch of the group, that is *LPE*; manuscript *F*, another very important — albeit heavily abridged — member of the Canterbury branch, includes four out of the eleven Bec letters in my selection.[12] From the Canterbury correspondence, I have selected *AEp*. 161 and 162. These have a special value above the other archiepiscopal letters, as they are the *only* two included in all the central witnesses to the tradition of the Canterbury correspondence in the major collections.

(Two.) I have used Schmitt's apparatus to help select some 700 passages of text, across the entire time span of the letter collection. These passages have been checked in each of the manuscripts

---

[12] *AEp*. 2, 8, 13, 37.

in question, since in most cases Schmitt did not include all the witnesses and at times the information in his apparatus is incorrect. Where possible, I have sought to select readings that resulted from alterations or scribal errors that would have been difficult or impossible to correct at a later date without recourse to another exemplar. Certain letters, disseminated in significantly different versions, are of particular importance.

The significant limitations of the genealogical method are well known. The most important of these results from contamination or horizontal transmission, a text's derivation from more than one source. Contamination is likely to affect texts that were frequently copied, as well as those that consist of several more or less autonomous textual bodies (such as letters) that could be easily removed and replaced. The possibility that an author might have produced several versions of his own work, by editing, elaborating, or enlarging it after first publication, constitutes another serious impediment. Our text, Anselm's letter collection, provides a good example of a tradition beset by these problems. On the one hand, we have his own testimony that he possibly authored more than one collection of his letters. On the other hand, there are a number of early survivors coming from a relatively short period (some contemporary to Anselm), which reflect active use of multiple sources; letters were sometimes gathered from several manuscripts and errors were occasionally corrected through recourse to secondary exemplars. As a result, the genealogical approach is not enough.

Therefore, I commissioned computer-based analyses of the letters I transcribed, applying the Compression-based method by Roos, Heikkilä, and Myllymäki (hereafter RHM). RHM does not generate a stemma along the principles of the genealogical approach, but produces a tree, with three edges connected to each of its nodes. An RHM-tree thus portrays the tradition in a different way from the genealogical stemma. It is particularly useful in determining groups of manuscripts and establishing their interrelationships. The position of the manuscripts in the RHM-tree is naturally determined by analysing the variants, although the RHM method differs from the classical approach in valuing all readings equally, and not classifying them as 'significant' or 'non-significant'. RHM has been further extended with the *Bootstrap method*, which is

implemented using the *Phylip programme*.[13] This method produces a consensus tree. Each edge of a consensus tree is determined by selecting a random sample of 100 passages from the material to be analyzed and establishing how often a particular result is achieved, with 100/100 the most definite result possible. The programme then uses its results to build the most convincing stemma possible. The report also indicates the statistical validity of the location of each of the manuscripts in the stemma (i.e., the number of positive matches out of the sample of 100). In a recent article, Roos and Heikkilä argue that the RHM method should be employed alongside the traditional tools of textual scholarship: standard textual criticism, palaeography, codicology, and the study of the historical context.[14] I agree: each of these approaches has contributed to my results. Computer-based analyses have enabled me to test the results achieved in traditional ways. Furthermore, they have refined my conclusions regarding the contamination affecting the earliest stages of the transmission, which is difficult to measure through Maasian approaches.

Textual evidence is crucial, but it is not always the only or even the most decisive criteria for the excavation and examination of texts. The codicology, palaeography, and provenance of manuscripts can probably more often than not make a significant contribution to our understanding of the tradition of any medieval text. A medieval manuscript necessarily supplies us with information as to the role of its text(s) in a historical context that is closer to the author(s) than is ours. I have not, then, resisted the temptation of providing the reader with such manuscript data even in connection with manuscripts that are not crucial to the understanding of the foundations of our tradition.[15] Yet I discuss and deploy this

---

[13] J. FELSENSTEIN, PHYLIP (Phylogeny Inference Package), 1993, version 3.64, distributed by the author. Department of Genetics, University of Washington, Seattle.

[14] T. ROOS & T. HEIKKILÄ, 'Evaluating methods for computer-assisted stemmatology using artificial benchmark data sets', *Literary & Linguistic Computing*, 24 (2009), pp. 426–430. T. ROOS, T. HEIKKILÄ & P. MYLLYMÄKI, 'A compression-based method for stemmatic analysis', *Proceedings of the 17th European Conference on Artificial Intelligence*, Amsterdam, 2006, pp. 805–806.

[15] As for palaeographical dating, I prefer to offer wide dates rather than to advance narrow and perhaps misleading ones. Occasionally I give the century alone (e.g. *s.* xiv); if a narrower span is justifiable, I use the following

evidence only rarely when dealing with manuscripts that I regard
as not essential.[16]

The group of major collections receives greater coverage in my
work. This emphasis seems natural to me, since the majority of
the letters are transmitted in the major collections and most of
the material in the minor collections is also known through the
major collections. The uneven treatment continues within the two
groups, as certain manuscripts are examined in greater detail than
others. Important manuscripts from a historiographical perspective
are those linked to Anselm and his inner circle in particular, while
manuscripts of stemmatic importance occur either close to the
original letters or at an important branching point in the stemma.
In practice, the same manuscripts often meet both these criteria.
This is because the various sub-branches of Anselm's letter collection took shape relatively quickly, already in the first third of
the twelfth century; subsequently, the sub-branches continued to
spread in the same form, with only relatively small alterations.

The descriptions of the contents of manuscripts observe the following system. When texts have been identified, the Latin titles
are in italics. 'Identification' here means that we are aware of the
author, title, and incipit of the text, and that we are able to com-
municate the identity of the text through (modern) research, most
often through an edition.[17] On certain occasions, my practice has
been flexible; for example, I have accepted some texts by anonymous authors into this category. Accordingly when an identified
text has no established title, its first words are given in quotation marks (and again in italics); for example, certain philosophical fragments associated with Anselm belong to this category. The
titles and/ or the initial words of unidentified texts are given in
standard typeface and in quotation marks. The identifications in
the group of the major collections are mostly mine. Those in the
group of the minor collections come mainly from catalogues, and

---

system: *s.* xi/xii = *c.* 1090–1110; *s.* xii^in = *c.* 1100–1120; *s.* xii^med = *c.* 1140–1160;
s. xii^ex = *c.* 1180–1200; *s.* xii^{1/2} = *c.* 1100–1150; *s.* xii^{1/3} = *c.* 1100–1133; *s.* xii^{1/4} =
c. 1100–1125, and so on.

[16] This features as the subject of my brief study 'Readers and editors:
the reception of Anselm's letter collections from *c.* 1090 to the early modern
period', (forthcoming).

[17] R. SHARPE, *Titulus. Identifying medieval Latin texts: an evidence-based
approach*, Turnhout, 2003, pp. 59–63.

if bibliographical data follow the title, I have checked the text because the catalogue reference was clearly erroneous, absent, or suspect for some reason. Finally, bibliographical data escort those Anselmian works that are absent from the *SAO* but present in the *Memorials of Saint Anselm* by Schmitt and Richard Southern, and the pseudo-Anselmian texts.

The transcriptions of the letters were made in an Excel spreadsheet to allow for the computer-assisted analysis of the texts. The spreadsheet table has over thirty columns, many containing nearly 7000 cells of data. This table is too unwieldy to be read easily by the human eye, and its great length also makes its publication unfeasible, given the need to keep this study to a reasonable length. The detailed textual evidence is therefore presented in the footnotes. Textual references are to Schmitt's edition.

4. Previous Research

Anselm's letter collection has been studied fairly intensively, with the two most recent monographs on the subject published in 2002.[18] My own research responds in detail to some of the earlier works for two reasons: first, many of my results are new and at odds with the previous scholarship; furthermore, consensus has not been reached, even on the questions generally recognized as the most important ones (and certain other 'lesser' questions have barely been considered at all). The possible origins of London, Lambeth Palace 59, manuscript *L*, have been the nub of the dispute, that is, whether Anselm may have edited this manuscript and its collection himself. Were this to be the case, we should have access to a political testament, which would reveal how Anselm wished to be remembered. At the time of writing, scholars working on broader questions that relate to this topic in some way, must choose whichever seems the better of two hypotheses. These two models were put forward by Richard Southern and Walter Fröhlich (largely building on the work of Anselm's modern editor, Schmitt). Subsequently, the positions have splintered to such an extent that

[18] S. N. Vaughn, *St Anselm and the Handmaidens of God. A Study of Anselm's Correspondence with Women*, Utrecht Studies in Medieval Literacy, 7, Turnhout, 2002; T. M. Krüger, *Persönlichkeitsausdruck und Persönlichkeitswahrnehmung im Zeitalter der Investiturkonflikte: Studien zu den Briefsammlungen des Anselm von Canterbury*, Spolia Berolinensia, 22, Hildesheim, 2002.

the victor of the debate is unclear. In fact, the conclusions of both parties are clearly mistaken in part, and a fully satisfactory interpretation of the internal relationships and origins of most of the more important manuscripts has yet to be presented.

The uncertain state of the question stems in part from a significant deficiency in Schmitt's edition. Although, by the inclusion of a critical apparatus, it theoretically meets the criteria of a critical edition, the work lacks a systematic and detailed analysis of the tradition and the manuscripts. Schmitt seems to have wished to add a seventh volume to the series, which would have discussed the manuscript tradition and the principles of the edition.[19] The idea was never realized, despite the fact that reviews of the various volumes had emphasized the importance of this.[20] As a result, the critical apparatus lost much of its significance: without any explanation of the manuscript tradition at all, the reader cannot weigh up the value of the readings Schmitt chose for his editorial text, or study the different branches of the tradition. In this case, the main function of the apparatus is to support the text by indicating the alternative readings the editor considered to be the most interesting, and some of Schmitt's editorial choices could have been rather better.[21] Furthermore, his apparatus contains

[19] Originally Schmitt possibly intended to include his articles in the sixth volume of the work; P. GROSJEAN, 'Franciscus Salesius Schmitt, O.S.B. Sancti Anselmi Cantuariensis archiepiscopi Opera omnia. T. I–III', *Analecta Bollandiana*, 65 (1947), p. 304. Since only the indexes were included in this volume, he seems to have hoped to add a seventh volume, but this was never published; C. VIOLA, 'Une réimpression des œuvres complètes de Saint Anselme', *Gregorianum*, 52 (1971), p. 555.

[20] M. CAPPUYNS, 'S. Anselmi Cantuariensis Archiep. Opera omnia...', *Bulletin de théologie ancienne et médiévale*, 6, 7, 9 (1951–65), pp. 322–323. Dom David Knowles likewise criticized the publication not only for its failure to provide solid historical commentary (*EHR*, 64 (1949), p. 364 and *EHR*, 67 (1952), p. 111), but also the method how the editor had dated the letters according to their arrangement, something that is weak both in theory and in practice (*EHR*, 68 (1953), p. 304). Knowles however praised Schmitt for his supposedly accurate work in editing the text and in the apparatus.

[21] In *AEp*. 1, Schmitt's editorial text reads '...quem *interiorem* sinu geritis, minime potestis fugere' (italics mine). The apparatus provides us with a better reading than the one Schmitt accepted. As for 'interiorem', Schmitt reports 'interiore *EL* (*corr. ex* interiorem) *P*'. This yields 'quem interiore sinu geritis, minime potetis fugere' ('the one whom you carry within your heart you cannot

inaccuracies and mistakes. In other words, the apparatus may not note variants of the type that are important in establishing the interrelationships of manuscripts. Furthermore, when studying the transmission of a letter collection, one needs to know in which manuscripts the letters survive and how the manuscripts arrange them. This is apparent neither from Schmitt's edition nor his studies, both of which fail to describe the contents of the manuscripts or even to address the issue.

The 1968 reprint of Schmitt's edition in part overcame the problems regarding the unclear state of research into the manuscript tradition. Schmitt's new German publisher offered him the opportunity to append his research on transmission to the first of the two volumes. In practice the *Prolegomena seu ratio editionis* merely reprints Schmitt's earlier articles, largely published in the *Revue Bénédictine*, with only minor alterations. Overall, the *Prolegomena* is confused and has been justifiably criticized.[22] Perhaps its most important new contribution to research is the inclusion of a list of the manuscripts employed in the editions. The list is not comprehensive and its details are superficial. The most obvious lapse is the absence of a clear and comprehensive account of the structure of the manuscript tradition. Unfortunately, as my research-visits to some of Europe's most important libraries have shown, the 1968 reprint of the *Opera omnia* met with surprisingly limited success, and the *Prolegomena* is rarely available, reducing its value to scholars. The largest libraries had naturally acquired the corpus of Anselm's texts as the volumes appeared in 1938–1961, and did not purchase a new edition published only a few years after the appearance of the final volume in the previous edition. In what follows, I therefore cite Schmitt's original articles, mostly published in the *Revue Bénédictine*.

4.1 *The debate in the* Revue Bénédictine

In the 1920s, Anselm's letter collection became the subject of modern textual scholarship in the *Revue Bénédictine*. The debate opened with an edition of a letter Dom Germain Morin OSB († 1946) believed Anselm to have sent; later, however, it became

---

escape'), which is superior to Schmitt's reading, as 'interiore sinu' is virtually idiomatic.

[22] VIOLA, 'Une réimpression', 1971, p. 561.

clear that he had been mistaken.[23] The series of articles by Dom André Wilmart OSB († 1941), the superb textual scholar, were to be of greater significance. Wilmart published material which had been omitted from the earlier editions reprinted in the *Patrologia Latina*,[24] analyzed the content of the letters,[25] and assessed the manuscript transmission.[26] His list of manuscripts was the first undertaken for Anselm and thus opened the academic debate continued in this study.

Wilmart also tempted a young (Benedictine) scholar to study Anselm's letters, and the bait was taken by Dom Schmitt.[27] There are some clues suggesting that Schmitt's participation in the enterprise was not achieved in perfect harmony. Wilmart published some of the hitherto unedited Anselmian letters in 1931, which would imply a desire on his part and at this date to undertake an edition. In the same year, both Wilmart and Schmitt published new editions of the first revision of *Epistola de incarnatione Verbi*, reflecting a lack of mutual understanding as to who was to edit what texts. Later they agreed that Wilmart would bring out only the Prayers and Meditations — which in the end Schmitt published under his own name.[28] In any case, it was Schmitt who became Anselm's modern editor. At the time, he was already working on an edition of Anselm's key treatises for the series the *Florilegium Patristicum*. Now he extended his publication project to include Anselm's entire literary output.

In his 1936 article, 'Entstehungsgeschichte der handschriftlichen Sammlungen der Briefe des hl. Anselm von Canterbury', Schmitt sought to determine the relationships between the most important

---

[23] D. G. MORIN, 'Lettre inédite d'A[nselme] à G[odefroy de Bouillon]?', *Revue Bénédictine*, 34 (1922), pp. 135–146.

[24] A. WILMART, 'Une lettre adressée de Rome à Saint Anselme en 1102', *Revue Bénédictine*, 40 (1928), pp. 262–266; and 'Une lettre inédite de S. Anselme à une moniale inconstante', *Revue Bénédictine*, 40 (1928), pp. 319–332.

[25] Especially A. WILMART 'La destinaire de la lettre de S. Anselme sur l'état et les vœux de religion', *Revue Bénédictine*, 38 (1926), pp. 331–334.

[26] A. WILMART, 'La tradition des lettres de S. Anselme. Lettres inédites de S. Anselme et de ses correspondants', *Revue Bénédictine*, 43 (1931), pp. 38–54.

[27] WILMART, 'Une lettre adressée', 1928, p. 262.

[28] *SAO*, vol. 1, p. vii and vol 3, p. vii. On the possible tension between the men, see R. SHARPE, 'Anselm as author. Publishing in the eleventh century', *Journal of Medieval Latin*, 19 (2009), pp. 7–8, note 12.

manuscripts comprehensively.[29] This proved to be his last wide-ranging survey of the subject. The chief observation was that the tradition of Anselm's letters from his Bec period divides into two main branches, which were labelled as the Canterbury and the Bec branch — a conclusion that would prove highly influential in subsequent research. Lambeth 59 was the most important witness to the Canterbury branch, as Schmitt had noted already in his first study of the subject; the most important witness to the Bec tradition was manuscript V.[30] Subsequent scholars have accepted this point, though their overall interpretations have varied substantially. My research shows that Schmitt's argument, though not completely mistaken, is in part misleading. Schmitt's last important contribution to the subject was an article that sought to identify the scribe of London, Lambeth Palace 59 and Oxford, Bodleian Library Bodley 271 as Thidricus, a monk of Canterbury and secretary to Anselm, and to establish that Lambeth 59 was drawn up under Anselm's direction.[31] These arguments were not flawless, and a long-lasting academic dispute ensued.

4.2 *The debate on Lambeth Palace 59*

After Schmitt's studies, the subject was almost entirely neglected for some 25 years. The only contributions made to the debate during the period came from two influential, although uneven scholars. Norman Cantor asserted that Lambeth 59, manuscript L, was formed under Anselm's assiduous supervision, 'with the intention of making known his views on church-state relations' in the English investiture contest.[32] Cantor based his assessment on Schmitt's article, although I should argue that he did not do full justice to all the nuances of Schmitt's interpretation. Schmitt had suggested

---

[29] The results of that study largely superseded those in F. S. SCHMITT, 'Zur Ueberlieferung der Korrespondenz Anselms von Canterbury. Neue Briefe', *Revue Bénédictine*, 43 (1931).

[30] F. S. SCHMITT, 'Zur Entstehungsgeschichte der Handschriftlichen Sammlungen der Briefe des hl. Anselm von Canterbury', *Revue Bénédictine*, 48 (1936), pp. 302–308.

[31] F. S. SCHMITT, 'Die unter Anselm veranstaltete Ausgabe seiner Werke und Briefe, die Codices Bodley 271 und Lambeth 59', *Scriptorium*, 9 (1955), pp. 64–75.

[32] N. F. CANTOR, *Church, Kingship, and Lay Investiture in England 1089–1135*, Princeton, 1958, p. 169.

that Anselm had certainly removed letters from Lambeth 59 on
political grounds, but that the letter collection in the manuscript
could not be considered a particularly well thought out work, at
least not in comparison with Oxford, Bodleian Library Bodley 271,
which contains Anselm's treatises and devotional texts and which
Schmitt considered to be *L*'s sibling.[33] At all events, the supposi-
tion that Anselm diligently supervised the making of *L* to seek
political advancement was to have far reaching consequences, as
we shall see. In his still highly enjoyable double biography, *Saint
Anselm and his Biographer*, Richard Southern sought to refute Cantor and Schmitt by stating that *L* had been compiled years after
Anselm's death.[34] Schmitt defended his own position against this
critique in the *Prolegomena* to the reprint of his edition.[35] Cantor
remained silent.[36]

---

[33] SCHMITT, 'Die unter Anselm veranstaltete Ausgabe', 1955, p. 74: 'So tref-
fen wir die äußerste Sorgfall für den Text, der wir in B [Bodley 271] feststellen
konnten, in L nicht an. Hier sind oft Zweifel am Platz und gar manchmal sind
andere Hss. im Recht gegen L...Die Sicherheit des Textes, die wir, namentlich dank des Cod. B, bei den systematischen Texten bis ins kleinste, fast
ohne Ausnahme, haben, vermissen wir überhaupt bei den Briefen. Offensicht-
lich war es dem hl. Anselm nicht mehr möglich, wohl infolge der Schwänchen
und Krankheiten der letzten Lebensjahre, persönlich die letzte Aufsicht und
Überprüfung des Briefregisters zu übernehmen...Briefe sind eben nicht sys-
tematische Werke und daher mehr wie diese Zufälligkeiten ausgesetzt. Manche
Briefe sind vorlorengegangen, namentlich aus der Zeit, ehe man anfing, Anselms
Briefe aufzubewahren und zu registrieren. Andere sind von ihrem Autor selber
ganz oder teilweise aus politischen Gründen, privater oder öffentlicher Natur,
unterdrückt worden.' Compare Cantor's statement cited in the text and CAN-
TOR, *Church, Kingship*, 1958, p. 169: 'Anselm carefully took a hand in selecting
the letters which went into his collected correspondence.' Cantor (*ibid.*, p. 169)
stated, furthermore, that Anselm had made two compilations of his letters in
the last five years of his life, namely *L* and Bodley 271. However, Bodley 271
contains none of the letters. The statement indicates only superficial acquaint-
ance with Schmitt's results, and hardly strengthens Cantor's assessment of the
character of *L*.

[34] R. SOUTHERN, *Saint Anselm and his Biographer. A Study of Monastic Life
and Thought 1059–c.1130*, Cambridge, 1963, p. 238, note 1.

[35] *SAO²*, 2 vols., Stuttgart — Bad Cannstatt, 1968, vol. 1, *Prolegomena*,
p. 239, note 35.

[36] In his autobiography, Cantor (*Inventing Norman Cantor: Confessions of
a Medievalist*, Tempe Arizona, 2002) hardly mentions his own book on the
English investiture contest. For his assessment of Southern, see N. F. CANTOR,

Walter Fröhlich, a German historian, brought the debate back to life at the Third International Anselm Conference at Canterbury in 1979. There he presented a paper that was published a year later in German.[37] Fröhlich's greatest merits were his clear presentation, and the *stemma codicum* which he drew up of the two partially intertwined textual families.[38] These *stemmata* were the first of their kind, but contained significant errors, as this study will show. Fröhlich also supported Schmitt's hypothesis as to the origin of *L*; they both thus held that this manuscript was compiled under Anselm by Thidricus of Canterbury. In general, his conclusions were founded on Schmitt but also on observations concerning the arrangement of the letters, and the dates and provenances assigned to the manuscripts in particular. Most regrettably, he did not take textual variants into account at all — or so it would seem. Despite its imperfections, Fröhlich's research made a big impact, which can be fairly attributed to the clarity of his argument and the convenience of his results for those engaged in researching Anselm's career as prior, abbot, and archbishop.[39]

In 1987, Sally N. Vaughn published a revisionist double biography, challenging Southern's earlier portrayal. Like Southern's study of Anselm, Vaughn's was a double biography. Her second figure was Robert of Meulan, while Southern's was Eadmer, a rather different (if no less complex) individual than Robert. Eadmer was Anselm's faithful friend and the author of *Vita Anselmi*,

---

Inventing the Middle Ages. The Lives, Works, and Ideas of the Great Medievalists of the Twentieth Century, New York, 1991, pp. 337–370.

[37] The title of his 1979 paper was 'The genesis of the collections of St Anselm's letters'. In 1984, the same study, with slight alterations, appeared in English in *American Benedictine Review*, and in 1990, in the introduction to the first volume of Fröhlich's translation of Anselm's letter collection.

[38] W. FRÖHLICH, 'Die Entstehung der Briefsammlung Anselms von Canterbury', *Historisches Jahrbuch*, 100 (1980), p. 459; W. FRÖHLICH, 'Introduction' in *The Letters of Saint Anselm of Canterbury*, 1, *Cistercian Studies Series*, 96, Kalamazoo, 1990, p. 29.

[39] It is hard to assess how much Cantor's interpretation of Lambeth 59 had influenced Fröhlich. He does not cite Cantor's book, and the materials for his arguments were all already present in Schmitt's studies. Fröhlich referred to Cantor's book in his PhD on Anselm's episcopal colleagues, however. In any case, Fröhlich himself saw the collection as more than a polemic within the investiture dispute. W. FRÖHLICH, *Die bischöflichen Kollegen Erzbischof Anselms von Canterbury*, [PhD diss., unpublished], Munich, 1971, p. 119, note 2a.

written to advance the cause of Anselm's sanctification; Robert
was one of the most active and capable sources of leadership and
lordship in the English kingdom of the Anglo-Norman kings, who
was excommunicated for working against Anselm and the pope.
The men placed alongside Anselm by the authors are indicative
of the general tone of each work and, perhaps, of the perspectives
and sympathies of the authors. Southern's presentation of Anselm
is, *mutatis mutandis*, almost identical to Eadmer's portrayal in his
time: Anselm was a good and pious monk, an outstanding theo-
logian, with a depth of human understanding, and an exemplary
Christian; in a word, a great man. There was only one flaw in the
picture: according to Eadmer, Anselm loathed the responsibilities associated with his high office. In medieval eyes, such a trait
was indeed a fitting quality in a man elevated to sanctity; for a
modern academic audience — perhaps especially one in Oxford — it
was a recommendation for an intellectual widely hailed as a gen-
ius. Southern emphasized this factor and sought to demonstrate
that as a ruler, Anselm was not only without ambition, but also
positively inadequate, and this interpretation was generally accepted.[40] In contrast, Vaughn's Anselm was a politician of completely
different calibre from Eadmer's and Southern's rather bloodless,
although brave, cloistered monk. Anselm was at least as effective
as his opponent, Robert of Meulan, 'the wisdom of the serpent'
in the subtitle of Vaughn's book referred to both men equally.[41]
Vaughn's interpretation took into account the possible bias in the
source material: medieval prelates were meant to feel distaste for
political power, and this *topos* shaped the world view of Anselm
and his students, as indeed of all committed medieval churchmen.
Since the sources for Anselm largely derive from the man himself,
or his immediate circle, we may assume that they also reflect this
topos. Fröhlich's conclusions, which appeared to show that Anselm
had carefully shaped his public image by selecting the material in
his letter collection, fitted very well with research undertaken from

[40] E.g. F. Barlow, *The English Church 1066–1154: a Constitutional History*,
London, 1979, p. 69: 'Anselm was a failure as bishop, metropolitan, primate
and even as abbot of Christ Church, but he was one of the best men ever to
occupy St Augustine's chair.'

[41] S. N. Vaughn, *Anselm of Bec and Robert of Meulan. The Innocence of the
Dove and the Wisdom of the Serpent*, Berkley 1987, p. 366.

starting points like Vaughn's.[42] The interpretation of *L* put forward by Schmitt, Cantor, and Fröhlich was one of Vaughn's most significant hermeneutic keys, with which she sought to lay bare Anselm's mystery. Naturally, an academic dispute followed, which gradually focused on the question of the origin of manuscript *L*.

Southern sought to reply to Vaughn's challenge, first through articles, and finally through a (partially) new biography of Anselm.[43] Disproving Fröhlich's assertions became a part of the project: already in his first critique of Vaughn's work, Southern also criticized Fröhlich's dating of manuscript *L* as too early.[44] Subsequently he undertook new research into the relationships between the most important manuscripts, presenting the results first in his article 'Verso una storia della corrispondenza di Anselmo' and a little later, in slightly altered form, in the revised biography, *St Anselm: A Portrait in a Landscape*.[45] The final version of the textual survey, too, was intended to be provisional only.[46] Southern's arguments will be analyzed in detail in the chapters on the individual manuscripts. The most striking feature of the stemma as sketched by him is that none of the surviving manuscripts were compiled under Anselm's supervision, or were even derived directly from a manuscript of this kind: this was because Southern assigned the manuscripts later dates than Fröhlich. For example, Southern placed manuscript *L* between 1123 and 1130, almost 20 years after Anselm's death.[47] The dating and the result obviously supported his interpretation of Anselm excellently, a man whose motivation could be summed up by the proverb *pax multa in cella, foris autem*

---

[42] VAUGHN, *Anselm and Robert*, 1987, pp. 3, 132.

[43] R. SOUTHERN, 'Sally Vaughn's Anselm: An Examination of the Foundations', *Albion*, 20 (1988), pp. 181–204; Verso una storia della corrispondenza di Anselmo', in *Anselmo d'Aosta Figura Europea, Atti del Convengo di studi, Aosta 1° e 2° marzo 1988*, eds. I. BIFFI & C. MARABELLI, Milano, 1989, pp. 269–289; *Saint Anselm. A Portrait in a Landscape*, Cambridge, 1990.

[44] SOUTHERN, 'Vaughn's Anselm', 1988, pp. 194–201. For a response to the critique, see S. VAUGHN, 'Anselm: saint and statesman', *Albion*, 20 (1988), pp. 205–220.

[45] Compare especially SOUTHERN, 'Verso una storia', 1989, pp. 282–285 and SOUTHERN, *A Portrait*, 1990, pp. 473–476.

[46] The presentation retained the same title as that of the original article: 'Towards a history of Anselm's letters'.

[47] SOUTHERN, *A Portrait*, 1990, pp. 459, 473–476.

plurima bella, and who would scarcely have bothered to pay heed
to his posthumous political reputation. Although some conclusions drawn by Southern may be shown to be incorrect, it is to
his credit that he does not oversimplify matters as Fröhlich did;
neither did he believe that he had solved the tradition, unlike his
opponent. The impact of the debate was thus to make the origin
of manuscript *L* seem to become the critical point, which could
indicate whether Vaughn's or Southern's interpretation of Anselm
was valid.[48]

Following this dispute, the academic community has been especially interested in Lambeth 59, and the other manuscripts have
attracted much less attention. Since the millennium, the subject
has been considered most extensively by the German scholar Thomas Michael Krüger in his PhD thesis, published in 2002. Although
Krüger's research largely focuses on the contents of the letters,
his principal argument is based in the main around the history
of manuscript *L*'s genesis, and therefore he analyzes the tradition
of the best known manuscripts. This discussion is almost entirely
based on Schmitt's studies, and Krüger successfully employs these
to bring out some important points not previously noted by other
scholars. While Krüger does distance himself from Fröhlich by
pointing out some of his mistakes, his interpretation of the origins of Lambeth 59 follows Fröhlich's suit. Krüger sought to prove
that *L* was in fact a register of letters, which was produced under
Anselm's active supervision.[49]

[48] McBride's unpublished PhD thesis, *Benevolent letters: Ecclesiastical epistles
to nobles in the early twelfth century* (Santa Barbara, 1998) on early twelfth-
century letters (1998) analyzed relations between members of the ecclesiastical
and lay elites, especially 'the ways in which the churchmen characterized their
roles as advisors and as prayer-givers, the manner in which they treated matters of benevolence and characterized the return on favours and gifts, and the
nature of frequency of their appeals to a noble's desire for honour or a good
reputation.' Her principal sources are the letters of Anselm and Ivo of Chartres, supplemented by those of Bernard of Clairvaux, Lanfranc and Peter the
Venerable. I have only been able to obtain the introduction to the work, which
clearly suggests that, insofar as McBride considers the manuscript tradition for
the letter collection, she follows Fröhlich's interpretation of it.

[49] KRÜGER, '*Persönlichkeitsausdruck*', 2002, pp. 73–82. Also in 2002, Vaughn
published a monograph on Anselm's correspondence with women, which, in my
view, leans too heavily on Fröhlich's stemma and Cantorian interpretations of

Since the publication of Southern's volume, English scholarship has, by and large, supported the view that Lambeth 59 was not authorial but postdated Anselm's death at least by ten years. When, moreover, the approach has been of palaeographical or codicological nature, Fröhlich has been met with severe criticism.[50] The most important contribution comes from Richard Sharpe, who has published a series of articles on the early transmission of Anselm's works, of his treatises in particular. He has also organised a one-day conference discussing five very early manuscripts, including Lambeth 59.[51] His work — especially the 2009 article 'Anselm as Author: Publishing in the Late Eleventh Century' — has redefined our understanding of how Anselm published and distributed his texts. Sharpe's results demonstrate that much previous scholarship on the transmission of Anselm's treatises, based on Schmitt, rests on insecure assumptions. We shall see that this applies to Anselm's correspondence as well.

---

what functions the letter collection has; see e.g. VAUGHN, *St Anselm and the Handmaidens*, 2002, pp. 20–21, 23–25.

[50] R. GAMESON, 'English Manuscript Art in the Late Eleventh Century: Canterbury and its Context', in *Canterbury and the Norman Conquest: Churches, Saints and Scholars 1066–1109*, eds. R. EALES & R. SHARPE, London, 1995, pp. 119–120, note 85. The Oxford scholar Ian Logan has very recently undertaken the most extensive analysis hitherto of the data for Thidricus, whom Schmitt and those of his mind believed to be the scribe of *L*. Logan's approach is palaeographical, and his conclusions pose serious problems both to the Cantorian perspective derived from Schmitt's work, and to that of Southern. I. LOGAN, 'Ms. Bodley 271: Establishing the Anselmian Canon?', *Saint Anselm Journal*, 2 (2004), pp. 67–80; and 'Anselm and Thidricus: Revisiting MS Bodley 271', in *Anselm and Abelard. Investigations and Juxtapositions*, eds. G. E. M. GASPER & H. KOHLENBERGER, Toronto, 2006. For the dating of *L*, see also R. GAMESON, *The Manuscripts of Early Norman England (c. 1066–1130)*, Oxford, 1999, p. 122, no. 581; and in P. R. ROBINSON, *Catalogue of Dated and Datable Manuscripts c. 888–1600 in London Libraries*, 1, London, 2003, no. 48, p. 41. See also P. HEALY, 'A Supposed Letter of Archbishop Lanfranc: Concepts of the Universal Church in the Investiture Contest', *EHR*, 121 (2006), pp. 1385–1407, p. 1388.

[51] The colloquium, convened to celebrate the 900th anniversary of Anselm's death, was held on 27 April 2009 in the Bodleian Library. Results from the discussions are briefly reviewed in R. SHARPE, 'Early Manuscripts of Anselm: A discussion with five manuscripts', *Gazette du livre médiéval*, 54 (2009), pp. 49–52.

Nice historiographical review

II. THE LETTER IN THE ELEVENTH
AND TWELFTH CENTURIES

1. A RENAISSANCE OF EPISTOLOGRAPHY

The eleventh and twelfth centuries are held to be the golden age of medieval epistolography: it has been suggested that letter writing increased markedly in both quality and quantity in this period.[1] The period also saw the birth of the *ars dictaminis*, the discipline that defined good prose style for letters and legal documents in particular.[2] While it is impossible to trace all the factors contributing to the growing popularity of letter-writing, the increased success can be associated with wider intellectual developments of the eleventh and twelfth centuries, developments often labelled the 'twelfth-century renaissance'. From the eleventh century onwards new schools were established in increasing numbers, especially at cathedrals. These reforms probably gave remarkable impetus to letter writing. As the learned community slowly grew, letters became an excellent tool allowing literate men and women to create and sustain networks and to debate issues over distances. One should not focus exclusively on cathedral schools at the expense of monasteries at this time, however, for a great number of the significant letter writers we know from the period were monks, Anselm and his circle being a case in point.

It has been assumed that the letter collections of Cicero, Seneca, and Pliny offered models for medieval epistolography.[3] Possibly

---

[1] CONSTABLE, *Letters and Letter-Collections*, 1976, p. 31. Constable (*ibid.*, p. 26) divides the history of the medieval letter into four periods: late antiquity, from the fourth to the mid-sixth century; the Carolingian period, from the mid-eighth century to the ninth; the Central Middle Ages, in the eleventh and twelfth centuries; and the late medieval and humanist period, in the fourteenth and fifteenth centuries. He considered that the times falling between his periods were characterized by a reduction in the quantity and/ or quality of letter writing.

[2] A fine introduction to the subject is M. CAMARGO, *Ars dictaminis. Ars dictandi, Typologie des sources du moyen âge occidental*, 60, Turnhout, 1991.

[3] F.-J. SCHMALE, 'Brief, Briefliteratur, Briefsammlungen: IV. Lateinisches Mittelalter', *LexMA*, vol. 2, Munich, 1983, col. 657.

so, but in the Anglo-Norman world of the late eleventh and early twelfth century, the direct inspiration for making a collection of one's own letters came from the late antique patristic authors, such as Jerome, Augustine, and Gregory the Great,[4] and naturally from other contemporary writers. If Cicero had any direct influence on medieval epistolography, this was surely worked through his *De amicitia*, which became fundamental reading when friendship was reinstated as a fashionable literary motif. The topic was ideal subject-matter for a letter: it was natural to analyze and praise friendship both generally and more personally in a letter to a friend.[5] Anselm is held to be a key proponent of this literary phenomenon, given the concentration on friendship in many of his letters, his original and elegant handling of the issue, his literary quality, and his letters' relatively wide dissemination during the first decades of the twelfth century.[6] His correspondence on the issue of friendship to the monks of Bec, who had transferred to churches and monasteries in England and Normandy, and to others must have had a formative influence on several individuals.[7] A new interest in the personal – of which the fresh attention to friendship was one feature – may also have increased the popularity of letters since an introspective approach is naturally suited to correspondence between friends. The spirituality of the day emphasized individual experience more strongly than before, a change reflected in devotional texts in particular.[8] This stance permeates

----

[4] From the Anglo-Norman period up to *c.* 1130, collections or compilations of letters by these authors survive in several English manuscripts, totalling roughly thirty. As for the classical authors mentioned above, we only know one Anglo-Norman manuscript from the same period, London, BL Egerton 654, which includes letters of Seneca. The medieval transmission of the letters of Cicero and Pliny was negligible.

[5] B. P. McGuire, *Friendship and Community. The Monastic Experience 350–1250*, Cistercian Studies Series, 95, Kalamazoo, 1988, p. xxix; Constable, *Letters and Letter-Collections*, 1976, p. 32.

[6] Anselm's (like virtually any monastic writer's) understanding of the subject was moulded by John Cassian's *Conferences*, its *collatio* xvi, *De amicitia*; see A. Fiske, 'Saint Anselm and Friendship', *Studia Monastica*, 3 (1961), pp. 259–290; Southern, *Saint Anselm and his Biographer*, 1963, pp. 67–76; McGuire, *Friendship*, 1988, pp. 210–227.

[7] McGuire, *Friendship*, 1988, p. 228.

[8] G. Constable, *The Reformation of the Twelfth Century*, Cambridge, 1996, p. 274.

all Anselm's literary output, and even his treatises are sometimes intensely personal in appearance. His prayers and meditations, and their compilations, are considered especially important, even 'revolutionary', in this regard.[9] Finally, improving communications certainly played a part in promoting letter writing. This was linked to progress in society more generally as more peaceful times followed the end of Viking, Magyar, and Saracen attacks around the turn of the millennium. Urbanisation, population growth, colonization, economic growth, and the expansion of trade were factors behind the increase in letter writing as well.

2. Writing Letters

The classical technique of letter writing had three stages. First, the mind formed thoughts into words (*componere*), which were then dictated (*dicere* or *dictare*), and finally written down (*scribere*). While the distinction between the first two steps of the process was often blurred,[10] *dictare* and *scribere* were still distinguished prior to the period this study focuses on: even if the author physically wrote the letter himself, he was thought to be doing so to his own dictation.[11] In the eleventh and twelfth centuries, conceptual blurring extended to the *dictare* and *scribere* steps as well, so that the verb *dictare* and its derivatives might also refer to writing. On the other hand, *scribere* too could signify not only the action of writing, but also the creation of text, even when an author dictated to a scribe.[12] The development of professional letter writers

---

[9] C. Morris, *The Discovery of the Individual 1050–1200*, London, 1972, p. 8; T. H. Bestul, 'The Collection of Private Prayers in the 'Portiforium' of Wulfstan of Worcester and the 'Orationes sive Meditationes' of Anselm of Canterbury', in *Les mutations socio-culturelles au tournant des* XIe-XIIe *siècles*, ed. R. Foreville, Paris, 1984, p. 360.

[10] E.g. Anselm's reference to the mental process involved in the verbalization of thoughts ('mentis siue rationis locutio') in *Mon.* (*c.* x, p. 24, lines 24–30). See also *AEp.* 28: 'Quidam frater...rogauit, ut de sancta Maria...orationem componerem.' Here the word refers to the whole process.

[11] Constable, *Letters and Letter-Collections*, 1976, pp. 42–43; A. Ernout, 'Dictare "Dicter" allem. *Dichten*', *Revue des études latines*, 29 (1951), p. 159.

[12] In *AEp.* 379, the verb *scribere* appears in both senses: 'Si aliud iuuante deo scripsero, suo tempore monstrabitur'; here the verb refers to the creation of a new literary work. 'Quod autem in libris quos scripsisti corrigis'; here the verb indicates copying.

strengthened this tendency, as most of the *dictatores* wrote their letters themselves. Though examples indicating that dictation and writing were understood as separate actions continue during and after Anselm's lifetime,[13] he too seems to have used the verb *dictare* to refer to both processes, albeit it is often difficult to determine the precise meaning of the word.[14] At all events, he certainly dictated letters to a scribe and sometimes possibly wrote them out himself, as was also the case with his other works.[15]

The first text dictated or written by the author could either be a draft or a finished letter.[16] Wax tablets were used both by scribes taking dictation and by authors writing their own texts, including Anselm, as the dramatic events surrounding the creation of the ontological argument reveal. First, Anselm probably wrote the argument he had received as a revelation into wax tablets himself ('scripsit in tabulis'). When the tablets were stolen, he either dictated, or himself wrote the text into wax tablets again ('Reparat Anselmus aliud...dictamen[17] in aliis tabulis'). This time, the tablets were destroyed, and Anselm then gathered up the fragments and

---

[13] CONSTABLE, *Letters and Letter-Collections*, 1976, p. 43. See e.g. Bernard of Clairvaux, *Epistolae*, in *Sancti Bernardi Opera*, vol. 8, eds. J. LECLERCQ & H. ROCHAIS, Rome, 1977, *Ep.* 90: 'Quiescant, inquam, a dictando ingenia, labia a confabulando, a scribendo digiti, a discurrendo nuntii.'

[14] See *AEp.* 6:5, 22:4–5; 39:5–12, 101:76, 116:5, 156:19, 325:32.

[15] At the outset of his ecclesiastical career, as well as writing his own letters, Anselm apparently had to act as his superior's scribe, a very common practice during the age. *AEp.* 17:52–53: '[Domnus abbas] cuncta hic a me scripta sua dicta uult esse.'

[16] CONSTABLE, *Letters and Letter-Collections*, 1976, pp. 43–44. Scribes could probably never keep up with the rate at which the fastest authors dictated. See Peter of Blois, *Epistolae*, PL 207, *Ep.* 92: 'Confidenter et sub testimonio plurium dico me semper dictare litteras solitum citius quam posset aliquis exarare.' It is uncertain whether this assessment is trustworthy, however, since the text forms part of the argument with which Peter sought to prove that the accusations of plagiarism made against him were unfounded. R. SOUTHERN, 'Towards an Edition of Peter of Blois's Letter-Collection', *EHR*, 110 (1995), p. 934. On the new shorthand scripts developed in the twelfth and thirteenth centuries see B. BISCHOFF, *Latin Palaeography. Antiquity and the Middle Ages*, trans. by D. Ó Cróinín & D. Ganz, Cambridge, 1990, pp. 80–82; M. PARKES, 'Tachygraphy in the Middle Ages: writing techniques employed for *reportationes* of lectures and sermons', *Medievo e rinascimento*, 3 (1989), pp. 159–169.

[17] In this context, *dictamen* could refer either to dictation or to the text.

gave the text to a scribe to be copied to parchment ('pergamenae iubet tradi').[18]

The next stage in the letter-writing process was for the dictated text to be copied on parchment, as in the example above. Although one person, possibly the author himself, could act as both the writer of the draft and scribe of the fair copy, the process could equally involve different people at every stage.[19] Sometimes the final version of the letter was written out by a calligrapher, working either from dictation, or by reading the draft for himself. When the process involved every step discussed here (especially if different individuals were involved at each stage), there was clearly significant potential for miscomprehension and the occurrence of scribal errors.[20] Thus Herbert Losinga († 1119), for example, checked the text of his letters personally before they were despatched: this is revealed by the addition in his hand of the word 'contuli', 'I have checked this', at the end of his letters.[21] Bernard of Clairvaux († 1153), on the other hand, pleaded overwork to account for his failure to correct the overly aggressive tone imparted to one of his letters by his scribes.[22]

3. ANSELM AS A LETTER WRITER

In one of his letters, Anselm complained that because of the *lex epistolae*, he could not discuss matters as extensively as he wished.[23]

---

[18] Eadmer of Canterbury, *Vita Anselmi*, ed. R. SOUTHERN, *OMT*, repr., Oxford, 1972 [1962], pp. 30–31.

[19] Eadmer, William of Malmesbury, and Orderic Vitalis all acted as their own scribes. William of Newburgh (1136–1198), on the other hand, complained that he could not find a scribe to copy his work on the Song of Songs off wax tablets and to parchment (*Analecta S. ordinis Cisterciensis*, 6 (1951), p. 223); information from SOUTHERN in Eadmer, *VA*, p. 30, note 2.

[20] J. DE GHELLINCK, *Patristique et moyen âge. Études d'histoire littéraire et doctrinale*, vol. 2, *Museum Lessianum, Section historique*, 7, Paris, 1947, p. 217; CONSTABLE, *Letters and Letter-Collections*, 1976, p. 46.

[21] L. WAHLGREN-SMITH, ' "*Ambrosianum illud*" in the Letters of Herbert Losinga', *Classica et mediaevalia*, 50 (1999), pp. 208–209.

[22] Bernard, *Ep.* 387: 'Multitudo negotiorum in culpa est, quia dum scriptores nostri non bene retinent sensum nostrum, ultra modum acuunt stilum suum, nec uidere possum quae scribi praecipi.'

[23] *AEp.* 101: 'Ad haec omnia, carissime, quid respondendum sit, uellem aliquanto diffusius scribere, nisi lex epistolae cogeret me breuitatem non excedere.'

This is the only occasion on which he referred to 'the law of the letter'; he was not an epistolary theorist. The following short discussions provide a sketch of what the concept meant to him.

3.1 *Language*

Without exception, Anselm's literary style has been considered of a very high or excellent quality.[24] His Latin is grammatically pure and his vocabulary is vast; the overall impression is one of deliberation as well as flexibility. Of the favourite authors of high medieval monastic scholars, Anselm's literary voice is closest to Augustine's, whose texts he must have digested in great quantities. Anselm's style was, naturally, thoroughly medieval. He commanded formidable rhetorical weaponry, and several repetitive techniques and parallelisms are his trademark. His letters employ such embellishments more often than his treatises, indicating that he possessed a distinct epistolary style. His early letters in particular are full of these mannerisms. Sometimes this happens at the cost of clarity and fluidity, which classical and medieval theorists regularly mentioned as key elements in epistolary expression.[25] A passage from his earliest surviving letter, *AEp.* 3, shows how repeatedly these devices might occur. The suprascript letters, running from a to k, indicate parallel expressions.

> Cuius bonus odor, iam per multos huius patriae suauiter diffusus, [a]quanto delectabilius animae meae [b]fragrat, tanto[a] ipsa ad eius amicitiam et notitiam ardentius[a] flagrat.[b] Quas iam ex quo uitam eius audiui, [c]habeo et amplector[c] [d]quantum possum, [e]et oro, oret et[e] ipse mecum, ut tanto nobis [f]crescant, quantum[d] in Deo crescere[f] possunt.[d] Ambo, karissimi, ualete. Obsecro, [g]in Babylonia sentite [h]id ipsum, ut in Ierusalem[g] participetis in id ipsum.[h] Non hoc dico

---

[24] There have been only very preliminary studies of the language and style of Anselm's letters, and the subject is too large to examine in detail here. See J. LOUGHLIN, *Saint Anselm as a Letter Writer*, [Ph.D. diss., unpublished], Washington, 1968. A. GRANATA, 'Anselmo d'Aosta: maestro di stile epistolare', *Anselmo d'Aosta Figura Europea, Atti del Convengo di studi, Aosta 1° e 2° marzo 1988*, eds. I. BIFFI & C. MARABELLI, Milano, 1989, pp. 247–268. Granata does not appear to be acquainted with Loughlin's work: see *ibid.*, p. 263, in particular note 18.

[25] For instance, Anonymous of Bologna, *Rationes*, in L. ROCKINGER, *Briefsteller und Formelbücher des elften bis vierzehnten Jahrhunderts*, 1, *Quellen und Erörterungen zur Bayerischen und Deutschen Geschichte*, ix/1, 1863, p. 19: 'Narratio uero expositio est rerum gestarum uel ut potius se geri uidebuntur.'

ⁱquasi timens ʲuobis ᵏaliquando discordiam uenire, sed uere cupiensⁱ a uobisʲ nunquam concordiam abire.ᵏ

The reader of this letter also encounters: 'ᵃCum considero, strenue miles dei et mihi carissime, cum consideroᵃ ᵇtuae prouectus strenuitatis et meae sterilitatem inertiaeᵇ'; and 'Quod ut efficacius efficias, precor, obsecro...'; and '...uenerabiliter amabilis et amabiliter uenerabilis...'. As Anselm's correspondence acquired a more official tone when he secured promotion to prior, abbot, and archbishop, these rhetorical embellishments became less frequent. To conclude, in Anselm's epistolary expression, such parallelism, by and large, served as an instrument by which to demonstrate affection.

While Anselm relished elaborate sentences, he was also able to express a complex matter in a few – often elegant – words. His letter of consolation written for his nephew on the death of his mother (and Anselm's sister) provides a fine example of this: 'Sollicitudinem et tristitiam quam tu habes de matre tua, ego quoque tolero.'[26] At its most concise, his Latin hardly translates. The phrase 'suus quod suus', with which he concluded his salutation to Lanfranc in several letters, has often been discussed, but only rarely satisfactorily rendered into the vernacular.[27]

Loughlin is the only scholar to have looked at the use of *cursus* in Anselm's letters, which she did on the basis of a small number of examples.[28] Her chosen passages allowed her to show that

---

[26] *AEp.* 327.

[27] The formula occurs in *AEp.* 23, 25, 27, 57, and 66, and slightly altered in *AEp.* 32 and 49. This example is from *AEp.* 23: 'Domino et patri, catholicis reuerenter amando et amanter reuerendo archiepiscopo Lanfranco, frater Anselmus suus quod suus'. I should translate the phrase as 'his brother Anselm as he is'. Southern's translation is 'Anselm sends all that he is', which is rather far from the original; *A Portrait*, 1990, p. 60. Cowdrey's rendition 'his own as owing his own self to him' is correct, but lacks in elegance; H. E. J. COWDREY, *Lanfranc: Scholar, Monk and Archbishop*, Oxford, 2003, p. 208. Aldo Granata translates the first three occurrences as 'Anselmo augura ciò che può augurare chi è suo', the fourth as 'Anselmo augura ciò che deve chi è suo', and the last as 'suo in quanto suo', of which the last in particular is very fine; *Anselmo d'Aosta: Lettere*, vol. 1, eds. I. BIFFI & C. MARABELLI, Milan, 1988. Henri Rochais renders each as 'Anselme, qui est sien parce que Lanfranc est sien', which is rather liberal; *L'œuvres de S. Anselme de Cantorbery*, ed. M. CORBIN, vol 6, *Lettres 1 à 147*, Paris, 2005.

[28] LOUGHLIN, *Anselm as a Letter Writer*, 1968, pp. 91–95.

Anselm used all the three fundamental cadences — *planus, tardus,* and *uelox* — and the rarer *trispondaicus.* Nevertheless, it is clear that any body of text as extensive as Anselm's correspondence will include all the cadences under investigation, whether the author used them consciously or not; Loughlin's evidence cannot therefore be used to draw watertight conclusions as to Anselm's use of cadences one way or the other.[29] A systematic evaluation of these questions in the form of Janson's statistical test would require significant work, however, and must remain outside the scope of this study.[30]

Anselm's correspondents often implicitly praised his letters by seeking to receive more of them. It is much harder to assess what impact, if any, his epistolary style had on letter writers outside his immediate circle.[31] The 'suus quod suus' salutation, however, is found in use within the circle of Bernard of Clairvaux († 1153) slightly later. The formula first occurs in a letter of William of Saint Thierry, a Benedictine abbot who wished to become Cistercian († 1148), then in three letters of Bernard, and finally in four letters of Nicholas of Clairvaux († 1178).[32] A standard work on medieval friendship observes that Prior Elmer of Canterbury († 1137) wrote of friendship that in tone and terminology corresponds to Anselm's. According to the same study, this shared style

---

[29]   See J. Howe, 'The alleged use of *cursus* by Bishop Arbeo of Freising', *Archiuum latinitatis medii aeui,* 42 (1982), pp. 129–131, proving that bishop Arbeo of Freising († 783) did not use *cursus* contrary to previous assumptions.

[30]   Naturally Anselm both knew and made use of *cursus.* Interesting questions may be whether he favoured *trispondaicus,* and whether he systematically avoided *planus* or not: in other words, did he continue to practise the traditions of his native region, like his teacher, the Lombard Lanfranc? T. Janson 1975, *Prose Rhythm in Medieval Latin from the 9th to the 13th Century,* Studia Latina Stockholmiensia, 20, Stockholm, 1975, p. 42.

[31]   See my forthcoming article 'Readers and editors: the reception of Anselm's letter collections from c. 1090 to the early modern period'.

[32]   Abbot William's letter is lost, but in response to it, the addressee, Bernard, wrote: 'Frater Bernardus de Clara-Valle, suo illi quod suo. Hanc mihi tu salutationis formulam tradidisti, scribendo "suus ille quod suus"', Bernard of Clairvaux, *Ep.* 86 (in 1123 or 1124). See also *ibid., Ep.* 178 to Innocent II (1136), and *The Letters of Peter the Venerable,* Cambridge, ed. G. Constable, vol. 1, Mass., 1967, *Ep.* 38 from Bernard to Peter (1138). Nicholas of Clairvaux, *Epistolae,* ed. J. Picard (*PL* 196), *Ep.* 42, 43, 52 (cross-referenced to the collection of Peter of Celle in *PL* 202), and 57.

contrasts with an anonymous letter collection from Bec, dating roughly from the middle of the twelfth century or slightly later: the Bec author's discussions of the topic are not Anselmian in character.[33] Likewise, the most recent editor of this collection did not detect any Anselmian citation or allusion in the letters.[34]

3.2 *Structure*

Around the turn of the eleventh and twelfth centuries, a relatively coherent set of guidelines for a recognised epistolary style were developed more systematically than before. These rules were called the *ars dictaminis* (or *dictamen* or *ars dictandi*).[35] It became a standard principal of the guidebooks that letters consisted of five elements, the *salutatio, captatio beneuolentiae, narratio, petitio*, and *conclusio*, although other structural theories were also established.[36]

---

[33] McGuire, *Friendship*, 1988, pp. 234–236.

[34] The editor attributes the collection to Alain de Lille whom she identifies as Alan of Tewkesbury. This is highly implausible. *Alain de Lille, Lettres familières (1167–1170)*, ed. F. Hudry, Paris, 2003, see especially p. 74.

[35] The earliest (known) guide books to the *ars dictaminis* were written a little too late to have been studied by Anselm. The earliest author is said to be either Alberic of Monte Cassino († 1105) or Adalbertus Samaritanus, who taught the *ars dictaminis* in the secular school of Bologna and wrote the *Praecepta dictaminum* for his students sometime between 1111 and 1115. For example Schaller ('*Ars dictaminis, ars dictandi*', *LexMA*, 1, Munich, 1980, col. 1035) and Camargo (*Ars dictaminis*, 1991, pp. 30–31) do not classify Alberic's work as an *ars dictaminis* manual. Camargo, however, emphasizes that the entire debate as to the father of the *ars dictaminis* is 'pointless', in that both Alberic and Adalbertus were building on the traditions of centuries. See Adalbertus Samaritanus, *Praecepta dictaminum*, ed. F.-J. Schmale, *MGH, Quellen zur Geistesgeschichte des Mittelalters*, 3, Weimar, 1961, p. 51, where Adalbertus criticizes the earlier traditions embodied by Alberic of Monte Cassino. The *ars dictaminis* spread beyond Italy with considerable speed. By the mid-twelfth century, it had reached France, and by the end of the century, it had probably crossed over to England; it was established in German areas by the end of the twelfth century and in the Iberian peninsula during the next century; Camargo, *Ars dictaminis*, 1991, p. 35. The first known 'English' guide is considered to be the one attributed to Peter of Blois († 1211/1212) and written sometime between 1181 and 1185. Schaller, *Ars dictaminis*, 1980, col. 1037; M. Camargo, 'Introduction' in *Medieval Rhetorics of Prose Composition. Five English* Artes Dictandi *and Their Tradition, Medieval & Renaissance texts & studies*, 115, Binghampton and New York, 1995, p. 3.

[36] The earliest known systematic presentation of the five parts of the letter appears in the *Rationes dictandi*, written in the mid 1130s by the Anonymous

I shall only discuss Anselm's use of the *salutatio* in detail, while providing short generalisations for the rest.

The five structural elements were, indeed, no novelties. For instance, the letter collection of Bishop Frothair of Toul (*c.* 813–847) shows that Carolingian epistolary writing recognised each of them, even if no individual letter in his collection necessarily includes all five.[37] Anselm's letters reflect comparable flexibility, the *salutatio* and *narratio* — the epistolary *sine qua non* — being the only elements to occur in all his letters. He also closed, as one expects, virtually every letter with a valediction. At its most straightforward, this was the very typical *uale* or *ualete*, while the most extensive valedictions are short prayers or blessings of a few lines.[38] The *captatio beneuolentiae* is far more frequent than the *conclusio*. Anselm was, however, quite prepared to omit the *captatio* if the *salutatio* had already achieved the objective.[39] At other times, he created an organic whole out of the *salutatio* and *captatio*, by developing

of Bologna and after that the five-part division became standard; Camargo, *Ars dictaminis*, 1991, p. 22. Besides the five-part structural theory, alternative divisions into three, four, or six parts were also known. J. Martin, 'Classicism and Style in Latin Literature', in *Renaissance and Renewal in the Twelfth Century*, eds. R. L. Benson & G. Constable with C. Lanham, Cambridge (Mass.), 1982, p. 538; Constable, *Letters and Letter-Collections*, 1976, pp. 16–17; Rockinger, *Briefsteller*, 1863, pp. viii–x.

[37] M. Goullet & C. Vulliez, 'Etude littéraire de la correspondance', in *La correspondance d'un évêque carolingien. Frothaire de Toul (ca 813–847)*, Textes et documents d'histoire médiévale, 2, Paris, 1998, pp. 42–48. Many of the rules that found their way into the *ars dictaminis* handbooks had been in use long before the earliest works were written. For a good, concise presentation of the debate, with references, see W. D. Patt, 'The early '*ars dictaminis*' as response to a changing society', *Viator*, 9 (1978), pp. 135–139. One writer who followed the rules of the 'later' *dictamen* in the tenth century was Gunzo of Novara: P. O. Kristeller, *Renaissance Philosophy and the Mediaeval Tradition*, Latrobe, 1966, p. 89, note 19.

[38] E.g. *AEp.* 434: 'Deum, pro cuius amore me diligis, oro ut ipse te diligat, ipse te ad bene uiuendum, quod a me petis, instruat, ipse te ab omnibus peccatis absoluat, et ipse te ad uitam aeternam perducat. Amen.'

[39] *AEp.* 385, 388, 389. This custom was acknowledged and approved in the *ars dictaminis*. Anonymous of Bologna, *Rationes*, p. 19: 'Est idem sepe numero maxima pars captandi beniuolentiam in ipsa salutationis serie. Ideoque taliter moderari debemus epistolas, ut quotiens in salutatione uel mittentis humilitas uel recipientis laudes largius apponuntur, uel statim a narratione uel a peticione reliquum epistole incipiamus, uel satis exiliter et modeste beniuolentiam denotemus.'

the ideas of the former in the latter.[40] Towards the end of his life, his *captationes* became simpler and shorter. The *petitio* occurred only when something had to be requested. A modern commentator admired Anselm's ability to present his requests so 'that at times he does not seem to be making a direct request at all'.[41]

The salutatio

The *salutatio* established who was writing to whom, and their relative positions in the social hierarchy.[42] Accordingly, modern scholarship interested in the medieval concepts of authority has looked rather closely at the *salutationes*, and the topic has recently been discussed in connection with Anselm too. A closer analysis is still needed, however.[43] In its simplest form, Anselm's *salutatio* is 'Gondulfo Anselmus'; at its longest, it extends to a few lines.[44] The *salutatio* in letters to Gundulf in particular, who was among Anselm's closest friends, is often particularly direct. Anselm indeed explains the motivation for the bare *salutatio* in the letter cited: 'Ideo tam amicus tam amico salutationem meam tam breuiter

---

[40] E.g. *AEp.* 7, 42.

[41] LOUGHLIN, *Anselm as a Letter Writer*, 1968, p. 60. A fine instance of this is an appeal to Lanfranc for a man given the death penalty: 'Volens igitur ego seruulus uester notam facere uobis domni abbatis, dilectoris uestri, in re praesenti uoluntatem et modestiam, simul miserans hominem in periculo graui positum, nolui uestrae pietati hanc miserendi opportunitatem tacendo subtrahere, ne et proximus noster per indigentiam auxilii damnaretur, et uestra sanctitas praemio misericordis operis fraudaretur, et mea negligentia pro reatu inmisericordis silentii puniretur.' *AEp.* 27.

[42] The early handbooks regarded the arrangement of the names of the sender and addressee as crucial. Alberic of Monte Cassino, *De dictamine,* in ROCKINGER, *Briefsteller*, 1863, p. 41: 'Antiqui mittentium nomina solebant preponere. Moderni autem humilitatis gratia, nisi excellentissima sit persona mittentis, consueuerunt postponere. Interdum excellentissime persone humilitatis gratia sua postponunt nomina.' Half a century later, the Anonymous of Bologna did not allow letter writers of higher status a similar right to demonstrate their humility; Anonymous of Bologna, *Rationes*, 1863, p. 11: 'Est item in salutationibus notandum, ut recipientium nomina semper mittentium nominibus preponantur, siue datiuo casu cum omnibus eorum adiectiuis, siue accusatiuo cum omnibus similiter eorum adiectiuis. Nisi tunc solummodo cum maior scribit minori. Tunc enim mittentis nomen proponendum est, ut eius dignitas ipsa nominum positione monstretur.' See also Adalbertus Samaritanus, *Praecepta*, pp. 33–42.

[43] KRÜGER, *Persönlichkeitsausdruck*, 2002, pp. 134–145.

[44] *AEp.* 7; see also *AEp.* 28, 34, 316.

praenotare uolui, quia sic dilectus dilecto affectum meum opulen-
tius intimare non potui.'

The short greeting cited above is from Anselm's time at Bec:
subsequently, he became less ascetic in his choice of *salutatio*.
The change was brought about by his new status as archbishop
of Canterbury, which made him a rather grand member of the
complex networks of power, within which communications were
more formal than in the Norman monastic world. Anselm's new
position also meant that the salutations in his letters reflected the
hierarchy of ecclesiastical office more clearly than previously: a
prelate as powerful as the archbishop of Canterbury, who considered himself the primate of Britain, could not cease to display his
authority on the grounds of humility or personal friendship. The
greeting Anselm used in a letter written in around 1104, again to
Gundulf (who had in the meantime become bishop of Rochester),
is an excellent example of this: 'Anselmus archiepiscopus, reuerendo episcopo Gundulfo salutem'.[45] This, the plainest *salutatio*
from the Canterbury years, reveals particularly clearly the changes
introduced by Anselm's appointment as archbishop: the offices of
sender and recipient are stated explicitly, and above all, the name
of the sender, with his higher position in the ecclesiastical hierarchy, precedes that of the lower-status recipient.

In addition to the rather conventional understanding of the
social hierarchy that the arrangements of names expose, certain
adjustments and exceptions to Anselm's general practice are wor-
thy of note. As prior of Bec, regardless of the rank of the recipient,
Anselm always placed his own name last, whether he was writing
to a novice or ordinary monk of lower status,[46] or an abbot[47] or
archbishop of superior status.[48] When he became abbot, initially
he placed his own name first when writing to novices,[49] individual monks,[50] or to monks of Bec despatched to other monasteries

---

[45] *AEp*. 316.

[46] *AEp*. 2, 3, 4, 5, 7, 8, 9, 16, 17, 21, 24, 28, 29, 33, 34, 35, 36, 37, 38, 40, 41,
42, 43, 44, 46, 47, 50, 51, 59, 60, 64, 68, 69, 74, 75, 76, 79, 84, 85.

[47] *AEp*. 18, 26, 52, 61, 62, 65, 80, 83.

[48] *AEp*. 1, 14, 23, 25, 27, 32, 39, 49, 57, 66, 72, 77.

[49] *AEp*. 99.

[50] *AEp*. 97, 101.

or daughter-houses.[51] In every other case, including letters to the monastery of Bec, his name followed that of the recipient. Later, perhaps around the mid-1080s, however, to all intents and purposes Anselm completely stopped placing his own name first,[52] the sole exception being a particularly curt letter of rebuke and command.[53]

In the letters sent between his nomination and consecration as archbishop of Canterbury, Anselm always placed his name second;[54] the surviving letters from this period were addressed to the monastery of Bec,[55] to an abbot,[56] to bishops,[57] to a former cantor who had become a monk,[58] and to one of the stewards of the king of England.[59] Once consecrated, however, Anselm placed himself first in letters addressed to churchmen below the rank of archbishop and to all laymen, apart from rulers of high status. The monastery of Bec was an exception to the rule: Anselm expressed the special affection he felt towards the community by placing its name first.[60] If the letter was addressed to the abbot or prior of Bec alone, however, the archbishop's name came first.[61] The practice reflects the fact that Anselm was no longer bound by obedience but he still belonged to Bec's fraternity. Anselm's letter to Archbishop Asser of Lund († 1137) is exceptional in the opposite regard. He departed from his usual practice of honouring other archbishops by writing his own name first: the reason lies in the general suspicion felt towards the periphery.[62]

---

[51] *AEp.* 96, 104.

[52] See *AEp.* 119, 121.

[53] *AEp.* 137.

[54] This was not a universal custom; Lambert of Arras, *Epistolae*, ed. É. Baluze, in *Miscellaneorum collectio ueterum*, vol. 5, Paris, 1700, *Ep.* 11: 'Manasses Dei gratia Remensis electus Lamberto eadem gratia Atrebatensium Episcopo.'

[55] *AEp.* 148, 151, 156, 157, 164.

[56] *AEp.* 158.

[57] *AEp.* 159, 160, 161.

[58] *AEp.* 162.

[59] *AEp.* 163.

[60] *AEp.* 173, 178 199, 205. There were also exceptions to this rule: *AEp.* 165 and 166, written shortly after Anselm's consecration, present his name first.

[61] *AEp.* 179, 468.

[62] Compare *AEp.* 176, 261, 266, 269, 271, 274, 279, 389, 419, 432. See also the *salutationes* of Lanfranc of Canterbury, *The Letters of Lanfranc Archbishop*

The most interesting adjustments to Anselm's earlier practice in the *salutatio* relate to rulers and their consorts. During his time at Bec, Anselm had always placed his name after that of a countess or duchess, but as archbishop his name came first.[63] A letter to countess Atla, for whom the archbishop seems to have had a particular respect, is admittedly an exception to this rule.[64] Where rulers were concerned, Anselm's practice was more fluid: sometimes their names appear first, sometimes second. It seems unlikely that this was the result of any general change in attitude on Anselm's part, as he alternated between the two practices. The distribution of these letters might perhaps hint, however, that in his last years the archbishop preferred to stress his ecclesiastical office, and not to show deference to temporal powers — something the investiture contest might have caused.[65] The order of the names was apparently connected to the content of the letter and the ruler's actual power. When Anselm wrote to the counts of Savoy and Flanders and to the duke of Normandy, who were among the most significant rulers in western Christendom, either with praise for their services to the church, or with a particular request, each ruler encountered his own name first in the greeting. In contrast, the Norman earls and counts, for example, whose attitude to the rights of the church was distinctly wanting, heard their names after that of the archbishop. The same applied to Count Robert of Meulan, Henry I's adviser, considered by Anselm to be his enemy in the investiture dispute. The king and queen, however, were always placed before Anselm's own name in the *salutatio*.[66]

---

of *Canterbury*, eds. H. CLOVER & M. GIBSON, *OMT*, Oxford, 1979, *Ep.* 9 and 10.

    [63] *AEp.* 10, 45, 82, 86, 114, 131 and 167, 244, 247, 249, 325.

    [64] *AEp.* 448. This is likely to be countess Atla/Adela of Blois and Chartres (SAO, vol. 5, apparatus; FRÖHLICH, *The Letters*, vol. 3, 1994, p. 232). She was king Henry I's sister, who apparently played an important part in the negotiations between him and Anselm in the English investiture dispute. VAUGHN, *Anselm and Robert*, 1987, pp. 289–291; 2002, *passim*.

    [65] The recipient's name first: *AEp.* 180, 248, 262, 273. Anselm's name first: *AEp.* 270, 369, 412, 449, 466, 467.

    [66] Lanfranc's practice had been very similar to that of Anselm, as one would expect. He put his name second in letters to his former communities, Bec and Caen, regardless of the status of the recipient (Lanfranc, *Ep.* 18 to the prior of Bec (Anselm); 19–21 to the monks of Bec; 61 to the abbot of Caen). In writing

3.3 *Length*

In theory, the length of the letter was constrained by *breuitas*. It is impossible to define *breuitas* precisely, or even meaningfully: according to the probably most exact definition possible, 'the standard length [of a letter] is that of not encroaching upon the fuller developments proper to other literary forms'.[67] While there was no recognised limit as to length, medieval letter writers themselves often noticed when overstepping it; Bernard of Clairvaux, for example, allowed his readers to decide for themselves whether his *De praecepto et dispensatione* should be called a *liber* or an *epistola*.[68] The rule favouring brevity was acknowledged, even when breached; Peter the Venerable (†1156) claimed that the rule was being overemphasized because of the laxity of his contemporaries.[69] For his part, Anselm often drew on the rule to justify his decision not to treat a subject in greater depth.[70] But equally, he might refer to *breuitas* in a short letter,[71] while writing at far greater

to other archbishops, Lanfranc placed his name second, except in the second of his known letters to Thomas of York (Lanfranc, *Ep.* 26). His practice in letters to bishops varied (e.g. Lanfranc, *Ep.* 24 and 42, both to the bishop of Thetford). It is interesting that the names of both Queen Margaret of Scotland, and King Toirrdelbach Ua Briain of Munster, were placed after the archbishop's (Lanfranc, *Ep.* 50, 10); this is probably the result of the suspicion felt towards peripheral areas, and in the former case, also of the gender of the recipient.

[67] M. M. WAGNER, 'A Chapter in Byzantine Epistolography: The Letters of Theodoret of Cyrus', *Dumbarton Oaks Papers*, 4 (1948), p. 137.

[68] Bernard of Clairvaux, *De praecepto et dispensatione*, in *Sancti Bernardi Opera*, vol. 3, eds. J. LECLERCQ & H. ROCHAIS, Rome, 1963, pp. 253–254.

[69] Peter the Venerable, *The Letters of Peter the Venerable*, vol. 1, ed. G. CONSTABLE, Cambridge (Mass.), 1967, *Ep.* 24: 'Additur difficultati studium breuitatis, qua moderni nescio qua innata segnicie delectantur, et concaeptus illos breui cogor compendio terminare uerborum...'

[70] *AEp.* 2:71, 5:25–28, 12:31, 13:42–43, 37:76–79, 54:9–11, 65:109–111, 101:40–41, 109:13–15, 160:28–29, 165:38–40, 192:4–5, 435:34–36. The matter is discussed in more detail in GRANATA, 'Maestro di stile epistolare', 1989, pp. 253–262. St Bruno (†1101), for example, did likewise: 'Epistolaris breuitatis excessi modum, quia, dum te corpore praesentem habere non possum, saltem diutius sermocinando tecum morabor.' A. WILMART, 'Deux lettres concernant Raoul le Verd, l'ami de saint Bruno', *Revue Bénédictine*, 51 (1939), p. 270. On Peter the Venerable see the previous note.

[71] *AEp.* 54:9–11.

length without mentioning it at all at other times.[72] The occasion, rather than the rule, thus dictated the length of individual letters.

We should also note at this point that the surviving material reveals that Anselm's letters lengthened slightly on average after his move from Bec to Canterbury, and then became significantly shorter towards the end of his life.[73] The disputes associated with Anselm's promotion from abbot to archbishop elongated the early letters of the Canterbury period. Long letters become rarer soon after the turn of the twelfth century, probably reflecting the increasing burden of office — and perhaps age and ill-health — on Anselm and his correspondence. His letters refer to *breuitas* most often during his Bec years, especially while he was acting as prior; paradoxically, his letters reached their greatest length only after his departure from Bec. His more frequent references to the rules in the early years of the correspondence may perhaps reflect the very human tendency of the less-experienced to be more mindful of the rules than the experienced.[74] It should be added that the use of messengers, who were entrusted with parts of message for oral delivery, prevented letters from becoming too long or ranging too widely in content.[75] Reasons for delivering messages in part orally were, however, associated rather with diplomacy, status and confidentiality than with obeying the rules regarding *breuitas*.

[72] See in particular *AEp.* 156, which is the longest of Anselm's surviving letters (184 lines).

[73] The Bec correspondence (*SAO*, vol 3) includes 138 out-letters, thirteen of which are longer than 50 lines of print (*AEp.* 2, 17, 37, 39, 63, 65, 97, 101, 112, 117, 120, 126, 137). *SAO*, vol. 4 covers the Canterbury correspondence roughly for 1093–1104. There are 129 letters sent by Anselm, of which seventeen exceed 50 lines (*AEp.* 146, 156, 169, 160, 161, 165, 168, 169, 176, 192, 193, 198, 204, 206, 210, 214, 231). *SAO* vol. 5 has the Canterbury correspondence roughly for 1104–1109, with 101 letters sent by Anselm, only four of which are over 50 lines long (*AEp.* 311, 331, 355, 414).

[74] On *breuitas* in Anselm's theological works, see B. PRANGER, 'Anselm's Brevitas', *Anselm Studies*, 2, *Proceedings of the Fifth International Saint Anselm Conference*, eds. J. C. SCHNAUBELT, T. A. LOSONCY, F. VAN FLETEREN & J. A. FREDERICK, New York, 1988, pp. 447–458.

[75] *AEp.* 54:9–11: 'Sed ea per huius schedulae latorem plenius poteritis discere et notificare, quam breuitas epistolaris sufficiat intimare.' See also *AEp.* 4: 'Quae autem erga me sint et pro quibus te uelim mecum gaudere uel esse sollicitum, melius disces per huius schedulae latorem quam per epistolae scriptorem.' See also GRANATA, 'Maestro di stile epistolare', 1989, pp. 254–255.

4. DELIVERING LETTERS

Only the largest medieval courts were able to employ permanent couriers or messengers, who carried letters on a regular basis.[76] This may have been the case for Canterbury: given its top position in the English church, it was essential to be able to transmit information swiftly and reliably, within England at least. In contrast, the monastery of Bec probably did not need, or was not able, to employ its own permanent couriers. In one letter to Lanfranc, Anselm used the lack of messengers to justify his infrequent letters to him.[77] Bec's connections with the English churches, to which Lanfranc had moved Norman monks (especially Canterbury and Rochester), were nevertheless very close for the period. Letters could be delivered by trusted individuals who were travelling by an appropriate route, as well as by monks of Bec.

The danger, inconvenience and expense of travel meant that it was very difficult to send letters far. It made sense to give as many letters as possible to messengers who were travelling long distances, and on one occasion the same man carried letters from both Anselm and the English king to Rome while they were in dispute with one other.[78] It seems to have been a different matter on occasions when each required his own representative at the papal curia, as in 1106, for example, as the result of the investiture contest. Even then, however, the couriers might travel together.[79] Letters might also be written if someone was travelling far on personal business. An opportunity of this kind may have given Anselm the impetus to send letters to Archbishop Asser of Lund and to King Baldwin I of Jerusalem.[80]

Estimating how long letters really took to reach their destinations is difficult, especially over longer distances. A fit courier could

---

[76] CONSTABLE, *Letters and Letter-Collections*, 1976, pp. 52–53.

[77] *AEp.* 39: 'Si tam facile dictare et scribere quam loqui possem, nunquam illi, cui tam saepe loquitur cor meum, epistolarum copia mearum deesset, nisi cum inopia mihi latorum adesset.'

[78] See e.g. *AEp.* 219: '...uestrum petii per epistolam nostrum [= *AEp.* 214] concilium, quam misi celsitudini uestrae per Willelmum regis legatum.'

[79] *AEp.* 376. See VAUGHN, *Anselm and Robert*, 1987, pp. 296–297.

[80] *AEp.* 235, 324, 447. Compare FRÖHLICH, *The Letters*, vol. 3, 1994, p. 37, note 1.

travel about 40 kilometres a day on foot, or about 60 kilometres on horseback. By water, it was possible to travel 150 kilometres a day with a favourable current, but only 25 kilometres a day at the outside, when travelling against the current; the fastest galleys might achieve as much as 200 kilometres per day. The journey between Bec and Canterbury took half a week, though it could take much longer with adverse weather conditions in the Channel. Thus on his departure into exile in late October 1097, Anselm had to wait at Dover for two weeks for the weather to improve.[81] The journey from England across the Alps to the pope and back seems to have taken roughly between three and six months, depending on weather, and how long the messengers had to stay in Rome. Pope Paschal II's letter, *AEp.* 281, was written at Benevento, some 200 kilometres southeast of Rome, on 12 December 1102, and it is known to have reached Canterbury at the beginning of March 1103.[82] On 12 October 1108, the pope, again in Benevento, registered his reply to a letter that Anselm had despatched to him in or around August 1108.[83] Although the preferred season for travel in central Europe was between spring and autumn,[84] couriers also had to travel in winter, as the above examples demonstrate.[85]

5. Receiving Letters

The courier did not only deliver the letter but also often read it aloud to the recipient, even if he or she could read. This custom derived from antiquity, when letters often consisted of notes or *aides-mémoire* made for the courier. Likewise many educated individuals of the medieval period probably preferred hearing to reading for themselves.[86] It is instructive that the meanings of the words *nuntius* and *epistola* were almost identical in thirteenth-cen-

---

[81] Eadmer, *VA*, p. 97.

[82] Eadmer of Canterbury, *Historia Nouorum in Anglia*, ed. M. Rule, *RS*, London, 1884, pp. 146–147. On journeys between England and Rome, see V. Ortenberg, 'Archbishop Sigeric's Journey to Rome in 990', *Anglo-Saxon England*, 19 (1990), pp. 197–246.

[83] *AEp.* 451 and 452.

[84] N. Ohler, 'Reisen, Reisenbeschreibungen: Westen', *LexMA*, 7, Munich, 1995, col. 674.

[85] E.g. *AEp.* 376.

[86] See Peter the Venerable, *Ep.* 2 and 151.

tury juridical texts.[87] Silent reading was simply not customary at this period, and the meanings of the verbs *legere* and *audire*, for example, were easily confused.[88]

The letter itself was far from containing all the facts that the sender wished to transmit to the recipient, and the courier's role included relating the matters which were either too sensitive or too pedestrian to be put in writing.[89] In the latter event, the writer often used *breuitas* to justify not writing at greater length, as was discussed above. The many reasons for omissions arising from a genuine need for confidentiality might include the ever-present risk of the letter falling into the wrong hands, and the danger of putting matters in writing that could subsequently be used by the recipient or some other party against the wishes of the sender. Certain witnesses to Anselm's correspondence reveal how he removed overly sensitive content from particular letters, possibly at the point when the final version was drawn up on the basis of the earlier drafts. Manuscript *N* gives far less guarded versions of certain letters than the manuscripts representing the later collections.[90] The most apt example of this occurs in *AEp.* 89, a letter addressed to Lanfranc: while *N* recounts the uncertainties concerning Bec's properties in detail, the text included in the later collections merely announces that the messenger will relate these matters in more detail.

We may expect that while Anselm was still prior of Bec, his letters to his monastic friends that related to personal and local affairs were not read out by a messenger but by the addressees. In contrast, we occasionally encounter references to business affairs that were trusted not to writing, but for a courier to report by word of mouth. Once promoted to archbishop, Anselm's addressees became in general grander, including kings and popes. The grander the addressee, the more likely it was for the letter to have been read out to the recipient, rather than to be read by him or her. If the addressee was a member of the laity, with only the most

---

[87] D. E. Queller, 'Thirteenth-century diplomatic envoys: *Nuncii* and *procuratores*', *Speculum*, 35 (1960), p. 199.

[88] Constable, *Letters and Letter-Collections*, 1976, p. 54. See also M. Clanchy, *From Memory to Written Record: England 1066–1307*, 2nd edn., Oxford, 1993 [1979], pp. 253–293.

[89] Constable, *Letters and Letter-Collections*, 1976, p. 53.

[90] *AEp.* 89, 97, 118.

limited understanding of Latin, the letter had to be rendered into the vernacular or reworded into a more digestible Latin expression. Anselm's lay addressees were generally of the highest social strata and they were likely to have possessed some sort of grounding in Latin. Whether royal officials to whom Anselm occasionally sent letters were able to understand his Latin is less certain (though they were presumably competent enough to read, translate, and execute writs and writ-charters of rulers and high-ranking laymen).

A common method of assuring the recipient of the authenticity of a letter, if this proved necessary, was to attach the writer's seal to it, though other means of authentication were also known.[91] The most important laymen, churchmen, and communities all possessed their own seals. A typical ecclesiastical seal depicted the owner or a saint of significance to the community in the centre, with a legend identifying the individual or community that owned the seal encircling the image. Anselm's archiepiscopal seal can be assembled from the surviving examples, none of which is perfect. The central image shows the full figure of the archbishop standing, in dalmatic and chasuble, holding a crozier and blessing with his right hand, and holding a book in his left hand. The seal is notable as the earliest seal to show an English bishop wearing a dalmatic (although no seal of Lanfranc, Anselm's predecessor, survives). Around the image is the text 'SIGILLVM ANSELMI GRATIA DEI ARCHIEPISCOPI'.[92] From the time of his abbacy onwards, Anselm's letters make several references to his own and his correspondents' seals. If something important was at stake, Anselm might request the recipient of his letter to affix his seal to the reply, for example.[93] While archbishop-*electus* of Canterbury, Anselm, who 'was no longer an abbot nor yet an archbishop', used no seal at all, lest he 'present [himself] as a person that [he was] not'.[94]

---

[91] CONSTABLE, *Letters and Letter-Collections*, 1976, pp. 46–48.

[92] M. BRETT & J. A. GRIBBIN (eds.), *English Episcopal Acta*, 28, *Canterbury 1070–1136*, Oxford, 2004, pp. lix–lx.

[93] *AEp*. 110, 111, 141, 191, 258, 306, 316, 337, 406.

[94] *AEp*. 159: 'Sigillum haec epistola non habet, quia abbas iam non sum et archiepiscopus nondum sum, nec me delectat pingi quod non sum.' Likewise *AEp*. 161.

6. Preserving Letters

The nature of a letter collection is obviously affected by the ways in which letters were preserved prior to their inclusion in the collection. Developments in bureaucracy naturally helped improve archival systems. The papal curia boasted the most advanced administrative system of the age. Accordingly, the earliest examples of surviving registers of letters come from the papacy. The practice of gathering papal letters may have been established already in the fourth century, and was certainly followed by Leo I (†461). It is difficult to assess how continuously the custom was maintained, because only Gregory the Great's *Registrum* is extant from the early period. His register, which we know only through later copies, consisted of fourteen books, each covering material from a year of his rule.[95] The next surviving register, known through a latter copy and only partially, comes from John VIII (†882). The first pope whose authentic register books survive is Gregory VII (†1085). His register, ASV Reg. Vat. 2, comprises nine books, each giving material from one year of Gregory's reign, arranged in chronological order, although some books follow this pattern rather flexibly. The letters were entered into the register in small batches rather than one at a time, and the collection is not comprehensive: it includes only a selection of Gregory's letters (which applies to the register of Gregory the Great as well). According to a recent study, it is impossible to establish any precise principle as to how the letters were selected for inclusion in the register. Moreover, the register includes some other material besides the letters Gregory sent, namely a few letters addressed to him, records of his Lent and autumn synods in the Lateran, copies of oaths, and some other items, including the famous *Dictatus papae*.[96] Various references show that Gregory's immediate predecessor and his successors kept similar registers, although the first to survive comes from Innocent III (†1216). From then on until the end of the medieval period, papal registers survive from almost every pope.

---

[95] D. Norberg, *Critical and Exegetical Notes on the Letters of St. Gregory the Great, Filologiskt arkiv*, 27, Stockholm, 1982, p. 3.

[96] H. E. J. Cowdrey, *The Register of Pope Gregory VII (1073–1085)*, Oxford, 2002, pp. xi–xv.

Scholars have often discussed whether authors retained copies of the letters they despatched or merely the drafts generated by the many-staged production process described above. The question prompted heated debate in the first half of the twentieth century, particularly in the case of the collection of Froumond of Tegernsee, with Erdmann arguing that the texts in the collection represented fair copies of the final letters ('Reinschriften') and Schmeidler suggesting that they represented drafts ('Konzepte'). The implications of this dispute were wider than the understanding of an individual collection. Schmeidler believed that medieval letter collections were typically based on registers of letters. These registers would have consisted of drafts added in one after another as they were produced.[97] In contrast, Erdmann considered that in the eleventh and twelfth centuries, letter collections were generally composed from single-sheet letters, which were gathered back from the addressees — often by their authors — for the purpose of publication. Erdmann observed that Schmeidler's conception was in part based on an anachronistic interpretation of the word *registrum*: in the Middle Ages, the term was used for any book containing letters, and did not refer to the way in which the book was actually produced.[98]

In most individual cases, it is inevitably difficult, if not impossible, to provide a watertight answer to this question concerning the use of drafts or fair copies.[99] We know that certain authors' collec-

---

[97] I know Schmeidler's arguments on registers only through a note in C. ERDMANN, *Studien zur Briefliteratur Deutschlands im elften Jahrhundert*, *MGH, Schriften des Reichsinstituts für ältere deutsche Geschichtskunde*, vol. 1, Stuttgart, 1938, pp. 10–11. See also B. SCHMEIDLER, 'Die Briefsammlung Froumunds von Tegernsee. Bemerkungen zur Beschaffenheit frühmittelalterlicher Briefsammlungen überhaupt', *Historisches Jahrbuch*, 62–69 (1942–49), pp. 226–227, 237–238.

[98] ERDMANN, *Studien zur Briefliteratur*, 1938, pp. 7–13.

[99] Southern suggested that the nature of a letter could perhaps be established from its *salutatio* and final greetings. He proposed that collections might present drafts if the salutations and final greetings were repeatedly given in summarised form, or completely omitted; R. SOUTHERN, Review: *The Letters of John of Salisbury*. Eds. W. J. MILLOR; H. E. BUTLER; C. N. L. BROOKE. *Vol. i: The Early Letters (1133–1161)*, *EHR*, 72 (1957), p. 496. The method may be useful, but it must be applied most cautiously. For example, manuscript *F*, BL Royal 5 F. IX, repeatedly abridges letters, often the *salutatio* and closing greetings in particular; however, it is apparent that the scribe was *abridging*

tions do include drafts, but have insufficient evidence to draw any wider conclusions.[100] The other available data on the transmission of letters, which is often equally fragmentary and difficult to interpret, suggests that the authors of the day were far from following uniform practices. The letters of Fulbert of Chartres originally seem to have been copied into separate quires and single sheets, and it has been possible to establish the existence of as many as eighteen of these earlier entities.[101] Gerhoh of Reichersberg perhaps used a regularly updated register. Prior Peter of the Augustinian house of Saint-Jean in Sens apparently archived his letters individually.[102] And even individual authors might have recourse to more than one method: thus Peter the Venerable both had his letters copied into books (which may have been separate quires of the type described above), but also had in his possession authentic letters, which the

the texts in his source. See e.g. *AEp.* 136 (fol. 132v), in which Anselm's name is the only part of the *salutatio* to survive and all the closing greetings are lost, and compare manuscripts *LECV*.

[100] On Gilbert Foliot see A. MOREY & C. N. L. BROOKE, *Gilbert Foliot and His Letters*, Cambridge Studies in Medieval Life and Thought, New Series, 11, Cambridge, 1965, p. 27; on Peter of Celle see J. HASELDINE, 'The Creation of a Literary Memorial: The Letter Collection of Peter of Celle', *Sacris erudiri*, 37 (1997), pp. 368–371; on John of Salisbury see SOUTHERN, Review: John of Salisbury, 1957, pp. 495–496. Southern ('Peter of Blois', 1995, p. 933) suggested that the letter collection of Peter of Blois differed from its predecessors in that it was no longer based on drafts. Southern cites the collections of Fulbert of Chartres, Lanfranc, Anselm, Ivo of Chartres, Hildebert of Lavardin, Bernard of Clairvaux and Peter the Venerable as examples of collections based on drafts. The argument is interesting, but difficult to prove.

[101] Fulbert of Chatres, *The Letters and Poems of Fulbert of Chartres*, ed. F. BEHRENDS, *OMT*, Oxford, 1976, 'Introduction', pp. li–lii. The letters of Lanfranc and John of Salisbury may also have been preserved in this way: GIBSON in Lanfranc, *Ep.*, 'Introduction', pp. 13 15; SOUTHERN, Review: John of Salisbury, 1957, pp. 495–496.

[102] Magnus of Reichersberg, *Chronica collecta*, ed. W. WATTENBACH, *Monumenta Germaniae Historica, Scriptores*, 17, Hannover, 1861, p. 494: '...quae [the letters of Gerhoh] etiam fere omnes adhuc inueniuntur in registro et epistolario suo libro in duobus uoluminibus.' Peter of St John, 'The Letter from Peter of St John to Hato of Troyes', ed. G. CONSTABLE, *Studia Anselmiana*, 40 (1956), *Ep.* 52: 'Litteras quas mee paruitati paternitas tua misit, debita cum ueneratione suscepi, lectas in archiuo meo reposui, futurum ut eas sepissime legam, et in carta manu tua tacta deosculer manum tuam.' See CONSTABLE in Peter the Venerable, *Ep.*, 'Introduction', pp. 8–9; M. DUCHET-SUCHAUX, 'Introduction' in *Bernard de Clairvaux, Lettres*, vol. 1, *Sources chrétiennes*, 425, 1997, pp. 41–42.

recipients had returned to him. Nor was Peter's archive without
its gaps: he had to admit that, to his regret, he had not preserved
the correspondence between himself and Hugh of Amiens, archbishop of Rouen.[103] Deficiencies of this kind in the preservation of
letters seem to have been fairly common, since many authors were
forced to ask the recipients of their letters to return them, including Anselm.[104]

7. COLLECTING LETTERS

Letter collections survive for more than 200 medieval authors.[105]
These are distributed unevenly across the medieval period: for
example, only the collection of Rather of Verona († 974) is known
from the time between the collections of famous Carolingian scholars and Bishop Frothair of Toul († 847), and those of Gerbert
(† 1003) and Froumond of Tegernsee († between 1006 and 1012).[106]
From the eleventh century, the number of letter collections grows
steadily, and the levels attained in the twelfth century indicate
that letter collections had achieved a recognised and independent
place among the literary genres of the day.

The letter collections of the eleventh and twelfth centuries
were characteristically compiled on the author's own initiative.[107]

---

[103] Peter the Venerable, *Ep.* 178: 'Debuissem plane quod me neglexisse non
parum paenitet, qualescumque libros meos epistolis uobis missis implesse et
rescriptis a uobis uelut gemmeis floribus adornasse.' *Ibid., Ep.* 153: '...mitto
uobis epistolas uestras, librum quoque domini abbatis Claraeuallis ad dominum
papam, epistolas etiam duas quas a eidem domino abbati et michi misistis hoc
anno.' *Ibid.*, 'Introduction', pp. 13–14.

[104] Arnulf of Lisieux, *The Letters of Arnulf of Lisieux*, ed. F. BARLOW, *Cam-
den Third Series*, 61, London 1939, *Ep.* 1; Herbert Losinga, *Epistolae*, in *The
Life, Letters and Sermons of Bishop Herbert de Losinga*, eds. E. M. GOULBURN &
H. SYMONDS, Oxford, 1878, *Ep.* 1; *AEp.* 104 and 147.

[105] Österley (*Wegweiser durch die Literatur der Urkunden Sammlungen*, Berlin, 1885, pp. 20–45) lists about 220 authors from between the fifth and the
sixteenth century. Collections composed of letters by several authors form a
category of their own, which is not considered here. Famous twelfth-century
collections including letters by various authors are those of St Victor, Tegernsee, Admont, and Becket, and the Codex Udalrici. CONSTABLE, *Letters and Letter-Collections*, 1976, p. 59. See ÖSTERLEY, *Wegweiser*, 1885, pp. 19–20.

[106] CONSTABLE in Peter the Venerable, *Ep.*, 'Introduction', p. 5.

[107] Such collections include Peter the Venerable, Bernard of Clairvaux,
Arnulf of Lisieux, John of Salisbury, Herbert Losinga, Anselm of Canterbury,

Many authors — e.g. Peter the Venerable, John of Salisbury, Gilbert Foliot, and Peter of Blois — also published their letters more than once.[108] Where an author did not put the collection together himself, almost without exception, the task was undertaken on his behalf by a member of his own community. In many cases the editor of the letter collection undertook other literary tasks for his superior: thus the collections of Peter the Venerable and Bernard of Clairvaux were probably compiled by their secretaries under their active supervision, with both men personally editing certain letters before allowing them to be included in the collection.[109] In contrast, the secretary of Gervase of Prémontré collected his superior's letters independently.[110] Likewise the collection of Fulbert of Chartres seems to have been put together posthumously by Hildegar and Sigo, his closest pupils, who — Hildegar possibly and Sigo certainly — had also served as his secretaries.[111] The use of an editor naturally distances the letter collection from the author, and in this regard Fulbert's collection, for example, has been considered to be 'as much the product of Fulbert's school as of Fulbert himself'.[112] It is often impossible to determine where the dividing line runs between the work of the author and that of the compiler who edited his letters, and therefore how far the decisions of either influenced the selection and the editing of the letters and their texts.[113]

Wibald of Stavelot, Guido of Bazoches, Nicholas of Clairvaux, Peter of Blois, William of Aebelholt, Gerard of Wales, Gilbert Foliot, and Thomas Becket.

[108] Gilbert Foliot: MOREY & BROOKE, *Gilbert Foliot*, 1965, pp. 26–27; John of Salisbury: *The Letters of John of Salisbury*, vol. 1, eds. W. J. MILLOR, H. E. BUTLER & C. N. L. BROOKE, *NMT*, London, 1955, 'Introduction', p. ix; 1979, xlvii; Peter of Blois: L. WAHLGREN, *The Letter Collections of Peter of Blois*: *Studies in the Manuscript Tradition, Studia Graeca et Latina Gothoburgensia*, 58, Gothenburg, 1993, pp. 63–65; Peter the Venerable: CONSTABLE in Peter the Venerable, *Ep.*, 'Introduction', p. 17. Possibly also Bernard: DUCHET-SUCHAUX, 'Introduction', 1997, p. 42.

[109] CONSTABLE in Peter the Venerable, *Ep.*, 'Introduction', pp. 15–17, 41; DUCHET-SUCHAUX, 'Introduction, 1997, pp. 41–42.

[110] C. R. CHENEY, 'Gervase, Abbot of Prémontré: A Medieval Letter-Writer', *Bulletin of the John Rylands Library*, 33 (1950–51), pp. 29–30.

[111] BEHRENDS in Fulbert of Chartres, *Ep.*, 'Introduction', pp. xxxviii–xl.

[112] BEHRENDS in Fulbert of Chartres, *Ep.*, 'Introduction', p. xxxix.

[113] On Herbert Losinga's role in completing his letter collection, see L. WAHLGREN-SMITH, 'On the composition of Herbert Losinga's letter collec-

If all the letters by an author were not published in a collection (as must usually have been the case), it is necessary to consider the grounds on which letters were selected. Four motives seem to have lain behind the selection process: literary, didactic, pragmatic, and reputation-related. A division of this kind is inevitably somewhat artificial: literary motives would encompass a didactic element, as the compiler's objectives would include demonstrating good epistolary style. Purely didactic collections, designed to teach the art of letter-writing, were probably unknown in Anselm's day; these would be the creation of the professional *dictatores*. The spiritual, social, and political needs of the compiler and his community determined pragmatic motives. But even distinguishing literary and pragmatic motives is not unproblematic: 'good' literature often discusses themes which are of innate interest, and the literary taste of the day favoured themes which were considered to be spiritually and morally formative. Motives arising from a concern for reputation emerge in a desire to include in the collection letters received

tion', *Classica et mediaevalia*, 55 (2004), p. 240. In principle it is also possible that the editors of collections produced letters in their superiors' names. Certainly well-known authors composed letters sent in the names of their respective superiors; for example, both John of Salisbury and Peter of Blois did this. As far as Anselm is concerned, the use of a ghost writer is improbable. Anselm's letters and other writings, as also Eadmer's accounts, suggest a man to whom writing came easily and who had a distinctive style. It is true, however, that towards the end of his career his correspondence became ever more official in character, losing the personal touch of his earlier letters. Nevertheless, manuscript Lambeth Palace 59 includes a potential forgery, *AEp.* 475, which purportedly records Anselm's surrender of rights in lands at Saltwood and Hythe in favour of the monks of Christ Church. The main cause for doubt is the use of plural 'we' in Anselm's salutation ('benedictionem Dei et nostram'), a usage that is unparalleled in his other salutations. Throughout the twelfth century, Saltwood was the subject of recurrent disputes between the archbishop and others, and there exists another suspect document dealing with the affair; this is in Lanfranc's name and restores Saltwood to him 'ad profectum ecclesie'; D. BATES (ed.), *The Acta of William I, Regesta Regum Anglo-Normannorum*, Oxford, 1988, no. 70. In Lambeth 59, *AEp.* 475 occurs, interestingly, in the section that was removed from (and subsequently reattached to) the manuscript. The letter is also absent from the copies of Lambeth 59, namely manuscripts *P* and *E*. In other words, *AEp.* 475 was excluded from Anselm's literary output, which again strengthens the suspicions regarding its authenticity. See BRETT & GRIBBIN, *Canterbury 1070–1136*, no. 17, see the footnote. F. DU BOULAY, *The Lordship of Canterbury. An Essay on Medieval Society*, London, 1966, pp. 366–368.

from, or sent to, famous men and occasionally famous women.[114] Although it is often hard to establish the motives behind a given letter collection for certain, it should be highlighted that studies of letter collections tend to emphasize literary factors over pragmatic ones.[115] Indeed, the genre would not have been so popular were it not for its literary merits.

Some collections indeed possess a distinctive literary character: for example, every letter in the collection of Guido of Bazoches († 1203), the first known medieval angler, apparently ended in a poem, and the letters were probably composed specifically for the collection.[116] Likewise the collection compiled by an anonymous author, probably at St Albans in the 1150s, consists of letters which may only have been written with a view to publication.[117] Literary models stretching back as far as the collections of Pliny the Younger and Sidonius Apollinaris have been observed in the collections of Herbert Losinga, Nicholas of Clairvaux, Arnulf of

---

[114] Gervase of Prémontré, *Epistolae*, in *Sacrae Antiquitatis Monumenta*, vol. 1, ed. C. L. HUGO, Étival, 1725, 'Proemium': '...aliquas litteras missas supradicto Abbati meo, in praesenti libello censui inferendas; non tam propter elegentiam dictaminis, quam propter mittentium dignitatem.' See CONSTABLE in Peter the Venerable, *Ep.*, 'Introduction', p. 11. Anselm's correspondence from the Bec period comprises 147 letters, of which only eight are addressed to him. Two of these are from the pope (*AEp.* 102, which appears in manuscripts *VELPMDC*; 125, present in collections *VELPC*) and one from archbishop Lanfranc (*AEp. 30*, appearing in manuscripts *VELPC*). The remainder are from abbots (*AEp.* 70, 88), monks (*AEp.* 19, 128) and an unidentified William (*AEp.* 135).

[115] CONSTABLE, *Letters and Letter-Collections*, 1976, pp. 60–61 and references. The term 'Briefliteratur', coined by Erdmann (*Studien zur Briefliteratur*, 1938, pp. 1–2 *et passim*) and widely accepted in subsequent research, also contains an emphasis of this kind.

[116] Guido of Bazoches, *Liber epistularum Guidonis de Basochis*, ed. II. ADOLFS-SON, *Studia Latina Stockholmiensia*, 18, Stockholm, 1969, *Ep.* 23; R. C. HOFF-MANN, 'Fishing for Sport in Medieval Europe: New Evidence', *Speculum*, 60 (1985), pp. 886–887. The endings of Guido's *Ep.* 16, 26, 36 are missing as a result of damage to the manuscript.

[117] M. L. COLKER (ed.), *Epistolae ad amicum*, in *Three Medieval Latin Texts in the Library of Trinity College*, *Analecta Dublinensia*, Cambridge (Mass.), 1975, *Ep.* 30, pp. 200–201: 'Petierat, pater, fateor, dilectio tua ut diuturnum otium alicuius utilitatis conuerteremur in studium...meliores efficeremur et aliquid quod delectaretur cum profectu legentibus profiteremur. Scripsi igitur petitioni tue epistolas per tricenas mei desiderium plurimorum et actus...'. COLKER, *Ep. ad amicum*, 'Introduction', pp. 65–67.

Lisieux, and Peter of Blois.[118] Even if the letters in the compilation were clearly business correspondence, literary motives might
prompt their publication: a well-known case is the collection of
Gervase of Prémontré; although the letters relate to the governance of the order, the compiler stated that his motive was literary.[119] Pragmatic motives only seem to dominate in exceptional
cases, of which one of the best twelfth-century examples is the
Becket collection.[120] Christ Church was the centre of another notable, pragmatically-biased collection, namely the *Epistolae Cantuarienses*. The collection includes letters of the prior and convent of
Christ Church and comes from the years 1187–99. The letters deal
with the dispute that arose when archbishops Baldwin and Hubert
attempted to establish a college of secular canons at Canterbury.
The emergence of these two pragmatic collections from Canterbury within a relatively narrow period of time suggests that Christ
Church circles regarded letter collections as an effective means to
present arguments for their case.

An important, if obvious, observation made by a recent epistolary scholar is that out-letters tend to outnumber in-letters in

---

[118] Wahlgren-Smith, 'On the composition', 2004, pp. 235–237; Barlow
in Arnulf, *Ep.*, 'Introduction', pp. lxii–; Wahlgren, *Peter of Blois*, 1993,
pp. 16–17.

[119] Gervase of Prémontré, *Ep.*, 'Proemium': 'tum quia audieram a pluribus
quod idem Abbas meus in modo dicendi, pariter ac dictandi commendatur a
multis…ut sicut ipse erat adolescentiae meae Doctor pius, & benignus instruc-
tor; ita & ego essem ipsius tam in moribus, si concederetur a Domino, quam in
dictandi scientia humilis & diligens imitator.' On the character of the letters in
the collection, see Cheney, 'Gervase, abbot of Prémontré, 1950–51, p. 28.

[120] A. Duggan, *Thomas Becket. A Textual History of his Letters*, Oxford, 1980,
p. 7. Duggan, the expert on Becket's letters, emphasizes pragmatic motives
more strongly than other scholars in the collections of Arnulf of Lisieux, Peter
of Blois, Gilbert Foliot, and John of Salisbury, each of which touches on the
Becket case (*ibid.*, pp. 6–7). On Gilbert Foliot see Morey & Brooke, *Gilbert
Foliot*, 1965, pp. 23–27; on John of Salisbury, see Mynors in John of Salisbury,
Ep., 'Introduction', pp. ix–x. The same tendency is apparent in Duggan's handling of the best-known twelfth-century continental letter collections (*ibid.*,
1980, pp. 5–6). Compare e.g. Constable in Peter the Venerable, *Ep.*, 'Introduction', p. 14, Morey & Brooke, *Gilbert Foliot*, 1965, p. 13; J. Leclercq, 'Lettres
de S. Bernard: Histoire ou literature?', *Studi Medievali*, 12 (1971), p. 72; *The
Letters of Peter of Celle*, ed. J. Haseldine, *OMT*, Oxford, 2001, 'Introduction',
p. xix.

the letter collections of eleventh- and twelfth-century authors.[121] The 147 letters known from Anselm's Bec period from *c.* 1060 to 1093, for example, include only eight letters received by him.[122] The collections of Thomas Becket, with good coverage of the letters he both sent and received, and the collections of Abbot Suger and Henry of Rheims, which largely consist of the letters they received, represent exceptions to the rule.[123]

Once the letters had been selected they had to be arranged. It is very rare for the material in eleventh- and twelfth-century letter collections to be arranged solely chronologically. Some chronological hints, however, may be discerned in the arrangement of most collections. This may be a consequence (albeit one that is difficult to establish) of the ways in which letters had previously been preserved.[124] It is obviously difficult to determine that a potential chronological arrangement is in fact correct, since it was exceptional for letters to be dated, apart from those of the papal curia. Letters could also be arranged thematically,[125] or by recipient, in which case the letters sent to, and possibly also received from, each person were grouped together; at the same time, or instead of this, letters could be arranged according to recipients'

---

[121] HASELDINE, 'The Creation', 1997, p. 336.

[122] *AEp.* 19, 30, 70, 88, 102, 125, 128, 135.

[123] The collections of Suger: *PL* 186, cols. 1347–1440; and that of Henry of Rheims: *PL* 196, cols. 1565–1578.

[124] According to Haseldine ('The Creation', 1997, p. 333), 'the organisation of letter collections is rarely chronological'. If the word *purely* is added before the word *chronological*, our perspectives are identical. Although it is rare for collections to follow chronological order faithfully, chronological elements may be observed in them: BEHRENDS in Fulbert of Chartres, *Ep.*, 'Introduction', p. lii; for Ivo of Chartres, see J. LECLERCQ, *Yves de Chartres: Correspondance*, 1, 'Introduction, Paris, 1949, p. xxx; MYNORS in John of Salisbury, *Ep.*, 'Introduction', p. lii.

[125] The letters in Lanfranc's collection are arranged into a dozen more or less identifiable thematic groups. The subjects include friendship, matters relating to English monasteries, the primacy of Canterbury and canonical rulings. Some of the themes, such as the canonical rulings, appear repeatedly. It is hard to discern any chronological or other principle behind the arrangement. It is true, however, that the first of the sections, which the editors of the letters have defined fairly loosely as gathering 'papal and primatial' letters, only includes letters that may be dated to the 1070s. Many of the letters in subsequent groups may only be dated very broadly, with the period often extending up to Lanfranc's death: GIBSON in Lanfranc, *Ep.*, 'Introduction', pp. 13–15.

status.[126] Purely literary motives could also leave their mark on the arrangement; here, *uarietas* was the organising principle. Ideals originating in antiquity insisted that content and style should not be shackled,[127] and an anonymous twelfth-century letter writer justified this approach on the grounds that 'uariatio hominis est recreatio: fastidium prouocat assidua sollicitudo et unius rei continua supersessio'.[128] Of course collections were not limited to the use of one organising principle, and several may appear side by side. My survey, which is far from definitive, suggests that the arrangement of most eleventh- and twelfth-century letter collections contains chronological traces, but that these have been broken up by many intentional or inadvertent interpolations and changes.

In many cases, the manuscript tradition has further shaped the arrangement of the letters. When a copyist drew on two or more dissimilar sources, a new arrangement of letters was born.[129] This also occurred where the exemplar was a manuscript that had fallen into disrepair and thus become disordered, or had lost some of its folios.[130] If a disunited body of materials, such as loose sheets and quires, was repeatedly used as an exemplar, each copy was likely to arrange the letters in a new way.[131]

The sources thus transmit a very varied picture of the ways in which letters were preserved and through which letter collections were created. This is hardly surprising in the twelfth-century context, when the preservation and collection of letters was still an individual rather than an institutional activity. Systematic and uniform practices could emerge only in institutions with bureaucratic archival systems that transcended transitions of power.[132]

---

[126] Peter of Celle's first (subsequently lost) collection (*Rc*) was arranged according to the rank of the recipients; HASELDINE, 'The Creation', 1997, p. 350. Likewise manuscript *M* of this study, compiled from several sources by William of Malmesbury and his team, partly followed the hierarchy of offices (see III.1.2).

[127] CONSTABLE, *Letters and Letter-Collections*, 1976, p. 60; HASELDINE in Peter of Celle, *Ep.*, 'Introduction', pp. xix.

[128] COLKER, *Ep. ad amicum*, 30, p. 203.

[129] E.g. manuscript *M*.

[130] E.g. manuscripts *LE*.

[131] BEHRENDS in Fulbert of Chartres, *Ep.*, 'Introduction', pp. l–lii.

[132] The papal curia was the most efficient bureaucratic institution of the period and the earliest authentic register of letters to be preserved is that of

We know that Anselm collected his letters on at least two occasions while he was abbot of Bec on account of his own words. In a letter despatched *c.* 1086 Anselm wrote: 'we are still waiting for our letters, which Dom Maurice should have sent us'.[133] Likewise, in a letter addressed to Bec from a visit to England in 1092, he requested: 'if Dom Maurice has any other of our letters which he has not sent, send [them] to me.'[134] As the following discussion will reveal, his letters were collected at different times for different reasons, drawing on sources ranging from single-sheet letters to earlier collections. These references to Maurice, though important, provide only one insight into the process as a whole.

Gregory VII. Many of his letters, however, were never included in the register. A. MURRAY, 'Pope Gregory VII and his Letters', *Traditio*, 22 (1966), pp. 168–175; compare *Das Register Gregors VII*, ed. E. CASPAR, *MGH, Epistolae Selectae*, 2 vols., 1920–23; and *The* Epistolae Vagantes *of Pope Gregory VII*, ed. H. E. J. COWDREY, *OMT*, Oxford, 1972.

[133] *AEp.* 104 (to brothers living in a daughter house of Bec in Conflans): 'Epistolas nostras, quas domnus Mauritius nobis mittere debuit, adhuc expectamus.'

[134] *AEp.* 147 (to brothers of Bec): 'Mittite mihi *Orationem ad sanctum Nicolaum*, quam feci, et *Epistolam* quam *contra dicta Roscelini* facere incohaui, et si quas de aliis nostris epistolis habet domnus Mauritius, quas non misit.'

III. THE MAJOR COLLECTIONS

This chapter will argue that, as abbot of Bec, Anselm twice re-collected his letters, that at least one, probably two, substantial collections were executed, and that as archbishop of Canterbury, he probably had a further collection made. I call the first two collections α and β and the third ω. These conclusions can be drawn from a combination of Anselm's own words and textual evidence. In his correspondence, there are at least two, possibly three, references to the collecting of letters, while our manuscripts provide textual traces of three very early large collections. No authorial manuscript survives, however, and no surviving manuscript is an intact witness to an authorial collection. Manuscripts tend to derive from more than just one source, resulting in considerable divergence between them and the authorial foundations. Indeed, only one collection, β, can be restored in full. The chief reason for this 'contamination' is that the first two collections, α (if it ever existed) and β, were not comprehensive. They both lacked the correspondence of Anselm's Canterbury years (with the exception of the few early archiepiscopal letters in the latter), and α's selection of the Bec letters must have been more limited than that of β. In the subsequent steps of the tradition, these deficiencies were to be made up through recourse to other sources.

The two subsequent sections will introduce the manuscripts so that the first deals with the hypothetical collection α, its witnesses and their derivatives, while the second focuses on the final Bec collection β and the Canterbury collection ω. Since our manuscripts do not group into clearly distinct branches but since branches overlap, this twofold — or indeed any other observable — division matches the structure of the tradition only imperfectly. For instance, manuscript M by William of Malmesbury, to be presented in the α group, also drew on a manuscript from the ω group.

Alongside the stemmatic questions, I also seek to resolve questions that are of interest for historical research. In many cases, these analyses also clarify the internal relationships between the manuscripts. In addition, I evaluate earlier research in the field. These debates all relate to questions which are fundamental in

weighing up both the quality of the current critical edition and the original intention of the most important manuscripts. Appendix IV gives the arrangement of the letters in manuscripts *NMFLPECVO*, which are the most important witnesses to the major collections.

1. THE FIRST COLLECTION: α

Preliminary remarks

THE COLLECTION: Our evidence suggests that a major collection, α, was compiled under Anselm's direction around 1086, while he was abbot of Bec. The existence of α cannot be positively determined since the evidence is open to various interpretations.

THE WITNESSES: There are either one or two witnesses to α: *N* and possibly *M*. *M* may have drawn on *N*, and if so, it bears no evidence for α. This would weaken, but not refute the argument for the existence of α. At all events, both *N* and *M* cover letters from multiple sources, so that we can only have impure witness to α.

THE DERIVATIVES: The anonymous author of *Vita Gundulfi* almost certainly used *N* as his source for Anselm's letters to Gundulf. *M* has two descendants, *D* and *U*, which drew on other sources as well.

1.1 *London, BL Cotton Nero A.* VII – N

1086 × 1093; origin: Rochester cathedral priory (OSB); parchment; v + 157 + iv; part A (fols. 1–39) and B (fols. 41–112): I–IV^8 V$^{8-1}$ / fol. 40 / VI–XIV^8; 155 × 120 (A: 120 × 85–90; and B: 120 × 80–90) mm; 22 (long) lines

Contents

Booklet A
fols. 1r–39v	Lanfranc, *Epistolae*
fol. 40r	'*Hic tumulus claudit*' (Lanfranc's epitaph)
fol. 40v	'*Si uis uerniculum facere*' (a fragment on the making of varnish and colours)[1]

Booklet B
fols. 41r–112v	Anselm, *Epistolae* (*N*)

---

[1] Dicussed in A. PETZOLD, '*De coloribus et mixtionibus*: The Earliest Manuscripts of a Romanesque Illuminator's Handbook', in *Making the Medieval Book: Techniques of Production*, ed. L. L. BROWNRIGG, Los Altos Hills, London, 1995, pp. 59–65.

BL Cotton Nero A. VII is the oldest of all surviving witnesses to our text and will be studied in greater detail than the rest of the manuscripts in this subgroup. The present volume consists of several originally separate entities. The first two booklets, A and B, were possibly already bound together in the Middle Ages; units C and D, not relevant to this study, were apparently added on the orders of Sir Robert Cotton († 1631), for the continuous, Cottonian foliation in Arabic numerals goes through the volume.[2] Cotton added these manuscripts to his collection in or after 1603.[3] The histories of the first two booklets were possibly intertwined from the outset, wherefore the codicology, palaeography, and content of Lanfranc's collection, booklet A, will also be analyzed in detail below.

While Lanfranc's letter collection is preserved in full, the booklet including Anselm's letters has lost an unknown number of folios and the end of the last letter preserved in the manuscript is missing.[4] At least some of the missing letters can be identified with certainty, as will be discussed below. The folios have been trimmed in both books; since units C and D share the same folio size, this probably happened on Cotton's orders. The leaves were cut down conservatively and thus the prickings often remain visible. The layout — the ruling and the size of written area — is almost identical in the two booklets. The inks are almost identical in colour, though the main text of Anselm's letters is written in a slightly darker brown ink than Lanfranc's letters. Likewise, almost identical colours are used for the initials in both booklets: usually red and occasionally green or purple. Both booklets open with an initial S, of strikingly similar colouring and ornament, though the initial S in Anselm's letter collection was never quite completed.[5] Identical symbols appear in the margins of both books, further-

[2] Compare the foliation of e.g. Cotton Claudius A. XI and Cotton Titus A. XXVII.

[3] On fol. 1r 'Bruceus' appears after Cotton's Christian name; he used this name after James I knighted him in 1603. See M. P. BROWN, *A Guide to Western Historical Scripts from Antiquity to 1600,* Toronto and Buffalo, 1999, p. 70; GIBSON in Lanfranc, *Ep.,* 'Introduction', pp. 11, 15–16.

[4] *AEp.* 133:15–21 aut minuere – incessanter memorare.] *om. N.*

[5] Fols. 1r, 41r.

more, though these are hard to date.[6] The symbols probably relate
to the shared later history of the booklets. Parchment of middling
quality was used for both manuscripts, though slightly better quality parchment was employed for Lanfranc's correspondence than
Anselm's.

There are certain significant differences between the two booklets. Where the last word on the page does not fit into the final
line in full, the end of the word is placed in the lower margin in
the Anselm booklet[7] and on the first line of the following page in
Lanfranc's letter collection.[8] A black and red symbol, not present
in Lanfranc's letters, appears beside the initial letters in Anselm's
correspondence.[9] The Anselm booklet employs letters as quire
marks, also in black and red ink, while in the Lanfranc booklet
these are Roman numerals.[10]

The letters of both Lanfranc and Anselm were not copied by
the same hand. In appearance the two hands, both writing late
Carolingian minuscule of average quality, are considerably similar.[11] A specimen of the hand in Anselm's collection is in plate 1.

---

[6] See e.g. fols. 1r–3r, 43v–44r.

[7] E.g. fols. 43v, 47r, 51r, 55v, 57v, 59r, 63r, 64r, 65r, 68v, 76r, 77v, 80r, 93r,
103r, 110r.

[8] E.g. fols. 11r, 16r.

[9] Fols. 48v–50v, 53v, 57r–58r, 67v, 73v–80r and 83v. See also fols. 91r, 91v,
93r, 99r, where the symbol is used within letters to indicate divisions into paragraphs.

[10] Only one of these has survived trimming, fol. 32v: 'IIII' (in black and red
ink).

[11] Fröhlich ('Introduction', 1990, p. 29) incorrectly argues that a single
scribe wrote the manuscripts. The palaeographical evidence does not determine
whether the scribes were English or Norman. See N. R. KER, *English Manuscripts in the Century after the Norman Conquest*, Oxford, 1960, especially p. 23.
On manuscripts by scribes of English and Norman origin working together:
ibid., pl. 1b, 2, 3, 11. See also T. A. M. BISHOP, *English Caroline Minuscule*,
Oxford, 1971, pp. xvi–xvii; M. GULLICK, 'Manuscrits et copistes normands en
Angleterre (xɪᵉ–xɪɪᵉ siècles)', in *Manuscrits et enluminures dans le monde normand (xᵉ–xvᵉ siècles)*, 2nd edn., Caen, 2005 [1999], pp. 83–91. As for Lanfranc's
collection, Brown argues (*A Guide*, 1999, p. 70) that 'the style and content
indicate an origin in S.E. England, although probably not Canterbury itself.'
Christ Church had an exemplar of Lanfranc's collection, accounted by a book
list from the first half of the fourteenth century, but this does not survive;
M. R. JAMES, *The Ancient Libraries of Canterbury and Dover*, Cambridge, 1903,
p. 33, item 106: 'Gesta Lanfranci. In hoc uol. cont.: Epistola Lanfranci Cant.

\

The rubrics of the two books were also the work of two different scribes.[12] The resemblance of the main hands, the virtually uniform layout, and the almost identical decorated initials imply that the two manuscripts came from the same centre. Richard Southern proposed that the origin was Rochester, and this suggestion must be correct.[13] I have recently identified the hand of Anselm's collection in Brussels, Bibliothèque Royale 8794–99. The Brussels manuscript, apparently, consists of two codicological units or booklets (fols. 1–17 and 18–71), and the hand in question is found in both.[14] A typical Rochester *ex libris* inscription from the fourteenth century on fol. 2r provides the first part of the manuscript with a definitive Rochester provenance.[15] Furthermore, on fol. 1r there is a copy of a letter from Archbishop Geoffrey Plantagenet of York (1191–1212) to Bishop Gilbert Glanvill of Rochester (1185–1215) in a contemporary or near-contemporary hand, indicating the manuscript's whereabouts at that time. There is also textual proof supporting the Rochester origin for N. The anonymous Rochester author of *Vita Gundulfi*, written apparently between 1114 and 1124,[16] incorporated into his work four pieces of Anselm's correspondence, and certain textual variants in the *Vita* reflect a close relationship to N.[17] Finally, the exemplars of Anselm's and

Archiep. de corpore et sanguine Domini contra Berengarium hereticum. Epistole et Gesta eiusdem. Anselmus de ueritate. Item Anselmus de libertate arbitrii. Anselmus de casu diaboli. [etc.]'

[12] Fols. 1r and 41r, 94r.

[13] SOUTHERN, *A Portrait*, 1990, p. 459. Fröhlich ('Introduction', 1990, pp. 26–31) argued that the manuscript is from Bec, but he could not support this argument with any firm evidence as far as I can see. N's selection of Anselm's letters is very disordered, which suggests that it was not authorial, and makes a Bec origin less probable.

[14] Fols. 2r–13r line 16 (end of a work), and fols. 22r line 12 (Et filius)–70v line 7 (end of a work).

[15] Fol. 2r: 'Liber de claustro Roffensi per [...]'. The word following 'per' is not legible from microfilm. Gameson (*The Manuscripts*, 1999, p. 56, no. 13) argues that the second unit of the manuscript is possibly 'Collationes diuersorum auctorum in uno uolumine' of the 1122/3 catalogue (B77.93), but his case remains unproven.

[16] R. M. THOMSON, 'Introduction' in *The Life of Gundulf, Bishop of Rochester*, *Toronto Medieval Latin Texts*, Toronto, 1977, pp. 3–5.

[17] *AEp.* 4, 7, 28, 41. *LP* provide a different version of *AEp.* 28 and 41 from that of *Vita Gundulfi* and *NECV* (the other main witnesses); *AEp.* 7:3

Lanfranc's letter collections in Cotton Nero A. VII appear to have been itemized — as Southern himself noted — in medieval book lists from the library of Rochester cathedral priory.[18] The book list of 1122/23 has an item 'Epistolae domini Lanfranci archiepiscopi cum aliis minutis opusculis. in .i. uolumine';[19] the book list of 1202 has an item 'Epistole Lanfranci et Anselmi cum aliis in .i. uolumine'.[20] Together the two entries correspond to the contents of Cotton Nero A. VII fols. 1–112, with its two letter collections and short texts. If we put together the evidence from the codicology of the manuscript and that from the book lists, it appears as if two originally separate booklets were joined together at some point between 1122/23 and 1202.[21]

Cotton Nero A. VII meets very few of the criteria of an average library book from Rochester in quality and in format. Among the roughly twenty early Rochester manuscripts I have examined, with the exception of Brussels, Bibliothèque Royale 8794–99, none is comparable to its palaeographical mediocrity and small size. The Cottonian and the Brussels manuscript together are likely to represent a communal rather than an individual undertaking, although this cannot yet be verified conclusively. While the manuscripts are very similar in palaeographical and codicological terms, they were the product of more than one hand. Second, both manuscripts are likely to be very early. Anselm's collection in Cotton Nero A. VII,

---

sic dilectus *NLP and Vita Gundulfi*] *om. ECV*; 28:13 nondum *NCV and Vita Gundulfi*] non *ELP*.

[18] SOUTHERN, *A Portrait*, 1990, p. 463.

[19] R. SHARPE, J. P. CARLEY, R. M. THOMSON, A. G. WATSON (eds.), Rochester: Catalogue of the library, 1122/3, in *English Benedictine Libraries: The Shorter Catalogues, CBMLC*, vol. 4, London, 1996, B77.79.

[20] SHARPE *et al.*, Rochester: Catalogue of the library, 1122/3, in *Benedictine Libraries*, 1996, B79.84.

[21] The fact that no collection of Anselm's letters occurs in the earlier catalogue is a complexity not easily resolved. The list is part of *Textus Roffensis*, a compilation of administrative texts, now Rochester, Dean and Chapter Library A. 3. 5, currently on deposit in the Kent Archives Office (Maidstone) as MS DRc/R1. The quire containing the catalogue lacks three folios, and on the evidence of other book lists, especially that of Reading (B71 of *Corpus of British medieval library catalogues*), it has been suggested that one of the missing leaves was likely to have listed biblical books and commentaries. In other words, Anselm's letter collection is unlikely to have been itemised. SHARPE *et al.*, *Benedictine Libraries*, 1996, p. 470.

as we shall see, precedes his promotion to archbishop in 1093, while Bibliothèque Royale 8794–99 has an early version of Gilbert Crispin's *Disputatio iudaei et christiani*, which bears a dedication to Anselm the abbot (subsequently replaced with a dedication to Anselm the archbishop).[22] On the other hand, the in-house book production undertaken at Rochester began on a large scale slightly later, either in the first or the second decade of the twelfth century.[23] The two manuscripts are likely, therefore, to represent the cathedral's scriptorium at a period before the generation that produced a number of high quality library books began working.

Rochester provided a substratum for collecting the letters of Lanfranc and Anselm. Several monks of the cathedral had come to Rochester from Bec or Caen, often via Christ Church. One of them was Bishop Gundulf (1077–1108), a Bec monk who had followed Lanfranc first to Caen and subsequently to Canterbury. He was not only Lanfranc's principal assistant, whom he installed as bishop of Rochester, but also one of Anselm's closest friends and most regular correspondents. Cotton Nero A. VII was possibly the work of Gundulf's circle.

Continuing with our review of the external characteristics of the Cottonian manuscript, the annotations that refer to Anselm's correspondence may be divided into four categories: (i) corrections made by the scribe or a contemporary; (ii) corrections made in a twelfth-century hand; (iii) marginal annotations made in fourteenth-century *Anglicana*; (iv) short additions and annotations, indicating where the text of *N* is shorter than that of later collections (such as '*desunt multa*'), made in a seventeenth-century

---

[22] Gilbert Crispin, *Disputatio iudaei et christiani*, in *The Works of Gilbert Crispin*, eds. A. S. ABULAFIA & G. R. EVANS, Oxford, 1986, p. 8.

[23] The editors of the book list in *Corpus of British medieval library catalogues* date the surviving items, including the Lanfranc collection, to s. xii^{in} with two exceptions. They date item 83, a collection of homilies in Anglo-Saxon (now Oxford, Bodleian Library Bodley 340 and 342) to s. xi^{in}, and item 26, a bible (now San Marino (CA), Huntingdon Library HM 62) to s. xi^2. Gameson gives a slightly earlier date to six manuscripts: London, BL Royal 2 C. III, fol. 5–172 (his no. 460), s. xi^{ex}; Royal 3 C. X (464), s. xi/xii; London, BL Royal 5 B. XIII (482), s. xi/xii; London, BL Royal 5 D. I (489), s. xi/xii (this has two companion volumes: D. II and D. III, which Gameson dates to xii^{in} and xii^1 respectively); London, BL Royal 5 E. X (499), s. xi/xii; London, BL Royal 6 C. X (527), s. xi/xii.

hand. Lanfranc's collection likewise has four corresponding layers of annotations: (i) corrections and additions made by the scribe himself or one of his contemporaries; (ii) short citations from the letters written in the margins in fourteenth-century *Anglicana*; (iii) short descriptions of the letters' content or type, written in a seventeenth-century hand; (iv) an addition written on fol. 7r, in a seventeenth-century hand.[24] The marginal annotations in *Anglicana* in both booklets are perhaps the work of the same hand.

Dating

The latest of the *datable* letters in *N* derive from Anselm's second visit to England, in spring 1086.[25] Furthermore, manuscript *M* implies that the missing leaves of *N* possibly (though not certainly) contained *AEp*. 130–132 and 134, as I shall argue later in this chapter. Of these four letters, at least *AEp*. 130 to Abbot Gilbert Crispin and probably also *AEp*. 131 were written after this visit to England. *AEp*. 130 includes a reference to a conversation Anselm and Gilbert Crispin had had in England in 1086 concerning Archbishop Lanfranc's nephew.[26] At the time of writing, Anselm clearly still had fairly detailed memories of his journey, and he was also able to rely on Gilbert Crispin to remember their conversation well. Since one can assume therefore that Anselm had returned to Normandy only recently, the *terminus a quo* for *N* falls in the second half of 1086. Interestingly, the latest datable letters in Lanfranc's collection are also from 1086.[27]

The opening rubric of *N* runs 'Incipit liber epistolarum domni Anselmi abbatis' (fol. 41r) while the rubric indicating the change from Anselm's correspondence as prior to his correspondence as abbot is 'Hactenus continentur epistolae domni Anselmi abbatis quas fecit donec prior Beccensis fuit. Quae uero iam deinceps se-

---

[24] GIBSON in Lanfranc, *Ep.*, 'Introduction', p. 16.

[25] *AEp*. 116 (*N92*), 117 (*N77*), 118 (*N94*), 119 (*N95*).

[26] *AEp*. 130:23–24: 'De domno Lanfranco nihil melius sciui aut potui, quam quod in Anglia feci et dixi.'

[27] The editors of Lanfranc's letter collection state that the *a quo* of the archetype for the collection is around 1086 and that the text in Cotton Nero A. vii is either the first exemplar or its copy, and was made in 1100 'at the very latest'; Lanfranc, *Ep.*, 'Introduction', pp. 11–12, 15–16. Subsequent estimates as to the date are by and large based on their arguments: BROWN, *A Guide*, 1999, p. 70: *s*. xi[ex]; GAMESON, *The Manuscripts*, 1999, p. 100, no. 389: *s*. xi/xii or xii[in].

quuntur, egit postquam abbatis nomen et officium suscepit'
(fol. 94r). Since the rubricator identified Anselm as abbot of Bec
but not yet as archbishop of Canterbury, Anselm's appointment as
archbishop on 6 March 1093 provides N with an *ad quem*.[28]

Material distinctive to N

N includes three letters which appear in no other manuscript:
AEp. 18 (*N16*), 26 (*N46*), and 27 (*N48*). The arguments to be presented below suggest that these letters were additional material
acquired by the compiler of N and incorporated by him amongst
the letters he copied from his principal source, an exemplar of *a*,
our first hypothetical authorial major collection; N's position in
the stemma will be established shortly. Furthermore, the texts
of twelve letters in N differ significantly from those preserved in
some later collections.[29] The existence of two versions seems to
account for about half of these instances where a draft or rejected
version survives alongside the letter that was actually despatched.
The remaining cases can be accounted for either by the existence
of drafts or rejected versions, or by scribal errors or revision, as
emerges from a study of the readings. Subsection III.3.1 *The sources
of the Bec correspondence for* αβω will discuss these letters in detail.

The arrangement of the letters

N arranges the letters in two divisions, corresponding to the
phases of Anselm's career: the first division includes the letters he
wrote as prior, the second those written as abbot, as the rubric
dividing the sections explains.[30] Southern discerned 'an attempt'

---

[28] It should be noted that medieval rubrics, presumably in particular in manuscripts of a considerably later date than the texts they contain, are sometimes
anachronistic, as in London, BL Cotton Claudius E. ɪ (*s.* xii/xiii), fol. 147r:
'Incipit prologus libri monologios editi ab anselmo uenerabili beccense abbate'.
If the rubrics in N should derive from a lost exemplar, the *ad quem* should be
extended to *c.* 1100 on account of the palaeographical evidence. Gameson (*The
Manuscripts*, 1999, p. 100) dates the manuscript as *s.* xi/xii or xii[in]. According
to Fröhlich ('Introduction', 1990, p. 29), the second rubric in N is written over
an erasure. The text on the reverse folio side is visible through the parchment,
and this may have given him the false impression of an earlier erasure.

[29] *AEp.* 17, 25, 29, 39, 89, 97, 98, 100, 109, 117, 118, 122.

[30] Fol. 94r: 'Hactenus continentur epistolae domni Anselmi abbatis, quas
fecit donec prior Beccensis fuit. Quae uero iam deinceps sequuntur, egit postquam abbatis nomen et officium suscepit.'

at chronological order, albeit very poorly realized, in the internal arrangement of the two sections.[31] Southern's suggestion has one weakness. Thematic and other connections between the recipients, such as their location, ecclesiastical office and family relationships, influenced the precise arrangement. Letters *N21–38*, written during Anselm's time as prior, were all addressed to recipients at Canterbury. The sections arranged by recipient or on thematic principles are usually much shorter than this, often formed from only two letters. For example, in both letters *N48* and *49* Anselm intercedes on behalf of a third party.[32] The recipients of letters *N50–52* were all members of Anselm's family.[33] Letters *N76–79*, though all addressed to different individuals, open with two letters encouraging the recipient to take up the monastic life, followed by two letters congratulating the recipients on taking this step.[34] In letters *N37* and *38* Anselm reports to Lanfranc upon the progress of the monks the archbishop had sent to Bec.[35] The theme of returning to one's own monastery links letters *N55* and *56*.[36] Two consecutive bishops of Rochester received letters *N59* and *60*.[37] In letter *N88* Anselm asked Countess Ida to assist a certain Richard in his plans to become a monk of Bec, and in letter *N89* he tempted a certain Wilencus to enter this monastery as well.[38]

Evaluation of earlier scholarship on N: *Schmitt and Southern*

Schmitt argued that *N* was made in about 1090, and was a copy of a collection put together under Anselm's direction in around 1085. His dating of *N* was based on observations concerning the relationship between *N* and *M*, our next manuscript to be discussed. Schmitt suggested furthermore that a sequence of letters in *M* (*M18–73*) came from *N* or a 'Duplikat' of it. Since some letters in this sequence were missing from *N*, he argued that these letters

---

[31] SOUTHERN, *A Portrait*, 1990, p. 462.

[32] *AEp.* 27 and 48.

[33] *AEp.* 54–56.

[34] *AEp.* 95, 117, 99 and 101.

[35] *AEp.* 39 and 66.

[36] *AEp.* 76 and 62.

[37] *AEp.* 78 and 53.

[38] *AEp.* 114 and 115.

must have been on the missing leaves of N.[39] The penultimate of
the missing letters, AEp. 146, can be dated roughly to 1090–1092,
and Schmitt considered this decisive in dating the manuscript.[40] I
must reject Schmitt's narrow dating of N to 1090 and also remould
the argument that N or its duplicate was necessarily M's source.
Schmitt's use of the term 'duplicate' is indeed problematic, as it is
unclear how much such an exemplar could differ from N. The following three points undermine Schmitt's argument.

(One.) More of the letters missing from N are included in the
relevant section of M ($M18$–71) than Schmitt noted: a total of
nine, not five.[41] These nine letters include two letters received by
Anselm, neither of which should have been included in N according to its rubric ('continentur epistolae...quas fecit...egit').[42] It is
therefore possible that this section of M drew on a source containing rather more diverse texts than N, in which case a 'duplicate' of
N is an inappropriate term to use for M's source.

(Two.) The arrangement of the letters in M reveals that material in the sequence in question, $M18$–71, was copied into M as
two consecutive sections.[43] AEp. 146 and 145, which are so central for Schmitt's dating of the manuscript N, follow the second
of these sections and thus could equally well belong with the four
subsequent letters.[44] These four letters, and thus perhaps also AEp.

---

[39] SCHMITT, 'Zur Entstehungsgeschichte', 1936, pp. 311, 313–314; SCHMITT,
'Die Chronologie der Briefe des hl. Anselm von Canterbury', *Revue Bénédictine*,
64 (1954), p. 178; SCHMITT, 'Die echten und unechten Stücke', 1955, p. 218.
Fröhlich (e.g. 'Introduction', 1990, pp. 29–31) simplified Schmitt's argumentation and results. He believed that N was the very manuscript that Anselm was
planning when he asked to have his letters back from Maurice in 1086. His
claim is clearly invalid and need not be analyzed here.

[40] AEp. 146 has two addressees, John and Boso, both brothers of Bec serving temporarily at Séez. Boso had become a monk at Bec at a late stage of
Anselm's abbacy since his name is 123rd out of 163 monks professed during
Anselm's period as abbot. Southern suggests a date *c*. 1090 for the profession
(Eadmer, *VA*, p. 61; for Boso's noviciate, see *ibid*., pp. 60–61). John had been
professed a little earlier as his name is 101st. Some time had probably passed
since Boso's profession before he and John were sent to Séez.

[41] AEp. 131, 130, *134*, *132*, *135*, 88, 96, *146*, *145*. The letters cited by
Schmitt ('Zur Entstehungsgeschichte', 1936, p. 311) are in italics.

[42] AEp. 88 and 135.

[43] First section: fols. 128r–141r; second section: fols. 141v–144v.

[44] AEp. 156, 148, 120, 425.

146 and 145, were either copied from an unknown source or from material added *later* to N or another witness to α. The fact that the other four letters derive from Anselm's time at Canterbury, from between 1106 and 1108 at the latest, clearly points to this conclusion.

(Three.) *AEp*. 146 and 145, and the four following letters, all differ from previous material in M in one significant regard: in these six letters the name of the recipient is abbreviated to a single initial (for example B for Bosoni),[45] whereas the letters immediately preceding these (that derive from N or α) all give the name of the recipient in full.[46] *AEp*. 146 and 145 may thus perhaps derive from the same unknown source as the subsequent set of the four letters.

To conclude, Schmitt's stance appears too tight. M did not *possibly* use N or its duplicate as its source; the source may have been a lost exemplar of collection α. There is no solid reason to suggest that the α source — be it N or a lost manuscript — would have included *AEp*. 146 and 145, wherefore Schmitt's dating of N to *c*. 1090 must be rejected, in favour of the broader dating given here.

In order to combat Schmitt, Fröhlich, and Vaughn, Southern argued against the assumption that N would be or descend from an authorial collection.[47] Although my understanding of N resembles that of Southern in several aspects, I am not in absolute agreement with him. On the one hand, the origin Southern ascribed to N indeed hits upon the truth; he held that N was a compilation made by 'an unauthorised admirer' in Rochester. On the other hand, it would be against his view that N is partly based on an

---

[45] *AEp*. 156, 120, 425 abbreviate the name of the recipient. *AEp*. 148 in contrast is addressed to the monks of Bec. The scribe and possibly also the source changes after these letters.

[46] The exception is *AEp*. 17, i.e. *M13*, in which M abbreviates the recipient, who is named in full in N.

[47] Southern tried to establish two things: first, that N could not have been the collection compiled by Anselm in the mid 1080s; second, that 'the compiler of N had access to Anselm's materials *in an imperfect state* [this would be α by implication], before he had finished making his collection of drafts and copies, and there are *no signs that he ever resumed it*' (my emphases); SOUTHERN, *A Portrait*, 1990, p. 463. He (*A Portrait*, 1990, pp. 464–465) considers it possible that Anselm arranged Bec's archives while in exile at the monastery in 1105, and that this accounts for the arrangement of the Bec correspondence in V.

authorial collection. Because between our positions divergence is clearly at least as significant as convergence, I need to comment on his argumentation on the subject. In support of his conclusions, Southern advances five arguments, each of which seems problematic to me.[48]

(One.) Southern argues that the arrangement of the letters within N's sections covering Anselm's correspondence as prior and abbot is 'chaotic', although it is possible to discern 'an attempt' at chronological arrangement. The argument is in part misleading. There was no generally accepted internal arrangement for letter collections, and letters could equally well be arranged according to non-chronological principles. A variety of principles appear concurrently in the arrangement of letters in N, with letters arranged by theme and recipient as well as by chronology.

(Two.) Southern suggests that too much material is missing from N for Anselm to have initiated its compilation. Anselm's own words reveal, however, that he did not possess copies of all his letters. Against this background, the coverage of N can be considered satisfactory. Twenty of the 87 letters known from Anselm's time as prior are missing. If we take into account the fact that according to its rubric, N is to cover only Anselm's out-letters, four of the twenty missing letters can be eliminated.[49] It is rather more difficult to assess how complete coverage N offered for Anselm's correspondence as abbot, since an unknown number of folios are missing from the end.

(Three.) The relationship between Southern's third argument and his overall thesis is not clear to me, and the argument is therefore cited in full:

> Among the missing letters are all those which Anselm wrote to Maurice, with the exception of a draft of one [AEp. 97], and the text of another which was written to several other monks besides Maurice [AEp. 51]. Of these, the draft may have been in Anselm's possession, and Anselm could have received the letter sent to several monks from one of its other recipients.

Southern's observations to my mind weaken rather than support his point, since the use of the a rejected version or a draft of

---

[48] SOUTHERN, A Portrait, 1990, pp. 459, 462–463.
[49] AEp. 19, 30, 31, 70.

the letter to Maurice included in N agrees with our information on Anselm's attempts to get Maurice to return him his letters.

(Four.) N includes too many drafts to have been compiled under Anselm's direction. In fact, the inclusion of the drafts or rejected versions again indicates Anselm's involvement rather than the opposite. The simplest solution is to consider that Anselm himself retained the versions that were not sent, and the case of Maurice also reveals that Anselm did not always request copies of all the letters he despatched.[50]

(Five.) N was not apparently preserved at Canterbury along with the rest of Anselm's literary legacy. This argument proves nothing. If N, as is very probable, was not at Canterbury, it was available elsewhere—*non plus ultra*.

Finally, Southern erroneously suggests that N includes letters from between 1070 and 1092. This misleading statement has brought the *a quo* to 1092, and regrettably has also influenced subsequent assessments of the dating of the manuscript.[51] In fact, though N includes a number of letters that are (at least for the nonce) datable only to Anselm's abbatial years 1078–93, its latest letters that can be dated more accurately are from 1086.[52]

1.2 *London, Lambeth Palace 224* – M

1119 × *c.* 1125; Malmesbury (OSB); parchment; ii + 210 + iii; I^{10} II–X^8 XI^4 XII^{10} XIII^8 XIV^4 XV–XVI^8 XVII^{10} XVIII–XXI^{8+2} XXII^{12-3} XXIII^{14-4} XXIV–XV^8 XVI^{10}; 275 × 175 (210 × 130) mm; 40–41 lines in two columns

---

[50] Admittedly Southern's argument fits the case of one possible draft or rejected version in N, *AEp.* 118, addressed to the monks of Bec. Thus the final letter should have been in Bec. The significance of this case should not be over-emphasized, however: the scribe of the potential collection a would have copied letters mainly from Anselm's own archives possibly in England while Anselm was there in 1086. Furthermore the sheer numbers of letters meant that he would inevitably be only superficially acquainted with the contents of individual letters. N (with an unknown number of folios lost from the end of the manuscript) contains 98 letters, and its potential precursor a would have contained about 60–100 letters.

[51] E.g. GAMESON, *The Manuscripts*, 1999, p. 100, no. 391: 'xi/xii or xii^{in} (?1092 × 1100)'.

[52] *AEp.* 116 (*N92*), 117 (*N77*), 118 (*N94*), 119 (*N95*).

Contents

---

[53] First lines 22–91, 'Si malum–quod fecit', then lines 1–2, 'Frater Anselmus–dei benedictionem', finally lines 17–21 'scriptum illud–epistolae direxi'. 97:21 direxi] destinaui *M* (fol. 86v). The text possibly occurs under the title *Si malum nihil est* in two book catalogues: R. H. Rouse, M. A. Rouse & R. A. B. Mynors (eds.), *Registrum Anglie de libris doctorum et auctorum ueterum*, CBMLC, vol. 2, London, 1991, R33.10; and Henry de Kirkestede, *Catalogus of Henry de Kirkestede*, eds. R. H. Rouse & M. A. Rouse, CBMLC, vol. 11, London, 2004, K3.36. William's version might mark the starting point of the tradition of the text.

[54] This includes the first version of *Epistola de incarnatione Verbi*.

London, Lambeth Palace 224 covers Anselm's key treatises and close to half his correspondence. The manuscript was copied by William of Malmesbury and his team of scribes.[55] William not only copied a significant proportion of the texts himself, but he also compiled the list of contents, corrected errors, and added marginal annotations to the texts copied by other scribes. The subsequent discussion will draw on the work of Rodney Thomson, the leading authority on William and his manuscripts.[56] The parchment is of poor quality and the quiring is irregular. The quire marks are in the bottom margin of the recto side of the first folio in each quire; these are letters in alphabetical order and are much later in date than the manuscript. The quires have been trimmed but the prickings remain; the lines and margins are ruled in dry point. The brown ink is sometimes slightly greyish in colour, while the simple initials are brown, red, or purple; there are just four larger, ornamented initials.[57] In comparison with William's other manuscripts, M is only of average quality. The second flyleaf has William's colophon, and below this is his list of contents, which concludes with the *Epistolae*. At the end of the fourteenth century, the list was extended to include the texts added to the manuscript at the time. The letters are followed by *De processione Spiritus Sancti*. The first part of the work was copied to fol. 174r–v in a contemporary or near-contemporary hand, which does not appear in William's other known manuscripts. Nor does the work appear in the original list of contents, suggesting that it did not form part of William's project. About a dozen folios were left blank by the team, implying that the collection of texts as originally planned was perhaps never completed.[58] The missing section of the *De processione* and the subsequent texts are in a fourteenth-century hand. Nine hands appear in the manuscript up to the fourteenth-century section. Two of these, Scribe A and Scribe B (as named by Thomson), and

[55]   The colophon in William's hand (fol. ii^r) reads 'Disputat Anselmus presul cantorberiensis. / Scribit Willelmus monachus malmesberiensis. / Ambos gratifice complectere lector amice.'

[56]   R. THOMSON, *William of Malmesbury*, 2nd edn., Woodbridge, 2003 [1987], pp. 76–96.

[57]   Fols. 1r, 40r, 53v, 103r.

[58]   The original ruling continues up to the last folio (187v) of the quire in question.

of course William himself, also worked on his other manuscripts. In Anselm's letters (fols. 120v–174r) we encounter four hands: William, Scribe A, Hand VII, and Hand VIII (see the table below). There were perhaps two rubricators.

The manuscript gives only the first words of certain papal letters and advises that the reader 'require in decretis pontificum'.[59] The work in question is William's edition of the *Liber pontificalis*, which he compiled in or shortly after 1119.[60] In other words, the *a quo* of *M* is 1119. The *ad quem* is slightly trickier to establish, but again William's other work proves helpful. In the *Gesta pontificum*, he relies closely on Eadmer's *Historia nouorum* and *Vita Anselmi* as his main sources for the life of Anselm, but the work also reports details not found in Eadmer or in any other work preceding the *Gesta* — apart from Anselm's letters. The *Gesta* (46.2 and 47.1) accounts that before his promotion to archbishop, Anselm had first been a monk for three years, subsequently prior for fifteen years, and finally abbot for another fifteen years. The only known source for these dates that precedes the *Gesta* is *AEp.* 156, which *M* includes. The manuscript shows that William had read this letter and the passage in question carefully. The scribe who copied the letter missed the crucial words 'quindecim in prioratu' (and wrote 'aut dominatione' instead). William, who corrected the manuscript, observed the error and added the missing words above the line (fol. 145va, line 15; plate 2). *M*'s *ad quem* is, therefore, the *Gesta pontificum, c.* 1125.[61] The sources *M* deploys — earlier compilations instead of archival letters — imply that William was working at Malmesbury, not at Christ Church, which he is known to have visited at least once.[62] He must also have had his *Liber pontificalis* at hand; otherwise the team could not have omitted the letters it covers.

---

[59] *AEp.* 281 (*M140*), 283 (*M142*), 303 (*M145*), 222 (*M148*), 223 (*M149*).

[60] On its dating, tradition and contents, see THOMSON, *William of Malmesbury*, 2003, pp. 119–136 and W. LEVISON, 'Aus Englischen Bibliotheken. II', *Neues Archiv der Gesellschaft für deutsche Geschichtskunde*, 35 (1910), pp. 410–411 and *passim*.

[61] Since Anselm is one of the main characters of the *Gesta*, it would have been natural to William to consider his letters necessary background reading.

[62] Cf. SOUTHERN, *A Portrait*, 1990, pp. 459, 470–473. On William's itinerary see THOMSON, *William of Malmesbury*, 2003, pp, 72–75.

1.3 NM *in the tradition*

Sources for N

Shortly before his journey to England in 1086, Anselm wrote a letter to the monks of Conflans, a daughter-house of Bec, in which he declares: 'Epistolas nostras, quas domnus Mauritius nobis mittere debuit, adhuc exspectamus.'[63] Anselm was evidently collecting his letters back home. He might have continued the project during his subsequent visit to England, where most of the recipients of his known letters lived. What this statement does not establish is whether or not a collection of letters was executed in the form of a book, in contrast to merely gathering out-letters back home. The surviving body of evidence implies that a book was made.

In 1092, during his second visit to England, Anselm was again engaged in collecting up his letters: he asked the monks of his own monastery to send him *any other* letters that Maurice had not *yet* despatched.[64] In other words, by 1092 Maurice had returned some but not all letters. It is unclear from the wording of the two passages alone whether Anselm's requests referred only to letters addressed to Maurice, and therefore preserved by him, or to letters Anselm had sent to others as well. The note from *c.* 1086 may have referred to letters of both types. The note from 1092 referred almost certainly to letters addressed to persons other than Maurice. By 1092, Maurice would certainly had more than enough time to return the letters Anselm had addressed to him.[65] The implication

---

[63] *AEp.* 104. The dating of the letter to *c.* 1085 is based on the passing comment that Anselm had lately recovered from a serious illness ('de aegritudine, quam nuper habui, bene conualesco'); *AEp.* 106, in which Anselm congratulates Gilbert Crispin on the abbacy of Westminster, which he received in 1085, also refers to the illness. Sainte-Honorine at Conflans was a dependency of Bec founded in 1080.

[64] *AEp.* 147:13–15 'Mittite mihi *Orationem ad sanctum Nicolaum* quam feci, et *Epistolam* quam *contra dicta Roscelini* facere incohaui, et si quas de aliis nostris epistolis habet domnus Mauritius, quas non misit.'

[65] It might perhaps be a possibility, although a rather far-fetched one, that the 1092 reference is to letters addressed to Maurice after *c.* 1086. Since the 1092 letter was sent to Bec (and not to Conflans), the impression is, however, that Maurice was now at Bec where he could easily have handed over his own letters to Anselm.

is that at some point before 1092, Anselm had commissioned Maurice to collect and return his letters from their addressees.[66] What we know about Maurice and what we know about the making of medieval letter collections would corroborate this perfectly. When he was living in Christ Church in the 1070s, Anselm had set him the task of obtaining and copying manuscripts for Bec.[67] At that time, he was also charged with helping Anselm publish his first substantial work, *Monologion*.[68] In the 1080s, when Maurice was at Conflans, he received a sketch towards *De casu diaboli* (*AEp.* 97). The impression is that Maurice performed the functions of a 'literary secretary' for Anselm. Men in similar positions are frequently found behind the letter collections of medieval authors, as chapter II demonstrated. Finally, Maurice's widespread networks, resulting from his peripatetic, cross-channel career, added to his suitability for the task. The 1092 letter, indeed, suggests that he was the keeper of Anselm's letter archive at Bec.[69]

Schmitt and Fröhlich completely overlooked the possibility that these references to Maurice revealed a process other than the return of letters addressed exclusively to Maurice himself. This led them to argue that the number of letters addressed to Maurice present in any manuscript could be taken as decisive evidence in plotting the evolution of the collections drawn up under Anselm's direction. But since the method is based on flawed grounds, it is likely to produce erroneous results. My inquiry, nevertheless, opens with a discussion on the letters addressed to Maurice.

N includes only *one* letter, *AEp.* 97, of Anselm's nine known letters to Maurice, and significantly, subsequent collections present a text that differs radically from *N*'s version of *AEp.* 97. *N*'s text is a rejected version, which Anselm could have retained him-

---

[66] Erdmann (*Studien zur Briefliteratur*, 1938, p. 10) and Southern (*A Portrait*, 1990, pp. 461–462) noted that Maurice could either have been charged with sending back the letters addressed to him, or collecting letters from other addressees.

[67] *AEp.* 42, 43, 60.

[68] *AEp.* 74.

[69] I am grateful to Prof. Richard Sharpe for drawing my attention to this point.

self.[70] The passages cited above show that by 1092, Maurice had returned at least some, and probably all his letters to Anselm. I shall demonstrate below that an authorial collection was drawn up soon after the letter of 1092 and that this collection covered all the known letters sent to Maurice and also the final version of *AEp.* 97.[71] Seen against this background, *N* fits the situation in the mid 1080s when, judging by the request Anselm sent to Maurice, he might not have had copies of any of his correspondence to Maurice. There are also other drafts or rejected versions of certain other letters in *N*, as section III.3.1 will show. Material of this type was most likely to be in the possession of Anselm himself, and it was most likely to wind up in a letter collection drawn up in his own monastery. *N* was not executed under Anselm's command, however. I call the hypothetical authorial collection of *c.* 1086 α. *N* is likely to derive from α, but its witness to α must be contaminated. The manuscript includes letters that were likely to be absent from the hypothetical α and may also lack letters found in α. The following five arguments support the view that *N* amalgamates a large authorial collection — that is, α — and a clutch of letters originating elsewhere.

(One.) *N* gives two letters twice, first on the initial folios and then again a little later.[72] This duplication is obviously an error. A recent study demonstrates how meticulously Anselm edited and published his texts.[73] He is unlikely to have authored a collection plagued with duplicates. The duplicates rather suggest that *N* (or its lost exemplar) drew on two sources. (Two.) The aforementioned duplicates occur in the context of a group of eighteen letters, all sent to Canterbury (*N21–38*). Since no comparable geographically oriented section emerges elsewhere, this raises the possibility that the sequence derives from another source than the material around it. There is some evidence suggesting that one of the sources for this sequence was *Schmitt 15* or, more likely, a clutch of letters

---

[70] *AEp.* 97 (*N80*). It must be unlikely, although still perhaps possible, that Anselm edited the letter thoroughly before publishing it in his subsequent collection.

[71] See III.3.1. The sources of the Bec correspondence for $\alpha\beta\omega$.

[72] *AEp.* 6 = *N5* and *N30*; *AEp.* 38 = *N9* and *N36*.

[73] SHARPE, 'Anselm as author', 2009.

behind *Schmit 15*.[74] (Three.) *N* includes drafts that were replaced by final versions in two subsequent collections, β and ω. Drafts were most likely to be preserved in Anselm's archive, and their presence in *N* implies an authorial collection somewhere behind it. A party without authorization from Anselm, working in Rochester while he was still abbot of Bec, could hardly have been able to put together as large a collection as *N* from scratch. (Four.) *N* includes three letters, *AEp.* 18, 26, and 27, that are found in no other manuscript. This too suggests a non-authorial pedigree, since there is no observable reason why Anselm should have suppressed these letters from his next collection. (Five.) It is *possible* that *M* derives from a source that preceded *N* and lacked the sequence of eighteen letters to Canterbury.

To sum up: when we combine our information on Anselm's efforts to gather his letters together with all the evidence discussed above, it appears likely that *N* had a predecessor, collection α. This collection was probably put together under Anselm's supervision in around 1086.[75] Although α must have resembled its descendant *N* in content, they were hardly identical. α probably included some letters received by Anselm, and it lacked some of the material later included in *N*. The letters missing from *M* and β but present in *N* are likely to belong to the material that *N* obtained from somewhere else than α. The compiler of *N* thus seems to have expanded the collection by a minimum of five letters. But he may have added rather more letters, maybe even about 40 (for the total number of letters included in *N* but missing from *M* is 42). In other words, α might have included some 60–100 letters.

Obviously no part of α can be persuasively restored. But if *M* proves to be independent of *N* (an issue to be discussed below), we may reach α's readings for the letters that are preserved either in the α-sections of *N* and *M*, or in β and the α-section of *M*. In this

---

[74] See the brief discussion '*The addition to* AEp. *41*: 'Vinculum coniugale' in chapter IV.1.

[75] On the basis of *M*, the latest datable letter in α was probably *AEp.* 130, which Anselm wrote shortly after his visit to England in 1086. Southern has argued that Anselm compiled a collection already during his journey to England, while staying with Gilbert Crispin, but the evidence is thin; 'St. Anselm and Gilbert Crispin, Abbot of Westminster', *Mediaeval and Renaissance Studies*, 3 (1954), pp. 87–88.

scenario, M's presence would be needed constantly, as it is unclear how far the material in β that is missing from M and found in N derives directly from individual letters archived or collected by Anselm and how far it derives (if it indeed derives at all) from α. β could rely entirely on the single-sheet letters or archived copies in his possession. This leads to the *provisional* conclusion that α's readings may be indicated by N, $M(18–71)$, and β according to the following agreements. α may be:[76]

    (1)   the agreement of $NM\beta$
    (2)   the agreement of NM
    (3)   the agreement of $M\beta$

Because M's α-section was contaminated by F (see the discussion below), which derives from ω, one must be even more cautious when reaching for the text of α through the third agreement. As a by-product, the third agreement might allow us to identify at least some of the letters that were included on the missing folios of N; these are $AEp.$ (96,) 130, 131, (132, 134). The case of the letters in brackets is more uncertain than that of those without, since these are also given by another source of M (namely by F or its unknown copy). Finally, it cannot be emphasized too strongly that any conclusion touching upon the selection and arrangement of letters and their texts in α is bound to be speculative.

The sources for M

M drew on three identifiable major sources and an unknown number of unidentified minor sources. Two of the major sources can be pinned down relatively straightforwardly: manuscript F or, less likely, its derivative, and Eadmer's *Historia nouorum*. The third was either manuscript N or a lost exemplar of α. In the following discussion, this source is referred to by the siglum α in quotation marks. The table below demonstrates the sources, the scribes (as Thomson has identified them) and arrangement the letters followed in M. A discussion substantiating these results follows the table.

---

[76] Note that here M refers only to the section $M18–71$.

Table 1: The sources, arrangement, and scribes of *M*

letters		source	arrangement	hand
M1–3		unknown		A
M4–17		*F*[77]	*F*	William
M18–71		'*a*'; possibly *N*; contamination from *F*	predominantly *F* until *M34*, then predominantly '*a*' or *N*	William until *M34*, then Hand VII
M72–79		unknown		Hand VII
M80–107[78]		*Historia nouorum*	*Historia nouorum*	Hand VIII
M108–137		*F*	*F*	William
M138–214				
M138–149	pope	*F*	original	William
M150–152	king of England	*F*	reversed	William
M153–162	queen of England	*F*	original	William
M163–164	rulers other than kingdoms	*F*	reversed	William
M165–166	Matilda of Tuscany	*F*	original	William
M167–171	archbishops and bishops	*F*	initially original, then reversed	William
M172–196	Canterbury	*F*	original	William
M197–203	prelates of other kingdoms	*F*	reversed	William
M204–210	monks	*F*	initially original, ending reversed	William
M211–214	nuns	*F*	original	William

The table demonstrates that letters from each source were copied as sequences of different lengths. In certain cases individual scribes were responsible for copying texts from particular sources; for example, only Hand VIII appears in the section coming from *Historia nouorum*. The first two letters are from an unknown source. These are followed by an early version of *Epistola de incarnatione Verbi*, composed before Anselm's promotion to archbishop and

[77] It should be noted that it remains beyond final verification whether it was *F* or its unknown copy that acted as *M*'s source.

[78] *M82* (*AEp.* 337) from an unknown source.

possibly sent to him from Bec in winter 1092/93.[79] M is our only witness to this version. Then follows a series of letters ($M4$–17) copied from F, either from the surviving manuscript or, less likely, from its unknown descendant. The relationship is revealed by the arrangement of the letters[80] and the shared readings.[81] Certain readings indicate that M's source was either the surviving manu-

[79] In this text Anselm recognizes himself as abbot (fol. 121v: 'Anselmus quamuis indignus diuina tamen dispositione dictus abbas beccensis'). The final version entitles him archbishop. When he came to England in 1092 he asked the Bec brothers to send him an unfinished draft (*AEp.* 147: 'Mittite mihi...*Epistolam* quam *contra dicta Roscelini* facere incohaui'). Anselm rewrote the text at Canterbury. On the evolution of the text, see SHARPE, 'Anselm as author', 2009, pp. 35–43, and F. S. SCHMITT, 'Cinq recensions de l'epistola de incarnatione verbi de S. Anselme de Cantorbéry', *Revue Bénédictine*, 51 (1939), pp. 275–287.

[80] The arrangement in $M4$–17 diverges from that in F twice (see *AEp.* 36 and 112).

[81] The evidence for the connection between FM abounds and I shall present only a small portion of it.
(1) FM are together weaker than the other branches. 9:10 congratulationem LP] passionem FM *corr. from* compassionem F; 49:1–2 reuerentiae–et filius] archiep. L. FM; 49:4–22 Sicut–oboedio *om.* FM; 121:3–19 Benedictus deus – commemoro *om.* FM; 121:20 igitur *om.* FM; 136:3–31 Audio–resipuerit *om.* FM; 137:4–15 *om.* FMD; 161:5–10 Quamuis – commonere *om.* FM; 272:21 eligunt] hoc *add* FM; 291:15 semper consolatione faciat uos FM semper uos consolatione faciat CV; semper consolatione faciat LPE.
(2) FM together offer a better reading than the other branches. 113:11 precantium FM] precantum $LPCVE$.
(3) F is better than M. M often omits passages that F includes or abridges the letters more extensively than F. The following list mentions only few cases: 9:2 quantum expedit et salutem animae quantum sufficit M; 31:3–14: Quia – deposcite] *om.* M; 121:49–50 Carissime–tardare. *om.* M; 136:41 ueneratur F ueneretur M; 161:18 breuiter *om.* M; 161:20 deus fortis *om.* M; 161:32 in eo conceptus M; 162:33–35 Lege–monacho. *om.* M; 320:22–26 qui–teneat *om.* M.
(4) Anomalies, i.e. M stronger than F. 121:22 calcantium $MCVE$] conculcantium FLP; 203:18 enim est M] est enim F; 249:2 Clementiae M] .C. F; 264:7 sic M] Si *ceterii cod.*; 266:7 habebamus M] habeamus F; 302:12–13 ostendet esse M] esse ostendet F; 311:53 Edmerus et Alexander M] E. et A. F; 333:21 hominibus M] omnibus F; 335:22 anhelabas M] hanelabas F; 335:26 Lanzoni M] .L. F; 354:6 promotioni MC] promonitioni $FLPE$; 361:8 ipsa M] ipsam F; 375:9 enim est M] est enim F; 385:1 reginae Anglorum Mathildi] M. Anglorum reginae F Mathildi reginae M; 413:1 Scottorum M] scotorum F; 421:19 etiam ea M] ea etiam F.

script or its descendant.[82] The relatively short time span between the manuscripts M and F, and F's distinctive character — owing to the manuscript's tendency to omit and abridge letters — imply that the source was the surviving manuscript F. At this early stage, when interest in Anselm remained strong, a compilation like F was probably not comprehensive enough to achieve a significant position in the tradition. It was, indeed, for this very reason that William also drew upon other sources. The letters derived from the F source (hereafter F) were copied by William, who apparently selected material from the manuscript with a view to providing letters which were missing from M's next source, which is 'a'. Of the fourteen letters in this group, only four appear in N.[83]

The following section, $M18$–71, derives mostly from N or 'a'. This is rather difficult to observe at first sight since the letters that are in William's hand follow for the most part the arrangement of F, which also serves as a source here. The textual evidence for the change of the main source, which is mostly present in Schmitt's apparatus, is nevertheless abundant. When Hand VII takes over, the arrangement becomes similar to that of N, so that section $M35$–58 resembles $N80$–98 and section $M59$–71 is close to $N66$–76. The question as to whether the whole section, $M18$–71, derives mostly from N or from the lost 'a' (which possibly fathered N as well) is an intricate one. In order to equip myself better for solving the problem, I picked out twelve additional letters for collation (that is $AEp.$ 80–84, 86, 87, and 90–94) and checked all the occurrences of N and M in Schmitt's apparatus that could shed any light on the problem. It should first be noted that N has a remarkably pure text, whereas M is almost as remarkable for the impurity of its text. Such a situation necessarily makes textual

---

[82] M agrees with certain corrections in F against other witnesses. 61:5 promta est, prout potest] prompta est F prout potest *inserts above the line* F prout potest promta est M; 113:4 esse FM] *corr. from* et[?] F et ELP *om.* V. The best reading 'esse' seems to be emended from et for the first time in F, which M then follows. 248:25 deueniunt?] deueniunt. FM *corr. from* deueniunt? F. 319:3–4 uestra dignatio $LECV$] dignatio uestra FM uestra *inserts* F. 421:21 hominem[2]] eum *add* MF *inserts* F.

[83] Since N also drew on an unknown source, it may have obtained these four letters from another source than 'a'. In other words, 'a' might have included only a few of the letters $M4$–17 — perhaps four at most — or none of them at all.

criticism more complicated and less effective, because a perfect copy never supplies textual evidence that could indicate whether an inferior copy of the same text may derive from it or its exemplar.[84] Where N seldom disagrees with the bulk of the tradition, M generally follows N. The very few cases where M disagrees with N and is *also* supported by other manuscripts may have been instances amended by William and his team without recourse to another source.[85] Under these circumstances, the obvious conclusion would be that N was William's source. Nevertheless, I have made four observations that make this solution far less obvious.

(One.) M sometimes gives the name of an addressee in full, whereas N only provides an initial. William and his colleagues could have correctly identified some of the addressees in question with very little effort, for example Archbishop Lanfranc. But there are certainly examples which are less obvious—at least to us. Where, for instance, $AEp.$ 81 is addressed to Humfridus, a member of a secular *fraternitas* and perhaps a teacher, and $AEp.$ 85 is addressed to Walterus, then a monk of Saint-Wandrille and later prior of the same monastery, N designates the men only by their initial, whereas M spells the names in full.[86] William and his team did, however, possess an instrument which may have helped them decipher and expand the initials: $AEp.$ 81 and 85 are both included in another source they were using, namely F. A more perplexing

---

[84] Interestingly the editors of Lanfranc's collection, who used Cotton Nero A. vii as their base manuscript, were unable to determine if BAV, Reg. lat. 285, a Bec manuscript serving as their other main witness, depended on the Cottonian manuscript or whether the two manuscripts derived from an urtext independently of each other. In calligraphic terms, the hand of the Lanfranc collection in Cotton Nero A. vii was of a slightly better quality than the one in Anselm's collection, but proner to errors. He or his contemporary corrected almost all errors, however, resulting in a very good text; Gibson in Lanfranc, *Ep.*, 'Introduction', pp. 26–27.

[85] 80:23 Nam *MCVL*] Non *on eras. N (the context shows that* Non *is incorrect)*; 80:29 uestra prudentia *MCVL*] prudentia uestra N; 80:42 dei *MCVL*] om. N *(the omission occurs in the middle of a frequent biblical citation)*; 86:4 nostris *MCVL*] uestris N; 86:8 domnus *MCVL*] dominus N; 91:22 Nec *MCVL*] Ne N. See also 2:54 amatissime *NCV*] amantissime *LPFM corr. from* amantissime P; 92:5 dedeceat *corr. from* deceat N *(possibly by the main scribe)*] deceat M.

[86] Also in $AEp.$ 111, addressed to Anselm's cousin Fulcherald, N provides only an initial while M gives the name, but the name occurs in the text of the preceding letter (110).

case occurs at the end of *AEp*. 78 where Anselm commends 'our Brother Richard' to Bishop Gundulf, the addressee of the letter. About Brother Richard *we* know nothing but that he was a monk of Bec who was removed to Rochester. *N* abbreviates the name and *M* gives it in full. Also this letter is in *F*, but one wonders whether William, who copied the letter, could have been motivated enough to consult another codex in order to check the name of a brother who had entered Rochester some forty years earlier.[87]

(Two.) The sequence of the eighteen letters to Canterbury in *N*, probably a non-authorial addition, is completely absent from *M*. In general, *M*'s *N* or '*α*' section only includes material from the first folios and the second half of *N*.[88] (Three.) The absence of *AEp*. 107 and 108 from both *M* and *β* — our next hypothetical authorial collection — appears to be of particular significance. In *N*, *AEp*. 107 and 108 appear in a sequence of 41 letters, of which 39 of the other letters appear both in *M* and *β*.[89] These parameters make it possible to calculate the probability that *M* and *β* would have omitted these two letters independently of each other.[90] The probability of the accidental omission is as low as 1:820, suggesting that the absence of the two letters from *M* and *β* was not caused by exclusion; rather, the letters were absent from the sources *M* and *β* deployed. (Four.) *M*'s '*α*' sequence includes also letters not in *N*, amongst which there are two *received* by Anselm.[91] We can-

---

[87] This impression is strengthened by the fact that in *AEp*. 17, *M* introduces the addressee with an initial while *N* gives the name in full. See also *AEp*. 119 where the full name of the addressee, which *N* provides, was subsequently added to *M*.

[88] *M* completely lacks *N16–39* and *N41–53* as well as certain shorter groups of letters; the aforementioned 'Canterbury section', consisting of letters sent to Christ Church, covers *N21–38*.

[89] *N58–98*. *AEp*. 101 (*N79*) had already been copied into *M* from another source.

[90] $1:(X \times (X\text{-}1):2)$, thus $1:(41 \times 40:2)$; X = the number of the letters in the sequence.

[91] *AEp*. 88 and 135 (which are absent from *F* as well). The other letters in *M* missing from *N* are *AEp*. (96), 130, 131, (132, 134); those in brackets are in *F*. *MCV* agree against the other manuscripts, suggesting a common source; *CV* indicate the authorial collection *β*. See e.g. *AEp*. 96:18 non mundi *MCV*] non *om*. *LPF*; 96:34 uestro *MCV*] nostro *LP*; 132:8 gaudet *MCV*] gaudeat *LP*; 134:36 quanto² *MCV*] quanta *LP*; 134:52–55 Omnipotens – dilecta *MCV*] *om*. *LP*.

not know precisely what letters *N*'s lost final folios included, but the manuscript has a rubric that states only Anselm's out-letters are covered.[92] In conclusion, taking a final stance as to whether *M* derived material from *N* or a lost manuscript that resembled *N* would be unreasonable. The problem may be solved only after both manuscripts have been collated in full, something that is beyond the parameters of this study.

As figure 8 below will demonstrate, the RHM algorithm places the section *M18–71* between *N* and *F*.[93] The suggestion is that *F* contaminated a part of this section, which is confirmed by our other evidence. William of Malmesbury personally copied material from both *F* and *N* or '*α*'. After finishing his work with *F*'s Bec letters, he did not put the manuscript completely aside. He arranged the letters from his subsequent source in accordance with *F*, and picked up individual letters from *F* or used its text for correction.[94]

The source for letters *M72–79* is unknown. The section includes material both from the Bec and Canterbury periods. After these letters, *M* moves on to Canterbury material for good. Letters *M80–107* were taken from books iii and iv of Eadmer's *Historia nouorum*, with the exception of a single letter.[95] This is *AEp.* 337 (*M82*), which is otherwise known through the family *Wilmart 14*.

---

[92] Fol. 94r: '...continentur epistolae...quas fecit...egit.' Compare Schmitt, 'Zur Entstehungsgeschichte', 1936, p. 311. Rubrics in the other manuscripts regularly use non-exclusive labels, such as *epistolae Anselmi*, which may refer to both in- and out-letters. One of the rubrics in manuscript *C* states incorrectly, however, that the subsequent sequence was reserved to include letters dictated by Anselm.

[93] The evidence for the descent of *M18–71* from '*α*' (perhaps *N*) is strong. Thus the results of the computer-assisted analysis should not be interpreted as indicating that the source for this section was *F* or an unknown collection that resembled it. The letters in which *NM/CV* present a different version to *LPF/CV* provide the strongest evidence for this conclusion: 17 'recensio I' *NMECV* 'recensio II' *LPF*; 97 'recensio I' *NMD* 'recensio II' *CVLPF*; 122 'recensio I' *NMD* 'recensio II' *CVLPF* (3–16 *om. F*).

[94] The main suspects are *AEp.* 2, 6, 8, 13, 17, 37, 53.

[95] Readings shared by *Historia nouorum* (*r*) and *M* include e.g. *AEp.* 392 where *rM* both refer to Anselm in the singular, but the descendants of *ω*, *LPEC*, have the plural; 392:9 permanserunt] permanserint *rM*; 392:10 Teste – Tonnebrigge] *om. rM*; 393:12–13 Omnipotens – Amen.] Valete *r om. M*; 401:10 dedit et Normanniam] et Normanniam dedit *rM*; 401:20 Teste – Wellebof]

I shall argue later that the *Wilmart 14* branch was established at Shaftesbury or somewhere nearby; in other words, the letter was circulating in the vicinity of Malmesbury. The arrangement in *M80–107* duplicates that of the *Historia*. Hand VIII, the scribe of this sequence, omitted those letters that were already in William's *Liber pontificalis*[96] and certain other letters that were not sent by Anselm.[97]

The material in the final part (*M108–214*) derives from *F*, and was again copied by William.[98] At first, up to letter *M137*, the arrangement generally agrees with that in *F*, and the few changes serve to improve the arrangement of letters slightly: William changed *AEp*. 240 and 241 around to bring them into chronological order, and he placed *AEp*. 382 after *AEp*. 267, as both were to Bury St Edmunds.

From letter *M138* onwards, the arrangement complies with the social hierarchy of the age. The correspondence between the pope and Anselm is placed first (*M138–149*), with royal courts following the papal curia. Letters *M150–152* were addressed to the king of England and letters *M153–162* to his consort, Queen Matilda. Letters *M163–164* continue the royal theme, and are addressed to the kings of Scotland and Jerusalem respectively. The last of the temporal rulers is the Matilda of Tuscany (*M165–166*). The final

---

om. rM. AEp. 367, 398, 442 and 470 are known only from the *Historia nouorum* and *M* (as well as the latter's descendant *D*).

[96] Absent from *M80–107* and present in *Historia nouorum* and *Liber pontificalis*: *AEp*. 216, 222, 223, 224, 281, 283, 303, 305. When William himself copied materials from *F*, he wrote only the first words of the letters that are in *Liber pontificalis* and advised the reader to consult it, *AEp*. 281 (*M140*), 283 (*M142*), 303 (*M145*), 222 and 223 (*M148* and *149*).

[97] *AEp*. 226 from Paschal to Bishop Osbern of Salisbury; *AEp*. 310 and 365, both from unknown senders to Anselm; *AEp*. 456 from Thomas of York to Anselm. To conclude, *M* omits the four letters in Book I and II of the *Historia* (*AEp*. 154, 171 and 201, 206); *M* includes only two out of nine letters from Book III and as many as 25 out of 29 letters from Book IV.

[98] 161:5–10 Quamuis – commonere] *om. FM*; 161:57–65 Saluto – non sum] Valete *F om. M*; 185:4–9 Gratis – Praeterea et] *om. FM*. There are significant numbers of comparable omissions, which are sometimes longer in *M* than those in *F*. The collections also share less dramatic variants; e.g. 272:21 eligunt] hoc *add. FM*; 421:5 scripsistis *FM*] scripsisti *LPEV^bC^b corr. from* scripsistis *C^b*. The last text, *Epistola de sacramentis eccelasiae* (*AEp*. 417), contains the anomaly: *SAO*, vol. 2, 240:10 quaeritur *M*] *om. F*.

part of M comprises ecclesiastical correspondence, opening with his letters to Anselm's episcopal colleagues ($M167–171$). These are followed by letters with a Canterbury connection ($M172–196$), which are addressed to the prior, the subprior, and/ or the monks of Christ Church, and to the bishop of Rochester, the *chorepiscopus* of Canterbury. This section also includes a letter to Haimo, the sheriff of Kent ($M191$), clearly placed here because its content was closely related to the following letter. The final letter in the section underlines the hierarchical principles underlying the arrangement: the addressee is a runaway monk from Christ Church. $M197–205$ are mostly letters directed to prelates across the Channel, including four abbots, a canon, and a bishop who had resigned his office; a letter to the abbess of the convent of the Holy Trinity at Caen concludes the section. The last sections comprise letters to ordinary monks ($M206–210$) and nuns ($M211–214$). The arrangement mirrored William's world view, which was fairly typical of the twelfth century: the first place was awarded to the pope, the next to temporal crowned heads, followed by higher ecclesiastical ranks, and finally other churchmen. Women, naturally, were deemed not equal to men.

M's hierarchically ranked sections follow the arrangement in F in an interesting way, summarised in the table above. With a couple of exceptions, the correspondence between Anselm and the pope, that is $M138–149$, faithfully follows the order in F.[99] The next small group of letters between Henry I and Anselm follows F's arrangement in reverse order, while the letters to Queen Matilda again take the order in F. The subsequent groups of letters are too short for firm conclusions to be drawn regarding their arrangement, but the relatively large section of Canterbury letters which comes next again shares F's order.[100] Thereafter, the letters addressed to prelates overseas again reverse the order in F.[101] Apart from the final two letters, which are reversed, the letters sent to monks follow the order in F, as does the final section of

---

[99] *AEp.* 283, 303, where M includes the first words and refers the reader to *Liber pontificalis* for the full text.

[100] With the exception of *AEp.* 336.

[101] With the exception of the last letter in the section, *AEp.* 285, William placed letters to women after those to men, so the female recipient of the letter (the abbess of Caen), may explain its location.

letters to nuns. In selecting his material, William leafed back and forth through his source

1.4 M's descendants: DU

Cambridge, Corpus Christi College 299 – D

s. xii$^{2/3}$; England; parchment; ii + (41 +)70; I^{8+1} II–V^8 VI^{10} / I–VIII^8 IX^6; 260 × 170 (190 × 120) mm; 32 lines in two columns

Contents

Unit 1

fol. 1r–v	'Intimo suo suus – cum christus apparuerit', an unidentified letter
fols. 2r–5v	Ivo of Chartres, *Sermo* 5 (entitled 'De conuenientia ueteris ac nouae legis sacramentorum', *PL* 162, cols. 535–562)
fols. 5v–52v	Ivo of Chartres, *Epistolae*

Unit 2

fol. 53r	Reginald of Canterbury?, '*Flete mecum precor. mea pignora*' (*Walther* 6619)
fols. 53v–122v	Anselm, *Epistolae* (D)
fol. 123	blank

Cambridge, Corpus Christi College 299 comprises two originally distinct manuscripts. Both are English and roughly from s. xii$^{2/3}$. The former contains some works of Ivo of Chartres, and the latter includes Anselm's letters. The discussion will focus on the latter.[102] The quire marks are Roman numerals, placed in the bottom margin of the verso side of the final folio in each quire. This numbering restarts at the beginning of Anselm's collection. The initials are blue, red, or green, and from fol. 69r onwards green and red initials alternate. The ink is brown. The ruling is in lead. Prickings are still visible, but the folios have been trimmed. There are two hands: A copied the epitaph (*Walther* 6619) on fol. 53r and fols. 53v–72ra, l. 10 of the letters, and B the remainder of the letters, that is fols. 72ra, l. 11–122v.

---

[102] The initials in the former part hint at a southwest origin. Michael Gullick, pers. comm. 9.4.2010. Ivo's collection has the same number of lines, but the written area is slightly larger, 195 × 130 mm. The manuscript must also have had slightly larger folios than Anselm's collection, since only the quire marks for the first two quires survived the trimming process, while all the quire marks in Anselm's letters are preserved. Ivo's collection has initials in red, green, blue, or light brown.

The two manuscripts had been joined together by 1405, as is known from the (erased) annotation on the first folio: 'De perquisito fratris Johannis Tille ordinis fratrum predicatorum anno domini 1405 scilicet epistole Yuonis Carnotensis et epistole beati Anselmi'. Likewise, both works are mentioned in the other annotations on the first flyleaf, though these are hard to date.[103] It is not known from where or from whom brother John Tille acquired the manuscript, but thanks to him it made its way to London's Dominican community.[104] The library holdings of the London Dominicans, like the English libraries of the orders of friars in general, are poorly known and no works by Anselm or Ivo appear in the surviving in catalogues.[105] After the dissolution, Archbishop Parker obtained the manuscript.[106] *D* includes 213 letters from Anselm's Bec and Canterbury period. The arrangement closely resembles that in *M*.

Cambridge, University Library Dd. 9. 5 – U

s. xii$^{2/2}$; England; parchment; (138 +)16; I–XVI^8 XVII^{10} / I–II^8; 315 × 215 (235 × 145) mm; (34 and) 41 lines in two columns

Contents

Unit 1

fols. 1r–25r	Anselm, *Monologion*
fols. 25r–31v	Anselm, *Proslogion*
fols. 31v–33v	Gaunilo, *Liber pro insipiente*
fols. 33v–36v	Anselm, *Responsio Anselmi contra Gaunilonem*
fols. 36v–49v	Anselm, *De processione Spiritus Sancti*
fols. 49v–51v	Anselm, *Epistola de sacrificio azymi et fermentati*
fols. 51v–52v	Anselm, *Epistola de sacramentis ecclesiae*
fols. 52v–53v	Anselm, *AEp.* 410, 403, 405, 414
fols. 53v–61v	Anselm, *Epistola de incarnatione Verbi*
fols. 61r–85v	Anselm, *Cur Deus homo*
fols. 85v–95v	Anselm, *De conceptu uirginali et de originali peccato*

---

[103] Also on the same folio in a s. xiii[?] hand: 'Vt ualeat uiuatque diu persona prioris / Det deus et uicium uelit omnis demere moris. Amen.'

[104] Three other manuscripts that Tille either gave to, or obtained for, his convent have been identified, see *BRUO*, vol. 3, 1876.

[105] K. W. Humphreys (ed.), *The Friars' Libraries*, CBMLC, vol. 1, London, 1990, p. xv.

[106] Parker's signum 'J 6' on fol. ii^r. See T. Graham & A. Watson, *The Recovery of the Past in Early Elizabethan England: Documents by John Bale and John Joscelyn from the Circle of Matthew Parker*, Cambridge Bibliographical Society Monograph, 13, Cambridge, 1998, pp. 70–71.

fols. 95v–96v   '*Bonus homo de omnibus*' (an adaption of *Similitudines Anselmi* clxii, *PL* 159, col. 691)[107]

fols. 96v–97r   Anselm, *AEp.* 109

fols. 97r–109v   Anselm, *De concordia praescientiae et praedestinationis*

fols. 109v–112r   Anselm, *Meditatio 3 de redemptione humana*

fol. 112r–v   Anselm, '*Praefatio beati Anselmi in tribus tractatibus*' (*SAO*, vol. 1, pp. 173–174)

fols. 112v–120v   Anselm, *De ueritate*

fols. 120v–126v   Anselm, *De libertate arbitrii*

fols. 126v–138v   Anselm, *De casu diaboli*

Unit 2

fols. 139r–154v   Anselm, *Epistolae* (*U*)

Cambridge, University Library Dd. 9. 5 consists of two originally separate manuscripts. They were, no doubt, joined because of their content: the first includes a broad selection of Anselm's treatises and a few letters, and the second has his letters, compilation *U*. *U* consists of only two quaternions and contains 49 letters. The manuscript has not survived completely, as the text of the last letter breaks off midway at the end of the last folio.[108] The initials are simple, in red or green ink, while the text is written in ink that varies between brown and dark brown. Prickings are still visible. The hand is from the second half of the twelfth century, and it does not appear in the first codicological unit (which contains numerous hands of the same or a slightly earlier period). *U* has a heading that refers to Anselm as a saint.[109]

DU *in the tradition*

It has only been possible to undertake a limited textual analysis of *U*; in contrast, much fuller information is available for *D*. The evidence I have obtained does, however, offer a relatively clear picture of the relationship between the manuscripts. *DU* include *M*'s weak readings plus some readings shared only by them; in addition, both *D* and *U* have readings not present in the other. We may conclude that *DU* are independent of each other and descend

---

[107] The same extract is found in manuscripts BAV Vat. lat. 310, fol. 148r (*R³* in this study) and Budapest, Bibl. Univ. Cod. Lat. 50, fol. 170r (*s.* xiv), see P. Tóth, *Catalogus Codicum Latinorum Medii Aeui Bibliothecae Vniuersitatis Budapestinensis*, Budapest, 2006, p. 90.

[108] *AEp.* 259:38–41 esse – uestris] *om.* *U*.

[109] Fol. 139v: 'Epistole sancti anselmi archiepiscopi'.

from M through a shared intermediary, a lost text that may be named $\varkappa$.[110] The content of $\varkappa$ can in part be reconstructed from DU. As a witness to $\varkappa$, D is superior to U; it must be closer to $\varkappa$ in size and arrangement than U is. For the similarities between MD are closer than those between MU (even taking into account the loss of an unknown number of leaves from U).

D has some material that is absent from M. In D, a letter which seems unrelated to Anselm's collection follows the Bec section.[111] Furthermore, either the compiler of D or of a lost intermediary had access to a source which contained a little more of the correspondence between Anselm and Hildebert of Lavardin than M: where M included only AEp. 240 and 241, D added AEp. 239. Apart from D, AEp. 239 is otherwise known only from the letter collection of Hildebert of Lavardin. Of its manuscript witnesses, I have consulted Troyes, Médiathèque 513 (= Z^1) and BAV Vat. lat. 6024 (= Z^2). The source from which D derived AEp. 239 was at

---

[110] (1) M is the family's hyparchetype. (a) Manuscripts MD. My collations of AEp. 1, 2, 3, 37, 65, 161, 162 and 337 reveal that D includes M's specific readings, for example the numerous omissions. In some cases, D extends M's characteristic omissions still further, or seeks to amend clearly weak readings. Schmitt's apparatus for DM is particularly problematic, since it often lists their shared otherwise isolated readings under only one manuscript or the other, although he stated that both were collated. I have observed one probable anomaly: AEp. 337:2 Eulaliae] .E. D .F.[?] M. This does not undermine the conclusion regarding the relationship between MD, which is based on substantial evidence. (b) Manuscripts MU. U follows M's readings, a result which was gained through comparing Schmitt's apparatus and U in AEp. 37, 89, 91, 99, 117, 146. Schmitt only used U in AEp. 89 and did not start reporting its readings until the second half of the letter, giving the misleading impression in the apparatus that U was independent of M. (c) Finally, one further strong piece of evidence confirms that M was the hyparchetype for this branch: 91:18 aut uere nulla aut fere nulla] aut uere nulla aut uere parua DU, a reading derived from M as follows: aut uere nulla aut uere parua *corr. from* aut uere nulla aut uere nulla M (parua *inserts in marg.* nulla^2 *del.* M)
(2) D does not derive from U. The arrangement and selection of letters in MDU is initially identical — for more than the first thirty letters — apart from U's omission of AEp. 49, 136, 131, 7, 83, 57. (3) U does not derive from D. AEp. 89:16 post obitum – similiter MU] *om.* D; 91:6 tumore MU] timore D. (4) Between M and DU there must have been (at least) one intermediary. Although DU do not arrange their letters absolutely identically, they often agree against M significantly.

[111] Fol. 82r: 'Caro suo D. F. sacerdos – debito mandes. Valete.' Published in Wilmart, 'La tradition', 1931, no. xvi.

times better than that behind Z^1Z^2, both of which, for example, omit the *salutatio*.[112] D's source seems to have been closer to Z^1 than Z^2 since in *AEp*. 240, DZ^1 present the farewells (completely missing from M) in a form that significantly differs from Z^2.[113] After Hildebert's letters, D again reverts to the text and arrangement in M; section $D192$–204 parallels that in M precisely. Before concluding, D adds one further letter not found in M, *AEp*. 450, drawn from an unidentified source.

For some letters from Paschal II to Anselm, M announces only the first words and instructs the reader to refer 'in decretis pontificum' for the full text. In two cases of this kind, *AEp*. 222 and 281, D presents the full text. Schmitt's apparatus suggests that D's source for these two letters could have been Eadmer's *Historia nouorum* or a collection closely related to it. Thus the source could have been the *Liber pontificalis* by William of Malmesbury, which is textually very close to Eadmer's work and was certainly available in Malmesbury, from where the subgroup stems.[114]

---

[112] 239:1–3 Venerabili – salutem] *om.* Z^1Z^2.

[113] *AEp*. 240:22–24 Vale – apud te.] *om.* M Vicem mihi, pater sancte, rependes, si tuarum participem me feceris orationum DZ^1. In this particular reading A^3, which is Bodley. Laud. Misc. 344 and which is briefly studied in Appendix I, agrees with DZ^1. On Z^2, I rely on Schmitt's apparatus here. It is not impossible that Z^2 too might unite with DZ^1A^3, although Schmitt's apparatus suggests the contrary; the matter needs checking. Other omissions in M not transferred into D: 240:12 nec] non M; 240:15 sane] *om*. M. Nevertheless, see 240:4–5 sanctissime pater MD] pariter $Z^1Z^2A^3$. Schmitt erroneously assigns this weak reading to D as well.

[114] On William's and Eadmer's sources for these letters, see Thomson, *William of Malmesbury*, 2003, pp. 132–133. In theory, this source for D could also have resembled one of the sources for Y^1Y^2, copies of letter collections of Ivo of Chartres that included some of Anselm's correspondence. *AEp*. 222:3 ut] quod Dr (Schmitt erroneously adds L to the group); 222:12 loquaris] perloquaris DY^1Y^2r; 222:24 reuerenda] ueneranda Dr; 222:29 procuretur] perducatur Dr; 222:33 plenum] pleniter Dr; 222:38 Data – Maii] *om*. Dr. Analysis is undermined by the absence of a critical edition of *Historia nouorum* (which is here r). Compare also 222:12 agas] peragas DY^1Y^2; the collation of *AEp*. 281's readings with D and Y^1Y^2 (the latter reported by Schmitt) did not reveal any significant agreement between them; in contrast 222:41 inuocarunt Y^1Y^2r] commutauerunt $DLPCVEFGA^6$. A^6 is London, BL Stowe 31, which includes letters touching on the investiture contest.

The arrangement of the letters in DU

In places, both *D* and *U* diverge strongly from how *M* arranges the letters. Since the arrangement in *DU* clearly differs from that in *M* in similar ways, *κ* must already have altered *M*'s arrangement. The motives for alterations can occasionally be established. For example, when *D* moves on to Canterbury correspondence at *D72*, it first presents five letters arranged in a way that shows clear traces of the order in *M*, derived originally from that in *Historia nouorum*; each letter relates to the investiture dispute, and was sent or received by either Paschal II or Henry I.[115] After this group, *M* presents letters from other individuals on the same theme.[116] *D* in contrast abandons the theme but continues with further letters from the same individual, Paschal II,[117] presenting a group of letters which occur much later in *M*. *U* likewise is initially strikingly faithful to *M*, and thus to *κ*, in the section of Bec correspondence (*U1–34*).[118] As for the subsequent letters (*U35–49*), the arrangement has close parallels with that in *D* and thus differs from that in *M*.

It is interesting to note that both *D* and *U* become much more independent immediately after the Bec letters. The English origins of the manuscripts probably account for this as the various turns that dramatically shaped Anselm's career clearly provided the impetus for the editorial selection and rearrangement. For example, the creator of *U* (or of a lost intermediary) opened the section of Canterbury correspondence by copying the letters between Anselm and the English episcopate, dealing with the archbishop's exile and the investiture dispute.[119] This was followed by two papal letters, of which the first is related to the investiture dispute and the second to the foundation of the diocese of Ely.[120] The next letters related to the dispute between Canterbury and York.[121] In contrast

---

[115] *D: AEp.* 367, 368, 353, 308, 282. *M: AEp.* 282, 308, [337,] 353, 367, 368.

[116] *AEp.* 369 (to Robert of Meulan), 386 (from the English bishops), 387 (to the English bishops).

[117] *AEp.* 280, 281, 222, 223, 283 etc.

[118] Anselm's letters as *electus* in this group: *AEp.* 148, 156.

[119] *AEp.* 387, 386 (*U35–36*).

[120] *AEp.* 397, 441.

[121] *AEp.* 443, 444, 451.

the order of the Bec correspondence was left almost untouched, possibly because the men behind the manuscripts had Norman ties not strong enough to undertake laborious editorial work.

1.5 *Conclusions: the* α *branch as* stemmata

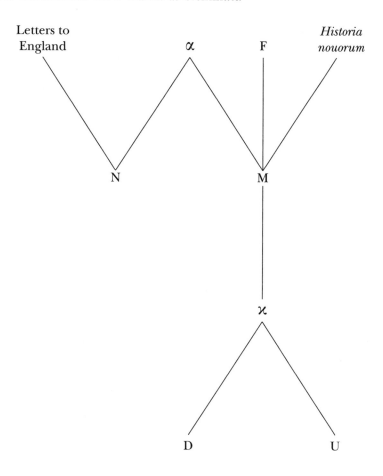

Figure 1: The α branch — preliminary conclusion A

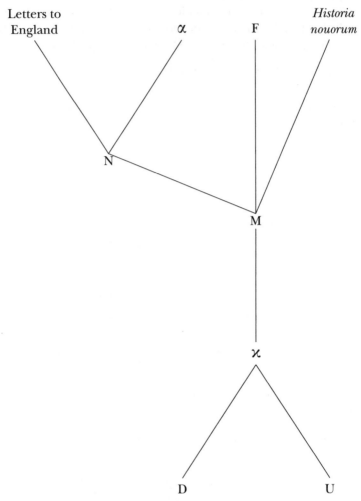

Figure 2: The α branch – preliminary conclusion B

2. THE SECOND AND THIRD COLLECTION: β AND ω

Preliminary remarks

THE COLLECTIONS: Anselm commissioned a collection of his letters at the outset of his time at Canterbury. This collection is β.
β covered most of Anselm's surviving Bec correspondence and a
few early Canterbury letters. The third collection, ω, was either
begun during Anselm's last years or, less likely, made soon after
his death.

THE WITNESSES: Since our manuscripts often unite materials from β and ω, they cannot be divided into two clearly distinct groups. The groups overlap and, what is more, they are governed by β and ω only in part. My division also reflects non-authorial transmission until the 1130s or a little later, and is founded on criteria predominantly geographical in character. One group stems from Canterbury and the other is connected to Bec. When using the labels 'Canterbury branch' and, in particular, 'Bec branch', one should keep in mind that the latter was in part rooted in Christ Church.

Subchapters 2.1–8 discuss the Canterbury branch, which derives mainly from ω. The best witnesses to ω are L and F. L is a Christ Church manuscript that has been a focus of an academic dispute. On the other hand, F has been undeservedly overlooked due to the fact that it presents a heavily abridged version of the collection. Textual evidence supplied by F is, however, crucial to the appreciation of the tradition. Subchapters 2.9–15 introduce the Bec branch. The main witnesses are manuscripts CV, covering Anselm's whole career, and O, including only his Canterbury letters. The Bec letters in CV derive from β, while the ultimate source for the great majority of the Canterbury material was ω. Manuscripts G and B cover too few letters to contribute significantly to our understanding of how the major collections were transmitted. They will be studied, therefore, only after the discussions of our textual evidence.

With respect to the Bec correspondence, the fact that the Canterbury group will be presented before the Bec group means moving backwards in the stemma. The decision to proceed in reverse is prompted by the fact that in establishing the interrelationships of the witnesses to the β stage, I repeatedly need to refer to manuscripts LE of the Canterbury group. Only when one appreciates the character of these manuscripts can β be discussed. Furthermore, several witnesses to ω antedate those to β.

The hybridity of our witnesses to β and ω resulted, at least in part, from the character of these collections. Since β included only a few archiepiscopal letters, other sources were needed as subsequent compilations were made. On the other hand, ω was probably a register, possibly consisting of separate codicological units. This would have reduced its applicability as a source, in particular for anyone who was not from Christ Church.

THE DERIVATIVES: Several manuscripts in these groups derive from other survivors. The derivatives are introduced after their (ultimate) source.

2.1 *London, Lambeth Palace 59* – L

c. 1120 × 1130; Canterbury cathedral priory (OSB); parchment; ii + 190 (+ 88); I–VI^8 VII$^{8-1}$ VIII–XXII^8 XXIII$^{8-1}$ XXIV^8 (originally the last three folios of XXIV came after XX; XXI–XXII were added upon the removal of XXIV); 350 × 240 (225 × 170) mm; 31 lines in two columns

Contents

fols. 1r–160v L^a	Anselm, *Epistolae* (L)
fols. 160v–161r	Anselm, *AEp.* 193
fol. 161r–v	Anselm?, '*Est considerandum*' (*Memorials*, pp. 334–336)
fols. 161v–162r	Anselm?, '*Laetaris quod*' (*Memorials*, p. 353:1)
fols. 162r–169v	Eadmer, *De beatitudine perennis uitae* ('second recension', *Memorials*, pp. 274–288)
fols. 169v–171v	Anselm?, '*Quattuor modis*' (*Memorials*, pp. 336–340)
fols. 171v–175r	Anselm?, '*Discipulus. Plura sunt*' (*Memorials*, pp. 341–351)
fols. 175r–176r	'*Haud habiture*' ('Versus ad laudem Anselmi', in R. SHARPE, 'Two contemporary poems on Saint Anselm attributed to William of Chester', *Revue Bénédictine*, 95 (1985), pp. 271–274, *Walther* 7673)
fols. 176r–177v	'*Presulis Anselmi*' ('Item uersus de eodem', in SHARPE, 'Two poems', 1982, pp. 274–279, *Walther* 14486)
fol. 177v	'Omnia maiorem – priusue fuerant' (two hexameter verses)
fol. 178r	Anselm, *Cur Deus homo: Commendatio operis ad Urbanum* (*SAO*, vol. 2, pp. 39–40, lines 2–17)
fol. 178r	Anselm, *AEp.* 411 (with a signum)
fols. 178v–179r	Canons of the Council at Westminster in 1102 (see *Councils and synods* no. 113, pp. 674–679)
fol. 179r–v	Primatial Council at London in 1108 (see *Councils and synods*, no. 116, pp. 694–704)
fols. 179v–182r	*AEp.* 331 (with a signum), 212 (with a signum), 255, 202, 200, 440, 207
fols. 182v–186v	blank
fol. 187r	Anselm, *AEp.* 471 (begins abruptly, the missing passage added in margin), 472
fols. 187r–188r	Anselm?, '*Est considerandum*' (*Memorials*, pp. 334–336)
fol. 188r	Anselm?, '*Velle eisdem*' (*Memorials*, p. 351:4)

fol. 188r	Anselm?, 'Laetaris quod' (*Memorials*, p. 353:1)
fol. 188r–v	Anselm, *AEp.* 469
fols. 188v–189r	Anselm?, '*Voluntas equiuoce*' (*Memorials*, p. 351:5)
fol. 189r–v	Anselm, *Epitaphium Hugonis* (*Memorials*, p. 351:B1)
fol. 189v	Anselm?, '*Quoniam corpus*' ('Idem ad interrogationem cuiusdam', *Memorials*, pp. 351–352:B2)
fol. 189v	Anselm?, '*Cum te plasmaui*' (*Memorials*, p. 352:B3)
fol. 189v	Anselm?, *AEp.* 475
fol. 189v	Anselm?, '*Anselmus. In spe auxilii*' (*Memorials*, p. 352:B5)
fols. 189v–190r	'*Haud habiture*' (lines 1–35, 'Versus ad laudem Anselmi', see above)
fol. 190r	'Que restant modici sunt scripta manu thiderici' (scribal note)
fol. 190r	'Tu solus timidis es medicina reis' (probatio pennae, from *Walther* 7673, line 34 above)
fol. 190v	blank

London, Lambeth Palace 59 or *L*, often referred to as the most important manuscript of our tradition, contains Anselm's letters (fols. 1–160v) and a rather mixed bag of Anselmian texts, including letters (fols. 160v–190r). Anselm's treatises follow in a manuscript, which dates from 1468; this does not form part of our study.[122] Certain characteristics related to the structure of the manuscript have posed major problems to scholarship, and particular features of its physical composition have been used to support arguments concerning the dating of the manuscript incorrectly. I shall discuss the codicology and palaeography of *L*, therefore, in somewhat greater detail than for the other manuscripts.

The manuscript comprises twenty-four quaternions, some of which have been reduced and rearranged.[123] Quires I–VIII or fols. 1–63 cover Anselm's correspondence from the Bec period; the last folio, 63v, is blank. Quires IX–XX or fols. 64–159, together with the recto side of the first folio (160) of the next quire, and the top two lines of its verso side, contain the letters from the Canterbury years. Folio 160v and quires XXI–XXIV, that is

---

[122] For a detailed exploration of the contents, see M. R. JAMES, *A Descriptive Catalogue of the Manuscripts in the Library of Lambeth Palace. The Mediaeval Manuscript*, Cambridge, 1932, pp. 95–96. On the dating, see fol. 230v and ROBINSON, *London Libraries*, 2003, no. 49, pp. 41–42.

[123] According to James's analysis (*Lambeth Palace*, 1932, p. 91), fol. 6 is missing from quire VII and fol. 8 from quire XXIII.

fols. 161–190, include letters from the Canterbury period, and
other texts almost certainly coming from his archive. This last section, fols. 160v–190, has been called L^a, and although the siglum
is somewhat misleading ($L^a = L$ appendix), it is probably too well-
established to be replaced. L^a itself divides into two sections, separated by the blank fols. 183r–186v at the end of the first. The
first section comprises fols. 161–186 and the second fols. 187–190.
Originally, fols. 187–190 followed fol. 159, and formed the final
section of the letter collection itself. In other words, the original
structure of the manuscript was fols. 1–159, 187–190, 182–186.[124]
Clear proof of this rearrangement survives: the bottom three lines
of the second column on fol. 159v have been erased. The opening of *AEp.* 469 is now written on the erasure, continuing to the
following folio. But the beginning of *AEp.* 471 may still be discerned beneath this text. The erased passage ends with the words
'per sanctam obedi[entiam]', and the same letter continues from
this point ('[obedi]entiam quam') on fol. 187r.[125] After the present
fols. 160–186 were added, fols. 187–190, which had been removed,
were restitched behind them.

Certain features reveal that this rearrangement took place soon
after copying. First, the main scribe of the manuscript (A) wrote
the text of both the original and the present endings, fols. 187–190
and fols. 159v–160r respectively. Second, although what is now
fol. 187r was originally the first leaf in a new quire, it has no quire
mark.[126] Third, unlike the rest of the manuscript, fols. 187–190
have no initials, marking that the folios were rearranged before the
initials were added and possibly even before the quires were bound
together. Finally, manuscript *P*, which was copied from *L* prob-

---

[124] The original centre fold of quire XXIV is now its spine fold and the
original central opening now forms the outside of the quire. In other words, the
quire has been turned inside out. The signatures from the seventeenth century
on fols. 183–184 give the *ad quem* to this alteration; Dr Teresa Webber, pers.
comm. 27.11.2008.

[125] This point was noted in F. S. Sᴄʜᴍɪᴛᴛ, *Ein neues unvollendetes Werk des
hl. Anselm von Canterbury, Beiträge zur Geschichte der Philosophie und Theologie
des Mittelalters, Texte und Untersuchungen,* 33, Münster, 1936, pp. 7–8. After
that, the issue was overlooked until the studies by Krüger (*Persönlichkeitsausdruck,* 2002, p. 76) and Logan ('Thidricus', 2006).

[126] The quire mark XXI on the present fol. 160r follows the arrangement of
the other quire marks.

ably very soon after its completion, follows *L*'s present, amended, arrangement of the final letters.

Each quire has quire marks, consistently placed in the lower margin of the recto side of the first folio. Quire marks I–XIX are in a twelfth-century hand, while quire marks XX and XXI may be in another hand of the same period. In contrast, quire marks XXII and XXIII and signatures XXIV.1. and XXIV.2. are in a seventeenth-century hand. The modern foliation in Arabic numerals runs through the entire manuscript, up to the final folio of the fifteenth-century manuscript, now forming a part of the volume. The ink is brown and sometimes black, and the initials are red, blue, or purple. The margins seem to be ruled with a crayon rather than with a plummet. Folio 63v has a rubric written in red rustic capitals. An illuminated initial S opens the first letter in the collection on fol. 1r. This is so incomplete that it is impossible to identify the subject properly, and the sketch may, in fact, be a later addition. The first words of the letter, '[S]uo domino et', are also absent, and an empty space is left for them next to the initial letter. *L* has a second illuminated initial on fol. 64r, marking the transition from the Bec correspondence to the Canterbury correspondence. This shows a dragon, twisted into a letter S. The initial perhaps remains unfinished. While the sketch is complete, it has no colours.[127] An initial with exactly the same theme is to be found in manuscript *P*, but this seems to be the work of a different artist.[128] Many of the initials in Cambridge, St John's College A. 8, which Dodwell dates to the period 1110–40, are close to the dragon initial in *L* (and especially in *P*) stylistically.[129] I doubt whether the same artist was responsible for these initials, however, since the initials in St John's College A. 8 seem somewhat lighter in touch and less forced than the one in *L*, though comparison is hampered by the fact that *L*'s initial is a sketch in one colour.[130]

[127] Published in *SAO*, vol. 5.

[128] *P* fol. 1r.

[129] See especially Cambridge, St John's College A. 8, fols. 164r and 219r reproduced in C. R. Dodwell, *The Canterbury School of Illumination 1066–1200*, Cambridge, 1954, pl. 42a and 37d. On the dating, *ibid.*, pp. 120–121, note 1.

[130] I am grateful to artist Anna Retulainen for her assistance in comparing the initials. According to Fröhlich ('Introduction', 1990, pp. 36–37), the

The similarity between the initials is also of interest given the fact that the scribe of the St John's College manuscript, named in the initial on fol. 103v as Samuel, has recently been identified as one of the scribes of Oxford, Bodleian Library Bodley 271; this is Christ Church's great collection of Anselm's treatises and devotional works.[131] Samuel's hand does not appear in *L*, however.

The first hand, Scribe A, copied virtually all of the original material in *L* and *L^a* (plates 3–5). He covered the Bec correspondence, ending on fol. 63r. Then he left fol. 63v blank and began copying the Canterbury correspondence on the first folio of a new quire. With the exception of certain very short passages, he copied fols. 64r–159v, and then fols. 187r–190r, which originally followed on from fols. 64r–159v directly. At this point he removed fols. 187r–190r and began a new quire, which was appended after fol. 159r. Scribe A copied the final letters into the first folio of the new quire (160), leaving the first column of the verso side blank after the first two lines of text. A desire to close the collection with the two chronologically latest letters — *AEp.* 471 and 472, which Anselm dictated shortly before his death,[132] and not *AEp.* 469 as had originally been the case — may have motivated the change. He resumed work on fol. 161r, copying first two of Anselm's theological texts and then *De beatitudine perennis uitae*, which Eadmer had compiled from Anselm's speeches. Scribe A completed his stint at the end of this text (fol. 169va, l. 12). He corrected his own

same artist was responsible for this Lambeth 59 initial and the L-initial in Cambridge, Trinity College B. 3. 32, fol. 42r. He cites the long ear lobes of both creatures in support of this point, and he considers this to be further evidence that a single *scribe* produced both manuscripts; he uses the term 'Thidrician ears'. Applying the Morelli method, which lies behind this conclusion, in the way Fröhlich does, is problematic. The most significant problem is of course that scribes and illuminators were often different people. Furthermore the 'long ears' Fröhlich noted seem to have been extremely popular among Canterbury's illustrators in general, and in many other scriptoria in England, and elsewhere as well.

[131] The hand also occurs in two Christ Church documents as not noted by T. Webber in BRETT & GRIBBIN, *Canterbury 1070–1136*, 2004, p. lxiv (see also LOGAN, 'Ms. Bodley 271', 2004, pp. 72–74). In Bodley manuscript he is the Scribe 2 who wrote fols. 15v–112v, 114r–139ra, line 10. Gullick dates the manuscript to between about 1110 and 1120, while Logan ('Ms. Bodley 271', 2004, p. 78) dates it to the years 1107–1114.

[132] Eadmer, *HN*, p. 206.

work, occasionally using a pen with a narrower nib than in the text, which makes his hand appear slightly different.[133] Michael Gullick has recently identified this scribe with a hand known from several Christ Church manuscripts and documents, some of which are datable.[134] The following table lists his other work so far identified.[135]

Table 2: Specimens by the Lambeth scribe

Canterbury Cathedral, Chartae antiquae A 182	a confirmation of a grant from Siwardus of Standon to Christ Church on his son's becoming a monk; n.d.
Canterbury Cathedral, Chartae Antiquae C 9	a bilingual charter of Henry I for Christ Church; 1121[136]
Canterbury Cathedral, Chartae Antiquae C 117, nos. 36 & 37	no. 36: the profession of Abbot Hugh of St Augustine's; 1126 no. 37: the profession of Bishop Gilbert of London; 1128
Canterbury Cathedral, Chartae Antiquae S 350	a charter of Archbishop Ralph for Christ Church; 1114 × 1122[137]
Dublin, Trinity College 98	a pontifical; ?1115 or 1123[138]

[133] E.g. fol. 47v: 'in bonis – Duo'; fol. 89r: 'scribere – dicens'; fol. 106v: 'et quia non debeo'.

[134] The most recent accounts of the work of this scribe (although not listing all manuscripts identified above) are by Teresa Webber in BRETT & GRIBBIN, *Canterbury 1070–1136*, 2004, p. lxiv, and M. B. PARKES, *Their Hands before Our Eyes: A Closer Look at Scribes*, Aldershot, 2008, pp. 95, 143; Parkes identified the Lambeth hand with a scribe in Bodley 160 and elsewhere independently of Gullick.

[135] A potential case is Oxford, Bodleian Library Add. C. 260, a Christ Church calendar that was finished before the dedication of the new choir in 1130. For the dating see, T. A. HESLOP, 'The Canterbury calendars and the Norman conquest', in *Canterbury and the Norman Conquest: Churches, Saints and Scholars 1066–1109*, eds. R. EALES & R. SHARPE, London, 1995, pp. 53–55.

[136] C. JOHNSON & H. A. CRONNE (eds.), *Regesta Henrici Primi, Regesta Regum Anglo-Normannorum*, vol. 2, Oxford, 1956, no. 1055.

[137] BRETT & GRIBBIN, *Canterbury 1070–1136*, 2004, no. 38; reproduction: *ibid.*, plate IIIa.

[138] M. GULLICK & R. PFAFF, 'The Dublin pontifical (TCD 98 [B.3.6]): St Anselm's?', *Scriptorium*, 55 (2001), p. 286 and pl. 59a.

[139] JOHNSON & CRONNE, *Regesta Henrici Primi*, no. 1388. G. F. WARNER & H. J. ELLIS, *Facsimiles of Royal and Other Charters in the British Museum*, vol. 1, London 1903, no. 6. Reproduced in *ibid.*, pl. 5 and C. JOHNSON & H. JENKINSON, *English Court Hand, A.D. 1066 to 1500*, vol. 2, Oxford, 1915, pl. Ic.

London, BL Campbell Charter xxi.6	a bilingual charter of Henry I for Archbishop William and the monks of Christ Church; 1123[139]
Paris, Musée des archives nationales ms. 138, no 4	an entry in the mortuary roll for Abbot Vitalis of Savigny; 1122 or 1123[140]
Oxford, Bodleian Library Bodley 160, fols. iiiʳ–51v and 61r–66v	fols. iiiʳ–46r: Bede, Commentary on the Acts of the Apostles[141] fols. 46v–51v: Bede, *Nomina regionum et locorum de Actibus Apostolorum* fols. 61r–66v: Ivo of Chartres, *De ecclesiasticis sacramentis et officis*
Cambridge, Corpus Christi College 371, fols. 3v–4r, 195r–v and corrections in fols. 221r–225v.	fols. 3v–4r: a letter from Nicholas of Worcester to Eadmer; 1121 at the earliest fol. 195r–v: the last miracle in and postscript to Anselm's *Miracula* by Eadmer; 1122 × *c.* 1130 fols. 221r–225v: Eadmer, *De reliquiis sancti Audoeni et quorundam aliorum sanctorum*; *c.* 1125 × *c.* 1130
Cambridge, Corpus Christi College 411, fols. 141r–142v	pericopes added to a psalter

The specimens demonstrate that the scribe may have begun working by the 1110s, that his most active years occurred in the 1120s, and that he continued to work at least until 1128. Since his hand is a mature representative of the full-grown Christ Church style, he was neither an adult convert nor a late-age monastic emigrant from Normandy, but he had entered Christ Church, where he must have received his education, at a young age. His apparent command of English, for which the two bilingual charters in his hand are proof, suggests an English origin, but that is by no means certain.[142] Although his writing represents the Christ Church style in a fully developed form, Lambeth 59 exhibits his hand in less good shape than most other specimens. Bodley 160 is important in this respect. Like Lambeth 59, it represents a library format by its size and layout, but on palaeographic terms, the Bodley manuscript is superior. In the Lambeth manuscript, the scribe's hand

[140] L. DELISLE (ed.), *Rouleau mortuaire de B. Vital, abbé de Savigny*, Paris, 1909, no. 105, pl. xxviii.

[141] The foliation counts the first two folios as flyleaves, numbering them as iii and iv. Fol. 8r reproduced in PARKES, *Their Hands*, 2008, pl. 68.

[142] See also his emendations in English to the letter from Nicholas of Worcester to Eadmer in CCCC 371, fol. 4r.

is variable, as the size, letter forms, and tilting are all subject to change. It is important to note that the changes in the aspect and in the letter forms do not coincide with the ends and beginnings of letters, but occur within them. The variation does not reflect the type of writing process involved in producing a regularly-updated register of letters, of the kind that Schmitt and his followers identified in *L*. Variations in the aspect and the general sloppiness were most likely due to deterioration caused by age, as will be argued in the discussion of the manuscript's dating below.

Hand B appears in the course of the main text copied by scribe A. B contributed only a few lines in four different places in the text: first the sixth from last line, starting from the penultimate word, and the five lines below it, on fol. 130rb; next lines 1–5 on fol. 132ra; then lines 10–11 on fol. 133ra, and finally lines 8–15 on fol. 155rb ('[ue]ram amicitiam – quod'). B's hand appears untidy and uncertain. The last (and to some extent the first) appearance of the hand give the impression that this man was being trained. He begins writing on fol. 155rb in the middle of a word ('[ue]ram'), and the hand is particularly careless and uncertain in appearance up to the word 'feci'. Thereafter the text (just under four lines of it) is written with a broader nib and is notably more even in quality.[143]

Scribe C began work probably some years after A. It appears as if C copied texts in two phases; fols. 160va, l. 3–161r (the lower margin)[144] and 169va, l. 16–180vb, l. 2 may represent the earliest phase of his work. He copied works including letters (*AEp.* 193 and 331) and other texts relating to Anselm. The letters on fols. 63r — *AEp.* 153 and 154 into the empty space A had left after the Bec correspondence (plate 3) — and 180vb, l. 3–182r, may represent the second phase of his work.[145] Scribe C was influenced by the Christ Church style, although the general appearance is not very angular.

---

[143] Likewise B's last word on fol. 130rb, 'quando', is sharper and more uniform in its appearance than his earlier writing.

[144] C began copying *AEp.* 193 on fol. 160v, which A had left empty apart from the two top lines. There was insufficient space, however, and C copied the end of the letter into the next folio's lower margin.

[145] I thank Michael Gullick for informing me that this was the work of the same scribe (pers. comm., 7.4.2007).

Annotations occur sporadically in near-contemporary and later hands. Folio 61v is annotated 'Osbernus': Schmitt took this perhaps to be 'the first hand', but in fact the hand does not appear in the main text and was none of the above hands.[146] Instructions were added in the margins and within the main text, indicating the points at which the letters subsequently added to the manuscript should be copied in future: there are five annotations of this kind, of which the first has been erased.[147] Both the erasure and at least two of the surviving additions were probably written by scribe C, although the hand is less formal than that in the main text.[148] The remaining two annotations are written even less formally and could likewise be the work of C, but this identification is less secure than for the others.[149] An informal twelfth-century hand has written 'hic incepi primo' on fol. 37r before the beginning of *AEp*. 85 and 'hic incipiendum iterum' in the right margin on fol. 38r referring to the final part of *AEp*. 89. These appear to be private reminders written either by a reader or a copyist using the manuscript as his exemplar.[150]

Christ Church *nota*-markings appear in the margins, some using the characteristic Christ Church form .a. and others the widely used form .N.[151] Marginal annotations written by Archbishop Cranmer

---

[146] See *AEp*. 149:3 (apparatus criticus).

[147] Fol. 70v: '[...] quae in fine libri habetur quae sic incipit Reuerendo ac reuerenter suscipiendo [*AEp*. 193]'.

[148] Fol. 75r: 'Ante istam [*AEp*. 194] ponatur illa epistola quae pene circa finem habetur ad hoc signum et sic incipit. Reuerendo ac reuerenter [*AEp*. 193]'. Fol. 119r: 'Hic scribatur illa epistola quae in fine libri habetur. quae sic incipit. Anselmus archiepiscopus reuerendo priori d[omno] e[rnulfo]. Ad hoc signum [*AEp*. 331]'.

[149] Fol. 78v: 'Ante istam scribatur epistola quae in fine habetur. quae sic incipit; Henricus dei gratia rex ad predictum signum [*AEp*. 212]'. Fol. 138v: 'Hic scribatur epistola quae circa finem habetur. Quae sic incipit. Amatissimo atque g[lorioso] ad hoc signum [*AEp*. 411]'; and on line 17: 'Deest de hac prescripta epistola'. See also fol. 170 where C wrote a note referring to a passage in '*Quattuor modis*': 'hoc tantum postea est scriptum ad hoc signum'.

[150] On similar annotations in Gloucester books, see R. M. THOMSON, 'Books and Learning at Gloucester Abbey in the Twelfth and Thirteenth Centuries', in *Books and Collectors 1200–1700: Essays presented to Andrew Watson*, eds. J. CARLEY & C. TITE, London, 1997, pp. 12–13.

[151] Examples of the former e.g. on fols. 119v, 146v, 147r, 148v, of the latter e.g. on fols. 105r, 133r.

also appear.[152] There are annotations next to certain letters, which had been published by Baluze, in a seventeenth- or eighteenth-century hand, possibly of Archbishop Sancroft, who compiled the list of contents. These notes state that the fourth volume of Baluze's series *Miscellanea* (published in 1683) includes this particular letter.[153]

The first lines of *AEp.* 471, which are missing from the main text, have been copied into the upper margin of fol. 187r (after the blank fols. 182v–186v). The marginal addition is made in a completely informal twelfth-century hand, which is somewhat reminiscent of the hand that wrote the verse at the end of the manuscript, on fol. 190r. Two hands seem to be responsible, however.[154] The verse on the final folio is a Leonine hexameter, which runs 'Que restant modici sunt scripta manu thiderici' (plate 4).[155] This hexameter is at the heart of the debate discussed in the introduction, in which the interpretation of Anselm's character is ultimately at stake: the central question is whether the Thidricus mentioned in the verse made *L*, and whether he worked under Anselm's supervision. I shall return to this problem below.

Dating

The original manuscript, fols. 1–160, 187–190

The internal evidence of *L* demonstrates that its concluding letters at least were copied after Anselm's death. As mentioned

---

[152] E.g. fols. 81r, 84v, 85r, 94r, 94v, 187r. D. G. SELWYN, 'Cranmer and the Dispersal of Medieval Libraries. The provenance of some of his medieval manuscripts and printed books', in *Books and Collectors 1200–1700: Essays presented to Andrew Watson,* eds. J. CARLEY & C. TITE, London, 1997, p. 285. Cranmer's annotations touch on the contents of the letters, and he was especially interested in Anselm's views on clerical marriage (fol. 94v, marg.: 'de clericis coniugatis'; and the underlines in the neighbouring *AEp.* 257, which deals with the matter), and in Canterbury's primacy (187r, marg.: 'de primatu sedis cantuariensis', referring to *AEp.* 472).

[153] Fols. 7v, 11r, 12v, 55v, 98r, 175r.

[154] Southern ('An Examination', 1988, p. 200) and Logan ('Thidricus', 2006, p. 71) argue the opposite. For an illustration of the hands, see SOUTHERN, 'An Examination', 1988, p. 200, pl. 1.

[155] Below this verse is a second, written in a different hand: 'Tu solus tum dis es medicina reis'. The verse derives from a poem further up the folio, and it cannot be the 'signature-phrase of [the] 'La' scribe', that Fröhlich ('Introduction', 1990, p. 35) suggests; it is clearly a *probatio pennae,* by a hand not otherwise encountered in the manuscript.

above, scribe A replaced the original ending of the manuscript, now fols. 187–190, with new folios in order to rearrange the final letters. Before the folios were moved, the letters and other texts appeared in the manuscript in the following order:

> *AEp.* 471 (fol. 187r)
> *AEp.* 472 (fol. 187r)
> '*Est considerandum*' (*Memorials*, pp. 334–336; fols. 187r–188r)
> '*Velle eisdem*' (*Memorials*, p. 351: 4; fol. 188r)
> '*Laetaris quod*' (*Memorials*, p. 353: 1; fol. 188r)
> *AEp.* 469 (fol. 188r–v)

The text preceding *AEp.* 469, '*Laetaris quod*', is a death-bed confession, which was probably written and used by Anselm himself.[156] The placing of *AEp.* 469 after the confession fits very badly with the hypothesis that Anselm himself supervised the production of the manuscript. Why would he have wished to include a confession and other assorted texts in his letter collection, moreover even before all the letters had been presented?[157] It is probable that several years passed between Anselm's death and the production of *L*. Textual criticism indicates that Canterbury had a collection of Anselm's letters incorporating the Canterbury correspondence, and which preceded *L*. This makes Southern's argument that *L* postdates Anselm's death a clear certainty. The palaeographic and codicological evidence suit this perfectly.

As stated above, we now know that the main hand in *L* was a prolific Christ Church scribe, the bulk of whose work fell in the 1120s. If compared to the other specimens, Lambeth 59 represents his hand in a somewhat degenerate shape — with one exception, which I shall discuss shortly. Gullick argues that the deterioration was most likely caused by age (and perhaps intensified by the variable quality of parchment), and places the manuscript towards the end of the scribe's career.[158] One should ask whether the story

---

[156] *Memorials*, p. 352.

[157] Cf. Krüger, *Persönlichkeitsausdruck*, 2002, p. 77. He considers it possible that Anselm himself ordered these letters (*AEp.* 471, 472 and 469) to be rearranged.

[158] The latest datable specimens of this hand are the copies of two episcopal professions from 1126 and 1128, both of which represent a better calligraphic quality than *L*. The professions were manifestations of Canterbury's archiepiscopal and primatial authority, and the roll in which they were made

could be reversed. In other words, could the sloppiness in Lambeth 59 ensue from professional immaturity at the beginning of the scribe's career? The answer, put simply, is no. In Eadmer's autograph manuscript, Cambridge, Corpus Christi College 371, our hand occurs thrice, and in one specimen his hand shows similar uneven quality as in Lambeth 59. This is an addition made to fol. 195r–v, constituting the last miracle of and a postscript to Eadmer's *Miracula Anselmi* (plate 6; cf. plates 3–5). Southern dates the addition to about 1123–4, but this is only a conjecture.[159] The miracle took place during a fire in the town of Bury St Edmunds and was added, says Eadmer, once he had heard of it. The fire is not recorded elsewhere, and the *Vita* tells us only that it occurred after the promotion of Anselm, the archbishop's nephew, to abbot of Bury in 1121. In the postscript — still in the Lambeth hand and evidently written in one campaign with the miracle — Eadmer states that his 'white hair and trembling fingers' made writing impossible for him. If this is to be taken literally, the addition postdates anything that we can see in Eadmer's own hand.[160] Southern dates the latest additions to CCCC 371 in Eadmer's hand to the years 1124–30, suggesting that the *ad quem* for the addition to the *Miracula* should be extended at least to 1130. This would permit Gullick's palaeographical dating for Lambeth 59. We may add that Lambeth Palace 224 (*M*), the collection of Anselm's works by William of Malmesbury, supports a late date for *L* as well. William drew on several sources for the treatises and letters, but these included neither Lambeth 59

---

was apparently of particular value to Christ Church. This and the fact that the two professions are only four lines long may in part explain their superior palaeographic standard to Lambeth 59.

[159] SOUTHERN, *Saint Anselm and his Biographer*, 1963, p. 369.

[160] There is a correction on fol. 179r that may be in Eadmer's hand, and if so, his statement as to elderly state should not to be taken literally, at least in absolute terms. The manuscript tradition implies that this correction — replacing 'mundalis' with 'secularis'—was later than the postscript (*VA*, pp. xxii and 110). The evidence comes from London, Harley 315, fols. 16r–39v, a contemporary copy of the *Vita*, and Lambeth Palace 410, an early modern but apparently very good copy of the Harleian manuscript. Harley 315 seems to have preserved *Vita Anselmi* in its second latest state, i.e. without the emendation in question. The manuscript has lost the folios covering the beginning and end of the *Vita*, but Lambeth 410 preserves the text, including the postscript, in full.

nor Bodley 271, which is Christ Church's omnibus of the treatises and devotional texts. Since William was well connected to Christ Church, we should expect him to have made use of Christ Church's collections of Anselm's works if they had existed. L's *ad quem* can be inferred from P, which is L's direct derivate. P was finished by early 1130, as will be shown below. All evidence considered, L can be dated tentatively to the final years of the 1120s and more securely to *c.* 1120 × 1130.

The appendix (L^a), fols. 160–182

All additions on fols. 160–182 apparently postdate P, and scribe C's work certainly postdates P; P draws on sources other than L^a for these items. In contrast, manuscript E, from *c.* 1120 × *c.* 1140, derived material from L^a. L^a thus falls in between P and E, or in other words *c.* 1120 × *c.* 1140.

Provenance

The first folio has a twelfth-century sign resembling a letter F, which was peculiar to Christ Church's library. On the first flyleaf, there is the pressmark 'D. ij^a. G. X^{us}' in a hand that is perhaps from the thirteenth century. In a fifteenth-century hand, there is the annotation 'Liber ecclesie christi cantuariensis de prima demonstracione' on the verso side of the second flyleaf; subsequently somebody has crossed these words out. Together, the signa provide the precise location of the manuscript within the library at Christ Church at these dates: the tenth *gradus* (shelf) of the second *distinctio* (press) in the first *demonstratio*. The seventy-first item in Prior Henry of Eastry's book list from 1326 is *Epistole Anselmi maiores*, a title which appears twice on L's flyleaves.[161] The same book was item 145 in William Ingram's list of 1508.[162] Ingram listed more or less all the books from a new, upper library room, constructed in the 1430s and 1440s. At the dissolution, the books Ingram listed came into circulation rather late. De

---

[161] JAMES, *Canterbury and Dover*, 1903, p. 24.

[162] JAMES, *Canterbury and Dover*, 1903, p. 157. The *Opuscula Anselmi maiora* are number 62 in Eastry's catalogue and number 144 in Ingram's list. This was Oxford, Bodley 271 (SCHMITT, 'Die unter Anselm veranstaltete Ausgabe', 1955, pp. 64–65), with the signum 'D. P^a monstra primus. D. II. G. VIII.' on its first folio.

Hamel suggests that the upper library may have been sealed off after a fire had broken out in 1535, when the royal commissioners had come to investigate the priory; afterwards the library would have been inaccessible for some thirty years, until funds were allocated for its restoration in 1569.[163] However, Archbishop Cranmer (1533–56) had probably appropriated *L* well before that year, for we find his annotations in the manuscript's margins.[164] The crown confiscated Cranmer's collection, which was transferred to Henry, twelfth Earl of Arundel († 1580) and onwards to his son-in-law, John, Lord Lumley († 1609). This was also *L*'s fate. A hand of the turn of the sixteenth and seventeenth centuries wrote 'Lumley' in the lower margin of the first folio; the 1609 catalogue of his library also mentions the manuscript.[165] Although the greater part of Lumley's collection went to the Royal Library and thence finally made its way to the British Library, *L* returned into possession of the archbishops of Canterbury. Credit for this is probably due either to Archbishop Richard Bancroft (in office 1604–10) or his successor George Abbot (in office 1611–33), both of whom are known to have developed the collections of their official library, where *L* was included in a catalogue drawn up soon after Abbot's death.[166] The manuscript also appears in a catalogue of 1647, and one drawn up a little later, both of which reflect the temporary migration of Lambeth Palace library to Cambridge after the abolition of episcopacy in 1646.[167] Folios 191–278 in the present volume had not yet been bound with *L* at this date; this only occurred after the book

---

[163] DE HAMEL, 'The Dispersal of the Library of Christ Church, Canterbury, from the Fourteenth to the Sixteenth Century', in *Books and Collectors 1200–1700: Essays presented to Andrew Watson*, eds. J. CARLEY & C. TITE, London, 1997, pp. 273–274.

[164] E.g. fols. 81r, 84v, 94r, 94v. SELWYN, 'Cranmer and the Dispersal', 1997, p. 285.

[165] *Lumley Catalogue*, item 40 (p. 43); Prof. Richard Sharpe (pers. comm. 27.11.2008).

[166] The annotation 'M 8' on the first flyleaf refers to this catalogue. See N. KER, 'Archbishop Sancroft's rearrangement of the manuscripts of Lambeth Palace', in *A Catalogue of Manuscripts in Lambeth Palace Library. MSS. 1222–1860*, ed. E. BILL, Oxford, 1972, pp. 1–2.

[167] KER, 'Sancrofts's rearrangement', 1972, pp. 2–4, 23; in the earlier catalogue *L* is 'E.β.2'. and number 207 in the latter.

collection had returned to Lambeth Palace.[168] The manuscripts were bound together by the order of Archbishop Sancroft (in office 1678–91), who arranged and reshaped the collection of his official library extensively, for example by binding different manuscripts together according to the fashions of the day. Sancroft also drew up the list of contents on the verso side of the second flyleaf, which includes the contents of both manuscripts.[169]

2.2 *Paris, BNF lat. 2478* − P

c. 1120 × 1130; Canterbury cathedral priory (OSB); parchment; ii + 138 + ii'; I[10] II–XVII[8]; 250 × 175 (190 × 130) mm; 38 (long) lines

Contents

fols. 1r–133r   Anselm, *Epistolae* (*P*)
fols. 133v–134r Canons of the Councils at Westminster in 1102 (see Councils and synods, no. 113, pp. 674–679)
fols. 134r–135r '*Haud habiture*' (SHARPE, 'Two poems', 1982, pp. 271–274, *Walther* 7673)
fols. 135r–136r '*Presulis Anselmi*' (SHARPE, 'Two poems', 1982, pp. 274–279, *Walther* 14486)
fols. 136v–138v 'Catalogus romanorum pontificum' (a list of popes)

Paris, BNF lat. 2478 or *P* contains Anselm's letters (fols. 1r–133r), texts relating to him (fols. 133v–136r), and a list of popes (fols. 136v–138v). The quiring is almost entirely uniform: the first quire is a quinion and the remainder are quaternions. Only two quire marks survive: IIII in the lower margin of fol. 34v and VI in the lower margin of fol. 50v. The text is written in a single column except for fols. 134r–138r, which contain the poems, running in two columns so that one verse takes one line. The ink varies between brown and dark brown in colour. The margins are ruled in lead, and prickings are still visible. The foliation is given in Arabic numerals in the top right corner. The illuminated initial on fol. 1r depicts a dragon twisted into the form of the letter S. The incomplete initial on fol. 64r in manuscript *L* shares the same theme; however, the initials are apparently the work of different artists. The initials in Cambridge, St John's College A. 8 also have similar

---

[168] 'E.α.3' and 204 in the same catalogues.
[169] JAMES, *Lambeth Palace*, 1932, p. 91.

stylistic traits to the initial in P,[170] though it is uncertain whether the same artist was responsible for these initials and the one in P. Samuel, the scribe of the St John's College manuscript, whose hand also appears in manuscript Bodley 271, does not appear in either P or L. Another ornamented initial occurs on fol. 53r, marking the transition from the Bec to the Canterbury period.[171] This initial is decorated with a clover leaf. The other initials in P are simple red, blue, green, or purple letters.

The top corner of the recto side of the first folio has a twelfth-century sign resembling the letters fr joined at the base. This sign is characteristic of Christ Church's twelfth-century manuscripts, as Patricia Stirnemann has observed.[172] The palaeography too indicates a Christ Church origin. There are four twelfth-century hands in the manuscript. Scribe A, who copied fols. 1r–135v up to the end of the first column in a typical Christ Church hand (plate 7), also occurs in BL, Cotton Cleopatra E. I, fols. 40–56; this is a copy of the famous Canterbury forgeries and has been dated to 4 April 1120 × 22 July 1123.[173] B commenced work at the beginning of the second column of fol. 135v, in the middle of Anselm's verse epitaph, and copied the final texts relating to Anselm in P. The angular aspect typical of the Christ Church scriptorium also dominates B's hand. C only inserted corrections, in a script more markedly angular than those of the previous scribes. D added a list of popes on fols. 136v–138v.

The list of popes is important with regard to the dating of the manuscript. The list originally ended with Gelasius II; subsequently his successors Calixtus II and Honorius II were added. Hand D

---

[170] Fols. 1v, 39v, 61r, 76v, 102r (DODWELL, *Canterbury Illumination*, 1954, pl. 14e), 164r (by another artist?, *ibid.*, pl. 42a), 180r (by the second artist), 191r, 219r (*ibid.*, pl. 37d).

[171] Fol. 53r.

[172] I thank Michael Gullick for this information (pers. comm., 7.4.2007). Wilmart ('La tradition', 1931, p. 40) assumed (erroneously) that the manuscript was from the monastery of St Augustine's, Canterbury. This may have been on the grounds that, because L was from Christ Church, P had to originate elsewhere; since the style indicated a Canterbury origin, St Augustine remained. Schmitt took up this view; 'Intorno all'Opera omnia di S. Anselmo d'Aosta', *Sophia*, 27 (1959), p. 228.

[173] R. SOUTHERN, 'The Canterbury forgeries', *EHR*, 73 (1958), p. 219.

probably added Calixtus II, while the addition of Honorius II was made significantly later (plate 8). The list gives not only the name of each pope, but also the number of years he ruled and the office was vacant after his death. Therefore, the original list must have been drawn up during the reign of Gelasius II's successor Calixtus II (1119–1124) at the earliest;[174] the entry referring to Calixtus II can only have been made after his death, upon Honorius's assuming the office.[175] Lists that were not up-to-date were sometimes made, which means that the last pope in our list can provide a watertight *a quo*, this is 1119, but not an indisputable *ad quem*. The Calixtus addition in the list, however, argues for an *ad quem* of 1130, since it is unlikely that the scribe (D) would have added Calixtus's name alone if his successor Honorius II had also died by that time; he died on 13 February 1130.[176] The catalogue may thus be dated to between 1119 and early 1130. Since the texts associated with Anselm continue right up to the recto side of fol. 136, and the catalogue of popes begins on the verso side of that folio, the letters must predate the catalogue. The *ad quem* for the letter collection part of the manuscript is thus 1130.[177] The *a quo* cannot be placed in a particular year. It is, however, clear, that P was produced after L, but before L^a, as P derived the material in L^a from other sources. Furthermore, P includes certain original readings from L, which were corrected in L itself before the preparation of E, for example at 433:20 coniuncti C^bV^bP] coniungi *LE corr. ex*

---

[174] Fol. 138v: 'Gelasius .ii. campanus sedit annum .i. et dies .v. cessauit episcopatus .iiii. dies.'

[175] Fol. 138v: 'Calixtus .ii. natus gallus. sedit annos .v. menses .x. dies .xii. et cessauit episcopatus dies .x.' Cf. the list of popes in Cambridge, Corpus Christi College 130, according to which Calixtus…'sedit annos .vi. Menses .x. dies xv…Cessauit autem episcopatus dies .iii.', fol. 219r–v. The main body of the manuscript is from *s.* xii[in] and the papal list was added between 1124 and, presumably, before the death of Honorius II.

[176] I thank Dr Teresa Webber for this observation (pers. comm. 27.11.2008).

[177] Krüger (*Persönlichkeitsausdruck*, 2002, pp. 72–73) draws on the same evidence to conclude that the *terminus ad quem* was 1119, stating 'war die Papstliste im Anhang bereits bald nach dem Tode Gelasius' II. im Jahr 1119 erstmals vorläufig abgeschlossen'; this assumption is, however, unfounded. Contra Fröhlich's ('Introduction', 1990, p. 39) suggestion, the manuscript was certainly not compiled in Anselm's lifetime, as its inclusion of *AEp.* 471 and 472, drawn up shortly before Anselm's death, in itself reveals.

coniuncti *L*. The palaeographical evidence suggests a date towards 1130 for *L*, although an earlier date, *c.* 1120 or later, is not impossible. To conclude, *P* should be dated *c.* 1120 × 1130.

Short marginal annotations, mostly at the beginning of letters, regarding their content, appear on fols. 1r–21r in an early fourteenth-century English cursive and in red ink.[178] The same hand also made nota marks on those folios. On fol. 72r–74r there are short annotations concerning the content,[179] and nota marks by the same hand in brown ink. Otherwise, the provenance of the manuscript is very poorly known. The marginalia in an English cursive mentioned above suggest that it may still have been in England in the fourteenth century. The manuscript did not, it seems, remain at Canterbury, since it does not appear in Prior Eastry's book list of 1326. The next certain information is not until the seventeenth century, when *P* emerges in the collection of the famous statesman and bibliophile Colbert († 1683), whence it too found its way into the hands of his librarian Étienne Baluze († 1718).[180] Baluze published certain texts from *P*, which will be discussed in more detail in chapter V.2 below.[181] In 1732 the manuscript entered the then royal library, today the Bibliothèque nationale.[182]

---

[178] E.g. on fol. 6v beside *AEp.* 13: 'Epistola de misericordia super pauperem'. English features include the use of a rounded s at the beginning of a word. I thank Professor Marc Smith (pers. comm. 18.10.2007) for the localisation and dating.

[179] Fol. 72r: 'De obedi[entia] monachi'; fol. 73r: 'De libertate ecclesie dei'.

[180] Fol. 1r: Codex Colb. 4195. The manuscript might have been purchased by Colbert's son, who bought about fifteen books from England in a sale of books from the library of William Cecil, Lord Burghley († 1598) in London in 1687. However, the 1687 sale catalogue has no Anselm. Richard Sharpe, pers. comm. 27.11.2008.

[181] According to the 1761 reprint of Baluze's work, the letters are 'Ex ueteri Codice MS. Ecclesiæ Atrebatensis' (p. v). This information is probably incorrect, since the original edition, published in Baluze's lifetime, does not mention Arras in connection with *P*. Furthermore the 1761 edition also includes material from the fifth volume of the original work; this included the letter collection of Lambert of Arras, which also included some of Anselm's letters. The source for this letter collection is introduced in the original edition in almost the same words: 'Ex ueteri Codice MS. Ecclesiæ Atrebatensis'.

[182] Fol. 1r: 'Codex Colbertus 4195. Regius 4090.'

2.3 *Cambridge, Corpus Christi College 135* – E

c. 1120 × *c.* 1140; Bury St Edmunds (OSB); parchment; a–b + i–ii +
165 + iii–v + c–d; I–XII^8 XIII^{8+2} XIV–XX^8 XXI$^{6-1}$;[183] 310 × 205
(220 × 135) mm; 36 lines in two columns[184]

Contents

fols. 1r–146v	Anselm, *Epistolae* (*E*)
2 fols. inserted between fols. 101 and 102	*AEp.* 216 (from Paschal II to Henry I), 319 (Anselm to Henry I), an unidentified Petrine tract 'Petre supra petram [n]ec inaniter edificasti – Ora pro nobis ad celica regna regressus.'
fols. 146v–147r	Anselm?, '*Est considerandum*' (*Memorials*, pp. 334–336)
fol. 147r	Anselm?, '*Laetaris quod*' (*Memorials*, p. 353:1)
fols. 147r–154r	Eadmer, *De beatitudine perennis uitae* ('second recension', *Memorials*, pp. 274–288)
fols. 154r–155v	Anselm?, '*Quattuor modis*' (*Memorials*, pp. 336–340)[185]
fols. 155v–160v	Anselm?, '*Discipulus. Plura sunt*' (*Memorials*, pp. 341–351)
fol. 160v	Anselm, *Cur Deus homo, Commendatio operis ad Urbanum* (*SAO*, vol. 2, pp. 39–40, lines 2–17)
fol. 161r–v	Canons of the Council at Westminster in 1102 (see *Councils and synods*, no. 113, pp. 674–679)
fols. 161v–162r	Primatial Council at London in 1108 (see *Councils and synods*, no. 116, pp. 694–704)
fol. 162v	*AEp.* 255
fols. 162v–164r	'*Haud habiture*' (SHARPE, 'Two poems', 1982, pp. 271–274, *Walther* 7673)
fols. 164r–165v	'*Presulis Anselmi*' (SHARPE, 'Two poems', 1982, pp. 274–279, *Walther* 14486)[186]
fol. 165v	'Omnia maiorem – priusue fuerant' (two hexameter verses)
fol. 165v	Anselm, *Epitaphium Hugonis* (*Memorials*, p. 351:B1)

---

[183] The two additional folios of quire XIII are contemporaneous with or a little later than the manuscript itself and they are not included in the foliation. They are 230 × 150 (200 × 125) mm in size.

[184] For a more detailed codicological description, see E. McLACHLAN, *The Scriptorium of Bury St. Edmunds in the Twelfth Century*, New York & London, 1986, pp. 284–285.

[185] The hand changes in the middle of the text on fol. 155va, l. 22.

[186] As in *L*^{a}, here too two blank lines are left between the verses, of which the first ends 'nocuere mali' and the latter begins 'Federa iura'.

fol. iii^r   two short extracts[187]
fol. iii^r–v   Tractatus beati Anselmi de uirtute corporis Christi;
                    Quia de sacramento altaris per sepe – gustus noster
                    dissimulare non potest. s. xiii^2/2
fol. iv^r   tables of letters designated by Roman numerals, para-
                    phrased extracts from letters, and a letter from brother
                    W, prior(?) and precentor of Ely to the abbot of Glas-
                    tonbury
fol. iv^v   extracts from Anselm's letters in two s. xii^2/3 hands[188]

Cambridge, Corpus Christi College 135 or *E* contains Anselm's
letters and some further texts relating to him. Folio 1r opens
with an incomplete initial S in red and green, which is larger in
size than the other initials. Folio 27r too has a decorated initial,
which marks the transition from Anselm's period as prior to that
as abbot; it is distinguished from the general run of initials by its
red, green, and purple colouring. The other initials are green, purple, or red, sometimes with the addition of silver. The text is in
brown ink. The margins are ruled with a stylus. Prickings are still
visible. There are no quire marks.

The letters were copied by a single scribe, who also corrected
the text. He wrote a late English Carolingian minuscule of the
twelfth century of high quality (plate 9). On palaeographical evidence, the manuscript has been placed within a group from Bury
St Edmunds that may be dated to the period 1120–40.[189] The same

---

[187] The first is a table to a treatise (*s.* xiv, inc. 'Ydropisi quarere auari-
cia comparatur'). The second is a short biographical note on Abbot Boso of
Bec (*s.* xvii [?], inc. 'anno etatis sue 23 factus est monachus Becci sub beato
Anselmo').

[188] The first hand: 35:6–21 (Cave – peruenias); 6:9–10 ([De obedientia.]
melius–inobedientiam); 37:46–53; 39–42 (Quapropter – uacet. Monachus –
ditescit). The second hand: 49:23–28 ([De elemosina.] si quis - mercedem.);
319:11–14 ([De prouidentia mortis.] Qualem – proficies.) The texts reflect devotional reading in Bury St Edmunds.

[189] E. McLachlan, 'The scriptorium of Bury St. Edmunds in the third
and fourth decades of the twelfth century: books in three related hands and
their decoration', *Mediaeval Studies*, 40 (1978), pp. 333–336. See also T. A. M.
Bishop, 'Notes on Cambridge Manuscripts. Part I', *Transactions of the Cambridge Bibliographical Society*, 1 (1953), pp. 432–433; R. Thomson, 'The Library
of Bury St Edmunds Abbey in the Eleventh and Twelfth Centuries', *Speculum*,
47 (1972), pp. 631–632; M. Brett, 'John of Worcester and his contemporaries',
in *The writing of history in the Middle Ages. Essays presented to Richard William Southern*, eds. R. H. C. Davis & J. M. Wallace-Hadrill, Oxford, 1981,

scribe also copied some of the texts following the letters. The hand changes on fol. 155vb, line 22, in the middle of the treatise 'Quattuor modis' (Memorials, pp. 336–340). Scribe B's hand has stronger proto-gothic features.[190] After he completed the text 'Quattuor modis', the process of selecting and rearranging the material found in the exemplar, L^a, began. The decision to end the manuscript with the poems in praise of Anselm, and Anselm's own epitaph in memory of Hugo, indicates a degree of forethought.[191]

Manuscript E may well have been commissioned by Anselm's nephew and namesake. The younger Anselm was abbot of Bury St Edmunds 1121–48, during which period the library experienced a campaign of expansion.[192] Already in around 1115 Anselm had commissioned a collection of his uncle's talks, the Dicta Anselmi.[193] The catalogue of the monastery library from the end of the twelfth century refers to a manuscript entitled the 'Epistole Anselmi archiepiscopi',[194] which is also included among Bury St Edmunds' books in the Registrum Anglie de libris doctorum et auctorum ueterum, a catalogue drawn up by the Oxford Franciscans at the end of the thirteenth century.[195] Furthermore the Bury St Edmunds ex-libris appears on the first folio, along with a list of contents of the manuscript, drawn up by Henry de Kirkestede, the

pp. 107–109; D. DUMVILLE, 'Introduction', in The Annals of St Neots with Vita Prima Sancti Neoti, Anglo-Saxon Chronicle, vol. 17, Suffolk, 1985, p. xvi; N. R. KER, Catalogue of Manuscripts Containing Anglo-Saxon, Oxford, 1957, pp. 133–134.

[190] E.g. the uncial d appears frequently.

[191] It has not been possible to identify Hugo with certainty; see Memorials, p. 351.

[192] Archbishop Anselm brought his nephew and namesake to England. Upon the older Anselm's death, the younger returned to Italy, where he rose to be abbot of the monastery of San Saba at Rome. In 1115–1119 he acted as the pope's legate to England and in 1138 he was briefly bishop of London; see D. KNOWLES, C. N. L. BROOKE & V. LONDON, The Heads of Religious Houses: England & Wales, 1. 940–1216, 2nd edn., Cambridge, 2001 [1972], p. 32. On the development of the library, see THOMSON, 'The Library of Bury St Edmunds', 1972, pp. 630–632. On E and Abbot Anselm see ibid., pp. 631–632 and SCHMITT, 'Zur Entstehungsgeschichte', 1936, p. 300, note 3.

[193] Memorials, pp. 25–26, 107.

[194] SHARPE et al., Bury St Edmunds: List of Books, late 12th cent. with later continuations, Benedictine Libraries, 1996, B13.28.

[195] ROUSE et al., Registrum Anglie, 1991, R33.23.

famous mid-fourteenth century armarius of Bury St Edmunds.[196] The manuscript is also mentioned in Henry's catalogue.[197] It was still in the possession of the monastery in the fifteenth century, as says an entry in a hand of that period on flyleaf iv[v].[198] After the Dissolution, the manuscript probably found its way into the collection of the famous antiquary John Bale († 1563). Bale's collection was dispersed when he was forced into exile. After his return to England, he succeeded in obtaining a royal decree for his books' return from Elizabeth, although this was never put into effect. On Bale's death, Archbishop Parker († 1575) managed to obtain parts of his collection for himself, which probably explains how *E* came into his possession.[199] Parker or somebody in his immediate circle clearly read the manuscript, as is apparent from marginal annotations, marks, and underlines in characteristic red crayon.[200] The archbishop bequeathed his collection to Corpus Christi College, Cambridge, where *E* is today.

2.4 *Conclusions: the subgroup* LPE

LPE all belong to the same stemmatic branch. The relationship between manuscripts *LP* is particularly interesting from the outset, since they were both compiled in the same scriptorium within

---

[196] Fol. i[v]: 'Liber sancti edmundi + martyris in quo continentur / CCCLXVIJ epistole Anselmi archiepiscopi. / Meditatio anselmi de eterna beatitudine. / Concilium prouenciale ab anselmo Londoniense celebratum.' On Henry of Kirkestede see Rouse *et al.* in *CBMLC*, vol. 11, pp. xxix–lxxxii and R. Rouse, 'Bostonus Buriensis and the author of the *Catalogus Scriptorium Ecclesiae*', *Speculum*, 41 (1966), pp. 480–490.

[197] Henry of Kirkestede, *Catalogus*, 2004, K3.35.

[198] Fol. iv[v]: 'De sorte Iohannis wickam monachi monasterii Sancti edmundi de buree actualiter scolatisantis oxoniensis et permansuri dum modo sit deputatus et legitime electus per capitulum.'

[199] The annotation 'L.8' on fol. i[v] is the Parker Library's signum. McLachlan, *The Scriptorium of Bury St. Edmunds*, 1986, p. 284; H. McCusker, 'Books and Manuscripts Formerly in the Possession of John Bale', *The Library*, 4th series, 16, 1935, pp. 146–148.

[200] Fols. 51v, 79r, 83r, 102r, 103r, 110r. There was also another early modern reader, possibly from Parker's circle, whose marginalia in grey pencil occur within the Canterbury correspondence, e.g. on fol. 45r. On Parker's and his son's annotations and reading, see R. I. Page, *Matthew Parker and his books*, Sandars Lectures in Bibliography, Western Michigan University, 1993, pp. 125–127.

a very short space of time. *L* and *P* arrange their letters likewise
and share a great number of distinctive textual variants.[201] When
P's text diverges from *L*'s, the former is inferior and isolated (with
the few exceptions discussed below).[202] The passage in *AEp*. 240,
lines 19–20, is a particularly informative example for the relationship between the manuscripts. The best reading is 'calamo scribae
uelociter scribentis omnia confiteor ascribenda cum psalmista
dicens a domino'. In *P*, the passage is truncated: 'calamo scribere
uelo a domino'. *L* reveals how the reading in *P* came about: there
originally appears to have been an omission in *L*, apparently running from the word 'scribae' and probably ending with the word
'psalmista';[203] this error was corrected by erasing the text after the
word 'calamo', probably the word 'dicens', to free up the end of
the line. Only the start of the omitted text, 'scribae uelo'[citer],
fitted into the space left by the erasure; and the corrector furthermore miscopied the first word as 'scribere'. He copied the end of
the passage '-citer scribentis [*corr. ex* scribentes] omnia confiteor
ascribenda cum psalmista dicens' vertically into the central margin between the columns. Thus the text in the column itself read
'calamo scribae [*corr. ex* scribere] uelo / a domino'. This reading
was taken into *P*, as its scribe either failed to notice the vertical
addition or did not connect it with the omission mark after 'uelo'
(plates 5 and 7).[204]

---

[201] There are too many readings of this kind to present a full list; see
Schmitt's critical apparatus.

[202] *P* frequently displays readings unique to it, although here Schmitt's
apparatus is not fully trustworthy. E.g. 44:5 rependere *NLCVE*] respondere *P*;
69:19 morum *LCV*] meorum *P*; 109:10–11 Monologion uocetis et alterum non
Alloquium *NMLCVE*] monoloquium *P*; 113:37 sui *LFCVE*] suam *P*; 118:23–24
est desiderium – uita uestra *NMLCVE*] *om. P*; 137:29 dedecorandi *LFMCE*]
dederandi *P* de^{c}corandi *V*; 192:26 nullus *LEFMV^b*] *om. P*; 197:3 temporalem
LEFMC^{b}V^b] corporalem *P*; 266:15 ipse *LEFMC^b*] *om. P*; 281:4 quod *LEFC^{b}V^b*]
om. P; 297:3 animae *LC^{b}V^b*] *om. P*; 321:5 pro *LEFMC^{b}V^b*] *om. P*; 343:24 deus
LEC^{b}V^b] *om. P*; 355:28 scandalo aut sine magna *LEFMC^{b}V^b*] *om. P*; 468:10
loquimur *LEFMC^{b}V^b*] loquitur *P*.

[203] The word following 'calamo' has been erased and is illegible. The original
reading in *L*, however, was probably 'calamo dicens a domino'.

[204] See also 297:5–6 saeculum] secundum *P*. In *L* (fol. 107vb, r. 5) the word
is abbreviated into the typical form *sclm*; the letter *c* is almost attached to
the *l* by the cross-stroke, so that the abbreviation looks like the letters *sdm*.

When the mistakes and inaccuracies are eliminated from Schmitt's critical apparatus,[205] a dozen anomalous readings remain;

P's scribe interpreted this abbreviation *scdm*, and wrote this into his own text (fol. 90v, r. 22).

[205] The witnesses incorrectly absent from Schmitt's reports are in brackets. (1) Where the apparatus notes that a certain reading appears in error in *P* alone, and in no other manuscript, the problem is not serious stemmatically. Examples include *AEp.* 5:18 delectatione] *Schmitt:* dilectione *P pro* dilectione *L* dilectioni *P*; 8:20 ueracius] ueraciter *P[L]*; 9:12 externi] aeterni *P[L]*; 16:20 nobis] *om. P[L]*; 23:8 mihi] *om. P[L]*; 44:14 debeam] debebam *P[L]*; 44:43 nomen meum] nomen domini *P[L]*; 78:31 rerum] *om. P[L]*; 80:21 multi praelati] praelati multi *P[L]*; 96:18 non mundi] non *om. P[L]*; 97:31 hoc ipsum] ipsum hoc *P[L]*; 97:69 non sunt] sunt non *P[L]*; 101:33 aliquantulum] aliquantum *P[L]*; 12:34 mercem] mercedem *P[L]*; 112:42 conglutinari] conglutinare *P[L]*; 112:67 aut] et *P[L]*; 113:20 conuersionem] conuersationem *P[L]*; 117:5 dominus] deus *P[L]*; 132:8 gaudet] gaudeat *P[L]*; 182:10 diuersae] deuersae *P[L]*; 182:13 ad regendum] ad regendam *P[L]*; 223:21 promouebuntur] promouehuntur *P[L]*; 227:4 et qui] et quia *P[L]*; 238:3 mi] mihi *P[L]*; 258:18 satisfacimus] *Schmitt:* satis facinus *P pro* satisfacimus *P*; 281:15 hoc immane] hoc in immane *P[L]*; 297:3 de salute animae uestrae] *om. P pro* animae *om. P*; 339:8 pro ea] pro eadem *P[L]*; 361:5 aliter] *om. P[L]*; 391:9 episcopis et] et *om. P[L]*.
(2) Mistakes where the apparatus links *P* and another manuscript against *L* are more serious. I have checked these cases in all the relevant manuscripts. Incorrect or incomplete references are: 5:7 in unam] *Schmitt:* uel (un)um *TP pro* in unam *P*; 6:1 Gundulfo] Gondulfo *L[P]*; 30:6 ac] et *L[P]*; 48:7 Gunfridus] *Schmitt:* Gufridus *L pro* Gunfridus *L*; 58:16 Gondulfi] Gundulfi *LV[P]*; 62:9 recta] est *add. PM[L]*; 74:33 haluuardum *L[P]*; 91:2 Gundulfo *sic simper DP[L]*; 95:12 '...quod in codi[cibus] *L[PE]* simul cum...'; 96:34 Gondulfi] Gundulfi *DP[L]*; 97:87 est nihil] nihil est *L[P]*; 112:74 proferre] proferri *L [corr. from* proferri *P]*; 113:11 precantium] precantum *EP[L]*; 116:35 scis] scit *EP[L]*; 120:51 fecerint] *Schmitt:* fecerunt *L pro* fecerint *L*; 132:12–13 uitam] *Schmitt:* uita *L pro* uitam *L*; 143:1 Waltero] Walterio *EP[L]*; 157:1 domno] domino *PV^b[LE]*; 160:20 diligit minus] minus diligit *PV^b[LE]*; 161:17 sapientiori] sipientiori *LE[P]*; 161:20 qui] quid *L[P]*; 180:14 praeeminet] praeminet *PV^a[LE]*; 182:2 subpriori] suppriori *PV[LE]*; 201:5 elegimus] *Schmitt:* eligimus *LE pro* elegimus *LE*; 201:7 cura] *Schmitt:* causa *LE pro* cura *LE*; 213:12 romana] ramana *L corr. from* ramana *E[P]*; 222:3 ut] *Schmitt:* quod *LDr pro* ut *L*; 223:25 aberrare] oberrare *PVF[LE]*; 242:2 septentrionalum] septentionalium *PV[LE]*; 242:2 Orcades] orchades *EP[L]*; 281:16 ut aliud] et aliud *PVFJ[LE]*; 286:14 consilii sui ui] ui consilii sui *PV [inversion signs in L]*; 299:23 si requisiuerit] si requisierit *PVFM[LE]*; 314:10 ambire] abire *PVFMD[LE]*; 317:13 non] *om. PF [inserts L]*; 318:10 domnino] domno *PV[LE]*; 333:21 hominibus] omnibus *PF[LE]*; 336:19 ab illis] ab allis *LE [corr. from* ab allis *P]*; 374:4 execrabilis] *Schmitt:* execrabili *L pro* execrabilis *L*; 391:12 parochias] parrochias *PF [parrochias from* parochias *L]*; 392:7 tecum]

that is, places in which *P* and another manuscript together disagree with the readings in *L*. These cases may be divided into two groups. First there are the variants, where *P* and one or more other manuscripts offer a reading better than, or of equal value to, the reading in *L*.[206] Each of these readings in *L* could have been corrected by *P* without recourse to an alternative source. The second group comprises readings shared by *P* and another manuscript, which are weaker than those in *L*.[207] Each of these could easily have occurred by chance. The opening of *AEp.* 1 is a case apart, however. *L* omits the first words of this letter, 'Suo domino et' (with the exception of the incomplete initial S, which may be of later date), which are however included in *P*. The scribe of *L*

Schmitt: uobis *LE pro* uobiscum *LE[P]*; 404:4 Heruaeus] herueus *PV[LE]*; 441:27 deum] *Schmitt*: dominum *LE pro* deum *LE[P]*.

(3) In certain cases, Schmitt did not collate *P*; *AEp.* 201, 206, 303, 353, 369, 392–394, 397, 401, 420–422, 425, 427, 429–431, 433–436, 441, 443, 444, 446, 450–452. *P* agrees with the readings in *L(E)* in these cases too. The list of these readings is too long to include here and I shall offer a single example. This case is rather more complicated than the other examples in this group, but of particular interest as it includes a reading not recorded in Schmitt's edition at all. 420:4 In quo recognosco] *Schmitt*: In qua recognosco *LEV pro* In qua re cognosco *LP* In qua recognosco *VE*.

(4) The divergences I have observed between *P* and the readings reported by Schmitt for *LE* are again the result of mistakes or deficiencies in the apparatus: 201:5 elegimus] *Schmitt*: eligimus *LE pro* elegimus *LE[P]*); 201:7 cura] *Schmitt*: causa *LE pro* cura *LE[P]*. 441:27 deum] *Schmitt*: dominum *LE pro* deum *LE[P]*. Furthermore, in some cases Schmitt's apparatus is expressed imprecisely and thus may lead the reader astray. See e.g. 320:6 quibus nebulis quippe *E* (*in L prius sic*) and the comparable instances at *AEp.* 401:3; 450:13 and 466:2. This would be better expressed *cum signis inuersionis L*, which would make it easier for the reader to discern *L*'s potential links to *P*.

[206] 25:2 amplectendo *PNCVE*] ampletendo *L*; 85:5 flagrant caritatis adore, tanto fragrant] flagrant caritatis adore, tanto flagant *L* flagrant caritatis adore, tanto flagrant *PMD*; 86:9 Lenis *PNMCV*] lems *LE*; 156:156 dilectorem *PC^aC^b-V^aV^bE*] delictorem *L corr. from* delictorem *E*; 157:17 per sanctam obedientiam praecipio *PC^aC^bV^aV^bE*] per sanctam obediendam praecipio *L*; 299:5 pertinent *PCV*] pernent *L* (*corr. from* pernent *E*); 392:7 tecum] *Schmitt*: uobis *LE pro* uobiscum *LE[P]*; 407:17 monstaruit *PCV*] mostrauit *L* (*corr. from* mostrauit *E*). The most difficult of the cases also belongs in this group: 86:11–12 dimittere militiam, immo malitiam, quam *NCVE*]...dimittere miliciam quam...*L* dimittere maliciam quam...*P*.

[207] 136:43 litteratum *LCV*] litterarum *PE*; 347:6 correptionis *LEF*] correctionis *PCV*; 445:19 debebo *LE*] debeo *PF*.

left a space for these words, which is blank to this day.[208] But he must have included instructions on what was to be written, from which the scribe of *P* copied the words. Instructions of this kind were often, though not always, written into the inner margin, close enough to the binding to be invisible in a (tightly) bound volume.[209] To conclude, the textual evidence indicates that *P* descends from *L*, and the production of these two manuscripts in close succession at Christ Church suggests that there was no intervening step in the transmission between them.

The same also applies *mutatis mutandis* to the *Canterbury* correspondence in *E*. In other words, *E* shares *L*'s textual idiosyncrasies[210] and also adds some new weak readings unique to itself.[211] Similarly, where *E* agrees with some other manuscript against *L*, the variants are few in number and not of a type to affect the conclusion, founded on substantial evidence, that the Canterbury material in *E* was copied from *L*.[212] The transmission of *E*'s Bec

---

[208] The first words were only intended to be in large, coloured letters here and in the first letter of the Canterbury correspondence (fol. 64r); the large letters at the start of the Canterbury letters were in fact completed. In the other letters, only the initial is coloured.

[209] The practice is familiar to everyone who has worked with manuscript fragments. Two randomly selected fragments from the collection of the Finnish National Library in Helsinki both have instructions to the rubricator placed so close to the lost binding that they must have been invisible when the manuscripts were intact: F.m. VII.24 (*s.* xii[ex.]); VII.28 (*s.* xiii[1]).

[210] Examples of readings common to *LE*: 156:156 dilectorem $PV^aV^bC^aC^bF$] delictorem *L* dilectorem *corr. from* delictorem *E*; 213:12 romana C^bV^b] ramana *L corr. from* ramana *EP*; 223:9 respondenda C^bV^bF] resplondenda *L corr. from* resplondenda *E* resplendenda *P*; 299:5 pertinent PC^bV^b] pernent *L corr. from* pernent *E*; 313:10 sunt FOC^bV^b] [sunt ~~sunt~~ C^b] sicut *PE* sicut *from* sunt *L*; 327:3 es C^bV^bF] *om. LPE*; 385:4 de fratre *LPE*] illo *add.* C^bV^bFM; 387:25 promulgari FC^bV^b] mulgari *LEP*; 413:19 repugnant C^bV^bF] regnant *LPE* (*in P a poster. manu corr. in* repugnant).

[211] Examples of readings unique to *E*: 156:78 Bene quia hoc feci in nomine domini $LPV^aV^bC^aC^bFMD$] *om. E* (quia] quod *MD*); 161:9 quid $LPV^aV^{b-}C^aC^bFMD$] mihi *adds E* (*not reported by Schmitt*); 374:12 excommunicationis percussit. Quam LPC^bV^bFM] *om. E*; 403:16 est LPC^bV^bFM] *om. E*; 433:17 protractae LPC^bV^b] pertractae *E*.

[212] 156:10 nostra EV^a] nostram LPV^bF; 156:15 habebam LV^aF] habeam *E corr. from* habeam V^b; 157:17 per sanctam obedientiam praecipio EPV^aV^b] per sanctam obediendam praecipio *L*; 161:20 qui $EFC^aC^bV^aV^b$] quid *LP* (*in E* qui *is in darker ink than the surrounding words and is possibly corrected*); 271:7

correspondence is another story: the Bec letters in E do not derive from L. Both the arrangement and the readings demonstrate that a lost manuscript, which closely resembled the source for manuscripts CV, served as E's exemplar. The relationship between the manuscripts will be discussed in detail below. Here it is enough to mention that L contaminated E's Bec correspondence; the main scribe of E corrected his text with the aid of L.[213]

PE omit the letters from Anselm's Canterbury period which were added to the end of L's 'liber primus' — that is, after the letters from Bec — at a later date.[214] E does, however, include five letters from L^a, that is, the appendix to L. Four of these, AEp. 193, 212, 331, and 411, are included with the Canterbury correspondence, and one, AEp. 255, is included in the section following the letter collection, comprising selected texts from L^a. The four letters within E's main sequence are placed at precisely the points where the marginalia in L instruct they should be.[215] These are also the only letters in L^a to have marginal annotations indicating their correct location. In contrast, P includes only one of the letters added to L^a, AEp. 331. P does not place the letter as L instructs, suggesting that the letter might come from somewhere else than L. Textual evidence supports this conclusion: P agrees with C^b (the second sequence of the Canterbury correspondence in manuscript C) against LE twice.[216]

In both P and E, the letters are followed by a group of texts relating to Anselm. The selection of texts in the two manuscripts differs slightly, but the common factor is that all the texts appear in L^a. Textual criticism demonstrates that L^a was the source of the

---

Eadmundi *EP*] edmundi *LV*. Schmitt's critical apparatus again includes some misleading errors and omissions: 161:17 sapientori] sipientori *L[EP]*; 162:1 pariensis *E[LP]*; 222:3 ut] *Schmitt:* quod *Dr pro* ut *L*; 240:2 ildebertus *L[E]*; 242:2 Orcades] orchades *EP[L]*; 374:4 execrabilis] *Schmitt:* execrabili *L pro* execrabilis *L*; 389:26 de iis] *Schmitt:* de hiis *EV pro* iis *E*.

[213] E.g. at 6:6 humiliter] *om. LP eras. E*.

[214] *AEp*. 153 and 154.

[215] *L* fol. 75r (regarding *AEp*. 193), 78v (regarding *AEp*. 212), 119r (regarding *AEp*. 331), 138v (regarding *AEp*. 411).

[216] 331:29 de debitis et de terris *L^aE*] de debitis et terris *C^bP*; 331:31 iuuenibus *L^aE*] iuuenculis *C^bP*.

additional texts in E, while P drew on an unknown source.[217] The

---

[217] The following analysis is based on the texts included in P.

(1) The canons of the Council of London of 1102 (*Councils and synods*, no 113, 674–679). The collation in *Councils and Synods* does not take PE into account. The common readings shared by L^aPE clearly indicate that the manuscripts represent the same branch of the tradition, which differs from the version in the *Historia nouorum*, as the editors indeed note; L^aEP contra the *Historia nouorum*: e.g. (introduction) iuxta] *om.* L^aEP; episcopo] *om.* L^aEP; (canon 1) Guido abbas de Perscore] Wido abbas de Perscole L^aEP; et Ealdwinus de Rammesei] *om.* L^aEP; pro sua causa quisque] quisque pro sua causa L^aEP; qui erat apud] de L^aEP (*Councils and Synods* does not note the variant in full); (canon 5) uero] *om.* L^aEP. L^a and P are independent of one another, since both include unique readings missing from the other. P contra the *Historia nouorum* and $L^a(E)$: (introduction) Gerardo] gerendo P; aliisque] aliis P; (canon 7) castitatis] castatis P; (canon 9) Ne] Nec P; (canon 17) sacretur] secretur P; (canon 22) ex[s]polient] expelient P. $L^a(E)$ contra the *Historia nouorum and* P: (introduction) Lundoniam] Lundonie $L^a(E)$; cultura] cura $L^a(E)$. E is a copy of L^a, since it includes all L^a's unique readings in addition to a group of readings unique to E. E contra L^aP and the *Historia nouorum*: (introduction) quo] qua E; (canon 19) quiuis] cuique *corr. from* cui E eis] eius E. This last reading may result from L^a's writing of the word *eis* with a superscript letter s very reminiscent of the *us*-abbreviation.

(2) *Walther* 7673 and 14486. A mostly similar distribution of readings between L^aEP is also attested in the poems, although there is no independent branch of the tradition with which to compare the readings. L^a includes the poem 'Haud habiture' (*Walther* 7673) twice, first in its entirety on fols. 175r–176r, to which I shall refer using the abbreviation L^{a1}, and in part on fols. 189v–190r, to which I shall refer as L^{a2}. The results of the textual criticism of 'Haud habiture' may be summed up as follows: L^{a1} is the best version. $L^{a2}PE$ each include a number of unique readings. Where L^{a1} has a weak reading, E follows it, but PL^{a2} do not. Verses 1–35. (i.) $L^{a1,2}E$ better than P: verse 10 sonent $L^{a1, 2}E$] sanent P; verse 17 australis $L^{a1, 2}E$] australes P. (ii.) $PL^{a1}E$ better than L^{a2}: verse 25 dulci] *om.* L^{a2}; verse 35 pater optime toto] *hic finit* L^{a2}. (iii.) $L^{a1,2}P$ better than E: verse 1 habiture $L^{a1,2}P$] dubiture E; verse 33 peccata $L^{a1,2}P$] pecata E. (iv.) There is however a disturbing anomaly: $L^{a1}E$ better than PL^{a2}: verse 19 Anglica tellus $L^{a1}E$] Anglica terra PL^{a2}. On the basis of Sharpe's critical apparatus, the same principles also apply to the epitaph 'Presulis Anselmi' with some exceptions. E diverges from the last principle cited once, although here a straightforward and easily amended scribal error is in question in L^a: 'Presulis Anselmi', verse 72: oderat omnino PE] oderat omnio L. Note that according to Sharpe's critical apparatus verse 54 reads sapiens fuerit] fuerit sapiens L; in fact this should be fuerit sapiens L *with inversion signs*. Additionally E does not note the last two corrections in L^{a1}, although it includes earlier corrections; SHARPE, 'Two poems', 1985, p. 267. Because of the 'Anglica tellus/terra' anomaly Sharpe argues that there were two sources for the poems, one for $L^{a1}E$ and another for PL^{a2}.

historical context makes it probable that the texts common to L^a and P derive from the same sources — although this is less certain for the two poems on Anselm.

Manuscript E was the source for the two letters included in Cambridge, Corpus Christi College 117 (s. xiv, Bury St Edmunds): AEp. 255, sent by Archbishop Gerard, and AEp. 256, Anselm's reply.[218]

2.5 *Why* L *and* P?

Two almost completely identical copies of Anselm's letter collection were drawn up at Christ Church for the community's own needs within a very short space of time. L, the earlier of the two, is more variable in quality than its direct copy P, judging by the external characteristics of the manuscripts as opposed to their readings. The main hand of L was inconsistent, as the many erasures overwritten with corrections and the generally uneven appearance of his hand attest. It should be noted, however, that some of the erasures clearly reflect editorial work. The selection of texts on the *original* final folios of L, now in L^a, is also very confused, with other Anselmian texts interspersing the letters at random. The incomplete ornamentation of the initials and the missing words at the start of the first letter emphasize the rather poor quality of the manuscript. P in contrast is notably uniform, both in its content and as to its codicological and palaeographical characteristics. Perhaps L was not fine enough to be the sole exemplar of the text in Christ Church, and it was felt that a more uniform and impressive manuscript was needed for the correspondence of the former archbishop, who was being groomed for sanctification. Some of the most influential monks in the scriptorium were, furthermore, former members of his inner circle. This impression is strengthened by the marginal annotations in L, which advise the correct locations for the letters included in the additional section L^a. The marginalia repeatedly state 'hic scribatur' or 'ponatur':[219] instructions

---

[218] CCCC 117, fol. 166r–v. Fol. 166v: 'Ex libro manuscripto quondam monasterij S. Edmundi martyris'. See WILMART, 'La tradition', 1931, p. 45.

[219] Fol. 75r: 'Ante istam [AEp. 194] ponatur illa epistola quae pene circa finem habetur ad hoc signum et sic incipit. Reuerendo ac reuerenter [AEp. 193].' Fol. 78v: 'Ante istam scribatur epistola quae in fine habetur. quae sic incipit; Henricus dei gratia rex ad predictum signum [AEp. 212].' Fol. 119r: 'Hic scribatur illa epistola quae in fine libri habetur. quae sic incipit. Anselmus

that were clearly written with a view to *copying*, not reading the manuscript.[220] One gains the impression that *L* was intended to be the instrument from which other manuscripts were to be copied, and that *P* is a fair copy.

Finally, attention must be drawn to the physical appearance of all three of Christ Church's surviving early Anselmian compendia, *L*, *P*, and Oxford, Bodleian Library Bodley 271. Bodley 271, which covers the treatises and devotional texts, and comes roughly from the second decade of the twelfth century, is a high quality book in palaeographical and codicological terms, and of considerable size, 400 × 285 (310 × 195) mm.[221] *L* and *P* do not fulfil these criteria. While *P* is of high palaeographical quality, its size is unremarkable, 245 × 175 (190 × 130) mm. Lambeth 59 is, on the other hand, of less fine quality, but of significant size, 350 × 240 (225 × 170) mm. The absence of a large, high quality exemplar of Anselm's correspondence may perhaps be explained by the existence of two exemplars of the same collection. Once Lambeth 59, the large but palaeographically and structurally rather weak book, was complete, there was perhaps no impetus to produce another big book, which would cost more in parchment than one in medium size.

L's title in Prior Henry of Eastry's catalogue apparently relates to the size of the manuscript: *Epistole Anselmi maiores*. In general, the term *maiores* could refer either to the size of the manuscript or the scope of the collection; in this case, it is the size of the manuscript that is in question. The heading also appears twice on *L*'s first flyleaf, in a twelfth-century hand above, and below in a later hand that is hard to date, but is perhaps also of the twelfth century. The older annotation of the two reads 'Epistole Anselmi MAIOR[ES]'. The erasure of the end of the final word clearly reflects the fact that Christ Church had two books of different size: *minor* and *maior*, *P* and *L*.

---

archiepiscopus reuerendo priori d[omno] e[rnulfo]. Ad hoc signum [*AEp.* 331].' Fol. 138v: 'Hic scribatur epistola quae circa finem habetur. Quae sic incipit. Amatissimo atque g[lorioso] ad hoc signum [*AEp.* 411]'; and on line 17: 'Deest de hac prescripta epistola.'

[220] Compare the marginal annotation in manuscript *C* (fol. 93r): 'hec epistola scilicet Henricus dei gratia rex anglorum deberet hic esse. Que est in fine libri ad tale signum [*AEp.* 212].' Unlike the annotations in *L*, the comment is directed to the reader.

[221] Dating by Michael Gullick; SHARPE, 'Early Manuscripts', 2010, p. 51.

2.6 *London, BL Royal 5 F.* IX – F

1109 × *c*. 1125; England; parchment; ii + 54 + 140 + ii'; I–VI^8 VII$^{10-4}$ /
I–II^{10} III–IX^8 X^{10} XI–XII^8 XIII^{10} XIV–XVI^8 XVII^4; 255 × 170 (195 × 105)
mm; (27–)28 (long) lines

Contents

Unit 1

fol. 3r–38r	Anselm†, *De humanis moribus per similitudines* (*Memorials*, pp. 39–93)
fols. 38r–45v	Anselm†, *De humanis moribus per similitudines*, Appendix (*Memorials*, pp. 94–104)
fols. 45v–52v	Alexander of Canterbury, *Liber de dictis beati Anselmi*, *c*. 5 (*Memorials*, pp. 127–141)
fols. 53r–55r	Augustine, *Ep.* 130 (excerpts)
fols. 55r–56r	Gregory the Great, *Moralia in Iob* (excerpts)
fol. 56v	blank

Unit 2

fols. 57r–76r	Anselm, *De concordia praescientiae et praedestinationis*
fol. 76v	blank
fols. 77r–95v	Anselm, *De processione Spiritus Sancti*
fols. 96r–108v	Anselm, *Epistola de incarnatione Verbi*
fols. 109r–189r	Anselm, *Epistolae* (*F*)
fols. 189r–192v	Anselm, *Epistola de sacrificio azymi et fermentati*
fols. 192v–194r	Walram of Naumburg, *Epistola Waleramni episcopi ad Anselmum*
fols. 194r–195v	Anselm, *Epistola de sacramentis ecclesiae*
fol. 195v	Pseudo-Clemens Romanus, *Recognitiones* v, 23 (extract, 'Si uere uultis honorare imaginem – memoribus sedas.')
fol. 196v	Hugh of Rouen, *Epistola* 11 (ends imperfectly, *PL* 179, col. 670)

BL Royal 5 F. IX consists of two originally separate entities.
Both books contain texts by Anselm; the second also includes
his letters. The following analysis concentrates on the latter unit,
fols. 57–196, noting details regarding the former, fols. 3–56, only
where they contribute to our understanding of the origins and
provenance of the second part. Palaeographical dating for both
books is *s*. xii$^{1/3}$. They must postdate Anselm's death, however,
since the first book includes two posthumous works, *De humanis
moribus* and *Liber de dictis beati Anselmi*, and the second covers his
last letters dictated on his deathbed. The *a quo* is thus 1109. Since
F predates *M*, the *ad quem* is *c*. 1125. The first unit, not including

the letters, may come from Lanthony. The monastery's catalogue, which dates from around 1355 to 1360, has the item 'Ancelmus de qualitate morum. Mediocre uolumen'; this is another title for *De humanis moribus per similitudines.*[222] The textual evidence from manuscripts *F* and *J*, the next manuscript to be discussed, which is from Lanthony, hints that the they might derive from the same source, a conclusion that is very far from certain, however.[223] On the other hand, manuscript *F* or, less likely, its unknown copy was one of the sources used by William of Malmesbury, apparently at Malmesbury rather than at Christ Church. It is interesting that one of William's autograph manuscripts, Cambridge, University Library Ii. 3. 20, seems to have ended up at Lanthony by the fourteenth century, leading to the thought that more Malmesbury material might have made its way to Lanthony Secunda, located comparatively near to Malmesbury.[224] To conclude, there is no positive evidence for (or against) Lanthony provenance; *F* cannot be attributed to any specific scriptorium for the present.

In the seventeenth century, some books from Lanthony's collection came into the possession of John Theyer of Gloucester († 1673), although the collection had gone largely to Richard Bancroft, archbishop of Canterbury († 1610).[225] This manuscript belonged to Theyer's collection, as the marginal annotation 'Johannes Theyer 1650' on fol. 38r, and the other marginal notes in his hand, reveal.[226] The second codicological unit, the subject of this study, may have entered Theyer's collection by a different route, however.[227] A parchment slip that is pasted to the first flyleaf and is in Theyer's hand reads: 'Johannes Theyer Cowpers in Commune Ciuitatis Gloucestrensis 1647. quondam liber Domini Thomae Moore militis ac[?] Domini Cancellarii Anglie tempore Henrici 8.'

[222] T. WEBBER & A. WATSON (eds.), Lanthony: Catalogue of the library, *c.* 1355–60, in *The Libraries of the Augustinian Canons*, CBMLC, vol. 6, London, 1998, A16.160.

[223] See subsection III.2.8.

[224] THOMSON, *William of Malmesbury*, 2003, p. 94.

[225] WEBBER & WATSON, *The Augustinian Canons*, 1998, p. 35.

[226] E.g. fol. 53r.

[227] Marginal annotations in Theyer's hand are found e.g. at 152r, 156r etc. It seems that it is precisely on Theyer's account that the manuscripts have been thought to derive from the same scriptorium. See *Memorials*, p. 15 and GAMESON, *The Manuscripts*, 1999, no. 505 and 506: '?Lanthony or Gloucester'.

The year mentioned here, 1647, disagrees with that given in the cited marginal annotation in the first codicological unit (1650). The patch thus appears to be associated with the second book, which contains the letters. If this manuscript did indeed belong to Sir Thomas More before coming into Theyer's possession, a Lanthony provenance becomes ever less likely.[228]

When the two manuscripts that now form Royal 5 F. IX were joined together remains unknown. The list of contents on the first flyleaf, which dates from the twelfth century, only gives the contents of the second unit.[229] The amalgamation possibly happened only after the crown acquired Theyer's collection in 1678. As part of the royal collection, the manuscript made its way to its present home in the British Library.

The second book, relevant to this study, was ruled in dry point; prickings are still visible. The ink varies in colour between brown and black; the initials are red, green, or purple. In the middle of the letters, slightly towards the end, quire XIV stands out from the other quires for its different codicological properties; for example, there is one less line per page, with 27 instead of 28 lines. The text in this and the surrounding quires is in the same hand. Three principal hands may be observed: hand A in *De concordia prae-scientiae* on fols. 57r–76r, or quires I–II; hand B in *De processione Spiritus Sancti* and *Epistola de incarnatione Verbi* on fols. 77r–108v, or quires III–VI; and hand C in the letters on fols. 109r–195r, or quires VII–XVI. In addition, hand D copied an excerpt from Pseudo-Clemens on fol. 195r and hand E copied a letter sent by Hugh of Rouen to the pope on fol. 196v. All hands are English Carolingian minuscule with pre-Gothic influences. Although hands A–C each copied different works into separate quires, the codicological

---

[228] The testimony of the parchment slip cannot be considered entirely reliable: since it is pasted into the manuscript, it is possible that it derives from some other manuscript in Theyer's collection and found its way into this manuscript in error upon rebinding. Also some other material related to More included in BL Royal 17 D. XIV had possibly come into Theyer's possession; see K. WARNER, *Medieval & Early Modern Women. Part 1: Manuscripts from British Library, London*, Marlborough, 2000, pp. 110–114.

[229] Fol. i^v: 'Haec est continentia huius uoluminis. / Anselmus De Concordia prescientiae et predestinationis et Gratiae dei cum libero arbitrio / Anselmus De processione spiritus sancti. / Item Epistola eius De Incarnatione uerbi. / Exeptiones Epistolarum ipsius.'

uniformity indicates that they collaborated on a single project. Theyer added numerous marginal annotations both to the letters and to Anselm's other texts, in both codicological units.[230]

Distinctive characteristics of F

Most of the letters in *F* are abridged. Often complete paragraphs or shorter parts of passages such as individual words are missing. Cutting occurs at the end of letters in particular. Furthermore, *F* has a notably relaxed approach to the texts, resulting in many unique readings. It is important to recognize that these readings are definitely the result of later editorial work; they by no means indicate that *F* descended from a collection including unique authorial versions of the letters (such as drafts, for example). This can clearly be seen from the fact that letters received by Anselm were also cut.[231] This editorial individuality appears to have been the work of scribe C. As mentioned above, quire XIV stands out codicologically from the other quires, although it probably formed part of the manuscript from the outset. Its disparate character may also be reflected in the way in which the final letters in it and in the preceding quire (XIII) fit precisely in each quire, finishing at the end of the final line of the last verso. Both letters were fitted into the available space by having their text abridged, something that no one but the scribe who copied the letters could have done.[232]

Editorial work was sometimes poor. A good example is *AEp.* 231. Contrary to the other manuscripts, *F* accommodates the words 'Oro. orate pro me' into the salutation of the letter. The passage derives from the previous letter, *AEp.* 230. In *F*, *AEp.* 230 omits the words by replacing them with the word 'Amen', a reading that no other manuscript supports (plate 10). I shall later demonstrate

[230] See e.g. 134v, 152r, 155v, 156r, 158r, 159r, 161r, 163v, 164r, 196v.

[231] E.g. *AEp.* 317 (from Queen Matilda): 317:1–3: Domino – obsequim] Domino et patri Anselmo Cantuariensi archiepiscopo Mathildis regina summae deuotionis obsequim *F(M)*; 317:38–39 Pax – abundare] Vale pater carissime *F*. Comparable examples may be found in many letters: see e.g. *AEp.* 320, 384 (from Queen Matilda), 350 (from Matilda of Tuscany to the pope), 386 (from the English bishops), 390 (from Hugo, archbishop of Lyon), 397 (from the pope).

[232] The concluding letter of quire XIII, *AEp.* 391:3–6 Ad me – mea, 14–15 sicut – uestrae, 26 secundum – suam.] *om. F*. The concluding letter of quire XIV, *AEp.* 397:28–50 Praeterea – Aprilis.] Valete *F*.

what caused this error, and here the example serves only to demonstrate F's flexibility with valedictions. In the valedictions of *AEp.*
262, 292, 329, 357, and 434, F differs from the other witnesses so
strongly that at first sight it appears as if it drew on otherwise
unknown versions of the letters. With the exception of *AEp.* 434,
however, F merely varies a standard valediction, which the scribe
happened to prefer to the original ones.[233]

With its 159 letters, F covers Anselm's correspondence rather
poorly. Its tendency to abridge individual letters suggests that
whole letters were also omitted. In other words, F's coverage does
not reflect the process of gathering back Anselm's letters to Christ
Church or their loss there.

2.7 *London, BL Royal 8 D.* VIII – J

c. 1110–1136, perhaps *c.* 1130; Lanthony (OSA); parchment; i + 175 +
iv;[234] 250 × 160 (200 × 130) mm;
45–47 lines in two columns

Contents[235]

---

[233] The closing greeting varied by F apparently was derived from *AEp.*
262:49–50 Omnipotens deus sic uos in hac uita dirigat et protegat, ut in futuro
ad aeternam beatitudinem prouehat.] uos in hac uita *om. F*; dirigat] uos semper *adds F. AEp.* 434 differs from these: 'Spiritus sanctus semper habitet in
corde tuo.' The valediction may be based on *AEp.* 418, which according to
LC^bV^b ended: 'Spiritus sanctus semper habitet in corde uestro, et semper uos
faciat gaudere et gratias agere deo de bono incepto.' F's scribe censored the
valediction to read 'Valete'. Compare the valedictions of this first group with
the following as well: *AEp.* 406:17–18 Omnipotens deus sua uos benedictione
assidue protegat et dirigat. Amen. *LPCVE*]; 414:71 Omnipotens deus sit semper custos totius uitae uestrae. Amen. *LPCVE*].

[234] The binding is too tight to determine the collation; there are no quire
marks.

[235] The library's catalogue of the Royal manuscripts (pp. 245–247) provides
a slightly fuller description.

[236] *Med.* 1, *Or.* 18, 19, pseudo-Anselmian prayer xlix in *PL*, *Or.* 2, 9, 11,
10, 13.

fol. 10v	Computistic circles
fols. 11r–13v	Computistic calendar
fol. 14r	Anselm, *Monologion* (extract: 'Cum igitur – cognoscit habere', *SAO*, vol. 1, pp. 77:7–79:6)
fol. 14r	Gregory the Great, *Moralia in Iob* (extracts)
fols. 14v–15r	Computistic tables
fols. 15v–16v	Anselm, *Epistolae* (*J*, part 1)
fols. 16v–18r	Gregory the Great, *Moralia in Iob* (extracts); Augustine: extract[237]
fol. 18v	Pseudo-Augustine, *Oratio ad deum*[238]
fols. 18v–23r	Anselm, *Orationes* and *Meditationes*[239]
fol. 23r–v	Anonymous, *Oratio sacerdotum*[240]
fols. 23r–33r	Ambrose, Gregory, Bede, Augustine, unidentified extracts
fols. 33r–40r	Hildebert of Lavardin, *De mysterio missae*
fols. 40r–49v	Jerome, Augustine, Gregory, unidentified extracts
fols. 49v–50r	Anselm, *Epistolae* (*J*, part 2)
fol. 50r–v	Anselm, *Cur Deus homo* (extract: 'Omnis uoluntas – quam abstulit', *SAO*, vol. 1, *c.* xi, p. 68:12–23, omits some sentences)
fols. 50v–61r	Various unidentified authors and extracts; one attributed to Anselm: 'Anselmus Archiepiscopus Hanc autem perfectae humilitatis celsitudinem – sicut consequenter orat cum dicit.' (fols. 52v–53r)
fols. 61r–81v	Robert de Braci?, *De similitudinibus* (cf. *Memorials*, pp. 37–104 and *PL* 159, cols. 605–708; on the evolution of this text, see *Memorials*, pp. 13–15, 296–297)
fols. 81v–82r	Jerome, *Epistolae* (extracts)
fols. 82r–89r	Caesarius of Arles, *Homiliae X ad monachos*[?]
fols. 89r–93r	'Eusebius Gallicanus', *Homiliae X ad monachos*[?] (*Serm.* 36–45, *CPL* 966)
fols. 93r–116r	Ivo of Chartres, *De ecclesiasticis sacramentis* (*Serm.* I–V) (omits some parts)
fols. 116r–124v	Augustine, Jerome, Gregory, Anselm, unidentified extracts and *AEp.* 53:1–21 (*J*, part 3; fol. 122r)
fols. 122r–129v	Pseudo-Basil, *Regula S. Basilii*

[237] Here and below, if the text is not identified, the name or the identification of the author comes from rubrics in the manuscript.

[238] Attributed to Anselm in *PL* 158, cols. 875–876; manuscript: 'ORATIO SANCTI AVGVSTINI'.

[239] *Or.* 6, 8, 14, 16 (16:26–90 qui uiuit–saecula saeculorum, amen. *om.*), 15 ('Ad sanctum Augustinum' instead of 'Benedictum' as in *SAO*), *Med.* 2, pseudo-Anselmian prayer xxix in *PL*.

[240] Attributed to Anselm in *PL* 158, cols. 921–924.

fols. 129v–164v Augustine, Cyprian, Gregory the Great, extracts
fols. 164v–170v Robert de Braci?, *De similitudinibus* (further additions
                 that later became part of the *De similitudinibus*, see
                 Memorials, pp. 13–15, 296–297)
fols. 170v–171v '*Dum quietum silentium*' (an exegesis on Wisdom 18,
                 rubric: 'Anselmus quomodo intelligitur Dum medium',
                 PL 91, cols. 1060–1062)[241]
fols. 171v–172v Bede, *Homilia* II, 3
fols. 172v–173v Augustine, Ivo of Chartres, unidentified extracts

BL Royal 8 D. VIII or *J* is connected with Robert de Braci
(† 1137), prior of Lanthony, as is indicated by the marginal annotation on fol. 1r: 'Exceptiones Rob[erti] de braci'. The manuscript
can be identified with 'Exceptiones Roberti de Braci, mediocris
liber' in Lanthony's late fourteenth-century library catalogue.[242]
The computistic calendar in the manuscript mentions Lanthony
twice: the entry for 4 June refers to the 'Dedicatio aecclesiae
lant.'; and to that for 10 August, a new hand has added 'Dedicatio
ecclesie nostre', referring to the consecration of Lanthony Secunda
in 1136.[243] From Lanthony, the manuscript entered the collection
of John Theyer, the Gloucester collector whom we have already
met as the owner of manuscript *F*; it is no. 116 in the Theyer sale-
catalogue.[244] Theyer's collection was acquired for the royal collection in 1678.

The manuscript covers a wide selection of extracts of differing
lengths from works by the patristic authors Gregory the Great
(whose *Moralia* is especially well represented), Augustine, Ambrose,
Jerome, Isidore, and Bede, as well as by contemporary early
twelfth-century authors, Anselm above all, but also Ivo of Chartres and Hildebert of Lavardin. The extracts are too many for me

---

[241] Reportedly several manuscripts give '*Dum quietum silentium*' after *De
similitudinibus* (London, BL Cotton Cleopatra C. XI and Paris, BNF lat. 15686;
Memorials, p. 297, note 2); Mews also mentions Hereford Cathedral O. I. 12);
C. MEWS, 'St Anselm and Roscelin: some new texts and their implications',
Archives d'histoire doctrinale et littéraire du moyen âge, 66 (1992), p. 71.

[242] WEBBER & WATSON (eds.), Lanthony: Catalogue of the library, *c.* 1355–
60, in *The Augustinian Canons*, 1998, A.16.233.

[243] Fols. 12v, 13r. *Memorials*, pp. 15–16.

[244] G. F. WARNER & J. P. GILSON, *Catalogue of Western Manuscripts in the
Old Royal and King's Collection*, vol. 1, London 1921. pp. 245–247. Theyer sale-
catalogue: BL Royal Appendix 80.

to present the contents in full.[245] Besides Anselm's works, I have identified passages from Gregory the Great's *Moralia*, of which more below. *J* includes twelve Anselmian letters, all of which have been abridged, some down to only a few lines. The letters appear in three separate sections: first on fols. 15v–16v, then on fols. 49v–50r and finally on fol. 122r.[246] As a witness to the correspondence, the value of *J* is extremely limited. The manuscript is one of our main witnesses to *De humanis moribus per similitudines*, however, its text being a stemmatic sibling of that in the first codicological unit of BL Royal 5 F. IX, discussed above.[247]

2.8 *Conclusions:* FJ *in the tradition*

The arrangement of letters in *F* is almost but not completely identical to that in *L*. In contrast, *F* is more distant from the branch of the tradition represented by *CV*; manuscripts *FL* arrange the Bec correspondence in the same way, which significantly differs from the arrangement of *AEp*. 51–72 in *CV*. The Canterbury correspondence in *F* has its own arrangement, which nevertheless is very close to that in *L* and *CV*.[248] The readings demonstrate conclusively that *F* is independent of *L* and other surviving manu-

---

[245] The data given in the catalogue of the British Library's Royal collection are also incomplete.

[246] Section 1: *AEp*. 185:11–13, 186:25–31, 230:13–28, 232:9–29, 450:1–33, 420:11–26, 91:23–29, 112:35–72, 2:30–70. Section 2: 414:13–65, 285:5–33. Section 3: 53:1–21.

[247] *Memorials*, p. 18.

[248] When divergences occur, *F*'s coherence must be adjudged generally weaker than that of *L* (and virtually identical *CV*). Letters *F51–53* form the first case: *AEp*. 241 (*L181*), 240 (*L180*) and 192 (*L149*). *AEp*. 241 is Anselm's reply to *AEp*. 240, the letter from Hildebert of Lavardin, and *F*'s arrangement is clearly weaker than that in *L*. In *F*, '.B.' is marked in the margin beside the former letter and '.A.' beside the latter: these symbols indicate the better, i.e. reversed order, for these letters. *AEp*. 192 is to Cardinal Bishop Walter of Albano. This letter is apparently unrelated to the previous letters in subject matter, nor is there any chronological link, as the former letters are from summer 1102 and the latter from the latter part of 1095 (SCHMITT, 'Die Chronologie', 1954, pp. 196, 198). Likewise *AEp*. 222 and 223 (*F154* and *155*) are clearly better placed in *L* than in *F* on both thematic and chronological grounds. *F* places *AEp*. 335 and 330 (*F67*, *68*) earlier than *L*, and the latter at least is chronologically better suited to its location in *L*. This also applies to *AEp*. 386 (*F99*). *AEp*. 368 may be better placed thematically in *L* (where it follows *AEp*. 364), than in *F* (*F123*), where its content is quite unconnected to that of the

scripts. It descends from ω independently of all the other known manuscripts.[249] This happened either directly or, less likely, through a lost exemplar.

letters before (*AEp.* 375) and after it (*AEp.* 380). There are no good grounds to indicate in which manuscript *AEp.* 336 is the better placed.

[249] (1) *L* is not *F*'s source (contrary to the understanding of Schmitt and Fröhlich), since *FCV* agree against *L*: (a) the Bec correspondence (*M* noted only for those letters where it is independent of *F*): 2:20 domine mi *FNMCVE*] mi domine mi *LP*; 2:83 constituetur *FNCV*] constituitur *LPE from* constituitur *P*; 13:5 domnum *FNVE*] donnum *C* dominum *LP*; 37:28 professus *FNMCVEG*] proffessus *LP*; 80:21 multi prelati *FNMCVE*] praelati multi *LP*; 97:31 hoc ipsum *FCVE*] ipsum hoc *LP*; 97:91 quod *FCV*] *om. LPE*; 112:42 conglutinari *FCVEM*] conglutinare *LP* glutinare *G*; 113:38 aliud *FCV*] alium *LPE*; 121:25 dicet *FCVEMG*] dicit *LP*; 122:20 Itaque *FNMCVE*] mihi *add. LP*; 122:30 sed et *FNMCVE*] et *om. LP*; 132:8 gaudet *FMCVE*] gaudeat *LP*; 134:36 quanto[2] *FMCVE*] quanta *LP*. Cf. also 9:10 congratulationem *LP (eras. in L)*] passionem *FMD corr. from* compassionem *F*. (Note the anomalies 2:83; 97:91; 113:38). (b) The Canterbury correspondence: 156:92 uiuerem *FC*[a]*V*[a]*O*] uiuere *LPC*[b]*V*[b] *corr. from* uiuere *E*; 156:154 dilexistis *FC*[a]*V*[a]*O*] dilexisti *LPEC*[b]*V*[b]; 156:179 nostram *FV*[a]*V*[b]*C*[a]] uestram *LPEC*[b] *corr. from* uestram *O*; 161:11 dominus *LPEOC*[b]*V*[b]] domnus *FC*[a]*V*[a]*G*; 161:22-23 cum illo in iudicio *FC*[a]*V*[a]*G*] in iudicio cum illo *LPEOC*[b]*V*[b]; 161:44 contra *FC*[a]*V*[a]*G*] aduersum *LPEOC*[b]*V*[b]; 162:1 parisiensis *FOV*[a]*V*[b]*C*[a]*C*[b]] pariensis *LPE*; 162:18 respicit retro *LPEOC*[b]*V*[b]] retro respicit *FC*[a]*V*[a]; 162:24 sequuntur *LPEO*] secuntur *FV*[a]*V*[b-]*C*[a]*C*[b]; 249:6 uestra *C*[b]*V*[b]*F*] uestrum *LPE*; 281:15 hoc immane *FGC*[b]*V*[b]] hoc in immane *LP corr. from* hoc in immane *E*; 285:19 est[2] *OC*[b]*V*[b]*FG*] *om. LPE*; 313:10 sunt *OC*[b]*V*[b]*F*] sicut *PE* sicut *from* sunt *L*; 322:26 faceretis *C*[b]*V*[b]*F*] facietis *LPE*; 327:3 es *C*[b]*V*[b]*F*] *om. LPE*; 355:6 laudabile *PE*] *corr. from* laudabilem *L* laudabilem *OC*[b]*V*[b]*F*; 385:4 de fratre *LPE*] illo *add. C*[b]*V*[b]*F*; 387:20 ostendet *C*[b]*V*[b]*F*] ostendit *LEP*; 387:25 promulgari *C*[b]*V*[b]*F*] mulgari *LPE*; 389:17 causae *C*[b]*V*[b]*F*] causa *LE corr. from* causa *P*; 389:23 illi *C*[b]*V*[b]*F*] *om. LPE*; 389:28 uestram[2] *C*[b]*V*[b]*F*] uestra *LPE*; 389:29 sententiam *C*[b]*V*[b]*F*] sententia *corr. from* sententiam[?] *L* sententia *E corr. from* sententia *P*; 389:30 deus *LPE*] *eras. in L* diu *add. C*[b]*V*[b]; 404:1 et regi *LPE*] et *om. C*[b]*V*[b]*F*; 406:11 ad me *C*[b]*V*[b]*F*] *om. LPE*; 407:1 archiepiscopus *LPE*] *om. C*[b]*V*[b]*F*; 418:18 corpus *OC*[b]*V*[b]*F*] cor *LPE*; 421:21 periculum *LPE*] pericula *OC*[b]*V*[b]*F*. In the letters absent from *V*, *F* also often agrees with *C* against *L*. 259:4 diligentibus *C*[b]*F*] deligentibus *LPE*; 336:19 ab illis *C*[b]*F*] ab allis *LE corr. from* ab allis *P*; 356:13 abstraxerunt *C*[b]*F*] abstracserunt *LPE*; 361:5 aliter *C*[b]*F*] *om. LPE*; 419:19 ipsi *C*[b]*F*] sibi *LPE*; 430:16 monstratis *C*[b]*F*] demonstratis *LPE*.

(2) *CV*'s common source δ, or δ's source γ, were not *F*'s source. (a) The Bec correspondence. The arrangement of the letters in itself indicates that *F* used a source independent of these witnesses; this source must have been the same, or similar to, *L*'s source. The readings agree with this understanding of the relationship: *F* clearly agrees with *L* more often than with the members of the former family. (b) The Canterbury correspondence. γδ[b] were not the source for

A scribal error allows us to deduce important facts regarding the external characteristics of *F*'s source.[250] As discussed before, *AEp.* 231 opens in *F* as follows: 'Anselmus archiepiscopus fratribus et filiis suis carissimis. *oro. orate pro me*' (my emphasis). The words in italics only appear in *F* (plate 10), and come from the end of *AEp.* 230, which precedes *AEp.* 231 in other manuscripts but is absent from *F*. *F*'s reading derived from the custom of placing the last words of the text that was concluding at the end of the first line of the new text, as occurred when less than a full line of text remained to be written. Since the passage 'oro. orate pro me' is too long to fit at the end of a line in a manuscript with two columns of text, the lost manuscript must have had long lines. Since the lay-out of the break between *AEp.* 230 and 231 corresponds to this in no surviving manuscript, the instance further supports the results of textual criticism: *F* derives from no known manuscript.[251] The only known derivative of *F* is *M* by William of Malmesbury, which was based on other sources as well.

Like *LPE* and *F*, *J* ultimately derives from *ω*. Determining its position in the stemma more accurately is hard and hardly very purposeful. The letters have been edited freely, as is generally the case with all the texts included in the manuscript, something that complicates the process of textual criticism. I have based my anal-

---

F, already on the grounds that these only included the Canterbury collection; furthermore, *F* and *Lδ^a* together now and then disagree with both *O* and *δ^b* or one or other of these witnesses; e.g. 156:36 non nouerunt *FLO*] inmouerunt *V^b* immouerunt *C^b*; 161:11 dominus *LPEOC^bV^b*] domnus *C^aV^aFMDG*; 161:22–23 cum illo in iudicio *FC^aV^aGMD*] in iudicio cum illo *LPEOC^bV^b*; 161:30 hortetur *FC^aV^aG*] ortetur *LPEOC^bV^b*; 161:34 clericos *FL*] clericis *OC^bV^b*; 161:38 intelligentes *FLO*] intelligens *C^bV^b*; 161:44 contra *FC^aV^aG*] aduersum *LPEOC^bV^b*; 162:14 persuadeat *FLO*] persuadet *C^bV^b*; 311:45 sed *LF*] et *add. C^bV^b*; 321:31 nec filius *LF*] (filius *interlinear in* L) filius non *C^bV^b*; 328:27 ostentando *LF*] ostendando *OC^b*; 332:14 indecens *LF*] indi *from* indicens[?] *V^b* indicens *C^b* (ind[?]cens *O*) 380:10 illi *LF*] om. *C^bV^b*; 397:10 manum *LF*] non *add. C^bV^b*; 414:60 ambulant *LFO*] ambulabunt *C^bV^b*. See also 281:31 uindicaret *LPC^bV^b*] uendicaret *FG* uendicaret *from* uindicaret *in another hand* E; *G* is, like *F*, independent of the manuscripts under discussion.

[250] It is of course possible that an unknown witness, which cannot be reconstructed, lies between *F* and the source I have posited for *F* in this study. In this case, the editorial process could have been carried out by the creator of the intermediate source.

[251] Given the date and contents, only *LP* come into question, and this passage of text is not suitably placed in either manuscript; *L* fol. 85v; *P* fol. 71r.

ysis on the collation of *AEp.* 2, of which *J* covers only lines 30–70, and, where the other letters are concerned, comparison of the text in *J* with the variants reported by Schmitt. Given the narrow sample and the limitations of Schmitt's apparatus, there is an element of uncertainty to my conclusions. In a nutshell, in *AEp.* 2, manuscripts *J* and *F* share one significant, although very far from decisive reading, which is not known to the other manuscripts,[252] and *J* does not agree with any other manuscript against *F* in any significant way. In the other letters, I observed a few weak readings, where *FJ* differ from the other manuscripts, either in sharing the same reading, or in offering their own unique readings. None of these instances have particularly strong evidential value.[253] The Lanthony provenance, which is secure for *J* but tentative for *F*, would of course support the case for a close relationship between the manuscripts. Finally, our evidence for the relationship of *F* and *J* is too insubstantial for any result to be recorded and for *J* to be included in the *stemmata.*[254]

2.9 *London, BL Cotton Claudius A.* xi – C

s. xiii$^{2/2}$; England (or France); parchment; iv + 163 + I' + iv';[255] I^8 II–XIII^{12} XIV$^{11(6+5)}$; 255 × 165 (165 × 115) mm; 37 lines in two columns

Contents

fols. 2r–7r	List of contents
fols. 9r–161v	Anselm, *Epistolae* (*C*)
fol. 162r	blank
fols. 162v–163v	Anselm, *AEp.* 206

---

[252] 2:40 uocatos] *om. FJ.*

[253] 91:1–23 Domino – feruere.] *om. J,* 4–23 Quamquam – feruere.] *om. F;* 91:23 enim] *om. FJ;* 414:49 redeant ad memoriam] ad memoriam redeat *J* ad memoriam redeant *FM;* 414:55 facillime] facilius *J* facile *FM;* 420:13 ac] et *FMJ.*

[254] *AEp.* 2 is followed in *J* by selections from Gregory's *Moralia.* This is of interest, since an extract from the *Moralia* also appears after *AEp.* 2 in the group of minor collections, presented below. Could the group of minor collections have derived the *Moralia* from Robert de Braci's manuscript or from a related manuscript? But since Robert de Braci's citations are from books 11, 16, 18, 19, 21 and 22 of the *Moralia,* while the excerpt in the minor collections is from book 35, this question must be answered in the negative.

[255] The flyleaves indicated in small Roman numerals are paper.

C is the most extensive surviving manuscript witness to Anselm's letter collection. It contains 418 letters, admittedly including seven duplicates, the *Epistola de incarnatione Verbi* in the midst of the letters,[256] and a later date copy of *AEp.* 206 appended at the end of the manuscript.[257] With the exception of the first and final quire, the manuscript consists of sexterns. The first quire, a quaternion presenting a detailed list of contents, is a later addition. From the second quire onwards the last verso of each quire has a catchphrase written at the inside edge of the lower margin. The line prickings are still visible and the lines were ruled with a plummet. The ink is black. Often, in typical Gothic fashion, red is also used for the first letter of the first word of a new clause or paragraph. The initials are red and blue, with the letter itself in one colour, and the ornamentation in the other, as is the fashion in thirteenth- and fourteenth-century manuscripts. The foliation is modern, and is given in Arabic numerals in the upper right corner of each recto. Folios 2r–7r have a detailed list of contents, which numbers the letters, names their sender and recipient, and sums up the contents of each letter in a few words, often also giving the first words of the *narratio*. The hand that wrote the list is *Anglicana* of the fourteenth century, possibly of the first half. Likewise *AEp.* 206 on fols. 162v–163r is the work of a later hand, of the late thirteenth or early fourteenth century.[258]

The text was copied by a single scribe, who also corrected it. He wrote a fine *Textualis* of roughly the second half of the thirteenth century. He was probably an Englishman or, less likely, a Frenchman.[259] By the second half of the fourteenth century, the manu-

---

[256] *Epistola de incarnatione Verbi*: fols. 67r–75v. This is the latest version of the text.

[257] The letter in question also appears in the main sequence at fols. 91v–92r.

[258] In this letter Anselm requested the pope to release him from his office. Grandisson commented on the letter: 'Vtinam nullus modo Episcopus posset sic scribere Vrbano V[I?].'

[259] Southern (*A Portrait*, 1990, p. 459) and Schmitt ('Verzeichnis der benutzten Handschriften', in *Prolegomena*, p. 217) date the manuscript to the thirteenth century. The hand includes features, however, that point to the second half of the century. The upper curve of the letter a is often closed, although an open variant also appears. Only the uncial form of the letter d appears (the hairline at the top points downwards, which is considered an English or French

script was in Exeter. On 9 April 1364, Bishop John Grandisson of
Exeter († 1369), gave it to Simon Islip († 1366), archbishop of Can-
terbury, as says Grandisson's autograph annotation on fol. 8r.[260]
From Canterbury, the manuscript moved to Maidstone College, an

characteristic (A. DEROLEZ, *The Palaeography of Gothic Manuscript Books from
the Twelfth to the Early Sixteenth Century*, Cambridge, 2003, p. 88). The cross-
stroke of the letter t has a shaft. The ampersand does not appear at all and
the vertical stroke of the tironian et-abbreviation already has a (single) cross-
stroke. The letter i has a diacritical stroke in places where it could be confused with the minims of letters u, n, or m. The straight s is deployed in the
final position. The feminine genitive plural ending arum appears as an orum-
abbreviation. The contemporary custom of dotting the y has been considered
an English feature (e.g. fol. 28rb, l. 18: 'ẏdolatrie'), although the practice was
common in France too. The use of the majuscule R at the ends of lines has
also been seen as an English characteristic (DEROLEZ, *The Palaeography*, 2003,
p. 91); in our manuscript, see e.g. 'approbetuR', fol. 13rb, l. 21 and 'tueatuR',
fol. 97va, l. 3; see 'iteR[um]' in the middle of the line, fol. 11vb, l. 10. This
custom was nevertheless not unknown in thirteenth-century France, either, see
e.g. Paris, Bibliothèque de l'Arsenal 3340, fol. 52rb, l. 14 (published in CARERI
et al., *Album de manuscrits français du* XIIIe *siècle. Mise en page et mise en texte*,
Rome, 2001, p. 4). An interesting feature — unknown, at least to me — is the
scribe's use of a punctuation mark resembling a *punctus flexus* within sentences
ending with a question mark (and nowhere else); this mark comprises a dot
with a mark resembling a figure 7 above. See e.g. 13v: 'Quomodo igitur possum
non transferre illum dolorem in animum meum . uel pocius quomodo non dicam
illum dolentem animum esse meum .[7] qui sic dolet propter amorem meum?'

[260] Fol. 8r: 'Registrum Epistole beati Anselmi, / beati Anselmj Cantuariensis archiepicopi / J. de .G. Ex. / concedo et lego cuicumque Archiepiscopo
Cantuariensis. / Vt memor sit miseri Johannis / de Grandissono. Exoniensis /
qui hoc manu sua scripsit, / hic infra potest uideri status / tam Ecclesie quam
Regni Anglie. / Vtinam renouet. per christum dominum nostrum / Qui uiuit
et regnat. rex / regum et summus Sacerdos et pon- / tifex in eternum. Amen.
Amen. Anno domini .mᵒ cccᵒ lxᵒ iiijᵒ. / Et etatis mee .lxxᵒiijᵒ. / Et officij mei
.xxxᵒ viijᵒ / mense Aprili. die nono.' Note too fol. 9r: 'Liber .J. Exoniensis episcopi' (*s.* xiv). Grandisson had also a copy of Anselm's posthumous *Liber de
similitudinibus*; this is London, BL Cotton Cleopatra C. XI. On Grandisson's
manuscripts, M. STEELE, *A Study of the Books Owned or Used by John Grandisson, Bishop of Exeter (1327–1369)*, unpublished doctoral diss., Oxford, 1994.
Building on Wilmart, Steele (*ibid.*, pp. 53–54) argues that Grandisson had
either copied Cotton Claudius A. XI himself or commissioned it, but the manuscript is too early for that. The words 'qui hoc manu sua scripsit' in his quoted
annotation must refer to the note, not to the letter collection. Marginal annotations in his hand occasionally occur, focusing on the ecclesiastical drama that
surrounded Anselm in England.

advowson of Canterbury.[261] Islip may have been behind the transfer since accommodation for the archbishop was built at Maidstone during his archiepiscopate. The manuscript came into the possession of Archbishop Cranmer in 1537 at the latest, when the crown acquired Maidstone.[262] Sir Robert Cotton acquired the manuscript for his collection in around 1616; the intervening owners between Cranmer and Cotton have not been identified.[263]

2.10 C's copies

After the publication of Picard's edition in 1612, at least four copies were made of manuscript C. Three of these seem to have been motivated by the fact that Picard had deployed manuscript V as his source; this is C's stemmatic sibling, which presents only slightly more than a half of the Canterbury correspondence found in C. The letters missing from V and Picard's edition were sought in C.

Oxford, Bodleian Library Add. C. 296, fols. 94r–123v – C[2] *(in* SAO: Add.*)* s. xvii[1]; England; paper; iii + 232 + ii'; 290–315 × 185–200 mm; 46 lines (in letter collection)

According to the Bodleian Library catalogue, Add. C. 296 was copied in part by Archbishop Ussher († 1656) and contains 'texts on the British Church', for example by Bede and Anselm. Ussher seems to have read Anselm's letters, as is suggested by the underlining of the name of the archbishop of Dublin in *AEp.* 277. C[2] consists of the Canterbury material absent from Picard's source, V, and thus from his edition. The letters follow the arrangement in C, and textual criticism also relates C[2] to C, as my sampling of readings demonstrated. The method used for this analysis is explained in the discussion of the following manuscript. Schmitt included this manuscript in his collation of *AEp.* 467 and 469, referring to it as *Add.*

Cambridge, Trinity College O. 10. 16, pp. 275–354 – C[3] *(in* SAO: Trin.*)* c. 1613; England; paper; ii + 648 pages + ii'; 310 × 205 (265–275 × 150–160) mm; 34–39 lines[264]

---

[261] Fol. 161v: 'Lib Colleg. de Maidston'.

[262] Fol. 9r: 'Thomas Cantuariensis'

[263] SELWYN, 'Cranmer and the Dispersal', 1997, pp. 288, 292 note 41.

[264] I am grateful to Dr Elina Screen, who undertook the codicological and textual analysis of the manuscript.

Trinity College O. 10. 16 contains the letters of Alcuin (†803; p. 1), Lanfranc (p. 225), Anselm (p. 275), Elmer of Canterbury (†1137; p. 355), and Osbert of Clare (†after 1139; p. 419), and various other texts.[265] The texts by the different authors are often interspersed with blank folios. The manuscript is largely the work of a single hand. The aim was clearly to gather together the most significant English letter collections from Alcuin to the first half of the twelfth century, chronological boundaries that meant leaving the letter collections touching on the Becket case to one side. The manuscript does, however, also contain a (possibly partial) copy of *Symbolum electorum* (p. 549) by Gerald of Wales (†1223). It has not been possible for me to check which part(s) of the work the manuscript includes; the context would naturally suggest the letter section of the *Symbolum*. Other hands appear alongside the main hand: for example, the final, incomplete letter in Anselm's collection is in a new hand, as are the final pages of the manuscript (635–648). The manuscript was 'almost certainly' commissioned by Patrick Young, the royal librarian. He seems to have planned an edition of the texts, possibly to be printed in Germany, but the project was never realized.[266] The manuscript came to Trinity College through the donation of the Gale collection of Latin manuscripts in 1738, and is possibly associated with Gale's (†1702) great work *Rerum Anglicarum scriptores ueteres*.

C^3 covers 122 letters. The arrangement follows manuscript C, and sampling of selected readings demonstrates the close relationship between the two. For this analysis, Schmitt's apparatus was used to identify readings particular to C in sixteen of the Canterbury letters, which are absent from V and therefore from Picard, beginning with the earliest such letters in C; subsequently, these readings were compared with manuscripts C^3 and C^2.[267] Both man-

---

[265] For a more detailed (but imperfect) list of contents, see M. R. JAMES, *The Western Manuscripts in the Library of Trinity College, Cambridge*, 3 vols., Cambridge, 1900–1902, no. 1468.

[266] GIBSON in Lanfranc, *Ep.*, 'Introduction', p. 24. The manuscript's Lanfranc collection derives directly from Cotton Nero A. VII.

[267] 171:15 exstitit] existit CC^2C^3; 171:19 haud] aut CC^2C^3; 198:45 proferri] perferri CC^2C^3; 214:8 Willelmo] Guillermo CC^2C^3; 214:13 susciperet] suscipere CC^2C^3; 214:21 Anglicae] Angliae CC^2; 214:37 praenomine] pronomine CC^2 pronomini C^3; 214:57 educerem] inducerem CC^2C^3; 219:11 se discessuros CC^2C^3] sedis cessuros *LPE*; 230:16 quia] *om.* CC^2C^3; 232:17 igitur] ergo CC^2C^3; 235:23–24

uscripts clearly descend from C. The two manuscripts are probably independent of each other, although it might be possible that C^2 derives from C^3.

Paris, BNF lat. 13415 – C^4
1673; London; paper

This is the transcript that Gerberon ordered from the Cotton Library in 1673.[268] Gerberon had requested a copy of the letters not found in Picard's edition. C, or more precisely its second section of Canterbury letters, C^b, served as the exemplar for this manuscript. Gerberon published the letters in C^4 in 1675, and subsequently the *Patrologia Latina* reprinted his edition. The *Patrologia* presents the material from C^4 in the fourth book of Anselm's letter collection (IV,1–101).[269] With two exceptions,[270] the letters in C^4 are absent from V and thus also from Picard's edition.

London, BL Stowe 33 – C^5
1670; London; paper; 268 fols.

C^5 was compiled under the oversight of Sir Roger Twysden († 1672), using C as the source.[271] The content of C^5 differs from

---

deus esse] esse deus CC^2 esse Deus C^3; 237:2 Athelitis] Anhelitis CC^2 *corr. from* Anhelis CC^2C^3. Note that the apparatus for C reports the following readings in letters included in the sample incorrectly: 214:57 quod C] (Schmitt: quod C); 214:62 sacrauit C] (Schmitt: consacrauit C); 230:7 spirituali C] (Schmitt: spiritali C); 230:11–12 proficere C] (Schmitt: perficere C); 232:15 suos C] (Schmitt: *om. C*), 232:17 in mente C] (Schmitt: in corde C); 232:34 mauis] maius *from* mauis C (Schmitt: maius C); 232:34 melius C] (Schmitt: *om. C*); 232:35 quia C] (Schmitt: quod C); 232:37 tuis C] (Schmitt: *om. C*); 234:2 patri C] (Schmitt: priori C); 234:12 meruerim C] (Schmitt: meruerimus C); 237:10 factam] (fcām) C (Schmitt: futuram (frām) C. Anomalies: 214:21 Anglicae C^3] Angliae C; 228:10 praeponendo ecclesiis dei personas C^2] proponendo ecclesiis dei personas C; 232:11 monachicum propositum C^2] monachum propositum C.

[268] See chapter V.2.

[269] Catalogue of the BNF: 'S. XVII, (1673). Paper. Aliquot Epistolae Diui Anselmi Cantuariensis Archiepiscopi qua nondum typis euulgatae sunt. Collectae ex antiquo manuscr. Codice Johannis Grandissoni e Bibliotheca Cottoniana.' See also WILMART, 'La tradition', 1931, p. 41.

[270] *AEp.* 31, 345.

[271] *Stowe catalogue* (via the BL website): 'ANSELMI Epistolæ ccccxvii.: a transcript of Cotton MS. Claudius A. XI, containing the complete collection of St. Anselm's letters; made in 1670 under the inspection of Sir Roger Twys-

that of the other members in this group: the manuscript includes all the letters in *C*.

2.11 *Paris, BNF lat. 14762* – V *(fols. 25r–204v) and* V² *(fols. 1r–23v)*

s. xii³/⁴; Saint-Victor, Paris (OSA); parchment; v + 338 + ii';[272] 255 × 175 (185 × 130) mm; 28 (long) lines

Contents (units 1 and 2)

fols. 1r–23v	Anselm, *Epistolae* (*V²*)
fol. 24r–v	blank
fols. 25r–204v	Anselm, *Epistolae* (*V*)

Paris, BNF lat. 14762 comprises five originally separate manuscripts. The first, *V²* (fols. 1r–23v), is an incomplete copy of Anselm's letter collection and the second is *V* (fols. 25r–204v), which fathered the former. The third book contains the *Regula* for the community of Grandmont[273] and the fourth the *Institutio seu Consuetudines* of Prémontré,[274] while the fifth covers the Pentateuch, Joshua, and Judges sections of *Quaestiones in uetus testamentum* by Isidore (fols. 241r–317r) and Bede's *In libros Regum quaestiones XXX* (317r–330v), and exegetical extracts on the Old Testament books ('Alie questiones in eosdem libros', fols. 330v–337r).[275] The following discussion focuses on the two Anselmian manuscripts and addresses the other sections only where relevant for this study.

---

den, who certifies its correctness in an autograph note at the end. A table of titles of the letters is prefixed. Paper; fols. 268. Inserted at the end (fol. 268) is a petition to Sir Roger Twysden from Margaret Snode, widow of Thomas Snode, complaining of the suppression of her Inn or Alehouse at Great Chart, co. Kent, belonging to the church of Canterbury.'

[272] The flyleaves i-iii and i' are paper.

[273] Fols. 205r–222v: *Regula Stephani Muretensis auctore Stephano de Liciaco*, (*CCCM*, 8, pp. 65–99).

[274] Fols. 223r–240r: *Institutio seu Consuetudines ordinis Grandimontis*, (*CCCM*, 8, pp. 515–525). In both, the written area is 210 × 140 mm; 33 (long) lines.

[275] Fols. 241r–317r. The written area is 210 × 140 mm; 30 (long) lines. The contents of the unit is given in a table (in *s*. xii/xiii hand) on fol. 331v: In hoc libro continentur libri isti. / Ysidorus super uetus testamentum seu .v. libros moysi. / Beda ad notellum de questionibus in libros regum / Item alie questiones de diuersis auctoribus in eosdem libros.

The manuscript is too tightly bound to be absolutely certain of the quiring. V^2 (fols. 1–24) has quire marks in the first two quires on the last folio; these indicate that the manuscript comprises three quaternions. (There are also catchwords at the end of the first quire.) As the text of the last letter ends abruptly and the last folio is blank, the manuscript was never finished. V (fols. 25–204) has quire marks only at the end of the first two quires, which are quaternions. The numbering recommences from 'I^{us}', which confirms that V^2 and V were originally separate entities.[276] Some of the quires and individual folios were confused when the manuscript was rebound at some point after being microfilmed.[277] I shall cite the folios according to their correct arrangement. The manuscript was ruled in lead; prickings are still visible. The ruling differs slightly in sections V^2 and V. The inks used in both parts vary from dark brown to black. The initials in the first four codicological units are strikingly uniform: they are red, and are simply decorated in blue. The initials in the fifth section differ in style from all the preceding ones; these are green with simple ornamentation. The foliation is in Arabic numerals, running throughout the manuscript, in the hand of André Hausselet, the late fifteenth-century librarian of Saint-Victor, who also wrote the list of contents on flyleaf ii^r. The list covers all the items in the manuscript today, and provides the *ad quem* for the amalgamation of the various parts.[278] Palaeographic analysis appears to suggest that V^2, V, and the monastic rules may already have been joined earlier. A single hand appears in V^2, scribe A, and two principal hands appear in V, scribes B (fols. 25r–169r line 22) and C (fols. 169r–204r). The monastic rules, the third and fourth codicological units in the present binding, were probably also copied by B (fols. 205r–240r). Scribe A resem-

---

[276] Fols. 32v, 40v. The third unit (fols. 205–222) has no quire marks. The fourth and fifth units include these; in both they are Roman numerals, and begin at I.

[277] The first quire is currently arranged fols. 1, 3, 5, 7, 2, 4, 6, 8; fols. 41–48 appear between fols. 73 and 80; fols. 74, 76, 75, 78, 77, 79 follow fol. 80.

[278] According to Gilbert Ouy, the modern expert on the library of Saint-Victor, the units were bound 'sans doute vers la fin du xve siècle'; G. Ouy, *Les manuscripts de l'abbaye de Saint-Victor, Catalogue établi sur la base du répertoire de Claude de Grandrue (1514)*, 2 vols., *Bibliotheca Victorina*, 10, Turnhout, 1999, vol. 1, p. 232). The flyleaves at the beginning come from an account book from 1496.

bles both B and C. The layout in V and V^2 is almost identical, and the ruling in V^2 and in fols. 25r–26r of V is completely uniform; then the ruling pattern changes slightly in V. Finally, as the text of V^2 derives from V (as will be shown), we may conclude that the two manuscripts originated in the same scriptorium.

The main hand of Paris, BNF lat. 15038 greatly resembles those of scribes A, B, and C in our manuscript, lat. 14762, both in general appearance and in several details. The similarities are so striking as to give grounds for deducing that the manuscripts were produced in the same scriptorium at about the same time. The extensive marginal annotations in lat. 15038 were written by another scribe, whose hand is known from innumerable documents and manuscripts from Saint-Victor, and whose activity may be dated to approximately 1166–1187.[279] Accordingly V and V^2 were both written at Saint-Victor, some time around the third quarter of the twelfth century. Many hands appear in the final section of the manuscript (fols. 241–337), writing a mid-twelfth-century French *Praegothica*, possibly of Saint-Victor.[280]

There are nota marks and marginal notes, referring to the contents of letters, to duplication, and to how certain letters should be rearranged. The time range of these markings is from the late twelfth century to the early modern period.[281] Folio 1r has an anathema text and fol. 1v has Saint-Victor's ex-libris and fif-

---

[279] F. GASPARRI, 'Le 'scribe G', archiviste et bibliothécaire de l'abbaye de Saint-Victor de Paris au XIIe siècle', *Scriptorium*, 37 (1983), p. 95 and pl. 10 (= BNF lat. 15038, fol. 123v; seen as a reproduction).

[280] Compare e.g. DEROLEZ, *The Palaeography*, 2003, pl. 13 = *CMDF*, vol. 7, pl. 51 (Tours, BM 244, fol. 12rb; seen as a reproduction). The dating of V has been problematic. Wilmart ('La tradition', 1931, p. 41) believed it to derive from the beginning of the thirteenth century, Schmitt ('Zur Entstehungsgeschichte', 1936, p. 301) from the twelfth century, and Southern (*A Portrait*, 1990, p. 459) from the thirteenth century. According to Schmitt, the hand that appears on fols. 169v–204r (C), and which he considered to be from Canterbury, is decisive for the dating. In fact, the hands changed already on the folio before and neither appears to be from Canterbury, although the latter of the hands is somewhat pointed in its general appearance.

[281] F. 124v: Due iste epistole (referring to *AEp*. 123 and 124) in superioribus scribi debuissent (roughly s. xii$^{3/3}$). Fol. 179r: Coronatio regis (early modern). At some stage, the text was punctuated to suit early modern standards better, and caudata were added to show the ae diphthong.

teenth-century arms.[282] The manuscript was in the possession of the monastery up to the French Revolution, and in 1796, along with the greater part of Saint-Victor's collection, it was transferred to its present home in the Bibliothèque nationale.[283]

The characteristics of V

The selection of letters from Anselm's Bec period in V is identical to that in its stemmatic sibling, manuscript C; each includes the same letters, in the same order. However, their selections of the Canterbury correspondence are not identical. Both manuscripts present the Canterbury material in two, partly overlapping sections (that is, some of the same letters appear in both sections); I shall refer to the first sections as V^a and C^a, and the second sections as V^b and C^b. V^a and C^a are identical in their selection and arrangement of the letters. C^b in contrast includes more letters than V^b, but the order of the letters is identical. I shall demonstrate below that V^b is a selective and C^b a faithful copy of their mutual ancestor, which may be called δ^b.

V^b covers 131 letters, where δ^b contained 258, as seen through C^b. The missing letters often appeared consecutively in δ^b. The longest of these stretches of omission comprises eight letters.[284] But here and there V^b omits also individual letters of δ^b. The editorial intention for the selection of letters is difficult to establish, and one gets an impression of not very conscious work. The selection could occasionally be thematic, however: for example, AEp. 323 and 327 are placed consecutively in V^b, in contrast to the arrange-

---

[282] Fol. 1r: 'Iste liber est sancti uictoris parisiensis quicumque eum furatus fuerit uel celauerit uel titulum deleuerit Anathema sit. Amen.' Fol. 1v: 'Jesus maria S. [arms, yellow lilies and a red centre on a blue field] uictor S. augustinus.' The anathema also appears on fols. 337v and 338v in a hand dated to the second quarter of the twelfth century; F. GASPARRI, 'Ex-libris et mentions anciennes portés sur les manuscrits du xiie siècle de l'abbaye Saint-Victor de Paris', *Scriptorium*, 44 (1990), p. 72. I personally consider a slightly later date could be possible, but accept Gasparri's dating. Manuscripts in the same hand as the anathema text on fol. 1r and the ex-libris and arms on 1v include BNF lat. 14502, fol. 1r, 2v, 181r, a manuscript which will be examined later in this work. See also Dresden, Sächsische Landesbibliothek P 46, fol. 1r (reproduced in OUY, *Les manuscripts de Saint-Victor*, vol. 2, 1999, pl. 8; before 1349).

[283] OUY, *Les manuscripts de Saint-Victor*, vol. 2, 1999, pp. 71–73, 97, 232.

[284] $C(297-306)$: AEp. 335, 330, 336, 315, 338–343. V^b only includes the first and last letters of the sequence.

ment in the exemplar δ^b, which gave *AEp.* 324, 325, 354, and 326 between those two letters. *AEp.* 323 is a letter from Queen Matilda to the pope, attempting to persuade him to soften his stance on lay investiture, which would, the letter argues, allow Anselm to return from exile to attend to his pastoral responsibilities. *AEp.* 327 is from the exiled Anselm to Ordwy, a monk of Canterbury, explaining that the rumours Ordwy had heard about the archbishop were unfounded; it had been claimed that Anselm himself had come up with the idea of forbidding lay investiture and that he had given churches to laymen and worthless clerics. In δ^b, four letters on completely different themes appeared between these letters.[285] At all events the selection of letters in V^b appears indiscriminate rather than carefully considered, an impression conveyed by the repeated inclusion and omission of sequences of letters in the source. It is interesting to note that the selection process left the Bec correspondence untouched, and this was copied in its entirety. There may be a geographical explanation for this: to Saint-Victor a Norman abbot may have been of greater interest than an English archbishop.

Characteristics of V^2

As stated before, V^2 is incomplete, and the text breaks off in the middle of *AEp.* 65. V^2 clearly contains a much thinned selection of the material in V. V^2 follows V's readings faithfully and we may assume that V was the exemplar from which V^2 was copied.[286] The arrangement of the letters is also almost identical in the two manuscripts: V^2 only diverges from V's arrangement twice on its first

---

[285] *AEp.* 324, 325, 354, 326.

[286] See e.g. *AEp.* 13:20 toleremus] tolleremus VV^2 (*corrected in* V *possibly by Picard*) 37:39 de loco] de lo V delo V^2. Compare also 65:40 Nec ullatenus] Nnec ullatenus V Nullatenus V^2. A good example of V^2's own corruption: 2:59–60 et retributioni totius uitae suae] *om.* V^2; 2:60 Sicut igitur uides] totius uitae sue. Sicut igitur uides *adds* V^2. V^2's ways of abbreviating the letters also reflect the direction of descent proposed here. I have noted one anomaly: 8:11 amicus huius seculi V] amicus seculi V^2F. According to Krüger (*Persönlichkeitsausdruck*, 2002, pp. 91–95), V^2 (which he names 'V1') is the earliest of all the surviving collections. He adduces no real evidence in support of this interpretation, which, I think, is unfounded. Krüger appears to know the content of V^2 through Southern (cf. 'Verso una storia', 1989, p. 274). Southern's description of the contents contains errors, one of which slipped into Krüger's study: both erroneously assert that the V^2 includes *AEp.* 9.

folios, where it presents an extract of only a couple of lines from these letters—and only these.[287] There are no further divergences in the arrangement of these two manuscripts from *AEp*. 13 onwards.

V^2 spans *AEp*. 1–65, but omits twenty of the 56 letters included in the same section in its exemplar, *V*. Stylistic factors, in part at least, dictated which letters were selected, as will emerge in the discussion of the abridged letters below. An inclination towards economy of effort also clearly influenced the decisions of the compiler, as both the included and the omitted letters usually appear in sequences in *V*, in stretches of a few letters.

Of four letters, V^2 presents only a couple of lines. The extracts reflect provisions regarding the structure of letters in the *ars dictaminis*; the editorial intention was to offer the reader texts which would be easy to utilize in writing letters. The first extract covers the beginning of the *captatio beneuolentiae* in *AEp*. 1, sent to Lanfranc.[288] The extract given in V^2 is general enough to be applied widely, since the passage breaks off immediately at the point where Anselm moved from the general and allegorical to the particular, and referred to Lanfranc's move to England. The third extract is also part of a *captatio beneuolentiae* which could be used as it stood in any letter sent to a friend.[289] This passage was also skilfully chosen, as it sums up the whole train of thought in that particular *captatio*: in the chosen extract, Anselm justifies both the preceding opening sentence of the *captatio* and the closing sentence which followed on from it. V^2 includes the *petitio* from *AEp*. 3 and the *conclusio* from *AEp*. 7. The latter passage, in particular, could not have been picked out with only a superficial knowledge of the text: the chosen extract, which summarizes the preceding *narratio* and links it to the Bible's promises of everlasting life, is embedded

[287] V^2(1–10): 2, 1, 3–6, 8, 11, 7, 13; *V*(1–11): *AEp*. 1–8, 11–13. The letters abridged by V^2: *AEp*. 1:4–7 Gloria – extinguatur. 3:36–37 Obsecro – ipsum. 4:5–8 Quidquid – desiderem; 7:29–33 Ut igitur – censemus.

[288] *AEp*. 1:4–7: 'Gloria in excelsis deo, qui fidei et sapientiae uestrae lucernam in eminenti constituit candelabro, ut luceat omnibus qui in domo eius sunt. Oramus itaque omnipotentem deum ut illa sic ardeat, ut non consumatur; sic luceat aliis, ut sibi numquam extinguatur.'

[289] *AEp*. 4:5–8: 'Quidquid enim de te sentio, dulce et iucundum est cordi meo; quidquid tibi opto, id est quod optimum excogitat mens mea. Talem enim te uidi, ut quomodo tu scis te diligerem; talem te audio, ut quomodo scit deus te desiderem.'

towards the end of the letter, before the greetings and closing fare-wells.[290] The valediction relating to the original recipients has been stripped out from the *petitio* to *AEp*. 3, so that the passage could be used as it stood.[291]

These excerpts give V^2 something of the flavour of the *ars dictaminis* manuals and collections of model letters. Typical guides to the *ars dictaminis* contained short model extracts of the different sections of letters, like the snippets picked out in V^2. Collections of model letters were produced both as sections within theoretical guides to the *ars dictaminis*, when the works are often entitled *summa dictandi*, and independently, when they may have been intended for use alongside the guides to the theory or other teaching aids for the subject. The greatest difference between 'real letter collections' and model letter collections is that the letters in the latter were chosen, written, or edited to serve a specific, didactic purpose. V^2 clearly abbreviates Anselm's letters for similar ends. This circumstance will be of interest for studies of the *ars dictaminis*, since 'real' and model letter collections have been assumed to have had clearly differentiated functions, although of course the didactic function of letter collections themselves has long been recognized.[292]

2.12 *Troyes, Médiathèque 836* – V^3

s. xiii[2/2]; (?)Clairvaux (OCist); parchment; i + 84 + i'; I–VII[12]; 275 × 195 (210 × 140) mm; 59 lines in two columns

---

[290] *AEp*. 7:29–33: Ut igitur tandem nostrum et — ut credo — tuam sententiam super tuorum actuum acceptione propalemus: quidquid erga nos uel quemlibet alium laudabiliter agis, gratissimum habemus; sed laudes eius in illum diem, cum 'laudabuntur omnes recti corde' et cum 'laus erit uniquique a deo', seruandas censemus.] corde – *Ps. 63:11*; a deo – *1. Cor. 4:5*.

[291] *AEp*. 3:36–39: '[Ambo, carissimi, ualete.] Obsecro, in Babylonia sentite id ipsum, ut in Ierusalem paricipetis in id ipsum. Non hoc dico quasi timens uobis aliquando discordiam uenire, sed uere cupiens a uobis numquam concordiam abire.'

[292] 'Collections of actual letters like theirs [namely Pietro della Vigna and Peter of Blois], though doubtless used for instruction in *dictamen* as similar collections were used long before the first theoretical treatises were written, should be distinguished from those collections composed by teachers of *dictamen* for the express purpose of illustrating their precepts.' CAMARGO, *Ars dictaminis*, 1991, p. 27. See also *ibid*. 20, 22, 23, 28, 43–46, and CONSTABLE, *Letters and Letter-Collections*, 1976, p. 57.

Contents

Troyes, Médiathèque 836 covers a fairly good selection of Anselm's treatises and a somewhat narrower selection of his correspondence. The letters appear in two sequences, with eleven on fols. 33r–35v and the remainder on fols. 76r–84v. The reason for the division is hard to pin down. The manuscript apparently survives in full, since the ending of its final text, *AEp.* 189, has been squeezed into an extra line in the lower margin, the only time such a device appears here. The margins are ruled in lead. The foliation is in Roman numerals, with the number 14 appearing twice and 53 completely omitted. The list of contents in the manuscript follows the foliation as marked. The initials are simple and the headings are in red ink. The text is in a single hand, dating from the thirteenth century, probably its second half. The manuscript appears in Clairvaux's library catalogues of 1471 and 1521.[293] The letters in *V³* extend from the beginning of the Bec period (*AEp.* 2) to the early years of the Canterbury period (*AEp.* 189). The arrangement of the letters and the readings indicate that *V³* descends from *V*.[294]

---

[293] A. Vernet (ed.), *La bibliothèque de l'abbaye de Clairvaux du XIIe au XVIIIe siècle*, vol. 1, Paris, 1979, item 662 in Pierre de Virey, 1472; item H 21 (p. 149); item 379a in Mathurin de Cangey, *c.* 1521), item K d V (p. 424).

[294] *V³* follows the readings common to *CV*, and in addition also the readings unique to *V*. See e.g. 6:11 est] etiam *VV³*; 79:1 filio] *om. VV³*; 161:38 est

V^3 contains just under a third of the material from the corresponding period in V, or 52 letters out of 171, including seven duplicates.

2.13 *The source for manuscripts* CV*:* δ

It has been suggested that manuscript C has no 'eigenständigen Wert'. This assessment was based on the erroneous identification of V and L as the sources for C.[295] The misconception had damaging consequences. Since Schmitt believed that C could be eliminated, it had very little influence upon his edition. C is, however, one of our key witnesses to Anselm's correspondence.

The structure of C is similar to V. After the Bec correspondence, C presents the Canterbury letters in two partially overlapping sections (C^aC^b). For the Bec material and the first section of Canterbury material, CV are identical in their arrangement and extent. However, C^a presents *Epistola de incarnatione Verbi* (fols. 67r–75r), which is not found in V, between AEp. 164 and 165. The arrangement of the second section of Canterbury material in C^bV^b is also similar,[296] but there are more letters in C^b than in V^b. The similarities continue at the textual level, in the readings: the manuscripts frequently agree against the other manuscripts (with the exception,

---

peccatum V^aV^3] peccatum est $C^aC^bV^bLPEF$; 161:44 enim] *om.* V^aV^3; 161:49 de ouili] *om.* V^aV^3; 179:6 usu] usui VV^3; 179:7 rogem VV^3] roget C.

[295] SCHMITT, 'Zur Entstehungsgeschichte', 1936, pp. 301–302: 'Cod. C hat also keinen eigenständigen Wert, wenngleich er unter allen Hss. die vollständigste Sammlung der anselmianischen Korrespondenz enthält.' Schmitt's interpretation influenced later German scholarship too. According to Fröhlich ('Introduction', 1990, p. 28) C 'appears to be a direct copy of L'. Krüger did not analyze the manuscript at all. Wilmart brought the manuscript into the field of modern research; he considered it to be a register compiled by Grandisson himself from many sources; A. WILMART, 'Les prières envoyées par S. Anselme à la comtesse Mathilde en 1104', *Revue Bénédictine*, 41 (1929), p. 35; and 'La tradition', 1931, p. 40. Southern (*A Portrait*, 1990, pp. 458, 477) saw the manuscript as a copy of a Bec archetype, a position very close to my understanding.

[296] Note that AEp. 212 (fol. 161r–v) is penultimate in C^b. The scribe placed a symbol beside the letter (a cross with a dot in each quarter); the same symbol appears in the lower margin on fol. 93r in association with text indicating the letter's position. The location is the same as in V. Fol. 93r: 'Hec epistola Henricus dei gratia rex anglorum deberet hic esse. Que est in fine libri ad tale signum.'

of course, of their derivatives).[297] Furthermore, each manuscript bears numerous isolated readings (again, with the exception of their derivatives, which naturally reproduce these idiosyncrasies).[298] The conclusion is clear: the two manuscripts derive from the same source, which we may call δ.[299]

δ was identical in structure to CV; in other words, it presented the Bec material first, followed by the Canterbury material in two partially overlapping sections. This overlap attests that δ was created by combining two sources. Both these sources may be reconstructed, as I shall demonstrate in detail below. The correspondence from Bec derived from manuscript β^1, and the first section of Canterbury letters, or δ^a, drew on both β^1 and on individual letters in Bec archives. The second and longer section of Canterbury correspondence, δ^b, drew on another lost manuscript, γ. The grounds and the principles for reconstructing these lost witnesses will be discussed shortly.

[297] C repeats the readings Schmitt reports for V; see the following notes for the exceptions.

[298] Some of the idiosyncrasies of V that are not found in C: 4:33 dulcissimo] dilectissimo V; 6:11 est] etiam V; 39:59 monachice] monachie V; 39:60 uellem] uelle V; 41:14 deus] dominus V; 42:24 ut] *om.* V; 46:15 inesse] non esse V; 48:15 dulcem] ducem V; 49:13 misistis] misticis V; 75:9–10 uel tempore] et tempore V; 79:1 filio] *om.* V; 137:36 factum tuum] factu V; 142:11 se V] sese *CELP*; 136:8 mihi] *om.* V; 148:13 uel] *om.* V^a; 148:13–14 confictiones] confectiones V^a; 149:18 infulae] insulae V^a; 156:12 illam] illa V^a; 156:60 tibi] mihi V^a; 161:38 est peccatum V^a] peccatum est $C^aC^bV^bLPEF$; 161:44 enim] *om.* V^a; 161:49 de ouili] *om.* V^a. The same dispersion naturally recurs in C^bV^b; e.g. 161:48–49 a multitudine – de ouili] *om.* V^b; 186:22 et amore] *om.* V^b; 205:9 ad quid] aliquid V^b; 205:13 diligo] *om.* V^b; 205:15 pariter] *om.* V^b; 318:16 Willelmo V^b] de war. *adds* C^b; 343:12 uirtutis tuae] *om.* V^b; 343:23 tuam] *om.* V^b; 368:11–12 gratia *om.* V^b; 380:16 enim V^b] ut *add.* C^bLPEF. It is unnecessary to present C's unique readings against V here, as C clearly could not have been the source for the much earlier manuscript V. Note that C shares many of the readings for V presented in Schmitt's critical apparatus.

[299] This was also Southern's understanding (*A Portrait*, 1990, pp. 458, 477), based on the analysis of the extent and internal arrangement of the manuscripts alone. Schmitt ('Zur Entstehungsgeschichte', 1936, p. 301) incorrectly believed that the Bec material in C and the manuscript's first section of Canterbury material, i.e. C^a, were copied from V. Schmitt thought that the second section of Canterbury material, i.e. C^b, was a copy of L. C^bV^b, however, clearly unite against L, as will be discussed in detail below.

The second section of Canterbury letters in δ, or δ^b, must have contained all the material in C^b, also the letters absent from V^b. Clear evidence for this survives in the choice of letters and the readings found in CV. Like L and its copies, C^b places an assortment of four Bec letters in the midst of the Canterbury material; these are AEp. 52, 135, 95, and 87. V^b retains only two of these letters (AEp. 52 and 95), which are likewise placed among the Canterbury material. V^b clearly abbreviates the group. The alternative explanation is unconvincing: that the Bec letters were erroneously copied consecutively into the Canterbury sequence at two different stages in the transmission process, first through the addition of the two letters found in V, AEp. 52 and 95, and then through the placing of AEp. 135 and 87 just after them, as they are found in C^bL. There is further evidence supporting the conclusion that V^b only provides a straitened testimony to δ^b, that a more substantial manuscript lay behind it. On the basis of the identical witness of C^bV^b, δ^b appended the last words of AEp. 277 to AEp. 276.[300] AEp. 277 is included in C^b but absent from V^b. The erroneous reading in AEp. 276 indicates, however, that the maker of δ^b did have access to AEp. 277.

The identical scope of C^b and δ^b is also supported by more detailed textual criticism. In the case of the letters absent from V^b, C^b's stemmatic position does not significantly change, judging by manuscript L and its copies, and manuscripts $FA^2(P)$ and the $Historia\ nouorum$, each of which is independent of L; A^2 is London, BL Add. 32091 and will be discussed in Appendix I.[301] $FA^2(P)$ and $Historia\ nouorum$ sometimes agree with C^bV^b against L and its descendants. This phenomenon also recurs in the letters not found in V^b; in other words, manuscripts FA^2 and $Historia\ nouorum$ agree with C^b against L.[302] Finally manuscript O, Troyes 1614, which will

---

[300] AEp. 276:13 possum] prebeat rogando et consulendo moneatis. Valete. $add.$ C^bV^b.

[301]   Unlike P's other letters, its AEp. 331 does not derive from L, and therefore it is included here.

[302]   (1) C^bF against L and its descendants: 259:4 diligentibus C^bF] deligentibus LPE; 336:19 ab illis C^bF] ab allis $LE\ corr.\ from$ ab allis P; 356:13 abstraxerunt C^bF] abstracserunt LPE; 361:5 aliter C^bF] $om.\ LPE$; 419:19 ipsi C^bF] sibi LPE; 430:16 monstratis C^bF] demonstratis LPE.
(2) C^b agrees with $Historia\ nouorum$ or A^2 against L and its descendants: 369:8 qui C^br] quia LPE [ex qui L?]; 423:3–4 Anglica C^bA^2] anglia LPE.

be studied shortly, confirms that δ^b was more extensive than V^b. O derives from the source of δ^b, that is γ. Like V^b, O too provides only a thinned selection of the letters in its (ultimate) source. On the one hand, V^b includes some letters absent from O and on the other, some letters in O are missing from V^b.[303] In conclusion, C has been hitherto unjustly overlooked and it is the fullest witness to δ given its breadth of material. The critical edition of Anselm's letters should take full account of the manuscript.

δ^b cannot be a copy of any of the known manuscripts: it descended from manuscript γ, which I shall discuss below. It is important to note that the group $\gamma\delta^b$ definitely cannot descend from L alone — a solution which would have suited Schmitt's understanding of the textual tradition. The witness of $\gamma\delta^b$ is often stronger than that of L, and, above all, it agrees with manuscript F against L.[304] Additionally AEp. 332 clearly indicates that the

(3) Compare also AEp. 331, where P is apparently independent of L^a: 331:29 de debitis et de terris L^aE] de debitis et terris C^bP and especially 331:31 iuuenibus L^aE] iuuenculis C^bP. C^b alone stronger than LPE: 340:11 poteritis C^b] poteris LPE; 358:9 restituas C^b] restuas LP corr. from restuas E; 388:10 ecclesiae C^b] ecclesiam LPE.

[303] OC^b om. V^b: AEp. 193, 196, 198, 206, 230, 232, 245, 254, 328. C^bV^b om. O: e.g. AEp. 211, 213, 218, 220, 222, 223, 227 etc.

[304] 161:17 sapientori $OV^aV^bC^aC^bF$] sipientori LPE; 162:1 parisiensis OV^aV^b-C^aC^bF] pariensis LPE; 161:20 qui $\underline{E}FOV^aV^bC^aC^b$] quid LP (in E qui is in darker ink than the surrounding words and is possibly corrected); 249:6 uestra C^bV^bF] uestrum LPE; 281:15 hoc immane C^bV^bF] hoc in immane LP corr. from hoc in immane E; 285:19 est² OC^bV^bF] om. LPE; 322:26 faceretis C^bV^bF] facietis LPE; 327:3 es C^bV^bF] om. LPE; 385:4; 387:20 ostendet C^bV^bF] ostendit LEP; 387:25 promulgari C^bV^bF] mulgari LPE; 389:17 causae C^bV^bF] causa LE corr. from causa P; 389:23 illi C^bV^bF] om. LPE; 389:28 uestram² C^bV^bF] uestra LPE; 406:11 ad me C^bV^bF] om. LPE; 418:18 corpus OC^bV^bF] cor LPE. C^bV^b clearly also diverge from the tradition of LPE in the letters which were subsequently added to L, i.e. to its appendix L^a. 193:10 cum L^aE] tum C^b corr. from tum V^b; (193:13 aegre ferat L^aE] egreferat C^b egre V^b); 193:36 onere C^bV^b] honere O onore L^aE; 212:4– Scias C^bV^b] Sciatis et sic omnia in persona plurali L^aE; 212:12 acciperem L^aE] susciperem C^bV^b. L's copies EP are naturally more distant from $\gamma\delta^b$ than L is. With regard to E especially see e.g. 223:15 sint. Si – parrochia] om. E; 262:38 et in eo Petri] om. E; 332:9 per hanc illum pacatis] om. E; 349:23 qui aperte et distincte scribat] om. E; 368:7–8 sed causa – non debeo] om. E. 374:12 excommunicationis percussit. Quam] om. E; 403:16 est] om. E; with regard to P, see e.g. 197:3 temporalem] corporalem P; 197:5 quanta] quanto P; 203:5 de uobis] uobis om. P; 261:6 de reditu] deritu P; 281:4 quod om. P; 343:24 deus] om. P; 345:15 aliud] illud P; 355:28 scandalo aut sine

compiler of γ had access to a fuller source than L. L omits the witness list at the end of the letter, which was included in γ on the evidence of δ^b (C^bV^b).[305] It is particularly interesting that *contemporary* corrections appear in L, beneath which the readings followed by $\gamma\delta^b$ emerge.[306]

On the other hand L was clearly independent of δ^b. For example in certain letters the king and queen of England addressed to Anselm, both L and δ^b occasionally use plural first person forms where other manuscripts use singular forms for both the verbs and the pronouns referring to Anselm.[307] However, L and δ^b do this occasionally in separate letters. In AEp. 242 from Queen Matilda, L and δ^b diverge: the former is content with the singular, the latter uses the plural. In δ^b an error at 242:8 reveals that the original reading was the singular which was used in $L(PE)$. When L reads 'didici te...cibum sumere', C^bV^b, in other words δ^b, give 'didici et... cibum sumere', which is clearly weaker. Since the pronoun 'te' clearly lies behind δ^b's weak variant 'et', the plural was editorial.[308] (To agree with the rest of the letter, δ^b should have amended the

---

magna] *om. P*; 402:4 quanto affectu possum deo a quo] *om. P*; 405:15 a conuersatione] auersatione *P*; 405:27 iuuent] uiuent *P*; 445:16 pallium *om. P*; 468:10 loquimur] loquitur *P*. Note, however, that P appears to derive AEp. 331 from a source that resembled C^b's source more than that of L^a. 331:29 de debitis et de terris L^aE] de debitis et terris C^bP; 331:31 iuuenibus L^aE] iuuenculis C^bP. Likewise F cannot have been the source for δ^b, since F presents some letters in a different order to that witnessed by δ^bL together, and includes fewer letters than these; see the notes in chapter III.2.8 for the manuscripts' divergent readings.

[305] 318:15–16 Teste Roberto – Willelmo C^bV^b] de war. *adds* C^b *om. LPE*. The letter is missing from O.

[306] 313:10 sunt OC^bV^bF] sicut *PE* sicut *from* sunt *L*; 355:6 laudabile *LPE corr. from* laudabilem *L*] laudabilem OC^bV^bF; 389:29 sententiam C^bV^bFP *corr. from* sententia *P*] sententia *LE corr. from* sententiam[?] *L*; 389:30 deus *LPE*] *eras. in L* diu *add.* C^bV^b; 433:20 coniuncti C^bV^bP] coniungi *E* coniungi *corr. from* coniuncti *L*.

[307] AEp. 212] *plural* L^aE *singular* C^bV^b; 242] *plural* C^bV^b *singular LPE*; 426] *plural* C^b *singular LPE*. See 392] *plural LPEC^b singular r*.

[308] AEp. 426, which is included in C^b but absent from V^b, has been edited similarly. Unlike *LPE*, C^b uses the plural but not entirely consistently: 426:3,4,6 tibi, tuis, tuae – tibi] uobis, uobis, uestre – uobis C^b; nevertheless, 426:6 succurristi. Scias tu C^b]. Since δ^b clearly tended to change forms into the plural (AEp. 242), the parallel tendency in AEp. 426 in C^b indicates that this letter is also derived from δ^b.

passage as 'didici uos...cibum sumere'.) In several other cases too, L is naturally stronger than δ^b, often agreeing with F against δ^b.

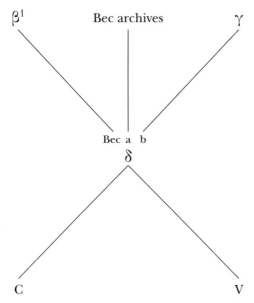

Figure 3: The sources for and witnesses to δ

2.14 *Troyes, Médiathèque 1614* – O

s. xvi[2/2]; (?)Saint-Claude, Jura (OSB); paper; iii + 96,[309] I–XII[8]; 23–26 (long) lines[310]

Contents

fol. 1r–v	Anselm's life in Latin
fol. 2r–93r	Anselm, *Epistolae* (*O*)
fol. 93v–97v	blank

O includes letters from Anselm's Canterbury correspondence only. Earlier scholarship has completely overlooked this manuscript, with the exception of d'Achery, who published certain letters from it in the seventeenth century. I was only able to consult the manuscript itself very briefly, and the detailed study is based on work with photocopies. This accounts for the incomplete codi-

---

[309] The foliation covers the flyleaves, ending at 99.

[310] The codicological data was noted from a photocopy and the collation was derived from the signatures. I do not have measurements for the manuscript.

cological description. The structure of the manuscript was deduced from the quire marks. In the first quire, the quire marks consist of a letter and a Roman numeral, which indicate each bifolium and thus go up to the number four, following the practice of quire signatures in a printed book. The following quires use letters alone as quire marks, placed on both the first recto and the last verso of the quire. All are placed in the centre of the lower margin and are the work of the same hand.

The text is in a single hand, writing a French cursive of the sixteenth century, probably of its second half.[311] The copyist was probably not from Normandy, since his error at *AEp*. 198:18 reflects ignorance of the Norman ecclesiastical hierarchy. Where the other manuscripts read 'metropolitani Rotomagensis', *O* gives 'Rotomagensis episcopi'. The origin or early provenance is Saint-Claude, Jura (OSB), as can be derived from the three following facts. First, in the list of contents of his *Spicilegium*, d'Achery states that the source for Anselm's letters, which is not otherwise identified, comes from Saint-Claude.[312] Second, textual evidence, as we shall see later, indicates that d'Achery's manuscript was either *O* or very close to it. Third, on its first flyleaf *O* has the inscription 'Codex MS. Bibliothecae Buherianae E. 82. MDCCXXI'. Jean Bouhier († 1746), a book collector, lawyer, and author, is known to have acquired several manuscripts from Saint-Claude.[313] In 1746, Bouhier's books went to Clairvaux, and — since the Clairvaux collection was eventually conveyed to Troyes — this seems to have been the fate of our manuscript too. The corrections, appearing both in between the lines and in the margins, are in the main hand. In addition, a few marginal annotations occur in three hands. Annotator A referred to the publication of certain letters in Danhauser's *editio princeps*.[314] Annotator B expanded certain abbreviations the

---

[311] See e.g. the letter r, which repeatedly is a small capital letter, and the dotted letter i. I am grateful to Professor Marc Smith for this analysis (pers. comm., 19.10.2007).

[312] L. D'ACHERY (ed.), *Veterum aliquot scriptorum qui in Galliae Bibliothecis maxime Benedictorum latuerant Spicilegium*, vol. 9, Paris, 1669, p. 24: 'Ex MS. Cod. Monasterii S. Claudii exscripsit R. P. Petrus Chiffletius S. I.'

[313] A. CASTAN, 'La bibliothèque de l'abbaye de Saint-Claude du Jura. Esquisse de son histoire', *Bibliothèque de l'École des chartes*, 50 (1889), p. 310.

[314] Fols. 8r, 20r, 27r, 48r, 59r, 74r, 79r.

copyist had made in the main text, often passages of scripture.[315] Annotator C contributed only two short marks, which recommend the reader to compare certain passages in *AEp*. 196 and 446 with one another;[316] in both, Anselm urges the recipient of the letter to refrain from overly severe ascetic practices, which endangered health.[317] Annotators A and B are possibly from the seventeenth century, whereas C appears slightly later, but the passage is so short that it is hard to determine the date.

Special characteristics

At the outset, *O* follows the arrangement of $C^b(V^b)L$. *O*'s immediate source (or a lost intermediary) arranged its letters identically to $C^b(V^b)L$. This source, which has been already referred to, and will be postulated in the next section, is called γ. Towards the end, *O* introduces small alterations to the arrangement, however. First, the section *O1–48* comprises letters which fall between *AEp*. 156 and 450 in Schmitt's edition. The arrangement is the same as in γ, but *O* must include significantly less material. Next, the copyist of *O* (or of an unknown intermediary) picked out *AEp*. 223. Then he returned to the beginning of the source to copy the letters between *AEp*. 157 and 210 that he had previously omitted. This section, *O50–63*, also follows the arrangement of γ.

The content and structure of *O* are individual in that clear traces remain of the compiler's motives. Within the section *O1–48*, the letters were clearly selected because of their subject matter. With the exception of *AEp*. 289 (*O19*), all letters to lay recipients are absent from *O*; this is remarkable, since Anselm's correspondence with the king of England and his court formed a substantial part of the corpus. Likewise Anselm's correspondence with the pope is completely excluded from this section, as are all the letters Anselm received. Letters *O1–48* almost without exception touch on monastic themes, including, for example, monastic vocations, obedience, and pastoral matters. Subjects which may best be described as relating to church(-state) politics are included more by chance than deliberately. *O* (or a lost intermediary) was clearly compiled for readers whose literary tastes were moulded by monas-

---

[315] Fols. 20r, 25r, 55r, 56r.

[316] Fol. 16r: 'confer cum epist. 47'; fol. 68v: 'confer cum epist. 7'.

[317] *AEp*. 196:5–9; 446:10–12.

tic life and who were not interested in Anselm's activity outside
monastic sphere. This motivation also explains why the copyist
stopped at *AEp.* 450. With one exception, thereafter the letters in
γ were on subjects that had no natural connection to monastic life,
for example the dispute between Canterbury and York over the
primacy, and ecclesio-political relations with both the ecclesiastical
and the lay nobility.[318] The editor was not interested in material
of this kind.

When the copyist had picked out the material he considered
interesting from his source, he returned to the beginning. The
first letter in the new sequence is *AEp.* 223, which could hardly
be more dramatically different from the preceding material in
its subject matter. The letter is from Paschal II and its contents
are entirely concerned with church politics; the letter deals with
detailed questions related to the central ecclesiastical and political problems of the day: priestly celibacy, lay use of ecclesiastical
power, and simony. Next the compiler returned to the beginning
of γ and continued up to *AEp.* 210, picking out all the letters that
were omitted when making the first selection. At the end of the
manuscript, its reader again gets an impression that this material
was not of real interest to the compiler: when he ceased work at
AEp. 210, the last five leaves of the final quire remained blank.

2.15 O in the tradition: γ

Stemmatically O is close to $C^b V^b$.[319] Despite its later date,
O descends from an earlier stage in the transmission than $C^b V^b$
and their source δ^b. For O sometimes offers stronger readings than
the agreement of manuscripts $C^b V^b$, that is δ^b, and agrees with the

---

[318] On the basis of $C^b(V^b)L$, γ continued after *AEp.* 450 as follows: *AEp.*
451, 452, 461, 462, 463, 464, 465, 466, 467, 468, 469, 471, 472. Of these, only
AEp. 468 touched on monastic life.

[319] See e.g. 160:52 siue episcopatum] *om. OC^bV^b*; 161:34 clericos] clericis
OC^bV^b; 187:11 me debere] *om. OC^bV^b*; 191:17 audio] audiero C^bV^b audiam O;
193:10 cum L^aE] tum OC^b *corr. from* tum V^b; 193:36 onere C^bV^b] honere O
onore L^aE; 193:53 Fulcone OC^bV^b] F *and lacuna* L episcopo Fulcone *in another
hand* E; 223:9 respondenda OC^bV^bF] respondenda L *corr. from* resplondenda E
resplendenda P; 285:19 est² OC^bV^bF] *om. LPE*; 313:10 sunt OC^bV^bF] sicut *PE*
sicut *from* sunt L; 328:27 ostentando *LF*] ostendando OC^b; 355:6 laudabile *PE*]
corr. from laudabilem L laudabilem OC^bV^bF; 418:18 corpus OC^bV^bF] cor *LPE*;
434:1 dilecto] *om. OC^bV^b*.

Canterbury branch of the tradition, i.e. manuscripts *LPE*, and manuscript *F*.[320] *O* must thus descend — either directly or through a lost intermediary — from the ancestor of δ^b itself; this is γ, which has already been mentioned above. In this sense, *O* is *recentior, non deterior*, and as such it should be taken into account in a critical edition.

γ, which contained Anselm's Canterbury correspondence, was more extensive than *O* and also arranged slightly differently; in other words, *O* only includes a selection of the material in its source, which it rearranges in part. There are three factors behind this conclusion. First, the selection and arrangement of letters are unique to *O* and are shared with no other known manuscript. Second, the arrangement followed in the manuscripts related to γ, that is δ^b (=C^bV^b) and *LPE* as well as (with certain alterations) *F*, may clearly be perceived in *O*'s background. Third, *O*'s selection and arrangement of letters reflect editorial individuality the character of which can be defined, as discussed above. The only straightforward explanation for the almost identical selection and arrangement of letters both in γ's Bec descendant δ^b and the Canterbury branch *LPE* is that γ closely resembled these. The same agreements can be applied to restore the selection and arrangement of the letters in γ as for its readings. In other words, γ is:

(1) the agreement of *O* with any of $\delta^b LF$[321]
(2) the agreement of δ^b with *L* and/ or *F*, where the material missing from *O* is concerned.

[320] 156:36 non nouerunt *OFL*] inmouerunt V^b immouerunt C^b; 161:38 intelligentes $FLPEC^aV^aO$] intelligens C^bV^b; 162:14 persuadeat $FLPEC^aV^aO$] persuadet C^bV^b; 162:23 quia sciunt] pascuunt V^b *om.* C^b (the evidential value of the passage is weakened by the fact that a biblical text is in question, John 10,4, which could have been corrected from memory); 188:18 absoluo *O*] absoluite VV^3 *corr. from* absoluite[?] *C*. 414:60 ambulant *LFO*] ambulabunt C^bV^b. Naturally the unique readings in V^b and C^b do not appear in *O*: (a) 160:47 mundi cont. deb. sed timor] *om.* V^b; 161:24 curis] cure V^b; 161:38 est peccatum V^a; 161:44 enim] *om.* V^a; 161:48–49 a multitudine – de ouili] *om.* V^b; 161:50 Mi reuerende – loquor] *om.* V^b; *AEp.* 196, 230, 232, 236 etc. *om.* *V*. (b) 156:152 nec debeo] *om.* C^b; 161:8 audio] audeo C^b; 162:23 quia sciunt] *om.* C^b; 203:11 seruandum] conseruandum C^b.

[321] Note however the following anomalies: 156:92 uiuerem FC^aV^aO] uiuere LC^bV^bP *corr. from* uiuere *E*; 156:154 dilexistis FC^aV^aO] dilexisti $LPEC^bV^b$.

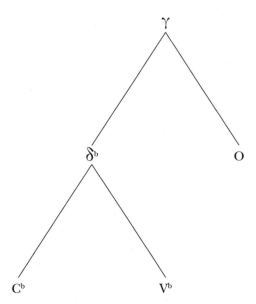

Figure 4: γ and its main witnesses

In the latter part of O, in the section comprising letters left out
in the first round, the compiler made an interesting error, which
might reflect γ's physical character. He copied a few lines of *AEp*.
206 within the text of *AEp*. 198. Having noticed this, he ruled
out the incorrect passage and continued his work from the correct
place.[322] One explanation for an error of this kind is that a page-
turn occurred in *AEp*. 198 in the exemplar, and that the copyist inadvertently turned over two leaves at once. In γ, *AEp*. 199
was placed between *AEp*. 198 and *AEp*. 206; O too includes the
letter, but in the earlier section of letters on monastic themes. If
this mistake occurred as I have suggested, and providing that no
unknown manuscript stood between O and γ, a single folio in γ
contained about 54 lines of the text as printed in Schmitt's edition. This appears rather low: the single column manuscript P fits
about 48 lines of text in Schmitt's edition per *page*.

According to Orderic Vitalis, Abbot William of Bec (1093–1124)
and his successor Boso (1124–1136), distributed Anselm's sermons

---

[322] Fol. 88r: '[*AEp*. 198:32]...sponte resiliant ditione. [*AEp*. 206:7–10] ~~Hac
igitur — sicut desidero.~~ [*AEp*. 198:32] et qui illis...'

and letters 'largiter'.[323] The making of γ and δ may have been part of this project. Since L, coming from $c.$ 1120 × 1130, provides the *a quo* for γ (as we shall see), either of the abbots could have commissioned γ and its descendant δ.

2.16 *The final authorial Bec collection:* β

In 1092[324] Anselm asked for his letters to be sent to England, which he was visiting in his capacity as abbot of Bec.[325] In this section I shall establish that Anselm did compile a new collection of his Bec letters at this time, and that the text of this collection may be restored with the assistance of the surviving witnesses. The following conclusions and observations presented above are central to this process.

(a) CV share a common source, δ.
(b) The Bec correspondence in each of the witnesses $LFE\delta$ is independent of the other members of the group (except that E was contaminated by L).
(c) $LFE\delta$ by and large contain the same material in roughly the same order, meaning that the manuscripts must be related to one another.

It should be noted that the existence of α, which our evidence suggests but cannot verify, is not a prerequisite for the argument that follows. For the sake of convenience, however, this discussion refers to α without addressing uncertainties about its existence.

As for the *Bec* correspondence, if manuscripts CV and their descendants are set aside, the Bec section of E is the most closely

---

[323] Orderic Vitalis, *Historia ecclesiastica*, ed. M. CHIBNALL, *OMT*, 1968–1980, vol. 2, p. 296: 'Dociles discipuli epistolas tipicosque sermones eius scripto retinuerunt, quibus affatim debriati non solum sibi sed et aliis multis non mediocriter profecerunt. Hoc Guillelmus et Boso successores eius multipliciter senserunt, qui tanti doctoris sintagmata insigniter sibi hauserunt, et sitientibus inde desiderabilem potum largiter propinauerunt.' However, Anselm's *Dicta* survive only from Christ Church.

[324] *GB* and the *editio princeps*, *a*, which ultimately witness to β, have not been taken into account yet at this point. In this context, these witnesses, containing only a small selection of letters, are of negligible evidential value. They will be considered below.

[325] *AEp.* 147 (to brothers of Bec): 'Mittite mihi *Orationem ad sanctum Nicolaum*, quam feci, et *Epistolam* quam *contra dicta Roscelini* facere incohaui, et si quas de aliis nostris epistolis habet domnus Mauritius, quas non misit.'

related survivor to δ (that is, the exemplar or ancestor for CV).[326] The identical arrangement of the letters and frequent agreement over minor and major variant readings in E and CV indicate this. $E\delta$ resemble α more closely than L does. Letters that survive in two versions provide compelling evidence of this. If we move through the witnesses in the order α–δE–L, the number of drafts or rejected versions reduces at each step: δE replace some of the rejected versions or the drafts in α with later, apparently final versions of these letters, while L repeats the process with the rejected versions of the drafts included in δE. In accordance with this conclusion, a more detailed analysis, founded in the minutiae of textual evidence, suggests that $E\delta$ represent an intermediate stage between α and L.[327] One must keep in mind, however, that

[326] Unless otherwise stated, references in this section are only to the Bec correspondence in each manuscript.

[327] There are too many readings of this type to present a comprehensive list here. See e.g. 2:17 debita *NMCVE*] dilecta *LPF*; 2:20 domine mi *NMFCVE*] mi domine mi *LP*; 2:54 amatissime *NCVE corr. from* amantissime *P*] amantissime *LFM*; 4:17 accipias *NCVE*] uideas *LP*; 4:39 Quod *NCVE*] Quo *LP*; 5:18 delectatione *NCVE*] dilectione *L* dilectioni *P*; 8:3 sapore *CVE*] a sapore *LPF*; 8:20 numquam *NCVE*] sic *add. LPF*; 8:20 ueracius *NCVE*] ueraciter *LPF*; 8:26 ponat *NCV*] ponet *LPFE (corr. from* ponat *E)*; 13:5 domnum *NCVFE*] dominum *LP*; 13:9 domino *NCVE*] domno *LPF*; 17:3 quam mihi *NCVE*] ipsi *add. LPF*; 17:11 haec *CVE*] est *L; eras. in P om. F*; 17:39–40 'Recencio 1' *NMCVE* 'Recensio 2' *LPF*; 28:1–2 Domno – Anselmus *NCVE*] Suo suus – felicitate *(cf. AEp. 41)*; *LP*; 28:15 sint longae *NCVE*] longae sint *LP*; 229:3 domnus prior *NCVE*] prior domnus *LPFM*; 29:4 Antiphonarium *NCVE*] secundum – artis *add. LPFM*; 36:15 nulli *NCVE*] non ulli *LP*; 36:18 Quamobrem *NCVE*] Quam propter rem *LP*; 37:15 dei dispositioni *NCVE*] dispositioni dei *LPF*; 37:19 Urso *NMCVE*] Ursione *LPF* [Schmitt's apparatus includes an error regarding *E*]; 37:81 Ursus *NCVE*] ursio *LPF*; 41:1–3 Suo – felicitate *NCVE*] Domino – Anselmus *LP*; 41:14 deus tibi *NEC*] dominus tibi *V* tibi deus *LP*; 44:9 quanta *NCVE*] quantas *LP*; 45:20 et carissima *NCVE*] et *om. LP*; 76:18 Amen *LP*] *om. NCVE*; 78:31 rerum *NCVE*] *om. LPF*; 80:21 multi praelati *NMCVEF*] praelati multi *LP*; 83:7 nec *NMCVE*] neque *LP*; 85:1 diligenti *NCVE*] et *add. LPF*; 85:24–25 quam ego uel loquendo uel scribendo *NCVE*] uel loquendo scribendo *LPF*; 86:12 militiam immo malitiam *NMCVE*] immo malitiam *om. L* militiam immo *om. P*; 93:9 erit *NMCVE*] fuerit *LP*; 96:18 non *CVEM*] *om. LPF*; 96:34 uestro *CVEM*] nostro *LP*; 101:24 scelerum *NMCVE*] *om. LPF*; 101:79 Amen. *NMCVE*] *om. LPF*; 104:9 nostro *NCVE*] *eras. L om. P*; 106:1 dispositione *NMCVE*] dispensatione *LP*; 117:5 dominus *NMCVE*] deus *LPF*; 117:48 rogo *NMCVE*] ergo *LPF*; 117:51 quia *NMCVE*] quoniam *LPF*; 117:74 quam te *NMCVE*] quam de te *LPF*; 118:35

a standard genealogical stemma cannot tell the whole truth of the transmission since archived letters were employed at various stages in the transmission, as will be discussed later.

Fröhlich identified the Bec portion of manuscript *E* as a direct copy of the collection for which Anselm may have been requesting Maurice to return him his letters in 1092. In this interpretation, *CV* (=δ), which contain more letters addressed to Maurice than *E*), represent a more extensive, updated version of the collection that *E* also represents; this compilation would have been put together at Bec.[328] These conclusions are both right and wrong. *CV*, their ancestor δ, and the lost source for *E* were once clearly absolutely identical in extent. This was so despite the fact that *AEp.* 58–70 are missing from *E*, and that on the evidence of *CV*, in δ these letters formed one continuous sequence between *AEp.* 57 and 71. This group included the three letters sent to Maurice, which have been held to be conclusive proof for Fröhlich's view.[329] Since *E* forms a single text out of an incomplete version of *AEp.* 57 (minus its two last sentences) and *AEp.* 71 (including only part of the last paragraph), a *lacuna* must be responsible for the omission of this group of letters, as *L* indeed confirms.[330] *L* contains *almost* the same letters from the Bec period in *almost* the same order as δ. *L*'s arrangement only diverges *significantly* from that in *CVE* at the point where *E* omits the thirteen missing letters. *L* includes ten of these letters,[331] one of which appears as *L41*,[332] with the remainder placed a little later, after *AEp.* 51 (*L49*). This group of letters is thus arranged as follows in the various witnesses:

honorando *NMCVE*] orando *LP*; 120:13 mea *CVEM*] *om. LPF*; 122:11 de dilatione *NCVE*] de *om. LP*; 122:30 sed et *EFCVNM*] et *om. LP*.

[328] Fröhlich's argument ('Introduction', 1990, pp. 30–32) clearly built on that of Schmitt ('Zur Entstehungsgeschichte', 1936, pp. 307–308), but extended it in a mistaken direction; according to Schmitt, manuscript *E* is the purest witness to the second stage of development of the collection, but the letters addressed to Maurice are missing because of an accidental omission ('versehentliche Auslassung').

[329] *AEp.* 60, 64, 69.

[330] Fol. 20v.

[331] *L* lacks *AEp.* 63, 64, 65.

[332] *AEp.* 61.

E43–50	AEp. **51**, **53**, **54**, **55**, **56**, 57/71, **72**
CV43–64 (=δ43–64)	AEp. 51, **53**, **54**, **55**, **56**, **57**, 58, 59, 60, 61, 62, 63, 64, 65, 66, 67, 68, 69, 70, 71, **72**
L49–65	AEp. **51**, 58, 68, **53**, 60, **54**, 66, 67, 59, 69, 70, 71, 62, **55**, **56**, **57**, **72**[333]

Three points are noteworthy. (One.) The letters in bold, AEp. 51, 53, 54, 55, 56, 57, and 72, appear in the same order in all three witnesses. (Two.) In L, these letters are interspersed with the sequence of letters missing from E, although L presents one of them a little earlier.[334] (Three.) L places AEp. 72 immediately after AEp. 57, a clear reflection of the limits of the *lacuna*, apparent from E.

It is evident, therefore, that a source containing a *lacuna* influenced the transmission of *both E and L* at some stage. I shall demonstrate below that collection ω stood between L and its damaged source; E, on the other hand, was copied directly from the lacunose (or, less likely, from a lost identical) manuscript. The compiler of ω noted the problem and attempted to remedy it, while the copyist of E failed to observe the *lacuna*. E, then, reveals that the *lacuna* stretches from the words 'Aut si servo' in AEp. 57 to the words 'in hoc saeculo' in AEp. 71.[335] The compiler of ω managed to restore the greater part of the material lost in the *lacuna*, that is ten out of the thirteen letters that had disappeared with the quire, as well as the incomplete AEp. 57 and 71. But he did not know the correct arrangement of the missing letters, only roughly where to put them, and thus the order differs substantially from that in δ, which was unaffected by the *lacuna*.[336]

Because the letters swallowed by the *lacuna* also included some of those addressed to Maurice the number of these letters cannot, contra Fröhlich, be used to determine the place and interrelation-

---

[333] F, which omits most of the Bec letters, has only AEp. 53 and 62 of those mentioned above. Like L, F places AEp. 61 before the sequence.

[334] AEp. 61 = L41.

[335] AEp. 57 line 12, AEp. 71 line 40.

[336] The *lacuna* has not been observed before, while attempts have been made to explain the deficiencies of L as deliberate censorship on Anselm's part. Schmitt, 'Zur Entstehungsgeschichte', 1936, p. 305, Krüger, *Persönlichkeitsausdruck*, 2002, p. 102.

ships of manuscripts *CVEL* in the stemma.[337] Furthermore, textual criticism forces one to conclude that δ, the source for *CV*, derives from an *earlier* stage in the textual tradition than *E*, since δ and α often group together against *ELF*.[338] In the final instance the readings, the arrangement, and the *lacuna* attested by *E* demand two witnesses of identical selection and arrangement of letters to be postulated: one source for δ and the other for *E* and ω, which is *L*'s source. Since the readings of δ's source were closer to the readings in α (or *N*), it was earlier than its copy, which served as the source for ωE. The source for manuscript δ may be called β^1, and that for ωE may be called β^2. Manuscript β^2 was a copy of manuscript β^1.

We may date manuscript β^1 unexpectedly precisely, yet with a fair degree of certainty. The β collection can be linked with Anselm's efforts to collect his letters in the winter of 1092–93. Manuscript β^1, probably the first witness to the β collection, is, however, a little later in date than this, because it and its copy β^2 included seven very early letters from Anselm's Canterbury period. That these letters were appended to β^1 slightly after the completion of its Bec sequence might, too, be a possibility.[339] As

---

[337] *E* lacks *AEp.* 60, 64, 69, all to Maurice, on account of the *lacuna*, and *L* lacks *AEp.* 64.

[338] 13:10 fratri *NCV*] suo *add. ELPF* 16:22 tibi retribuat *NCV*] retribuat tibi *ELP*; 33:4 nostrum *NCV*] domnum *add. ELP*; 34:1 Anselmus *NCV*] quod Gondulfo Anselmus *add. ELP*; 51:28 quicumque *NCV*] qui *ELP*; 51:40 caritatem *NCV*] ueritatem *ELP*; 53:9 ustionem *NMCV*] exustionem *ELPF*; 53:16 enim *NCVM*] *om. ELPF*; 80:39 Si *NMCV*] Et si *LPF* Et. Si *E*; 84:11 ipse *NMCV*] *om. ELP*; 85:10 me *NMCV*] *om. ELPF*; 85:17 merear *NMCV*] uobis *add. ELPF*; 86:7–8 memorari *NMCV*] commemorari *ELP*; 86:14 puniatur sine fine *NMCV*] sine fine puniatur *ELP*; 93:3 de uera *NMCV*] de uestra *ELP*; 101:76 dignitate *NMCV*] uoluntate *ELP om. F* (*M*'s source is unknown); 104:7–8 pro nostro amore si redierit *NMCV*] si redierit pro nostro amore *ELP*; 105:3–4 paenitens et ad *NM*] penitens ad *CV* penitus ad *ELP*; 105:6 intra *NMCV*] inter *ELP*; 109:7 debeant eadem opuscula *NMCV*] eadem opuscula debeant *ELP*; 111:6 mandaui *NMCV*] madauit *ELP*; 111:8 aut litteras *NMCV*] aut *om. ELP*; 115:23 tuam et meam *NMCV*] meam et tuam *ELP*; 117:25 festino in eis *NMCV*] in eis festino *ELPF*. See also 112:25,52; 113:4; 114:14; 120:20,23,47; 121:15,22,23,48; 140:17,23,40; 142:1,10,11,13;143:21; 146:22; 147:11; these letters are missing from *N* and thus also possibly from α. Relying on Schmitt alone is problematic here too, e.g. 117:34 et in] *in om. ELP*; in fact, et in *V*] *in om. ELPFNMC*.

[339] *AEp.* 156–158, 160–162, 180.

has already been observed, δ presented the Canterbury material in two, partially overlapping sections, and there is good reason to believe that the sections derived from two different sources.[340] The first Canterbury section, δ^a, broke off in around 1094 (while the second, δ^b, only ended upon Anselm's death). The following table presents the actual arrangement of all the letters in δ^a and that of the comparable section in $\gamma\delta^b$ and L. The letters in bold appear in each of these witnesses.

δ^a (=C^aV^a) and $\gamma\delta^b$ (=C^bV^b)	AEp. 148–152, 155, **156–158**, 159, **160–162**, 163, 164, 165–167, 170, 172–176, 209, 178, 179, **180**, 123, 124 and $\gamma\delta^b$: AEp. **156–158**, **160–162**, **180**
L	AEp. **156–158**, **160–162**, **180**[341]

Most of the letters in δ^a given in ordinary type in the table are not present in $L\gamma\delta^b$ at all.[342] The simplest explanation is that the letters in ordinary type were material only added to the corpus by the compiler of δ. The content of the letters, of which more shall be said below, also supports this conclusion. Second, δ^a and $\gamma\delta^b$ and L all include the letters in bold, AEp. 156–158, 160–162, and 180, in the same order. The identical order cannot have emerged by chance; rather, it evidences that δ^a and $\gamma\delta^b$ and L are interrelated in some way.[343] The only persuasive explanation is that δ^a

---

[340] The layout of the texts in the witnesses to δ, especially V, clearly reflects the use of two different sources. Two empty lines are left after the final letter of the Bec period (AEp. 147) on fol. 99v, and a much larger initial letter than normal is used for the first letter from the Canterbury period (AEp. 148) on fol. 100r, to mark the change from letters of Bec to those of Canterbury, i.e. the start of V^a. The next break occurs on fol. 116r, indicating the end of the *electus* period. Two misplaced letters from the Bec period conclude V^a. V^b begins on fol. 125r and the break is flagged by empty lines and a larger initial than normal. Since Anselm had already attained Canterbury and full consecration as archbishop, the change in layout no longer reflects his developing career, but must reflect another kind of break, such as a change in the source.

[341] L also incorporates AEp. 149, 153, and 154 among the Bec correspondence, the last two of which were added at a later date.

[342] The following letters appear in δ^a (C^aV^a) only: 123, 124, 150–152, 155, 159, 163–167, 172–176, 178, 179, 209.

[343] It is clear from the context that δ^a and δ^b did not share the source. Textual evidence too shows traces of two distinct sources. Readings unique to δ^a (=C^aV^a) follow; the underlined O variants are anomalies. 156:69 dixi *FLPEOC*^{b}*V*^{b}] me *add. C*^{a}*V*^{a}; 156:69 male me *FLPEC*^{b}*V*^{b}] me *om. C*^{a}*V*^{a} male *om. O*; 156:76 Dicunt *FLPEOC*^{b}*V*^{b}] enim *add. C*^{a}*V*^{a}; 156:92 uiuerem *FOC*^{a}*V*^{a}]

took those seven letters from manuscript β^1 and that $L\gamma\delta^b$ received them from β^2 via collection ω. Consequently the group of the letters in bold gives β^1 the date of late 1093 × 1094 — something that fits very well with our information on Anselm's attempts to collect his letters at the turn of 1092 and 1093.[344]

It is also possible to establish the origin and early provenance of our two lost witnesses to β. β^1 was made in England, where Anselm had requested material to be sent from Normandy. The origin is probably Christ Church, which became Anselm's new home community. β^1, however, ended up in Bec, as may indeed have been the original intention since Anselm was still its abbot when the project commenced.[345] The fact that δ, which used β^1 as its source, was from Bec, provides evidence of this transfer from England to Normandy. In order to demonstrate the Bec origin of

uiuere LPC^bV^b *corr. from* uiuere E; 156:131 deus illum $FLPEOC^bV^b$] illum deus C^aV^a; 156:154 dilexistis FQC^aV^a] dilexisti $LPEC^bV^b$; 156:163 regulam C^aV^a] oboedientiam *add.* $FLPEOC^bV^b$; 156:178 Expedit $FLPEOC^bV^b$] enim *add.* C^aV^a; 156:180 de me $FLPEOC^bV^b$] *om.* C^aV^a; 160:20 diligit minus C^aV^a] minus diligit $LPEOC^bV^b$; 160:26 Delectat C^aV^a] me *add* $LEOC^bV^b$ (*I prefer the reading* Delectat me, *which Schmitt rejected*);160:36 securius uos C^aV^a] uos securius $LEOC^bV^b$; 160:64 si mea me $LEOC^bV^b$] me *om.* C^aV^a; 162:31–32 Omnipotens – Amen] *sequitur propositionem* Lege – monacho C^aV^a. Where F and δ^a agree, the text of β^1 emerges: 161:11 dominus $LPEOC^bV^b$] domnus FC^aV^a; 161:22–23 cum illo in iudicio FC^aV^a] in iudicio cum illo $LPEOC^bV^b$; 161:30 hortetur FC^aV^a] ortetur $LPEOC^bV^b$; 161:44 contra FC^aV^a] aduersum $LPEOC^bV^b$; 162:18 respicit retro $LPEOC^bV^b$] retro respicit FC^aV^a.

[344] *AEp.* 156–158, 160–162 are from the period between Anselm's nomination on 6 March 1093 and his consecration on 4 December 1093, as is clear from their content. The remaining *AEp.* 180 was addressed to Count Robert II of Flanders after his father, Robert I, had died in October 1093 and before he embarked on the first crusade in 1096. The letter, an exhortation for Robert to govern righteously, appears to have been drafted soon after his promotion to count, either in December 1093, after Anselm's own consecration, or in early 1094, as noted by Marabelli in *Anselmo d'Aosta, Archivescovo di Canterbury: Lettere*, eds. I. Biffi & C. Marabelli, vol. 1, Milano, 1990, pp. 206–207, note 1. Such dating is supported also by the style deployed by Anselm; the same phrase 'seruus seruorum Christi Jesu, uocatus archiepiscopus Cantuariae' appears in *AEp.* 169 and 170, the latter of which may be dated to the beginning of 1094 (Schmitt, 'Die Chronologie', 1954, p. 195). Although the case presented here is not absolutely watertight, the combination of evidence — the letter's aim, its salutation, the dating of the other letters in the group — provides an adequately solid dating for *AEp.* 180.

[345] *AEp.* 147.

δ, I must return to the previous list of letters. The non-emphasized letters in δ^a are in the main known only from its derivatives, and it is indeed striking how often this material is associated with Bec. Out of twenty-three letters, fourteen are directly connected with the monastery: ten are letters from Anselm to the monks of Bec,[346] one is from a monk of Bec to Anselm,[347] one from Bishop Gundulf of Rochester to the monks of Bec,[348] while two date from Anselm's Bec years.[349] A further four or five letters are directed to lay magnates and prelates in Normandy and elsewhere in France, and two of these letters touch on Bec's affairs.[350] These letters, one may assume, reached the Continent via Bec. Thus only four letters without a possible connection to Bec remain.[351] I dare suggest that in the list of Bec's books, compiled in the mid twelfth century, either β^1 or γ is itemized. The entry in question reads 'in alio epistole eiusdem ad diuersos'.[352] No known manuscript bears the title 'Epistole Anselmi ad diuersos', nor should the statement that the collection consisted exclusively of out-letters be taken as conclusive evidence. The great majority of the letters in all our manuscripts are out-letters, which was likely to lead to false generalisations of this kind.[353] Furthermore, many of the titles in the list

[346] *AEp.* 148, 151, 164–166, 173, 174, 178, 179, 209.

[347] *AEp.* 155.

[348] *AEp.* 150.

[349] *AEp.* 123, 124.

[350] *AEp. 159* (to the bishop of Evreux), *163* (to William the Conqueror's steward), 167 (to the countess of Boulogne), 175 (to the abbot and monks of the monastery of St Martin, Séez), 176 (to the archbishop of Lyon). The letters in italics are related to Bec in that Anselm entrusted the monastery to the protection of the recipient. The recipient of *AEp.* 163, Eudo dapifer, possessed extensive estates in both Normandy and England; he died at his castle of Préaux and was buried at Colchester.

[351] *AEp.* 149, 152 (letters to Anselm from Osbern, a monk of Canterbury, in 1093), 170 (to the bishop of Worcester at the start of 1094), 172 (to the bishop of Exeter, 1094–97).

[352] H. OMONT (ed.), *Tituli librorum Beccensis almarii*, in *Catalogue général des manuscrits des bibliothèques publiques de France*, vol. 2, Paris, 1888, p. 382.

[353] *C*, one of our two key witnesses to δ, has a title 'Epistole quas dictauit beatus anselmus post adeptum pallium sui archiepiscopatus' (fol. 81r). The title is incorrect on two counts since, first, the subsequent sequence begins with letters preceding Anselm's reception of the pallium and, secondly, it also includes several in-letters.

are very generic in character, being succinct rather than precise. If encountered in a manuscript, the title by which the Bec's book list designates Anselm's letters would be too generic for a conclusive identification without further evidence.[354]

I shall shortly demonstrate that ω, which drew on β^2 as one of its sources, was from Canterbury. Thus β^2 was made for Christ Church, possibly immediately upon the completion of its exemplar β^1. The fact that β^2 must have lost a quire before the creation of ω makes it possible to put forward some relatively strong suggestions as to the manuscript's external characteristics. For example, in manuscript V, the material included in β^2 occupies 167 pages in total, and the material lost in the *lacuna* takes up some 19 pages. On the basis of these figures, β^2 may be calculated to have had around 141 pages or 70 folios.

β^1 and its descendant β^2 together established a homogenous basis for the Bec and Christ Church branches of the tradition of the Bec correspondence. The letters added at the subsequent stages in each scriptorium and the damage to β^2, however, differentiated the two branches. The text of β^1 — from which β^2 must be derived — can be restored through the following principal agreements.

(1) β^1 is the agreement of C and/ or V with E.
(2) Where CV agree against E, β^1 is either the agreement of CV and $L(F)$, or of E and $L(F)$, although the latter combination may reach only β^2.[355]

2.17 *The final collection:* ω

Our textual evidence requires a third collection to be postulated. This is ω. The collection comprised both the Bec and the Canterbury correspondence. If ω was authorial, Anselm commissioned it in the last years of his life.

---

[354] We may note, however, that the title in V, the second of our two key witnesses to δ, is closer to that found in the list than those found in any other surviving manuscripts. V reads: 'Epistole sancti Anselmi quondam Cantuariensis archiepiscopi ad diuersos et plurimum ad ipsum ab i usque 289'. The hand is of André Hausselet, the late fifteenth-century librarian of Saint-Victor, but he might have constructed his entry from an earlier title.

[355] One must take into account E's contamination from L. If the passage in question was contaminated (at least some and perhaps all cases are indicated by later corrections than those made by the scribe of the manuscript), then the agreement of LE has no evidential value.

The Bec correspondence

The Bec correspondence is arranged identically in LF, although F presents a more limited selection of letters than L. F too was clearly influenced by the same *lacuna* in its source as L, and the same changes to the arrangement of the letters, resulting from attempts to fill the gap, are visible in F as well as in L. As discussed above, F and L are independent of each other; each of the two occasionally agrees with manuscripts $NCVE$ against the other. Both manuscripts LF thus clearly descend from the same source independently of each other. This source is collection ω.

As demonstrated previously, E is the closest to ω of the witnesses to the β-stage. Both E and ω relied on the same damaged manuscript, β^2. Thus the Bec correspondence in ω may be reconstructed according to the following principles. ω is:

(1) the agreement of LF
(2) the agreement of L or F with E[356]
(3) for the material missing from E, the agreement of L or F with CV.

The Canterbury correspondence

The following conclusions and the results of the analyses presented above are central to the argument of this discussion.

(1) The first sequence of Canterbury correspondence in the Bec branch is δ^a (the agreement of $C^a V^a$)
(2) The second sequence of Canterbury correspondence in the Bec branch is δ^b (the agreement of $C^b V^b$).
(3) As δ^b derives from γ (the agreement of $OC^b V^b$), δ^b can be eliminated.
(4) As PE derive from L, PE can be eliminated.
(5) L, γ, δ^a and F are at least partly independent of one another.

Since the letters appear in an almost identical order in the witnesses L, γ, and F, it is clear that ultimately all must be influenced by the same source. This is the aforementioned ω. With the aid of δ^a, which is independent of ω as it derives from β^1 (and the Bec archives), we can adjudge the relationship between ω's witnesses

---

[356] E's contamination from L undermines the evidential value of LE agreements.

L, γ, and F.[357] Three letters alone appear in each of these four witnesses, L, γ, F, and δ^a. These letters are AEp. 156, 161, and 162. Only a comparison of these letters can reveal the internal relationships within this group. I have analyzed AEp. 156 by picking out the variant readings reported in Schmitt's apparatus, which evidence I then rechecked in the manuscripts. I have collated AEp. 161 and 162, taking into account all the branches or our tradition (and not only those manuscripts discussed in this chapter). The results of the analysis are presented most clearly with reference to δ^a's relationships with ω's three witnesses. If the anomalies discussed in the footnote are accepted, then:[358]

(1) δ^a does not agree with L against $F\gamma$.
(2) δ^a does not agree with γ against LF.
(3) δ^a agrees in certain cases with F against $L\gamma$.[359]

There are two straightforward explanations for the agreement of δ^aF against $L\gamma$. Either $L\gamma$ descend from ω via a lost intermediate manuscript independently of each other, while F descends from ω independently of that intermediate, or the tradition is contaminated. The latter alternative is much more likely, as γ contains clear traces of L in particular and of its 'appendix' L^a. Four arguments favouring this position set out the case.

(One.) As was noted above, L's original arrangement was changed by the insertion of AEp. 469 between AEp. 468 and 471 at the end of the manuscript. The first copy of AEp. 469 in L, which is now in L^a on fol. 188r–v, contains a number of readings which are not known in any other copy; that is, they do not appear in

---

[357] Without the fourth witness, the disagreements between $LF\gamma$ could be explained as errors made by their copyists. We may only suspect contamination if one witness presents a reading that is clearly stronger than those in the other two.

[358] 156:92 uiuerem FC^aV^aQ] uiuere LC^bV^b; 156:119 Forsitan $F\underline{V^aV^b}$] Forsan $L\underline{OC^aC^b}$; 156:154 dilexistis FC^aV^aQ] dilexisti LC^bV^b; 156:179 Hanc epistolam nostram $FV^a\underline{V^b}C^a$] Hanc epistolam uestram LC^b corr. from uestram O.

[359] 161:11 dominus LC^bV^b] domnus C^aV^aFMD; 161:22–23 cum illo in iudicio FC^aV^a] in iudicio cum illo LC^bV^b; 161:44 contra FC^aV^a] aduersum LC^bV^b; 162:18 respicit retro LC^bV^b] retro respicit FC^aV^a. At least one instance cited among the anomalies can be included here: 156:179 Hanc epistolam nostram $FV^a\underline{V^b}C^a$] Hanc epistolam uestram LC^b corr. from uestram O, in which V^b's opposing location may be explained by an improvement made on the basis of the context.

$LPEC^b$. L^a's unique readings are clearly erroneous, with one exception, however. In the *salutatio*, L^a designates Anselm plainly as 'archiepiscopus', where all the other copies have 'archiepiscopus cantuariensis'.[360] The longer reading arose when AEp. 469 replaced AEp. 471 in L. The opening of AEp. 471 was erased from the end of fol. 159v, apart from its first line, which read 'Anselmus archiepiscopus cantuariensis'. This passage was preserved because it was close enough to the original reading in AEp. 469, which did not include 'cantuariensis'. We may conclude that γ followed the reading that had emerged solely because of the rearrangement in L.[361]

(Two.) Contamination from L to γ may also be indicated by γ's inclusion of letters only added to L^a at a later date. If these letters had been available in L's source, they would likely have been included in the original selection of letters in L.[362] Furthermore, γ only included some of these letters, namely those for which the correct place in the sequence was indicated by the marginal instructions in L.[363] The 'correct' arrangement of these letters, which γ followed, may only have been established when the letters were copied into L^a. The evidence of P supports this conclusion. Of the additional letters in L^a, P, which is slightly older than these additions, includes only AEp. 331. P appears to have derived the letter from an unknown source, and does not place it in accordance with the instructions in L and L^a.[364] The arrangement of these letters was thus only finalized with the copying of L^a, and γ followed suit.

---

[360] Both the forms 'Anselmus archiepiscopus' and 'Anselmus archiepiscopus Cantuariensis' appear in many letters, the former occurring in tens of letters even.

[361] The end of F supports this view. The last four letters in the collection, with which L also originally ended before the addition of AEp. 469, are AEp. 467, 468, 471 and 472. F's testimony is however weakened by the fact that the manuscript omits several letters.

[362] Perhaps with the exception of AEp. 193, the contents of none of these letters are such as to suggest that the compiler of L might have censored them.

[363] On the basis of δ^b, AEp. 193, 212, 331, and 411.

[364] The context of AEp. 331 in $P(234\text{--}236)$: AEp. 297, 331, 298; in LEC^b: AEp. 303, 331, 334.

(Three.) The arrangement of this group of letters in $\gamma\delta^b$ indicates the influence of L in another way as well. C^b suggests that at least one of these letters was placed at the end of γ and furnished with a marginal annotation, close to those in L, indicating its correct location. Again γ follows a practice created by L^a.

(Four.) The marginalia in L and C^b differ considerably, however. While the annotation in L was clearly intended to aid future copyists, that in C^b has no such explicit intention. Rather, C^b's entry might have been intended for readers.[365] It is more natural to consider that L lies behind γ's marginal annotation than vice versa.

All these points suggest that L contaminated γ.[366] The data from the computer-assisted analysis support this conclusion, although the algorithm is unable to demonstrate contamination. In the RHM stemma, OC^bV^b, the witnesses to γ, appear between L and F. In contrast, F lies nearer to the witnesses to δ^a than to L and γ, because it is not tainted by L. The analysis also takes into account manuscript M (at this point in part a copy of F), the group GB (to be discussed at the end of this chapter), and L's descendants EP. The fact that E is positioned at a point on the line a little apart from L, towards the Bec branch, might indicate contamination from manuscript β^2 in E.

---

[365] L fol. 78v: 'Ante istam scribatur epistola quae in fine habetur. quae sic incipit; Henricus dei gratia rex ad predictum signum [*AEp.* 212].' C fol. 93r: 'hec epistola scilicet Henricus dei gratia rex anglorum deberet hic esse. Que est in fine libri ad tale signum [*AEp.* 212].' One should again recall that γ was not apparently solely dependent on L, even for the letters in L^a. In *AEp.* 331 the readings of C^b and P both agree against L^a in a way that raises the suspicion that they were influenced by a source other than L^a; 331:29 de debitis et de terris L^aE] de debitis et terris C^bP; 331:31 iuuenibus L^aE] iuuenculis C^bP.

[366] The direction of contamination may also be tested in another way, by drawing up the various possible *stemmata* for the manuscripts suggested by the analysis of δ^a's potential relationships above. There are twelve such potential *stemmata* in all, of which eight can be rejected since they cannot explain the disagreement between δ^aF and $L\gamma$. The four remaining solutions are: (1) F was contaminated by δ^a; (2) L was contaminated by γ; (3) δ^a was contaminated by F; (4) γ was contaminated by L. The provenance and content of the manuscripts allow the three first solutions to be eliminated.

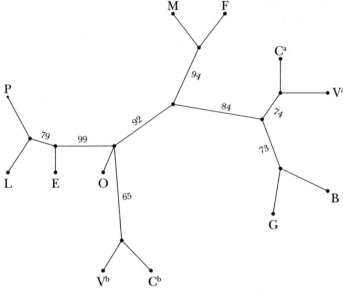

Figure 5: *AEp*. 161 and 162 in an RHM consensus tree

The previous leads to the conclusion that ω's readings are indicated by L, δ^a, γ, and F according to the following agreements. ω's Canterbury correspondence is:

(1)   the agreement of F with one or more of the witnesses $L\delta^a\gamma$.
(2)   the agreement of δ^a with one or more of the witnesses $L\gamma F$.

Both F and δ^a, particularly the latter, are regrettably weak in containing only some of the letters in ω. Furthermore, F abridges most of the letters, which are sometimes also edited in other ways. Fortunately ω's readings may also be restored from Eadmer's *Historia nouorum*, which is completely independent of the surviving Anselmian letter manuscripts, and possibly to some extent also of ω.[367] (The *Historia nouorum* is to be discussed briefly in Appen-

---

[367] Certain letters present in both *Historia nouorum* (referred to as *r*) and the witnesses to ω reveal the independent transmission of *Historia nouorum*: e.g. *AEp*. 171:5–11 Nouit − defendant *r*] *om. LC^b*; 201:19–20 a uestra paternitate *r*] *om. LC^b*. In addition, *r* includes seven Anselmian letters that are not known to the witnesses to ω, plus five letters in which Anselm is neither the recipient nor the sender of the letter. The Anselmian letters are: *AEp*. 282 (Paschal II to Anselm), 310 (prior Ernulf to Anselm), 365 (from an anonymous sender to

dix I.) Thus the further agreement may be added to the foregoing, that ω is *probably*:

(3)   The agreement of *Historia nouorum* with one or more of the witnesses $L\gamma F$.

The extant manuscripts do not permit us to draw up a complete picture of the contents of ω, or to measure the full extent of the contamination in γ. Since $F\gamma$ agree against L fairly often, it is likely that ω served as γ's principal source and that for the most part the text was contaminated only by individual readings from L. In this case ω would by and large be the agreement of $L\gamma$ $(=LC^b V^b)$.

2.18 *The minor representatives of the group:* GB

Trier, Stadtbibliothek 728/282, fols. 103r–136v – G

s. xii$^{2-3/3}$; (?)St Eucharius / St Matthias, Trier (OSB), parchment; 151 fols.; 165 × 110 (110 × 70) mm; 20 (long) lines

Contents

fols. 1r–102v	Hugh of Saint-Victor, *De sacramentis christianae fidei* (*PL* 176, cols. 173–618, sections do not follow the order in *PL*)
fols. 103r–136v	Anselm, *Epistolae* (*G*) (capitula on fol. 103r–v)
fols. 136v–137r	Anselm?, '*Si mihi transituro fluuium*' (SCHMITT, 'Eine fruehe Rezension', 1936, pp. 69–70)
fols. 137r–139r	Anselm?, '*Est considerandum*' (*Memorials*, pp. 334–336)
fol. 139r	Anselm?, '*Velle esse eisdem*'[368] (*Memorials*, p. 351:4)
fol. 139r–v	'De usu pallii', unidentified, 'Pallii usus inter caetera tantae uirtutis est – ad tantae perfectionis priuilegium peruenire non meruit.'
fols. 139v–145r	Pseudo-Cyprian of Carthage, *Epistula ad Turasium de morte filiae suae consolatoria*[369]

Anselm), 367 (Henry I to Anselm), 442 (Anselm to bishop Ranulf of Durham), 456 (archbishop-*electus* Thomas of York to Anselm, a fragment), 470 (Henry I to Anselm).

[368] The *Memorials* share *L*'s reading 'Velle eisdem'.

[369] Here attributed to Jerome, as this text often was. After the text (fol. 145r): 'Expliciunt omnia feliciter in domino. AMEN', an annotation which may have referred to the entire manuscript. The following text may be a little later addition, as the general appearance of the hand changes slightly.

fols. 145v–151v Petrus Pictor, *Liber de sacramentis* ('Prologus' and l. 1–136, *CCCM* 25, pp. 11–22)

Trier, Stadtbibliothek 728/282 is a German compilation from the mid or later twelfth century.[370] An anathema on fol. 1r in a slightly later hand identifies the monastery of St Eucharius / St Matthias as the owner of the manuscript.[371] The manuscript very likely originated, then, in Trier. A single hand copied all texts and perhaps carried out the corrections, which are slightly less formal. No quire marks are visible and the quiring remains unknown. But, because there is only one hand, we may presume that the manuscript represents a single book. The book has lost an unknown number of folios, however, since the last text, *Liber de sacramentis* by Petrus Pictor, ends abruptly. G comprises 14 letters, including *AEp*. 168, known only from this manuscript and its sibling B.[372] An even rarer text is '*Si mihi transituro fluuium*', our earliest sketch towards the *De concordia*, which is unique to this manuscript.[373]

Brussels, Bibliothèque Royale de Belgique 8386–96, fols. 212r–217v − B

s. xii[3/3]; ?Flanders; three codicological units; parchment; (ii + iv +) 220[374] + iii'; c. 255 × 175 (c. 175 × 120) mm; 30 (long) lines

[370] For example the letter g is a straight-backed *Rücken*-g and the *punctus eleuatus* is of German type, although the latter is not quite the basic 'point and seven' type. Here the upper element is a straight stroke, rising diagonally, sometimes with a small crossbar to the left. Absolutely identical *punctus eleuatus* is known from the monastery of Fulda in 1176–77: Leiden, Universiteitsbibliotheek Vulc. 46, fol. 130v, 131r, reproduced in *CMDNL*, 1, pl. 91, 92.

[371] Fol. 1r: 'Codex sancti Eucharii primi treuirorum archiepiscopi quem siquis furto abstulerit. auctoritate dei omnipotentis et omnium sanctorum eius. anathemati subdatur. atque aeterna careat mansione quam preparauit deus his qui diligent illum. nisi restituerit furtum. Amen.'

[372] *AEp*. 101, 112, 417 (*Epistola de sacramentis*), 121, 168, 258, 231, 37, 65, 160, 161, 188, 281, 285.

[373] F. S. Schmitt, 'Eine fruehe Rezension des Werkes De concordia des Hl. Anselm von Canterbury', *Revue Bénédictine*, 48 (1936), p. 54. The two subsequent Anselmian texts are also rare; they survive only in G and the final part of Lambeth Palace 59.

[374] Fol. 104 twice.

Contents

Folio 2r has an entry in a seventeenth-century hand, according to which the manuscript was brought to Belgium from the 'churches robbed bare' of England, and sold; initially owned by Abraham Ortelius († 1598), the famous cartographer and humanist, it was later acquired by the Jesuits of Antwerp. The Jesuits purchased the manuscript at the auction held shortly after Ortelius's

---

[375] *Sermo in honorem sanctae crucis in die nostrae redemptionis* (Odo of Canterbury, *Latin Sermons of Odo of Canterbury*, ed. C. DE CLERCQ with R. MACKEN, *Verhandelingen van de Koninklijke Academie voor Wetenschappen, Letteren en Schone Kunsten van België, Klasse der letteren*, 105, Brussels 1983, pp. 41–85); *Sermo de muliere Chananea* (*ibid.*, pp. 265–298); *Sermo de penitentia Dauid* (*ibid.*, pp. 299–307).

death.[376] Once in Antwerp, it was natural for the manuscript to make its way to the Bollandists, whose signum was previously to be found on the binding.[377] The palaeographical evidence suggests that the manuscript is not English, however. For example, the straight-backed *Rücken*-g and the relatively late use of the e-caudata favour a continental origin, perhaps in the German-speaking world or in Flanders. The hand is also very like some samples of hands known from Bonne Espérance, dated between 1178 and 1183.[378] A Flemish origin is further supported by a short epitaph after the letters, which is also known from the manuscript Brussels, Bibliothèque Royale de Belgique 9119.[379] In Brussels 9119, the epitaph follows Eadmer's *Vita Anselmi*, and according to the modern editor of the *Vita*, Brussels 9119 probably belongs a family that was disseminated particularly in Flanders.[380] Also the small group of short excerpts from texts related to penitence placed in the middle of the letters appears to have a connection to Flanders. The texts seem related to *Collectaneum miscellaneum* by Sedulius Scottus (*s.* ix), who had served as a teacher in Liège, and possibly to Pseudo-Augustinus Belgicus (*s.* xii). It should also be noted that the annotation attesting to an English origin is of significantly later date, in 1598 at the earliest. Insofar as Ortelius ever owned the manuscript, he could have acquired it in Belgium or Germany, where he travelled extensively, though he is known to have vis-

---

[376] F. 2r: 'LIBER HIC MEMBRANACEVS EX ANGLIAE calamitate uastatis ab Iconoclastis Ecclesiis sub Henrico VIII. Rege, in Belgium uerum allatus, e Bibliotheca Abrahami Ortelii redemptus est. in auctione publica ab And[rea] Schotto Antuerpiano, Soc. Iesu.' F. 7r: 'Collegij Societis JESU Antuerpiae 1598'.

[377] *Catalogus codicum hagiographicorum bibliothecae regiae Bruxellensis: codices latini membranei*, eds. Hagiographi Bollandiani, Brussels 1889, p. 208: '✝ Ms 200'.

[378] Cf. The Hague, Koninklijke Bibliotheek 76 E 15, fol. 37v, 54v, 56r, 96r = *CMDNL*, pl. 96, 97, 99, 100.

[379] Fol. 217v: 'Extitit anselmus. uir laude per omnia dignus. / Claruit in clero. fuit illi fortior ordo. / Monachus egregius. fuit abbas. postea summus. / Anglorum presul. Sapiens. & religiosus.'

[380] Information from: Eadmer, *VA*, p. xviii. It should be noted that Southern did not see the manuscript himself; he assigned the manuscript the date *s.* xii.

ited England as well.[381] *B* has only a small selection of Anselm's texts, and it likewise abridges certain letters considerably. The letter section includes: *AEp.* 121:1–2, 14–50; extracts on penitence from various authors, Sedulius Scottus?; and *AEp.* 112, 37:1–80, 161, 162, 168.[382]

The source for GB*:* ε

On the basis of the selection of letters and their arrangement, *B* and *G* seem closely related. *B* includes six letters, while *G* has fourteen letters in total. Five of the letters in *B* also appear in *G*, which only omits *AEp.* 162. The arrangement of the letters is identical with one exception: in *B AEp.* 121 precedes *AEp.* 112 and comes after it in *G*. The otherwise unknown *AEp.* 168 and my collations of *AEp.* 37 and 161, too, provide clear proof of a kinship between the manuscripts.[383] Textual criticism of *BG* and the other manuscripts produces some surprising results, however. I shall begin with the Bec correspondence.

In the letters from Anselm's Bec period, *B* and *G* fall at opposite ends of the sequence *β¹*–*β²*–ω, which begins in Bec and ends in Christ Church. *B* approaches the Bec manuscript *β¹*, while *G* on

---

[381] On the relationship between Ortelius and the library of the Antwerp Jesuits, see C. A. LADD, 'The 'Rubens' Manuscript and Archbishop Ælfric's Vocabulary', *Review of English Studies*, New Series, 11/44 (1960), pp. 357–358.

[382] I have not been able to locate an identical text to the extracts on penitence, and this could well be a potpourri perhaps made up out of six sections. Sedulius Scottus (fl. 848–860) seems the best represented author. (1) Penitentia est medicamentum – luctus et lacrimarum: Defensor Locogiacensis, *Liber scintillarum*, *CPL* 1302, cap. 9, sententia 55; cf. Pseudo-Augustinus Belgicus, *PL* 40, col. 1315 and Sedulius Scottus, *Collectaneum miscellaneum*, *CCCM* 67, Diuisio 13, subdiuisio 20, sententia 5. (2) Cor enim contritum – non despicit: cf. Ps 50,19. (3) Veruntamen quantum in peccando – esse in penitendo; unidentified. (4) Sed et qui circa finem suum – quam ueniat penitentia: Isidore of Seville, *De ecclesiasticis officiis*, *CPL* 1207, lib. 2, cap. 17, linea 73 ff. (5) Sicut enim nulli iustorum – medicamenta confugerit: Caesarius of Arles, *CPL* 1008, *CCSL* 103, *Sermo* 56, cap. 2. (6) In qua enim die – illius obliuioni tradetur: cf. Ez 18,21–22 and Sedulius Scottus, *Collectaneum miscellaneum*, Diuisio 13, subdiuisio 20, sententia 6a.

[383] 37:1 fratri frater] frater fratri *GB*; 37:4 consolatur] consolabitur *GB*; 161:26 alio] aliae *GB*. See also 161:53 suo canonico] canonico suo *G* suo *om.* B.

the other hand supports the Christ Church tradition.[384] Nevertheless, G agrees with the Bec tradition against that of Christ Church
in some cases.[385]

The Canterbury correspondence common to both manuscripts
includes material from the earliest years alone. In *AEp.* 161, G and
B clearly represent the same branch, with an obvious connection
to the Bec tradition (the surviving manuscript witnesses to which
are V and C).[386] *AEp.* 162, which is found in B but not in G, supports the result produced by the Bec correspondence: B not only
represents the Bec branch of the transmission,[387] but it descends
either from manuscript β^1 — at least one generation above δ^a from
which $C^a V^a$ derive — or the Bec archives.[388] *AEp.* 160 is absent from

[384] 37:19 Urso *NMCVEB*] Ursione *LPFG* (there is an error in Schmitt's
apparatus for *E*); 37:81 ursus *NCVE*] ursio *LPFG lacuna in B*; 101:33 ali-
quantulum *NCVE*] aliquamtum *LPFG* (*101 not in B*); 101:61 flecti possit
NCV] possit flecti *ELPFG*; 101:76 dignitate *NCV*] uoluntate *ELPG om. F*;
101:79 Amen. *NCVE*] *om. LPFG*; 112:34 mercem *CVEB*] mercedem *LPFMG*;
112:52 uero *CVB*] *om. ELPFG*; 112:67 honorari aut *CVB*] honorari et *ELPFG*;
112:69–70 illum amorem habere *ELPFG*] habere illum amorem *CVB*; 121:22
calcantium *CVB*] conculcantium *ELPFG*; 121:24 simul *CVEB*] *om. LPFMG*.
See also 101:24 scelerum *NECV*] *om. LPF* peccatorum *G*; 112:42 conglutinari
CVEFB] conglutinare *LP* glutinare *G*.

[385] 37:15 dei dispositioni *NCVEGB*] dispositioni dei *LPF*; 101:21 ponere
NCVEG] proponere *LPF*; 101:47 monachicae *NCVEG*] monasticae *LPF*. Cf.
also 37:93 conspectui *LPECV*] in conspectu *FMDG lacuna in B*. Moreover, in
the case of *AEp.* 65, which ω and its descendants lacked because of the damage to β^2, *G* is closer to β than to 'α' or the minor collections, referred to as
SWH and to be discussed later. 65:1 abbati reuerendo *NMDSWH*] reuerendo
abbati *CVG*; 65:47 contenderint *NMDSWH*] contenderunt *CVG*; 65:92 bene
NMDSWH] *om. CVG*.

[386] 161:11 dominus *LPEOC^bV^b*] domnus *C^aV^aFGB*; 161:17 sapientiori
C^aV^aC^bV^bFMDGB] sipientiori *LPE*; 161:20 qui *C^aV^aC^bV^bEFMDGB*] quid *LP*;
161:22–23 cum illo in iudicio *FC^aV^aGB*] in iudicio cum illo *LPEC^bV^b*; (161:30
hortetur *FC^aV^aGB*] ortetur *LPEC^bV^b*;) 161:44 contra *FC^aV^aGB*] aduersum
LPEC^bV^b. Cf. also 161:45 eligit *LPEFMC^bV^b*] elegit *C^aV^aOG lacuna in B. AEp.*
162 in B (not present in *G*) clearly represents the Bec tradition.

[387] 162:1 parisiensis *FOV^aV^bC^aC^bB*] pariensis *LPE*; 162:14 persuadeat
FLPEC^aV^aO] persuadet *C^bV^b*; 162:18 respicit retro *LPEOC^bV^b*] retro respicit
C^aV^aBFMD;162:33–34 monachicam uitam *FLPEOC^bV^b*] uitam monachicam
C^aV^aB.

[388] 162:31–32 Omnipotens – Amen *sequitur propositionem* Lege – monacho
C^aV^a, where B follows the reading in the other manuscripts.

B but present in *G*; in this letter *G* conversely distances itself from the Bec tradition and represents the Christ Church branch.[389] *G* seems to reach back to Anselm's archive.[390] This conjecture is corroborated by *G*'s inclusion of '*Si mihi transituro fluuium*', an otherwise unknown sketch towards the *De concordia*, and, above all, by its other unfinished Anselmian pieces, which are also found in *L*[a] and must come from his archive.[391] In these texts, the witness of *G* is often stronger than that of *L*[a].[392] The only plausible conclusion is that this material was derived from Christ Church's archives independently of *L*.

Since *G* is of German origin, it is likely to derive from a lost identical or near-identical compilation. Otherwise we must raise the possibility that a scribe from Trier came to Canterbury in order to copy texts of Hugh of Saint-Victor, and after having completed his task, appended to his manuscript Anselmian letters and miscellanea, some directly from the Christ Church archives. The *editio princeps* of the letters (Nuremberg 1491), which may be called *a*, includes the same selection of letters as *G*, and indeed seems to be based on *G*'s lost exemplar. This is because *a*'s text is sometimes stronger than *G*'s.[393]

---

[389] 160:20 diligit minus C^aV^a] minus diligit $LPEOC^bV^bG$; 160:26 Delectat C^aV^a] me *add* $LEOC^bV^bG$; 160:36 securius uos C^aV^a] uos securius $LEOC^bV^bG$; 160:64 si mea me $LEOC^bV^bG$] me *om.* C^aV^a.

[390] 281:15 hoc immane FGC^bV^b] hoc in immane *LP corr. from* hoc in immane *E*; 281:31 uindicaret LPC^bV^b] uendicaret *FG* uendicaret *from* uindicaret *in another hand E*; 285:19 est² OC^bV^bFG] *om. LPE*.

[391] '*Si mihi transituro fluuium*' possibly reaches beyond ω to the Christ Church archives.

[392] '*Est considerandum*' (*Memorials*, pp. 334–336) and 139r '*Velle eisdem*' (*Memorials*, p. 351:4). In certain places, *G* has better readings than L^a. (Where superscript numbers are attached to siglum L^a, they denote either the first or second occurrence of the given text in Lambeth 59.) '*Est considerandum*': 335:7 uolendi *G*] uolundi L^{a2}; 335:8 eam *G*] eum L^{a2}. '*Velle eisdem*': 351:6 sex *G*] sed $L^{a1, 2}$; 351:7 diuersitatibus *G*] diuersitati L^a; 351:9 uolumus salutem *G*] uolutem L^a. *G*'s own weak readings include: 335:28 Quando] Quod; 351:7 quot] quod.

[393] My collation of *AEp.* 65 only notes *a* where there are weak readings in *G*. *AEp.* 37:11 quo *a*] quem *G*; 37:33 mutari non ualet *a*] non ualet mutari *G*; 65:4 mihi dulcis sit *a*] mihi dulcis mihi sit *G*; 161:24 oneratos *a*] onerates *from* onerantes *G*; 161:43 dominus dicit *a*] dictum est a domino *G*; 161:64 pingi *a*] depingi *G*.

The following conclusions may be drawn from the discussion above:

(1) *GB* both descend from a single source, derived from $\beta^{\prime}$; this is ε

(2) There is at least one step in the transmission between ε and *G*; this is ζ

(3) *G* and *a* (*editio princeps*) derive from ζ

(4) ζ received contamination and additional material from ω or the Christ Church archives

The near-identical arrangement of the letters in *GB* suggests that ε was likely to be a coherent manuscript, not a mass of loose leaves. While ε cannot be restored with certainty, it must have contained the letters shared by *GB* at least. Both ε and ζ are likely to be very early since even ζ appears to precede ω. ζ's latest text is *Epistola de sacramentis ecclesiae*, providing it with the *a quo* of 1101 × ?1103.[394] *AEp.* 168, which ε included, is otherwise unknown and of great interest. In this letter Anselm sought to persuade King Harold's daughter Gunhild to return to monastic life in surprisingly violent language. A misunderstanding about Gunhild's status obviously lay behind the letter, and the case must have been embarrassing for Anselm.[395] The compiler of ε was either unaware of or unconcerned with the problems surrounding the letter. He was hardly an Englishman, a conclusion that supports the results from the above textual analyses. *AEp.* 168's availability in Bec would also comply with our understanding of how the earliest extant archiepiscopal letters were transmitted; they survive predominantly through the Bec tradition.

---

[394] Sharpe, 'Anselm as author', 2009, table 2.

[395] See R. SHARPE, 'King Harold's daughter', *Haskins Society Journal*, 19 (2008), pp. 1–27.

2.19 *Conclusions:* β *and* ω *as* stemmata

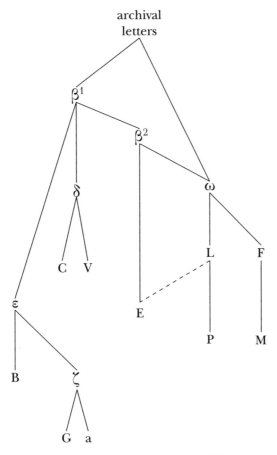

Figure 6: The Bec correspondence[396]

[396] *N* also used another source; *M* also used *F* and one or more other sources; for the *α* branch see figures 1 and 2. The broken line indicates contamination.

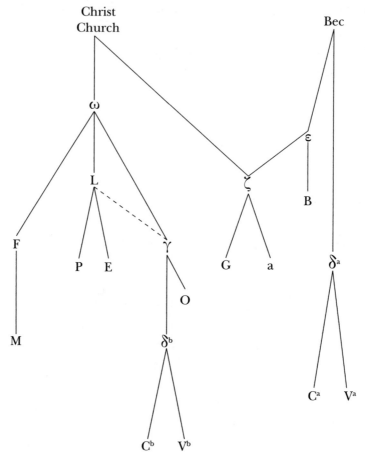

Figure 7: The Canterbury correspondence[397]

3. THE MAKING OF THE MAJOR COLLECTIONS AND MANUSCRIPT L

3.1 *The sources of the Bec correspondence for* $\alpha\beta\omega$

$\alpha\beta\omega$ appear to have drawn on single-sheet letters, although ω also depended on β in part. (This discussion too refers to α without addressing uncertainties about its existence.)[398] This is reflected by

---

[397] M also used the *Historia nouorum* as a source; for the α branch see figures 1 and 2. The broken line indicates contamination.

[398] If α never existed, the siglum α should be replaced by N in this discussion.

how the numbers of possible drafts or rejected versions decline as one proceeds through the collections in the order $\alpha\text{–}\beta^1\text{–}\beta^2\text{–}\omega$. This phenomenon is probably in direct relationship with the gradual return of the actual letters to Anselm. The texts of twelve letters in the α stage (NM) differ significantly from those either in $\beta\omega$ or in ω. Usually $\beta\omega$ offer identical readings, with α differing, but sometimes the readings of $\alpha\beta$ differ from ω.[399] In contrast, $\alpha\omega$ never agree in such readings against β. At least in four cases, the appearance of two versions of given letters in our manuscripts is best explained by the fact that Anselm had not apparently commissioned copies of all the letters he sent, and the gradual process by which the letters were returned to him.[400]

(One.) The version of AEp. 89 in α gives full details of King William's demands for watertight evidence regarding certain donations to the monastery of Bec.[401] $\beta\omega$ replace the passage with the statement that the courier bringing the letter would have more to

---

[399] AEp. 17, 25, 29.

[400] When the alternative versions of the letters differ only in length, with α preserving the shortest text, we cannot be sure whether a rejected version or a draft of a given letter in α, or scribal revision (possibly under Anselm's guidance) in α, β, or ω is responsible. If the latter is true, the scribe of α may be responsible for these differences, as he may perhaps have omitted the odd word or passage from his source; it is perhaps less likely that the scribe of β or ω would have added short passages to clarify the contents of the letters. AEp. 98:11 offers a good example of a case that is difficult to characterize in this way. The reading in $\beta\omega$ (CVE and L) states that Lanfranc received Anselm 'apud uillam ipsius, nomine Limingis'. The words 'apud – nomine' are missing from N and the words 'apud – Limingis' from M. The scribe of M left space to allow the words to be added later, but this was never done. See also AEp. 117:59 olim cum similiter, ut modo sum, in Angliam essem $\beta\omega$ (CVE and LF)] nuper postquam iui in Angliam α (NM). The letter is from Anselm's visit to England in 1086. The reading in α gives the impression that Anselm was referring to his current visit, whereas $\beta\omega$'s text points out that the reference is to a previous visit. As the change touches a minor and hardly well known point, Anselm himself is likely to have been behind the change, even if this was an addition made by the copyist of β. In AEp. 29:4, $\alpha\beta$ (N and CVE) agree against ω (LF). In both texts, the recipient of the letter is urged 'ad notandum Antiphonarium', which ω qualifies 'secundum regulam musicae artis'. M received this letter from its F source, and therefore it does not witness to α.

[401] AEp. 89:25–38 α (NM).

say regarding 'the affairs of our church'.[402] Such revision implies that the version attested by α was earlier and never despatched whereas $\beta\omega$'s version represents the text sent to the addressee.[403]

(Two.) The text of *AEp.* 97 in α discusses one subject only, the case of the monk Theduinus, who had left his monastery for the court of the French king. In contrast, the version in $\beta\omega$ phrases the matter differently and at slightly greater length, but without naming Theduinus; Anselm also appended a sketch towards the treatise that would become *De casu diaboli* to the new version of the letter, as Maurice, its recipient, had asked for a copy.[404]

(Three.) A more complex case is *AEp.* 25. Schmitt believed the letter to survive in three successive versions: one in N, a second in β, and a third in ω. (As M does not include the letter, it may have been absent from α as well; therefore N is referred to here.) Behind our manuscripts, there were apparently only two authorial versions, however; one is attested by ω and the other, albeit imperfectly, by $N\beta$. N's text may have been deliberately edited when the letter was copied, while β's text is imperfect — it lacks lines 23–31 of Schmitt's edition — most likely because of a scribal error. The section missing from N explicitly reveals that Archbishop Lanfranc had placed his nephew in Anselm's care at the monastery of Bec.[405]

---

[402] *AEp.* 89:26–37 Mortuo enim − quia] In iis uidelicet ecclesiae nostrae negotiis, quae per uiuam praesentium latoris uocem uobis necesse habuimus intimare. $\beta\omega$ (*CVE* and *L*).

[403] In α, *AEp.* 118 openly states that the fate of the bequest left to Bec by Hugh, count of Meulan currently was hanging in the balance, and that negotiations would have to continue; Anselm also advised on the action to be taken if another party attempted to take possession of the goods in question. This entire passage is omitted from $\beta\omega$. It is unclear whether this revision was due to the existence of two texts (a rejected letter and a sent letter), or later scribal revision. *AEp.* 118:12–16 De rebus domni Hugonis quas saisistis, cum Rogero, nepote eius, et cum rege, sicut oportere sciui, locutus sum; sed quamuis uerba bonae spei responderint, nondum tamen finem quem expeto sum assecutus. Quadpropter si quis alius resaisierit quod saisistis, nihil amplius inde faciatis quam fecistis; sed mobilia tantum tenete quam inde habuistis. α (*NM*)] om. $\beta\omega$ (*CVE* and *L*).

[404] *AEp.* 97:17–21 Scriptum illud...per presentium latorem tibi modo, ut postulasti, huic annexum epistolae direxi. $\beta\omega$ (*CVE* and *LF*)] om. α (*NM*).

[405] *AEp.* 25:9 assereretis.] Nam dilectissimum uobis nepotem uestrum, domnum Lanfrancum, ad nos misistis et eum magis in nostro monasterio quam in quolibet alio monachum fieri uoluistis *adds* β (*CVE*). See also line 9 namque α

The monk Lanfranc proved to be a persistent troublemaker and one of Anselm's greatest failures as a monastic mentor. We see him disobeying his uncle, the old archbishop, shortly after his entry to Bec.[406] *AEp.* 130, addressed to Abbot Gilbert Crispin soon after Anselm's visit to England in 1086, tells us that the man was again being a nuisance; the letter is silent on the nature of this trouble.[407] Finally, Lanfranc's schismatic promotion as abbot of Saint-Wandrille against the will of the community in 1089 constituted a serious scandal and doubtless a significant embarrassment to Anselm and his monastery.[408] In around 1086, therefore, when Anselm apparently commissioned collection α, relations were inflamed, and matters were about to get worse. Perhaps there was no desire to parade current tensions and Anselm's failure to bring up Lanfranc properly before the readers of the letter collection, and thus *AEp.* 25 could have been censored to disguise who was under discussion. Alternatively, it is possible that the letter was completely absent from collection α, as it does not appear in *M*. In this case, the letter would have been edited by the creator of *N* (or an unknown intermediary), whose sources probably included α and a body of letters addressed to Canterbury. *N* may well coincide with Lanfranc's scandalous Saint-Wandrille affair, which would explain why his name was suppressed in the manuscript. The section in question differs stylistically in collections β and ω: for example, in ω the passage concerning the arrival of the young Lanfranc at Bec appears a little later and is worded differently than in β.[409] β differs from both *N* and ω as a result of the apparently erroneous replace-

---

(*N*)] ergo $\beta\omega$ (*CVE* and *L*); this follows the censored passage which probably explains the variant: after an α scribe had omitted the aforementioned passage he changed *ergo* to *namque*. 19 inaequale α (*N*)] prioratus *add* $\beta\omega$ (*CVE* and *L*); this could be a scribal error or the result of censorship by the α scribe, or alternatively a later addition in order to clarify the meaning by a β scribe. ω (*L*) has two further readings that diverge from α (*N*) at the end of the letter, which was missing from β (lines 25 and 26).

[406] Lanfranc, *Ep.* 19

[407] *AEp.* 130:23–24: 'De domno Lanfranco nihil melius sciui aut potui, quam quod in Anglia feci et dixi.'

[408] *AEp.* 137 and 138.

[409] See also line 21 sub pondere $\alpha\beta$ (*NM* and *CVE*)] sub iniuncti sibi per uos prioratus pondere ω (*L*).

ment of the final paragraph (lines 23–31) with the last paragraph
of *AEp*. 23 (lines 14–30) apparently by the scribe of β^1.[410]

(Four.) The most complex case is *AEp*. 17, where even β^1 and
β^2 diverge from each other, a divergence that is otherwise unparalleled. The letter was written to Henry, a monk of Canterbury,
who was planning a journey to Italy in order to help his sister.
Anselm opposed this on the grounds of *stabilitas loci*. $\beta^2\omega$, or *EL*,
have a line of argument in favour of Anselm's point of view not
found in $a\beta^1$, or *NMCV*.[411] Yet, in a further line of argument, ω,
or *L*, diverges from $a\beta^1\beta^2$, *NMCVE*.[412] Finally, William of Malmesbury made slight revisions to the text, which was not unusual
for him.[413] How these divergences were brought to pass remains
unclear, but later editorial emendation may have played a part
not only in *M*, but also somewhere behind $a\beta^1\beta^2\omega$.[414] What we
learn from a slightly later letter to Henry, *AEp*. 24, might perhaps account for the motivation for the revisions. He had paid no
heed to Anselm's advice in *AEp*. 17 and probably regarded it as
offensive. A tension between these two men was no small matter,
since Henry was clearly considered a man of talent and virtue. He
was destined, indeed, to become a leading figure in Anglo-Norman
monastic circles. Lanfranc, who made him prior of Christ Church
c. 1074, also dedicated his monastic constitutions to him, and in
1094, William II promoted him to abbot of Battle at the instiga-
tion of Anselm.

---

[410] Alternatively, such an error may have resulted from the use of archival
drafts. The parchment for these drafts may not have been large enough to
accommodate substantial sections of text.

[411] *AEp*. 17:42–48 Quotiens – opponere *EL*] *om.* $a\beta^1$ (*NM* and *CV*). *E* suggests that β^2 included the passage.

[412] *AEp*. 17:38–40 'Crede igitur, carissime, plus consiliis amicorum, si te
solum sapientiorem omnibus illis non aestimas, quam tuae deliberationi.' $a\beta$
(*NM* and *CVE*) 'Crede igitur, carissime, plus consiliis amicorum tuorum quam
tuae deliberationi, nisi forte solum te sapientiorem aestimes omnibus illis. Quod
non ita tuae fraternitati uideri intelligo' ω (*LF*).

[413] In particular: *AEp*. 17:13 Vis – Anglia] Hoc ideo dico, quia dictum est
mihi te uelle ire *M*.

[414] One possibility is that the passage 17:42–48 Quotiens – opponere, absent
from the witnesses to β^1, was added to *E* from *L*, in which case β^2 would not
have covered it. This is quite possible, since *L* contaminates *E* elsewhere.

At the level of single letters, our manuscripts do not in general differ from one another. This means that the great majority of the surviving letters base their texts on the same versions. A computer assisted RHM analysis appears to demonstrate the tendency in the main branches to base the texts of their letters on the archived letters rather than earlier collections.

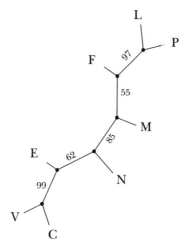

Figure 8: *AEp.* 1–5, 8, 13, 37, 41, 45, and 65 in an RHM consensus tree

Provided that α — the hypothetical source for $N(M)$ — and β the source for group CVE — and ω — the source for group FLP — all used primarily archival letters as their sources, the agreement of these groups comes closest to the original text of the letters. Through the RHM approach, this situation would best be depicted by a stemma with three branches, with all the representatives of a given subgroup located on one arm. The parameters of the RHM algorithm prevent such a stemma from emerging out of eight witnesses, since each node calls for three edges (for which we should need one witness more). The analysis, however, produced a result that is close to a tripartite division: CVE and LPF are placed at either end of the sequence, with NM appearing between them.[415]

---

[415] The location of CV beyond E is the result of two factors: E's source β^2 was also a background influence upon ω, which drags E and FLP closer to each other, and δ, which introduced new weak readings that distance its descendants from the original letters, lies between CV and β^1. In contrast, LP

The results concerning both ends of the stemma are solid, as is — to a slightly lesser degree — the bond between N and M. The intermediate position of NM between CVE and FLP is rather less certain. Given my previous results, I should prefer that CVE occupy the place at the centre between NM and FLP; even so, the stemma in no way alters my previous conclusions. N's inclination toward CVE agrees very well with my overall thesis and M's bent toward FLP results from contamination by F.

As for its Bec letters, collection ω from Christ Church in part leaned on collection β — more precisely on the broken manuscript β^2 — which covered Anselm's Bec era. As shown above, the *lacuna* in the lost manuscript is still visible in L, the direct offspring of ω. The reason for the double parenthood behind ω is obvious: Anselm's Bec correspondence was mainly in the archives at Bec and not at Christ Church.

3.2 ω's character and Anselm's Christ Church archives

If ω was authorial, the chronological distribution, which admittedly can only be established imperfectly, both of all the known letters and of those included in the witnesses to ω, is likely to reflect the date the collection was begun. The subsequent chronological categorizations of the Canterbury letters are based on Schmitt's datings, which are, of necessity, considerably broad and in some cases misleading. The numbers must therefore be considered indicative rather than exact. Since the material is rather extensive, however, sufficiently solid conclusions can be drawn. The table below presents the figures for Anselm's Canterbury career, sliced into six periods. (One.) The first group includes letters addressed between Anselm's nomination by King William II on 6 March 1093 and his consecration at Canterbury on 4 December. In terms of periodization, this is the most reliable of our six groups, thanks to the salutations of the letters in question. Before his consecration, Anselm never referred to himself as archbishop: before the enthronement at Canterbury on 25 September, his title was brother, and after that he introduced himself as archbishop-elect or possibly as brother. (Once he had been consecrated, he began to use the title of archbishop.) Schmitt's *AEp.* 148–160 fall in this period and the group

fall at the opposite extreme, beyond F, because L was subsequently edited, and most of the corrections introduced into it found their way into P.

consists of twelve letters.[416] (Two.) The next group covers Anselm's archiepiscopal period roughly before his first exile, that is between 4 December 1093 and 30 October 1097. The letters are *AEp.* 161–205. (Three.) In the third group, covering Anselm's first exile from 30 October 1097 to 23 November 1100, we have only seven letters. (Four.) The fourth group comprises sixty-eight letters, which seem to date from the period between the first and second exiles, that is between 23 September 1100 and 27 April 1103.[417] (Five.) The next group includes 109 letters, all dating apparently from Anselm's second exile from 27 April 1103 to August 1106.[418] (Six.) From the period after the second exile, there appear to survive seventy letters.[419]

Table 3: The chronological distribution of the Canterbury correspondence

period	estimated number of letters	estimated number of letters in ω	estimated coverage of ω as %	estimated ratio of letters to time[420]
6.III.1093–4.XII.1093 (9 months)	12	6	50	12:9 or 1.33
4.XII.1093–30.X.1097 (47 months)	45	20	44	45:47 or 0.96
First exile (23 months)	7	3	43	7:23 or 0.30
23.IX.1100–27.IV.1103 (31 months)	68	63	93	68:31 or 2.19
Second exile (40 months)	109	101	93	109:40 or 2.75
Aug. 1106–21.IV.1109 (33 months)	70	56	80	70:33 or 2.12

Despite the limitations of the evidence, the sharp decline in the ratio of letters to time during the first exile is, indeed, surprising. One would expect the opposite, that the exiled archbishop would

[416] *AEp.* 150 must be excluded, since the letter is from Bishop Gundulf to the monks of Bec, and does not belong to Anselm's own correspondence.

[417] I have subtracted from the group the letters in which Anselm appears as neither the sender nor the recipient: *AEp.* 215, 216, 221, 224, 225, 226.

[418] *AEp.* 305, 348, 351, 352, 362, 398 were excluded from the group on the same grounds as above.

[419] *AEp.* 457 and 460 were excluded for the abovementioned reason, and *AEp.* 469 because it is a later insertion by the main scribe of *L.*

[420] Measured in months.

have communicated with his subjects through letters more frequently than the archbishop present in Canterbury. The fact that
the ratio peaks during Anselm's second exile strengthens this consideration. I think that only the absence from the Christ Church
archives of Anselm's correspondence during his first exile can
explain the low number of the known letters, and that ω's coverage seems to be lowest in this period. Perhaps Anselm did not send
copies of his letters from his first exile to Canterbury, or perhaps
his archives travelled with him, but did not return to England and
Christ Church with him.

The second remarkable feature is the increase both in the esti-
mated coverage of ω and in the ratio of letters to time after the
first exile. The relatively low number of surviving letters from the
periods preceding the first exile may mean that the need for correspondence was simply lower than it was to be after the exile.
This explanation does not, however, account for why the *coverage*
of ω seems much lower before (and during) the first exile than
afterwards. The Christ Church archives clearly had an incomplete
record of the correspondence prior to Anselm's return from the first
exile. The year 1094 and perhaps the year 1095 appear particularly
significant, for the letters probably dating from that period survive
mostly through the Bec branch of the tradition, in other words via
δ^a ($C^a V^a$). Most of these letters were to recipients from Bec or Normandy, which explains their tradition.[421] The relatively poor coverage of ω as to the material from the first half of 1093 may be due
to Anselm's status at that time. The king had nominated Anselm
for Canterbury and in the church's view, he was merely a candidate for election. In this sense, there would have been no official
need to collect and store Abbot Anselm's correspondence in Christ
Church before his enthronement by the community. This cannot
of course account for the period between the consecration and the
first exile, when ω's coverage and the ratio of letters to time was
very close to that of the pre-consecration era. After the first exile,
the numbers in the ratio of letters to time and the coverage of ω
increase remarkably. We may assume that from then on the letters were preserved meticulously. The variations in the numbers in
the last three periods, which postdate the first exile, are generally

---

[421] The topic was discussed in III.2.16.

too small to reflect reliably any changes in how the letters were preserved. Nevertheless, we should note that the ratio of surviving letters to time peaks during the second exile, which perhaps mirrors how the exile augmented the need for correspondence.

The previous investigation reveals that ω cannot have been commenced before Anselm's return from the first exile in September 1100. It is unclear, however, whether the subsequent increase both in the survival of letters, and in the coverage of ω, resulted from the making of a collection or an intensification in the archiving Anselm's letters. In other words, these figures cannot show whether ω was a book or an archive. The latter appears less likely, however. An indication of this is that ω included mainly letters sent by Anselm, while its few letters addressed to him must represent a very narrow selection of his in-letters, which are now mostly gone. Active selection reflects more likely a book than an archive. Moreover, as noted above, the Bec correspondence in ω depended partly on the broken manuscript β^2; ω clearly did not present its Bec material in single-sheet letters. Lastly, had ω comprised loose letters, one would expect the arrangement to have undergone more marked alterations than our sources reveal.

If ω was a book, we must ask what kind of a book it represented — an updated register or perhaps a fair copy of the archive? The question is ultimately this: was ω authorial or posthumous? In order to discover the answer, we need to look into the preservation of Anselm's letters at Canterbury. Our investigation is materially assisted by the survival of letters despatched by the archbishop to his officials in Christ Church during his two phases of prolonged exile. Some of these letters of exile bear directly on the issue of archival preservation at Canterbury, evidence that rarely survives from this period.

Ernulf and Christ Church archives

From his second exile, Anselm sent some of his correspondence to Prior Ernulf, who was responsible for the governance of Christ Church in his absence. In *AEp.* 307, he informed Ernulf that he was sending a privilege from the pope 'ad transcribendum et diligenter custodiendum'. The document referred to was Christ Church's much desired papal confirmation of the primacy of Canterbury, as granted by the pope in *AEp.* 303, albeit only condi-

tionally.[422] The papal letter was a special case in many ways, and the cited passage cannot confirm that Anselm had a register or a regularly updated archive with originals or their copies *in* Christ Church while he was absent in exile. It is, nevertheless, important to note that *AEp*. 307 and 303 appear consecutively in *Lδ^b*, the witnesses to *ω*.[423]

In *AEp*. 357 of around 1105, Anselm informed Ernulf that 'exemplaria epistolarum quas misi, de iis quorum notitiam litteris fecistis, uobis mitto'. The letter from Ernulf to Anselm mentioned here is not preserved, but it is clear that Ernulf had *asked* to receive *certain* letters. In other words, Anselm did not send routinely all his letters to Christ Church at this stage. What were the 'exemplaria epistolarum'? Immediately before the passage cited, Anselm went over the dispute between Christ Church and a certain William Calvellus, and the 'de iis quorum notitiam litteris fecistis' may thus refer to the quarrel. In the witnesses to *ω*, *AEp*. 356, a letter related to this dispute that Anselm sent to the superior of William Calvellus, sheriff Haimo, precedes *AEp*. 357.[424]

Again in *AEp*. 364, dating from 1105, Anselm wrote that he had already sent the prior a copy of a certain letter from the pope. The subject matter of the text reveals that the letter in question was Paschal II's *AEp*. 353, which was dated 26 March 1105, at the Lateran.[425] The placing of the papal letter in *ω* is likewise again of interest, as it appears near the letter received by Ernulf discussed

---

[422] *AEp*. 304 is on the same subject; the letter has been preserved outside the main tradition and is known from a collection of papal correspondence, BL Cotton Vespasian E. IV, fol. 209r.

[423] *δ^b* restored here from *CL*; the letter is missing from *V*.

[424] In his letter to the sheriff, Anselm mentioned that he had written to him on the matter earlier. Although this letter has not been preserved, it may have belonged among the group of 'exemplaria epistolarum'. This also applies to *AEp*. 358 to William Calvellus, which followed the discussed letter to Ernulf in *ω* (*LC^b V^b*). It is true that *AEp*. 358 could equally have been composed in response to Ernulf's complaint and thus at the same time as the letter received by Ernulf.

[425] *AEp*. 364: 'Sin autem, ab introitu ecclesiae tantum illum arcebat [papa], sicut facerat prius de illo et de aliis complicibus eius consiliaris regis in litteris, quarum exemplar misi...De aliis uero nec aliquis nominatur in praefatis litteris...' On the dating of the letter, see SCHMITT, 'Die Chronologie', 1954, p. 202. *AEp*. 353: 'Quam nimirum sententiam nos sancti spiritus iudicio in comitem de Mellento et eius complices promulgauimus.' In principle this letter could also

above, *AEp.* 357. *LCF* attest that these letters appeared in ω in the order *AEp.* 353 (from Paschal II), 355 (to certain monks of Christ Church), 356 (to sheriff Haimo), 357 (to Ernulf). These letters perhaps arrived at Christ Church in a single shipment.[426]

To conclude, Anselm clearly sent copies of his letters to Prior Ernulf when important matters were at stake, either generally or from the point of view of the governance of Christ Church.[427] At least some of the letters addressed to other parties, but included in these shipments of letters to Ernulf, wound up in ω, in association with the letters sent to the prior himself. This cannot yet confirm whether ω may already have been started before or during the second exile. We only know that during the exile, some texts of Anselm's correspondence were archived under Prior Ernulf's oversight in Christ Church. The Christ Church archives probably covered only a limited portion of Anselm's ongoing correspondence, for Ernulf, at least occasionally, had to ask for his letters.[428] In addition, Anselm probably kept some kind of archive, or a more or less regularly updated register, which accompanied him on his exiles. At all events, although letters appear to have been preserved under Ernulf's stewardship during the archbishop's second exile, as prior of Christ Church, he would hardly have found time

be *AEp.* 354, although the recipient of this letter was the archbishop of York, not Anselm. FRÖHLICH, *The Letters*, vol. 3, 1994, p. 111, notes 6 and 10.

[426] In *LC*, *AEp.* 353 is preceded by *AEp.* 349 addressed to Ernulf and *AEp.* 350 to Matilda of Tuscany. *AEp.* 349 is slightly earlier than the papal *AEp.* 353, since its text reveals that the Lenten council at Rome in 1104 had not yet taken place and that the pope intended to consider Canterbury's situation then; *AEp.* 353, drawn up in conjunction with the council, states the papal position on the matter. Thus it is improbable that *AEp.* 353 and 349 would have arrived in Canterbury together.

[427] Southern (*Anselm and his Biographer*, 1963, p. 68) also takes this view; for the opposite position, see FRÖHLICH, *The Letters*, vol. 3, 1994, pp. 97–98, note 3.

[428] See also the reference in *AEp.* 307 to Ernulf: 'Litteras tamen nostras mitto regi, quarum exemplar uobis mitto.' The letter in question to the king was *AEp.* 308, in which Anselm justified his exile. Bishop Gundulf of Rochester also received a copy of the letter in advance; in *AEp.* 306 Anselm advised him as to whom the copy could be shown before the king received it. Here again the primary purpose in sending the letter to Canterbury was not the upkeep of a register, but was related to the needs arising from a particular political situation. On the basis of *LC*ᵇ, ω presented the letter to the king after the letter to Gundulf; twenty letters appear between these and *AEp.* 307 to Ernulf.

to maintain in person the archive or indeed the register, duties
which required long hours in the scriptorium.

3.3 Thidricus, ω, and L

Ernulf was not the only member of the Christ Church community to receive advice on the preservation of Anselm's writings
during his second exile. Thidricus, whom Schmitt and his followers
believed to be the maker of Lambeth Palace 59, was also the recipient of Anselm's counsel on this matter. There is no real evidence
binding Thidricus and Lambeth 59 together, and Schmitt's argumentation on the monk's doings is in many ways invalid, as will
be shown in detail briefly. Nevertheless, his belief that Thidricus
 was responsible for the actual work of compiling Anselm's letters
in Christ Church may have hit the mark.

Thidricus's duties included copying Anselm's theological and
philosophical texts, and correcting earlier copies of these works.[429]
Schmitt and his followers argued that a certain passage in *AEp*.
379, a letter sent to Thidricus, confirms his responsibility for keep-
ing up the register also. Here is the text.

> Litteras quas quaeris regis ad papam, non tibi mitto, quia non intel-
> ligo utile esse, si seruentur. Si quid aliud iuuante deo scripsero, suo
> tempore monstrabitur. Quod autem in libris quos scripsisti corrigis,
> fac ut, si qui ex illis transcripti sunt, in illis quoque corrigatur.

Schmitt included two letters from Henry I to the pope to his
edition, whereas the witnesses of *ω* have none.[430] The editor accordingly concluded that in the cited passage Anselm advised which
letters were not to be appended into *his* register or archive. There
is a serious problem in this interpretation, however: why should
Thidricus add correspondence between the king and the pope into
Anselm's register or preserve it in his archive? It is perfectly possible that Anselm was referring to a papal letter collection, of which
there must have been many at Christ Church, as there are still four
surviving early twelfth-century witnesses.[431]

---

[429] *AEp*. 334 and 379.

[430] *AEp*. 215, 221.

[431] Durham Cathedral B. IV. 18; BL Cotton Claudius E. v; Cleopatra E. i;
Faustina B. vi.

Nevertheless, Thidricus does appear to have collected Anselm's letters during the second exile. First, this would dovetail with what we know of his function in Anselm's household. The passage just quoted states that he was to see whatever Anselm would write in the future; and in *AEp.* 334, Anselm gave him meticulous advice as to how to correct a certain passage in *De conceptu uirginali*.[432] In other words, he acted as Anselm's 'literary secretary' in Christ Church, much in the same way that Maurice, another collector of Anselm's letters, had done at Bec. What is more important, in ω — on the basis of $LC^b(V^b)$ — *AEp.* 379 addressed to Thidricus was preceded immediately by four letters from the Bec period.[433] Implanting Bec material in the middle of the Canterbury correspondence was completely erroneous from the point of view of the structure of ω, and is otherwise unparalleled. There seems to be a simple explanation for this: Anselm could have sent the four Bec letters to Thidricus in the same consignment with the letter addressed to him, and then Thidricus, responsible for copying Anselm's texts, added all five letters — the four from the Bec era and the one addressed to him — to the register or the archive.[434] Anselm sent *AEp.* 379 to Thidricus from his second exile, and the letter has been dated to Anselm's stay at Bec where the four letters may have been found. Although probably two collections of Anselm Bec correspondence ($\alpha\beta$) had already been made, some material from the period may well have remained unpublished;

[432] *AEp.* 334: In sententia quarti capituli in libro De conceptu uirginali pone integre uerba apostoli, sicut hic reperies. Dicit enim idem apostolus 'nihil damnationis' esse 'iis qui sunt in Christo Iesu, qui non secundum carnem ambulant'.

[433] *L305–310, C332–337*: *AEp.* 378, 52, 135, 95, 87, 379. *V251–254*: *AEp.* 378, 52, 95, 380 (*V* omits *AEp.* 135, 87 and 379). A point of interest is that Thidricus had made his request concerning the letter(s) from the king to the pope by letter, referred to in *AEp.* 379 ('Dulcia sunt mihi uerba epistolae tuae').

[434] The passage cited above may provide an implicit reference to a text or texts delivered to Thidricus in the same consignment with the letter. The statement in question reads 'si quid aliud iuuante deo scripsero, suo tempore monstrabitur'. Should 'quid aliud' be understood as 'something new' or as 'something else'? If the latter rendition is correct, then, by implication, one could read it as 'something other than what we have here'. This would suggest that Thidricus received not only the letter, but also one or more of Anselm's other texts, perhaps the four Bec letters in question.

while visiting England and collecting letters for his second collection in 1092, Anselm still expected some of his letters to return from Maurice. Moreover, the four letters in question were not included in Anselm's earlier collections, except perhaps for *AEp.* 87, which may have been in α but was no longer included by the β stage of the transmission.

This evidence cannot yet confirm whether ω was posthumous or authorial: Thidricus might have updated Anselm's archive, and someone else could have made a fair copy, our ω, of this material at a later date. The manuscript tradition would suggest, however, that ω was begun while Anselm was still alive. For if the collection was posthumous, there would be a surprisingly high number of early posthumous exemplars of the collection in Christ Church: three altogether, with L and P. This, in turn, suggests that Thidricus was working on a register book, which would be ω. Indeed, the two surviving Christ Church witnesses could indicate that ω was not an adequate exemplar. A register updated over a period of years would have been more prone to codicological and palaeographical and other irregularities than a book made in a single campaign of production.

In conclusion, my argument concerning Thidricus builds on too many uncertainties to be completely watertight. Its most solid component is that Thidricus had a role in preserving Anselm's letters during his second exile. The next step, that ω was begun before Anselm's death, appears slightly less strong. If these arguments hold, ω was probably an updatable register book, although it also seems to have included letters from the period before its creation, even the Bec correspondence, which was partly taken from β^2. The earliest date for ω, then, would be Anselm's return from his first exile in September 1100, although Prior Ernulf's requests to receive certain letters from him in 1105 suggests that no register book was being systematically updated at that time. ω could have been instigated soon afterwards, in around 1106 when Thidricus received *AEp.* 379.

Thidricus possibly executed ω, but Schmitt and those who have shared his identification have associated him with manuscript *L*. The critical evidence for Schmitt's identification is found, first, in Anselm's letter advising Thidricus on the preservation of a letter from the king to the pope and, secondly, in a hexameter verse on the last folio of Lambeth 59. Although incorrect, these arguments

have proved tenacious. I shall attempt to refute Schmitt's view and then, after discussing our evidence for Thidricus, to construct a new argument as to how the famous hexameter should be understood.

I have already demonstrated that Anselm's advice to Thidricus relating to 'litteras regis ad papam' does not *necessarily* refer to the business of collecting Anselm's letters, but *possibly* to the assembling and archiving of papal and royal correspondence.[435] On its own, the passage cannot then serve as proof that Thidricus was actively collecting and preserving Anselm's letters. Schmitt argued that the Leonine hexameter 'Que restant modici sunt scripta manu thiderici' on the last folio of Lambeth 59 was a scribal colophon, identifying the scribe of the manuscript.[436] But the verse is in a hand that occurs nowhere else in *L*, and does not therefore represent a scribal colophon. It is rather to be associated with the poem '*Haud habiture*' (*Walther* 7673), which immediately precedes it.[437] The next step in Schmitt's argument was to identify Thidricus as the scribe of Oxford, Bodley 271.[438] He based this suggestion on Anselm's instruction to Thidricus to correct a particular passage in *De conceptu uirginali et de originali peccato* and on the parallel correction found at the relevant point in the Bodley manuscript.[439] This was again in error. The hand of the Thidricus verse does not appear in Bodley 271, and nor do any of the hands of Bodley 271 appear in *L*. In Bodley 271, there are also several overlapping layers of correction in the passage that Anselm had pointed out, further complicating the situation.[440] A third Christ Church manuscript, Cambridge, Trinity College B. 3. 32, roughly from 1120s, also formed part of Schmitt's thesis. This includes a poem on the

---

[435] *AEp.* 379.

[436] SCHMITT, 'Die unter Anselm veranstaltete Ausgabe', 1955, pp. 70–75.

[437] JAMES, *Lambeth Palace*, 1932, p. 95; SHARPE, 'Two poems', 1985, p. 270.

[438] GAMESON, *The Manuscripts*, 1999, no. 653; s. xii[1], Canterbury, Christ Church.

[439] SCHMITT, 'Die unter Anselm veranstaltete Ausgabe', 1955, pp. 67–70. *AEp.* 334: 'In sententia quarti capituli in libro De Conceptu uirginali pone integre uerba apostoli, sicut hic reperies: Dicit enim idem apostolus nihil damnationis esse iis qui sunt in Christo Iesu, qui non secundum carnem ambulant.'

[440] LOGAN, 'Ms. Bodley 271', 2004, pp. 70–71.

verso side of the first flyleaf, in which the name Thidricus appears once more.

> Seruus thiodricus dominis[441] me scripsit amicus
> Pro quo dic lector. sibi parce deus pie rector
> Huic et parce deus qui sic fuerit memor eius

This colophon is, however, again in a hand that is not encountered in either of the other manuscripts in question, Lambeth 59 or Bodley 271. To date, the hand of the colophon in the Trinity College manuscript has only otherwise been identified on fols. 114v–117v of the same manuscript.[442] In addition, 'thiodricus dominis' is written over an erasure in a non-book hand, which has not been identified elsewhere in the manuscript. Despite the irregularities in the colophon, it is the best witness to the hand of Thidricus. We may now conclude that Schmitt's argument concerning Thidricus is clearly indefensible. We cannot identify Thidricus's hand in the surviving witnesses to Anselm's letters.

Ian Logan has recently (2006) surveyed all the known sources related to Thidricus, and so most of these need only be discussed briefly here. The sources, many of which have been already introduced, may be listed as follows:

(1)   Anselm's letters to Thidricus: *AEp.* 334 (*c.* 1104) and 379 (*c.* 1105–1106)
(2)   A charter of Archbishop Ralph d'Escures, 1114 × 1122[443]

---

[441] 'Thiodricus dominis' is written on an erasure in a new hand. 'Thidericus' appears above the line in another new hand. Both corrections are early, Gameson (*The Scribe Speaks? Colophons in early English manuscripts*, Cambridge, 2002, p. 49) dating them s. xii[1]. Expanding the abbreviation 'dnis' or 'dms' after 'thiodricus' has proved problematic. James (*Trinity College*, 1, 1900, p. 132), Schmitt ('Die unter Anselm veranstaltete Ausgabe', 1955, p. 66), and Southern ('Vaughn's Anselm', 1988, p. 195) expand it as *dominis*, interpreting the three minims as the letters ni. The word *dominus*, which Gameson mentions as an alternative, would rhyme better with the final word. In this case, the manuscript would originally have read 'dns', corrected into the form 'dms'. I should impose no correction, rhyming 'thiodricus' with 'amicus' by suppressing the final s in 'seruus' and stressing the second syllable of 'thiodricus'. At any event, the medieval corrections too must have related to prosody.

[442] Michael Gullick and I made the identification independently of each other (Gullick, pers. comm. 6.5.2007), though Gameson (*The Scribe Speaks?*, 2002, p. 49) considers the identification uncertain.

[443] *EEA, Canterbury*, no. 49.

(3)   Two scribal notes: *'Que restant'* in *L* and *'Seruus thiodricus'* in
        Trinity College B. 3. 32
(4)   Two separate volumes listed in the Christ Church catalogue of
        c. 1170
(5)   Two references in Prior Eastry's book list from 1326

I need to begin with a proviso. The name Thidricus enjoyed
good currency in Normandy; when Anselm was prior of Bec, for
example, two men of this name took monastic habit there. In
Christ Church, too, there may have been more than one man bearing this name. If the sources listed above relate not to one but to
several men, what follows is seriously undermined.

Items 1–3 demonstrate that in the first quarter of the twelfth
century, Christ Church had a monk named Thidricus, who worked
actively in the scriptorium. He was one of Anselm's confidants
and apparently served as the monastery's subprior under Ralph
d'Escures.[444] Thidricus may have maintained Anselm's letter
archive or register, as discussed above. Since he asked Anselm
to send him a letter from 'the king to the pope', he may have
either planned or made a compilation of their correspondence as
well.[445] He was also responsible for checking and correcting copies
of Anselm's works.[446] The colophon of Trinity College B. 3. 32 is
our most reliable witness to his hand.

Items 4 and 5 add further details to our picture of Thidricus's
activity in the scriptorium. In the catalogue compiled in around
1170, Thidricus's name appears twice.[447] The catalogue opens with
entries for ten consecutive manuscripts of Priscian, often also naming the individual who had given the manuscript. The reference to
Thidricus reads: 'Priscianus magnus Theodorici, in asseribus'. Three
of the other individuals connected with these Priscian manuscripts

---

[444] Ralph d'Escures (archbishop 1114–1122) charter *EEA, Canterbury,*
no. 49: 'Theoder' priore Cantuar''. The then prior of Christ Church is known to
have been called Conrad. Thus Thidricus was probably subprior or third prior,
which are known to have been offices at Canterbury in the twelfth century. In
Lanfranc's *Constitutions,* the term prior was also used to distinguish senior and
junior monks, as Logan ('Thidricus', 2006, pp. 78–79) notes.

[445] *AEp.* 379.

[446] *AEp.* 334. See also *AEp.* 379: 'Quod autem in libris quos scripsisti corrigis: fac ut, si qui ex illis transcripti sunt, in illis quoque corrigatur.'

[447] Logan, 'Thidricus', 2006, pp. 72–75.

may be identified: Lanfranc, William Brito, who first appears in the sources in 1159 and who became subprior of Christ Church at the end of the 1160s, and Walter Duredent, who was prior of Christ Church in the 1140s and later became bishop of Coventry/Lichfield.[448] The 1170 catalogue also includes a second manuscript related to Thidricus, the 'Versus Theodorici', in a group of assorted theological works; Thidricus was the author of this work.

In Prior Eastry's book list from 1326, Thidricus appears in the section listing manuscripts of the *Parabole Salomonis*.[449] Again, the catalogue names some individuals in conjunction with the manuscripts. All names mentioned — Baldwin, Alexander, Eadmer, and Thidricus — are found in Anselm's circle of friends, and this is therefore likely to be a group of works from the beginning of the twelfth century. The catalogue further provides a list of contents for the manuscript associated with Thidricus, which reads in full:

> Parabole Salomonis Thodoricii; In hoc uol. cont.:
> Ecclesiastes
> Liber Sapientie
> Sentencie vii prudentum
> Laus monastice uite, uersifice
> Ephitafium sancti Anselmi
> Seneca de Institucione morum
> Liber Fulgentii Episcopi ad Cal[ci]dium grammaticum
> Excerpta de Ecclesiastico
> Liber Martini episcopi de iv uirtutibus principalibus
> Paradoxa Tulli
> Epistole Simathi
> Beda de naturis rerum
> Epistole Alexandri et Dindimi regis Bragmannorum
> Tractatus Tydericis, uersifice
> Exortatio ad studium sapientie
> Regule de primis sillabis exceptiones Prisciani
> Versus de Euangelio, Missus est Gabriel

---

[448] Items 1–9: 'Priscianus magnus Lanfranci, in asseribus. Priscianus magnus Willelmi morsel, in asseribus. Priscianus magnus Theodorici, in asseribus. Priscianus magnus Warini, in asseribus. Priscianus magnus imperfectus, in asseribus. Priscianus constructionum Britonis, in asseribus. Priscianus constructionum Ilgerii, in pergameno. Priscianus constructionum, in pergameno. Priscianus constructionum Duredent, in pergameno. Priscianus constructionum imperfectus, in pergameno.'

[449] LOGAN, 'Thidricus', 2006, pp. 75–78.

Metrum de beata Maria
Prouerbia Senece secundum ordinem Alphabeti

The most obvious candidate for the 'Ephitafium sancti Anselmi', the sixth title on the list, is the poem *'Presulis Anselmi'* (*Walther* 14486), which both *L* and *P* transmit independently. In the manuscript described in the catalogue, the epitaph is preceded by the unidentified 'Laus monastice uite, uersifice'. It is not impossible that the praise poem *'Haud habiture'* and the 'Laus monastice uite' are in fact the one and same text. The *'Haud habiture'* and the epitaph appear consecutively in two Christ Church manuscripts, *LP*, and the hexameter *'Que restant'* suggests that Thidricus had something to do with the poem. The mistaken title may be partially explained by observing that *'Haud habiture'*, to which our manuscripts attach no title, makes no mention of Anselm by name, and the rare references to his personal history are elusive and entirely unspecific; the hexameter could refer to any influential churchman in England with a claim to wider fame. Furthermore one should note that *'Haud habiture'* breathes a deep respect for, and also a fair knowledge of the classical tradition. The poet places himself in the tradition of the lyric poetry of antiquity, by borrowing the imagery of Helicon; the muses, Homer, the Hippocrene spring, and Apollo all appear in the introduction.[450] The panegyrical poem *'Haud habiture'* would have fitted perfectly into the manuscript 'Parabole Salomonis Thodoricii', in which both Christian and pagan texts cohabited. Of the other texts, the 'Tractatus Tydericis, uersifice' may be the 'Versus Theodorici' of the earlier catalogue. The 'Regule de primis sillabis exceptiones Prisciani' would also agree with the information provided by the 1170 catalogue, that Thidricus had owned or made a copy of Priscian.

It has been noted that the heading 'Epitaphium sancti Anselmi' may postdate our Thidricus, because Anselm became recognized as a saint around the mid-twelfth century.[451] If my speculation on 'Laus monastice uite' and *'Haud habiture'* hits the mark, there were no headings in this manuscripts or they were added at a later

---

[450] *'Haud habiture'* (SHARPE, 'Two poems', 1985, pp. 271–274), lines 1–12.
[451] LOGAN, 'Thidricus', 2006, p. 76, note 39.

stage. If so, the reference to sainthood is no evidence as to the date of the manuscript.[452]

The final aim of this discussion was to answer how the hexameter on the last folio in L — 'Que restant modici sunt scripta manu thiderici' — should be understood. It must have become clear that Thidricus's involvement in the making of L is unsubstantiated. The evidence deriving from AEp. 379 — Anselm's refusal to send Thidricus the king's letter to the pope and, what is more, the four Bec letters immediately preceding AEp. 379 in ω's witnesses — may connect him to ω, but not to L. This leaves the hexameter as the only remaining link between Thidricus and L. The palaeographical evidence, that the hand of the hexameter occurs nowhere else in the manuscript, implies that the verse is not a colophon identifying the scribe of the manuscript. Furthermore, our most reliable witness to Thidricus's hand is the colophon in Trinity College B. 3. 32, a hand that never appears in L. The hexameter is, as said, to be associated — in one way or another — with the preceding text, the poem '*Haud habiture*'. I can see two possible solutions: either the verse designates Thidricus as the author of the poem '*Haud habiture*', the verb 'scribere' denoting the act of composition; or the reference is to a lost exemplar of the poem in Thidricus's hand. While there is no way of identifying the author of '*Haud habiture*' (and that of Anselm's epitaph which often follows the poem) with any degree of certainty, the strongest candidate is not Thidricus, but William of Chester, a monk of St Werburg.[453] The identification, first proposed by John Leland († 1552), rests solely on Anselm's letter to William, AEp. 189. This rebukes William for having composed a poem in Anselm's honour: 'ne laudes hominem in uita sua'. An alternative solution to this question — my preferred solution — is that the source from which L got the poem was in Thidricus's hand. This could have been ω.

3.4 *Eadmer and* L

A better candidate than Thidricus as the potential creator of L is Eadmer. It must immediately be noted that Eadmer, whose

---

[452] It is unclear from the manuscript tradition whether the source (or sources) of LP included headings: L^a has headings, while P has none. The incomplete copy in L^a has no heading, but space has been left for that.

[453] SHARPE, 'Two poems', 1985, pp. 269–271.

hand is known from several specimens, was not one of the hands in *L* or *P*, and no sources refer to his working on Anselm's letter collection — apart from including many of Anselm's letters in his *Historia nouorum in Anglia*. Despite this, Eadmer is more likely to be responsible for the existence of manuscripts *LP* than any other of the monks of Christ Church that we know by name. Eadmer was Anselm's friend, secretary, and biographer-cum-hagiographer.[454] Their friendship developed into something close to mutual dependency. The anecdote recorded by William of Malmesbury is revealing (though apparently not to be taken literally): when lying in bed, Anselm would not even roll over without word from Eadmer.[455] Anselm's death on 21 April 1109 did not loosen the bond of friendship in the least: Eadmer cherished the memory of his late friend by writing two substantial works, *Vita Anselmi*, which he had commenced earlier but put to one side on Anselm's command in around 1100, and *Historia nouorum in Anglia*. The first version of the *Vita* was apparently completed between 1112 and 1114, and the *Historia nouorum* by around 1115.[456]

In 1116, Eadmer was part of the entourage of Archbishop Ralph d'Escures as he sought to confirm the primacy of Canterbury, first from the king in Normandy, and then from the pope in Italy. The mission failed, and Ralph d'Escures remained south of the Channel, apparently in order to avoid any danger of having to consecrate the *electus* of York and thereby admit Canterbury's defeat. When Eadmer fell seriously ill in 1119, he was permitted to return to Christ Church. He did not expect to receive a warm welcome, since he took with him a letter of recommendation, in which Ralph d'Escures attested that the man had done his all on Canterbury's behalf.[457] Southern reckoned that responsibility for this failure ultimately lay with Anselm, as he had not succeeded

---

[454] On Eadmer, see SOUTHERN, *Saint Anselm and his Biographer*, 1963, pp. 229–240.

[455] William of Malmesbury, *GP* 65.3: 'cuius [Eadmeri] Anselmus iussa tanti fatiebat ut cum eum cubili locasset, non solum sine eius precepto non surgeret, sed nec latus inuerteret.'

[456] SOUTHERN, *Saint Anselm and his Biographer*, 1963, pp. 298–299, 316 (followed in A. TURNER & B. MUIR, 'Introduction' in Eadmer of Canterbury, *Lives and Miracles of Saints Oda, Dunstan, and Oswald*, *OMT*, Oxford, 2006, p. xxiii).

[457] Eadmer, *HN*, pp. 250–251.

in establishing the primacy of Canterbury permanently.[458] Anselm's poor posthumous reputation is reflected in a miracle recorded in the *Vita Anselmi*, concerning a man who had become a monk at Christ Church after the archbishop's death. This man wished to revere Anselm as a saint, but he was not sure whether he should ask the dead archbishop to intercede for him or himself offer prayers for Anselm. Nobody was able to reassure the monk as to Anselm's sanctity, and he was only convinced when he received a divine revelation in a dream.[459] John of Salisbury also reports that the monks of Christ Church were very cold towards Anselm, already in his lifetime (something that also applied to his successors as archbishop).[460] These negative feelings may have stemmed, too, from Anselm's failure to provide effective leadership for the English church and unwillingness to collaborate with the king in a manner that would have enriched and advanced the same church, and in particular Christ Church. From this perspective, Anselm was a failure, whose achievement was plainly outshone by that of his predecessor, Lanfranc.

Eadmer recovered from his illness, and in 1120 the king of Scotland, Alexander I, invited him to become bishop of St Andrews. As *electus* he demanded to be consecrated by the archbishop of Canterbury, not of York. This demand was completely uncanonical and was never realized, and in 1121 Eadmer gave up and returned to Christ Church.[461] Combining evidence from Eadmer's texts and his personal manuscript, Southern argued that a new active period of literary creativity began when he came back to Canterbury.[462]

---

[458] SOUTHERN, *Saint Anselm and his Biographer*, 1963, p. 236.

[459] Eadmer, *VA*, pp. 167–168.

[460] John of Salisbury, *Ep.* 244 (p. 486): 'monachi Cantuarienses hoc quasi hereditarium semper habent, ut archiepiscopos suos oderint...Anselmo...bis pro iusticia exulanti, nichil unquam solacii contulerunt. Contempserunt Radulfum, oderunt Guillelmum, Theobaldo tetenderunt insidias, et ecce, nunc Thomam gratis insatiabiliter persequuntur.'

[461] Eadmer followed — certainly knowingly — Anselm's command *mutatis mutandis*. In *AEp.* 442, Anselm had prohibited the consecration of St Andrews' bishop elect, 'nisi a me', until the electus of York would have been consecrated and sworn obedience to Canterbury.

[462] SOUTHERN, *Saint Anselm and his Biographer*, 1963, pp. 369–371. See also TURNER & MUIR in Eadmer, *Oda, Dunstan, and Oswald*, 'Introduction', 2006, pp. xxvii–xxviii. In addition to the internal evidence, Eadmer's texts can be

Eadmer added two new books to the *Historia nouorum* and the *Miracula* to the *Vita Anselmi*. He also composed hagiographical texts, mainly relating to Canterbury's saints, and devotional works, such as *De conceptione sanctae Mariae*.

Gervase of Canterbury († 1210) mentions that Eadmer acted as *cantor* or precentor in Christ Church,[463] an office that involved responsibility for liturgical music, as well as supervision of the library and book production in the scriptorium.[464] We are not provided with a date for Eadmer's holding of this office. Southern argued that he was possibly assigned the office upon his return from Scotland, that is in around 1121,[465] but Eadmer's most recent editors suggest that he perhaps acted in the office already during the period between his return from Normandy and his episode as a bishop, in the turn of the 1110s and 1120s.[466] The evidence is too thin to supply a decisive answer, but what concerns us is that Eadmer's literary output suggests that he still held (or had recently been appointed to) the office of precentor in the 1120s, during the last discernible period of his activity. His works at this time reflect the duties of a precentor more closely than do his earlier writings.

dated with some degree of certainty by way of his autograph manuscript, Cambridge, Corpus Christi College 371. The arrangement of the texts, the quires added to the manuscript subsequently, and finally the script itself, which becomes tremulous towards the end, all witness to the dating of the works.

[463] Gervase of Canterbury, *The Historical Works of Gervase of Canterbury*, ed. W. Stubbs, 2 vols., *RS*, London, 1879–1880, vol. 1, p. 7; vol. 2, p. 374. Southern, *Saint Anselm and his Biographer*, 1963, p. 237; Turner & Muir in Eadmer, *Oda, Dunstan, and Oswald*, 'Introduction', 2006, p. xxvi. William of Malmesbury, Orderic Vitalis, and Symeon of Durham also held this office; M. Gullick, 'Professional Scribes in Eleventh- and Twelfth-Century England', *English Manuscript Studies 1100–1700*, 7 (1998), pp. 1–2.

[464] Lanfranc of Canterbury, *The Monastic Constitutions of Lanfranc*, ed. D. Knowles, *NMT*, London, 1951, p. 82: 'De uniuersis monasterii libris curam gerat, et eos in custodia sua habeat, si eius studii et scientiae sit, ut eorum custodia ei commendari debeat.' See also *ibid.*, p. 18; and R. Sharpe, 'The medieval librarian', in *The Cambridge History of Libraries in Britain and Ireland*, vol. 1, ed. E. Leedham-Green & T. Webber, Cambridge, 2006, pp. 221–222 and *passim*; E. M. Fassler, 'The Office of the Cantor in Early Western Monastic Rules and Customaries: A Preliminary Investigation', *Early Music History*, 5 (1985), pp. 29–51, at pp. 44 *sq.*

[465] Southern, *A Portrait*, 1990, pp. 418–419

[466] Turner & Muir in Eadmer, *Oda, Dunstan, and Oswald*, 'Introduction', 2006, p. xxvi.

The precentor was responsible for many aspects of the liturgy and above all for the music. The hymns Eadmer wrote at the beginning of the 1120s for King Edward the Martyr were clearly intended for the liturgy. The unpublished '*Ymnus de sancto Edwardo rege et martiro*'[467] also includes musical notation; likewise the '*De reliquis sancti Audoeni et quorundam aliorum sanctorum quae Cantuariae in aecclesia domini saluatoris habentur*' was undoubtedly produced for Christ Church's liturgical use.[468] Eadmer also 'almost certainly' wrote the miracle collection for St Ouen that was incorporated into the passional written at Christ Church in the late 1120s.[469] It is possible that the lectionary too was compiled under Eadmer's direction.

Manuscripts *LP* were produced in the Christ Church scriptorium roughly at the time when Eadmer appears to have been acting as a precentor. Furthermore, Eadmer's personal manuscript shows that on at least three occasions during the 1120s — which would again coincide with his assumed time as precentor — he assigned scribal work to the man who wrote *L*.[470] Eadmer's participation would help explain the existence of two almost identical copies of the letter collection — why, in other words, the scriptorium was so ready to invest so much parchment and labour upon a single text. Investment like this in Anselm's affairs would perhaps be unexpected in a community which held reservations about the man. Strong determination and genuine enthusiasm for promoting Anselm's legacy must lie behind the project. Eadmer had both the motive and the opportunity.[471]

Admittedly this argument relies more on a series of arguable suppositions than incontrovertible evidence, and it is possible that I have overemphasized both Eadmer's role and the negative atti-

---

[467] CCCC 371, pp. 5–6.

[468] CCCC 371, pp. 441–450.

[469] TURNER & MUIR in Eadmer, *Oda, Dunstan, and Oswald*, 'Introduction', 2006, p. xxviii; SOUTHERN, *A Portrait*, 1990, p. 420. Fragments of the lectionary survive: London, BL Cotton Nero C. vii; Harley 315 and 624; Canterbury Cathedral Archives Lit. E. 42.

[470] Cambridge, Corpus Christi College 371, fols. 3v–4r, 195r–v and corrections in fols. 221r–225v.

[471] We might also speculate that *L* was compiled during Eadmer's visit to Scotland and that on his return he had the new, better manuscript (i.e. *P*) compiled.

tudes towards Anselm at Christ Church.[472] Many monks who had
known Anselm personally, and continued to admire him, were
active in Christ Church and its scriptorium in the 1120s. The making of the manuscripts could equally have been sparked by a reali-
sation among Anselm's ageing inner circle, many of whom we do
not know by name, that they would soon be gone; they could have
therefore taken the decision to commission one last literary monu-
ment in their hero's honour. In any case *L* and its copy *P* indicate
that several scribes participated in the project in Christ Church.
The manuscripts thus reflect the prevailing literary tastes, and per-
ceptions of the dead archbishop, at their birthplace in Canterbury.

[472] The evidence for tensions between Christ Church and Anselm should be
treated with a degree of caution, however. In the *Miracula* Eadmer may have
built up such tensions for the sake of his narrative, while John of Salisbury was
a polemicist of the highest calibre.

IV. THE MINOR COLLECTIONS

Preliminary remarks

COLLECTIONS: Three collections, namely *Schmitt 15*, *Wilmart 14*, and *Sharpe 5*, together with manuscript *H*, append to *AEp*. 2 an extract from the *Moralia in Iob* of Gregory the Great, beginning 'In ipsa quippe' and ending 'curamus ablatam'.[1] The addition was not perhaps arbitrary, as the excerpt's subject closely relates to *AEp*. 2. The letter exhorts its addressees to keep their path straight, while the extract from the *Moralia* states that the religious life with all its hardships is a prerequisite for salvation. Since the letter does not refer to the extract, its attachment appears to be later editorial work, quite possibly by Anselm himself. While each of the three collections and *H* cover only a very limited number of letters, they share much of this material as well. Coverage in the group ranges from the three letters in *H* to the fifteen in *Schmitt 15* — hence the title 'the minor collections'. The implication is that the four are stemmatically related.

Unlike the major collections, the minor collections cannot be linked with information on Anselm's efforts to collect his letters. It is naturally possible that he had published a collection represented in this group or closely related to it. This may have taken place early in his career since the letters almost exclusively come from his years as prior of Bec. On the other hand, as we shall see, *at least* one of the minor collections, *Wilmart 14*, cannot be authorial.

Since the birth of the group can be sketched only imprecisely, the label 'collection', which I have denied to manuscript *H*, is somewhat problematic in association with *Schmitt 15*, *Wilmart 14*, and *Sharpe 5*. For example, *Schmitt 15* appears to have been preceded by a near identical collection, and if so, a 'derivative' or a 'compilation' would be a more fitting category. Yet, since at this stage of the argument all hypotheses concerning the sources behind

---

[1] Gregory the Great, *Moralia in Iob*, ed. M. ADRIAEN, *CCSL* 143B, Turnhout, 1985, 35.14.43–44. Schmitt published the excerpt separately from the letters without identifying the author, SCHMITT, 'Zur Ueberlieferung', 1931, p. 225, II.

what I call the minor collections can only be provisional, the term 'collection' is appropriate.

At all events, the minor collections are significant historical sources for the early transmission of Anselm's correspondence. They demonstrate what forms the correspondence took outside the key Anselmian bastions of Bec and Canterbury, probably already in his own lifetime and certainly soon afterwards. Their coherent selections of high-quality letters were admirably suited to the needs of communities outside the focus of Anselmian influence. And eventually, after Anselm's circle had faded away, they served the needs of the public better than the major collections, as the numbers of surviving manuscripts testify.

WITNESSES: The extant witnesses to *Schmitt 15* and *Sharpe 5* derive from surviving manuscripts; the former group was fathered by Cambridge, Trinity College B. 1. 37 and the latter by London, BL Harley 203. Both manuscripts are very early and they may, indeed, be the archetypes of their branches. Our witnesses to *Wilmart 14*, more numerous than those to *any* other collection, derive ultimately from a lost manuscript. In each group, the manuscripts will be introduced first, and then a textual discussion will follow. A word of warning deserves to be heard before we turn to the manuscripts themselves: I have only seen reproductions of some of them, and my encounters with some of those that I was able to see in person were at times too brief to allow a full analysis of the contents, codicology, and palaeography. The subsequent descriptions of manuscripts often rely on library catalogues.

1. SCHMITT 15

Contents
AEp. 136, 1, 3, 11, 13, 4, 5, 6, 38, 8, 45, 61, 41 (adds '*Vinculum coniugale*'), 37, 2 (adds '*In ipsa quippe*')

Schmitt introduced manuscripts Trinity College B. 1. 37 and Royal 5. E. XIV in his article of 1931. Although the selection of letters in the two manuscripts is completely different for the Canterbury period, their Bec material, fifteen letters in all, is identical.[2]

---

[2] SCHMITT, 'Zur Ueberlieferung', 1931, pp. 224–225.

Cambridge, Trinity College B. 1. 37 – S¹

1093–*s.* xii$^{1/4}$ (booklet 3); Salisbury cathedral; parchment; ii + 116 + ii';
a⁸ (wants 1; 8 now misbound at beginning of vol.) b¹⁰ c¹⁰ d¹⁴ (2, 3, 6, 8
cancelled) / 1–3⁸ 4¹² (4, 5 canc.) 5² / 6¹² 7¹² 8¹⁰ (4, 8 canc.) / A¹² (wants
12); quire 8 should follow c;³ 210 × 140 (180 × 110) mm (trimmed);
28–42 (long) lines

Contents

Booklet 1 (*s.* xii^{in})
fols. 1r–37r and 98r–105v Anselm, *Cur Deus homo*
fol. 37v   blank
Booklet 2 (*s.* xii¹)
fols. 38r–45r   Anselm, *Epistola de incarnatione Verbi*
fol. 45r–v   Anselm, *AEp.* 65:1–82 (ends abruptly: 'ad quod mul-
                 tos')
Booklet 3 (in or after 1094–*s.* xii$^{1/4}$)
fols. 46r–54v   Anselm, *Proslogion*
fols. 54v–55v   Anselm, *Sumptum ex eodem libello*
fols. 55v–57v   Anselm, '*Cur Deus magis assumpserit*', (a sketch
                 towards the *Epistola de incarnatione Verbi, c.* 10–11; in
                 MEWS, 'St Anselm and Roscelin', 1992, pp. 82–85)
fols. 57v–68r   Anselm, *Epistolae* (*S¹*)
fol. 68v   blank
fols. 69r–73r   Prosper of Aquitaine, *Responsiones ad capitula obiectio-
                 num Vincentianarum* (*PL* 51, cols. 177–186)
fol. 73v   blank
Booklet 4 (*s.* xii^{in})
fols. 74r–97v   Anselm, *Monologion* (imperfect)
Booklet 5 (*s.* xv)
fols. 106r–117r unidentified authors and texts (see JAMES, *Trinity Col-
                 lege*, vol. 1, 1900, 47–48)

Cambridge, Trinity College B. 1. 37 or *S¹* is one of the earliest manuscripts containing works by Anselm. Although Schmitt
knew and employed the manuscript, he did not recognize its
real importance, which was noted only recently.⁴ In its current
form, the manuscript consists of five booklets, the third of which
(fols. 46–73) includes Anselm's letters and other texts. The letters themselves divide into two groups, the *Schmitt 15* collection

---

³ JAMES, *Trinity College*, vol. 1, 1900, no. 35.
⁴ SHARPE & WEBBER, 'Four early booklets', 2009, pp. 58–72.

(fols. 57v–66v) and some later additions (fols. 67r–68r).[5] At least two hands appear in *Schmitt 15*: A (fols. 57v–66r, 66v from line 14 onwards) and B (lines 1–13 of fol. 66v). Four hands appear in the letters added later, each of them of a rather poor quality. These hands copied complete letters: C reproduced *AEp.* 177, D *AEp.* 190 and 183, E *AEp.* 195, and F *AEp.* 184 and letter Schmitt 1931, VI, which is possibly not by Anselm. It has recently proved possible to link the booklet with Salisbury, since some of the hands appearing in it have been identified in Salisbury manuscripts dated tentatively *s.* xi[ex]–xii[in] and xii[1/4].[6]

The palaeographical evidence demonstrates that the collection originally consisted of fifteen letters. Certain features regarding the additional letters deserve discussion here. In all, six letters were added to the collection later; of these, three are addressed to Bishop Osmund of Salisbury, one to the nuns of Shaftesbury and one to an unidentified nun M; the sixth letter, which is perhaps misattributed to Anselm, is also to Osmund.[7] The additional letters, thus, also connect the booklet to Salisbury. The additions were not made all at once but gradually. The palaeographical evidence suggests, however, that the letters were not appended to the manuscript as they arrived in Salisbury between 1094 and 1096, since at least some of the additions date from the first quarter of the twelfth century.[8] In any case, it is virtually certain that the

[5] The original collection: *AEp.* 136, 1'3, 11, 13, 4, 5, 6, 38, 8, 45, 61, 41 (adds '*Vinculum coniugale*'), 37, 2 (adds '*In ipsa quippe*'). Later additions: *AEp.* 177, 190, 183, 195, 184, and SCHMITT, 'Zur Ueberlieferung', 1931, no. vi.

[6] SHARPE & WEBBER, 'Four early booklets', 2009, p. 60.

[7] *AEp.* 177 (Osmund), 190 (Osmund), 183 (Abbess Eulalia and the nuns of Shaftesbury), 195 (Osmund), 184 (nun M); SCHMITT, 'Zur Ueberlieferung', 1931, no. vi (Osmund): '.A. Cunctipotentis disposicione uocatus cantuariensis archiepiscopus'. 'Cunctipotentis' does not otherwise appear in Anselm's (or Lanfranc's) letters.

[8] SHARPE & WEBBER, 'Four early booklets', 2009, p. 60. The letters to Osmund are possibly in the order in which they were received. *AEp.* 177 is from either March 1094 or September 1096, of which the earlier date is the better, although only on account of the order in S^I; see SHARPE, 'King Harold's daughter', 2008, p. 14, note 60 on *AEp.* 177. *AEp.* 190 was written during William II's campaign to Northumbria in 1095. *AEp.* 195 was written after the council of Clermont in November 1095. See also SCHMITT, 'Die Chronologie', 1954, p. 195. It is impossible to date the letters to Eulalia of Shaftesbury and nun M precisely.

original letters that had arrived in Salisbury served as the sources for the appendix to S^1.

London, British Library Royal 5 E. XIV – S^2

s. xiii$^{1/3}$; England; parchment; iv (paper) 190 + iv' (paper); four codicological units: A fols. 1–8, quire I (s. xiv); B fols. 9–53 quires II–VII; C fols. 54–181 quires VIII–XXII; D fols. 182–190 quire XXIII. Unit C: 230 × 165 (160 × 95) mm (trimmed); 44 lines in two columns; initials not executed

Contents

Unit A

fols. 1r–8v	'De uirtutibus in genere', unidentified, *inc.* 'Multis modis diffinitur seu describitur uirtus'

Unit B

fol. 9r–v	Table of contents of unit B
fols. 10r–13v	Table of chapters of Anselm's works
fols. 14r–30r	Robert de Braci?, *De similitudinibus* (*PL* 159, cols. 605–708)
fols. 30r–31r	'*Dum quietum silentium*' (an exegesis on Wisdom 18, *PL* 91, cols. 1060–1062, see Royal 8 D. VIII above)
fol. 31r–v	Bede, *Homilia* II. 3
fols. 31v–35r	Ambrosius Autpertus, *De conflictu uitiorum atque uirtutum* (*CCCM* 27B, pp. 909–931)
fols. 35v–50r	Hugh of Saint-Victor, *Adnotationes elucidatoriae ad Threnos* (*PL* 175, cols. 255–322)
fols. 50r–52r	Extracts from various theological treaties, some from St Bernard
fols. 52v–53v	blank

Unit C

fols. 54r–69v	Anselm, *Monologion*
fols. 70r–74r	Anselm?, *Disputatio inter christianum et gentilem* (in MEWS, 'St Anselm and Roscelin', 1992, pp. 86–97)
fols. 74r–81v	Anselm, *Epistolae* (*S²*)
fols. 81r–82v	Anselm, '*Cur Deus magis assumpserit*', a sketch towards the *Epistola de incarnatione Verbi*, *c.* 10–11 (in MEWS, 'St Anselm and Roscelin', 1992, pp. 82–85)
fols. 82v–87v	Anselm, *Proslogion*
fols. 88r–99r	Anselm and Pseudo-Anselm, *Meditationes* (*PL* 9, 10, *Med.* 1, *PL* 34, 50, 52, 63–65, 67–69, 72, 74, 75, 23, 24)
fols. 100r–105r	Anselm, *De ueritate*
fols. 105r–109v	Anselm, *De libertate arbitrii*
fols. 109v–118v	Anselm, *De casu diaboli*
fols. 119r–125v	Anselm, *Epistola de incarnatione Verbi*

Royal 5 E. XIV or S^2 is made up of four originally distinct units, of which B and C contain Anselm's works. On the basis of the hands, these two are from the first third of the thirteenth century. The provenance is unknown. The contents of B may suggest some kind of connection to Lanthony and Robert de Braci's manuscript Royal 8 D. VIII, discussed above.[10] In the seventeenth century, unit A was in the possession of Walter Stonehouse, whose name appears on fol. 1v, but it remains unknown when the units were joined together.[11] The letter compilation in S^2 has two elements: the first element is *Schmitt 15*, which we also find in manuscript S^1;[12] the

---

[9] According to a rubric this is the prologue to the next treatise, *De institutione nouiciorum* ('Incipit prologus in tractatum de[...] Hugonis prioris de institutione nouiciorum'). The prologue given by the *PL* edition follows this text, however. According to *In Principio*, Lambeth Palace 149, fols. 178v and 397 give the text as a prologue to the *De institutione nouiciorum* and Bordeaux, BM 272, fol. 74r as a 'Prologus expositionis regule sancti Augustini'.

[10] For *De similitudinibus*, '*Dum quietum silentium*', and Bede, *Homilia* II, 3, compare Royal 8. D. VIII; see *Memorials*, pp. 11–13 and MEWS, 'St Anselm and Roscelin', 1992, p. 71.

[11] On Stonehouse's other manuscripts, see MEWS, 'St Anselm and Roscelin', 1992, p. 70 note 37.

[12] *AEp*. 136, 1·3, 11, 13, 4, 5, 6, 38, 8, 45, 61, 41 (adds '*Vinculum coniugale*'), 37, 2 (adds '*In ipsa quippe*'). The second stage: *AEp*. 216, 306, 308, 224, 333.

second element comprises five letters from Anselm's time at Canterbury. The material in the second stage is outside the scope of my collations, and I shall not comment on its place in the tradition.

Date and structure

AEp. 136 provides *Schmitt 15* with the *a quo* of 1090×1092.[13] The *ad quem* can be derived only from the dating of our earliest manuscript, S^1. This is *s.* xii[1/4].[14] S^1 may be the archetype of the family. Its text is generally superior to that of S^2.[15] While in a few cases S^2 is stronger than S^1, there is strong proof that S^2 derives from S^1. This evidence comes from certain corrections to S^1 in its main hand. For examples, at 5:18 fruentes] S^1 originally read 'fluentes', unsupported by any other manuscript. The copyist corrected the mistake so that he wrote '[ue]l r' above the line. For the word uel he used a common abbreviation, the letter l crossed with

---

[13] SHARPE & WEBBER, 'Four early booklets', 2009, pp. 65–66 and SHARPE, 'Anselm as author', 2009, pp. 25–27 and 42–43.

[14] If the collection is authorial — which I doubt on account of the supplementation of the notes from Ernulf's *De incestis coniugiis* — it may be presumed that the *ad quem* is the *Epistola de incarnatione Verbi*, which would date the collection to either 1093 or 1094. For it appears unlikely that Anselm would have circulated a sketch (the '*Cur Deus magis*' extract) of a finished work (the *Epistola de incarnatione Verbi*). Another incomplete version of the *De incarnatione*, much larger than '*Cur Deus magis*', survives in Lambeth Palace 224. Since this text styles Anselm abbot, the version was completed either before his coming to England late in 1092 or shortly after that; this may be inferred from the often cited passage in *AEp.* 147: 'Mittite michi *Orationem ad sanctum Nicholaum*, quam feci, et *Epistolam* quam *contra dicta Roscelini* facere inchoaui, et si quas de aliis nostris epistolis habet domnus Mauricius, quas non misit.' In the final version of the *De incarnatione Verbi*, however, Anselm tells us that 'some brothers' had transcribed and circulated an unfinished version. The reference is apparently to the version in Lambeth Palace 224, but the '*Cur Deus magis*' must remain a possibility. Finally, although we possess several leads, watertight conclusions as to the relationship between the *De incarnatione*, *Schmitt 15*, and their date are hard to draw.

[15] 2:6 acquirere aut] *om.* S^2; 2:32 tuam] tua S^2; 2:43 prodat] perdat S^2; 2:55 quam] iam S^2; 2:appendix: percaepit] perceperit S^2; 3:9 in] *om.* S^2; 3:21 Si] Etsi S^2; 3:32 ipsa] ipse S^2; 4:10 pulsas] pulsa S^2; 4:17 et tanto – saepe accipias] *om.* S^2; 4:35 anima eius] *om.* S^2; 4:38 et precor[2]] *om.* S^2; 8:20–21 contra te tu] contra tu S^2; 13:8 liceat] *om.* S^2; 37:10 peregratione] peregrina- S^2; 37:13 diuinam] *om.* S^2; 37:15 reniti sed] renitis S^2; 37:25 rationis] ratione S^2; 37:78 quietem] quiete S^2; 41:5–6 inuicem] *om.* S^2; 41:9 uideo] *om.* S^2.

a near-horizontal stroke. Since the bottom of his l curves to the
right, the sign somewhat resembles the letter e, and the interlinear
correction could easily be read as 'er'. This explains S^2's isolated
reading 'feruentes'.[16] It is probable, however, that the maker of S^2
or — perhaps more likely — of a lost intermediary had recourse
to another manuscript by way of which he amended several weaknesses in the text.[17]

S^1

S^2

Figure 9: The manuscript tradition of *Schmitt 15*

Richard Sharpe has argued that the booklet in Cambridge, Trinity College B. 1. 37 that covers *Proslogion*, '*Cur Deus magis*', and
Schmitt 15 was copied from one or two primary booklets, which
Anselm had sent to Osmund, the number depending on whether
the *Proslogion* had already been associated with the other texts.[18]
This suggestion can be taken further, since certain structural features of *Schmitt 15* hint that it incorporates several units that were
originally distinct. The table below groups the letters, presented in
the order they appear, into clusters that may have derived from
separate sources.

[16] A similar case occurs at 5:23 karissime timendo]. S^1 has again a correction
above the line, '[ue]l non', while S^2 reads 'karissime non timendo'. See also 4:17
et tanto amore – saepe uideas] *in marg. S^1 om. S^2.*

[17] 2:18 sed S^2] si S^1; 2:21 meum S^2] meae S^1; 2:82 cornu S^2] cornum S^1; 4:4
allocutionem S^2] ad locutionem S^1; 4:6 opto S^2] obto S^1; 5:13 exigit S^2] exiit S^1;
5:18 fruendos S^2] fruendis (*corr. from* fruendus) S^1; 8:8 per os S^2] per hos S^1; 8:9
sic S^2] si S^1; 8:13–15 absunt...adsunt...absunt...adsunt S^2] absum...assum...
absum...assum S^1; 13:4 qua S^2] *om. S^1*; 13:16 nostra cohibitatio S^2] nostro
cohibitatio S^1 (uestra[?] cohibitatio S^2); 13:40 uidendi S^2] uiuendi S^1; 37:6 de
tua S^2] deuia S^1; 37:27 monachicum propositum S^2] monachi cum propositum
S^1; 37:29 uersutiis S^2] uersutus S^1; 37:38 ualens S^2] uolens S^1; 37:47 nisi S^2] non
S^1; 37:53 sedulo S^2] sedula S^1.

[18] SHARPE, 'Anselm as author', 2009, p. 25.

(1)   *AEp.* 136

(2a) *AEp.* 1, 3, 11, 13, 4, 5, 6, 38, 8, 45, 61, 41 (adds '*Vinculum coniugale*')

(2b) *AEp.* 37, 2 (adds '*In ipsa quippe*')

The first letter, *AEp.* 136, differs from the others in its subject. While *AEp.* 136 attends to a doctrinal issue, the other letters deal with monastic matters. The subject matter associates the letter with the preceding text, an extract beginning '*Cur Deus magis*'. This is a sketch towards the chapters 10 and 11 of *Epistola de incarnatione Verbi*, Anselm's contribution to the trinity dispute provoked — and eventually lost — by Roscelin of Compiègne. In *AEp.* 136 Anselm dissociates himself from Roscelin's view. Also *AEp.* 136's chronological distance from the other letters — it is from *c.* 1090, whereas the rest antedate Anselm's promotion to abbot in 1078 — suggests that it did not originally share the source with the subsequent letters. The chief reason for the division between 2a and 2b is the supplementary text '*Vinculum coniugale*' appended to *AEp.* 41. The text is a melange of citations from Prior Ernulf's study *De incestis coniugiis*. The excerpts, which will be discussed below, have absolutely nothing to do with *AEp.* 41 or with any other letter in the collection, and therefore their supplementation appears to reflect an earlier codicological break between *AEp.* 41 and the last two letters, *AEp.* 37 and 2. The suggestion is that *Schmitt 15* derived *AEp.* 41 from a source in which a few empty lines following the letter had later been filled by the extracts from Ernulf. Another explanation is that the notes could have been copied into an empty gap after *AEp.* 41 in the archetype of *Schmitt 15* — or of *Schmitt 14* (that is, *Schmitt 15* minus *AEp.* 136). Such a gap might also have occurred if the letters had not been copied in one campaign of production — which would again imply the use of multiple sources. In this scenario, Trinity B. 1. 37 could not be the collection's archetype, since it features no palaeographical or codicological break between *AEp.* 41 and 37. Finally, the addition of the extracts implies that *Schmitt 15* is not an authorial collection.

The addition to AEp. 41: 'Vinculum coniugale'

The extract '*Vinculum coniugale – corpus et una caro*' relates to the dissolution of a marriage. The text has been published as it stands on two occasions, but it has not previously been iden-

tified.[19] It is a compilation of excerpts from a tract *De incestis coniugiis*, written by Ernulf, prior of Christ Church (1096–1107), abbot of Peterborough (1107–14) and finally Bishop of Rochester (1114–1124). The study is on the question whether or not the bond of matrimony is dissolved if a wife has had intercourse with a stepson.[20] The passage consists of five excerpts, which are not copied in the order in which they appear in Ernulf's work; the first passage is in fact the last in Ernulf.[21] There is no observable connection between the subject of Ernulf's study and the content of *AEp*. 41, which is addressed to Gundulf. The notes must have been appended to an unknown copy of the letter. When and where did this occur?

In his preface, Ernulf, who does not reveal his office to the reader, states that the writing of the work was triggered when Bishop Walkelin of Winchester raised the question tackled in the work during a visit to Christ Church. According to Ernulf, there were also present 'regi exequutores…Caesari quae sunt Caesaris, et Deo quae sunt Dei reddentes'. In *Historia nouorum*, Eadmer tells us that just such a council was held at Christ Church in 1097, in which Walkelin participated too.[22] Walkelin died at the very beginning of the following year, however, and thus the incident Ernulf recalled could have occurred earlier. Possible contexts include the visitation of the Domesday circuit judges in 1085–86 and the vacancy at Canterbury after Lanfranc's death in 1089–93.[23]

Likewise, it is hard to discover how widely available Ernulf's treatise was. At all events, he himself must have had a central part in the process of dissemination. The work survives in manuscripts from the libraries at Rochester and Peterborough; the mid-

---

[19] SCHMITT, 'Zur Ueberlieferung', 1931, p. 225; MEWS, 'St Anselm and Roscelin', 1992, pp. 72–73.

[20] On the handling of the subject and the sources for this study, see P. CRAMER, 'Ernulf of Rochester and Early Anglo-Norman Canon Law', *Journal of Ecclesiastical History*, 40 (1989), pp. 494–510.

[21] (1) Vinculum coniugale – incestus in sua uita. *PL* 163, col. 1473A; (2) Dicit aliquis eum – peccauit cum uxore. *PL* 163, col. 1465A–B; (3) Quod ille peccauit – sed tamen iusta. *PL* 163, col. 1465B; (4) Ideo fortassis uoluit – in eterna uita. *PL* 163, col. 1465B; (5) Preterea etsi de coniugis – et una caro. *PL* 163, col. 1465C.

[22] Eadmer, *HN*, p. 81.

[23] Compare CRAMER, 'Ernulf of Rochester', 1989, p. 494.

twelfth-century list of books at Bec attests a copy;[24] Christ Church
and Winchester certainly possessed exemplars as well. The Bec
manuscript survives in part, but Ernulf's works, once closing the
manuscript, are now lost. The extant parts, now Vatican, Biblioteca Apostolica Vaticana Reg. lat. 285 and 278, have been dated
s. xii[med], and they thus postdate the addition in *Schmitt 15*.[25] It is
unlikely therefore that the supplementation of the notes occurred
at Bec. Christ Church, which almost certainly had a copy, would
be our prime suspect, if four of the five passages extracted from
De incestis did not coincide exactly with what is highlighted by
way of a vertical stroke in the outer margin in Brussels 8794–99,
the Rochester exemplar of Ernulf's work. On fol. 7r, a vertical line
and an underline cover exactly the passages two, three, and four in
Schmitt 15 (as well as the text that occurs between these extracts
in Ernulf's original). The first extract appears on fol. 12v and is
likewise precisely pointed out by a vertical line. The last extract,
on fol. 7v, is not highlighted. Furthermore, there are a rather similar stroke (as can be judged from microfilm) on fol. 5v, and underlines on fols. 2r, 3r, and 5v. Although the correspondence between
the extracted passages in *Schmitt 15* and the highlighted text in
Brussels 8794–99 is not absolute, it is too remarkable to have
emerged solely by chance. The palaeographical evidence makes the
matter even more fascinating. Brussels 8794–99 is written partly
in the hand that copied Anselm's letters in *N*, Cotton Nero A. VII,
the Rochester compilation, which derived letters from more than

[24] Rochester = Brussels, Bibliothèque Royale 8794–99, fols. 1–17, *s.* xi/xii
(GAMESON, *The Manuscripts*, 1999, p. 55, no. 12). Peterborough = London,
Lambeth Palace 191 (*s.* xii), which also appears in the monastery's late four-
teenth-century library catalogue (BP21.25h).

[25] The Bec item: 'in alio epistole Lanfranci. / in eodem epistole Fulberti
Carnotensis / et Hildeberti Cenomanensis episcopi. / in eodem liber Ernufi
de incesti coniugiis / item .iiii. questiones diuine solute ab eo', OMONT, *Tituli
librorum Beccensis*, 1888, p. 382. The dates for the Vatican manuscripts were
proposed by Gibson in Lanfranc, *Ep.*, 'Introduction', pp. 20–21, while the identification of Reg. lat. 285 and 278 as being parts of a single Bec manuscript
was made by Helen Clover. Wilmart, who authored the catalogue of the *codices
reginenses latini*, dated Reg. lat. 278 to *s.* xii[ex] and 285 to *s.* xii–xiii. I have not
verified whether the manuscripts are in the same hand. That this is not the
case is suggested by the fact that Wilmart did not recognize their potentially
mutual origin, by the divergence of his dates for their production, and by his
slightly different measurements of the manuscripts.

one source and which can be dated to 1086 × 1093. In Brussels 8794–99, this hand appears on fols. 22r–50r and probably also on fols. 2r–16v, which include Ernulf's study. On the other hand, *N* has two duplicates, *AEp.* 6 and 38, both found also in *Schmitt 15*. While there are several ways to account for these facts, the simplest explanation is that *Schmitt 15* or, more likely, an earlier version of the collection served as a source for the compiler of *N*. If so, the extracts from *De incestis* were added to an early version of *Schmitt 15* probably at Rochester.

2. WILMART 14

Contents
AEp. 65, 2 (adds '*In ipsa quippe*'), 37, 4, 5, 41, 45, 8, 13, 1, 3, 183, 208, 337

Wilmart's ground-breaking 1931 article on the transmission of Anselm's letter collection identified five manuscripts including a collection of fourteen letters.[26] At the moment, we know of eleven surviving manuscripts, which makes *Wilmart 14* the most widely disseminated of all Anselm's letter collections. The scope and the contents of the collection may partly explain its success. The relatively low number of letters made dissemination moderately easy, a crucial factor at a time when Anselm the letter writer had become less popular. The contents of *Wilmart 14* may best be summed up as Benedictine. The monastic tone accounts for the Cistercian interest in these letters at least in part; we know of three Cistercian manuscripts from the twelfth century. On the other hand, that same Benedictine emphasis in the letters may have reduced the popularity of Anselm's correspondence in other circles, as the focus of epistolary literary culture moved ever more towards the world outside the cloister.

As for the stemmatic structure, *Wilmart 14* is the most complex case of all the minor collections. While a number of manuscripts survive, the witnesses to the earliest steps are lost. I shall introduce the manuscripts according to their stemmatic position, beginning with those that are closest to the top. In consequence, the arrangement is not chronological.

---

[26] London, BL Cotton Claudius E. I; Paris, Arsenal 984; BNF lat. 4878 and 15694; Worcester Cathedral F. 132. WILMART, 'La tradition', 1931, p. 42.

London, BL Cotton Claudius E. i – W[1]

s. xii/xiii; provenance: ?Tewkesbury (OSB); parchment; iv + 186 + ii';
quires V, XIV and XX misplaced; 450 × 305 (335 × 210) mm; 52–53
lines in two columns

Contents

In codicological terms, Cotton Claudius E. i, from the turn of
the twelfth and thirteenth centuries, is a uniform book, although
at some point a number of leaves have been mixed up. The main
text is at least in two hands, both of good quality. The hands,
together with the hand responsible for the list of contents, appear
to be English. The manuscript may be from Tewkesbury, as has
been inferred (first by Ker) from the reference in the list of contents (fol. 1v), 'De dono domni Alani abbatis'. 'Alanus abbas' may
well be the master Alan, who served as prior of Christ Church in
1179–86 and as abbot of Tewkesbury in 1186–1202 and edited the

earliest version of Thomas Becket's correspondence.[27] John Prise
(† 1555), a noted collector, is the first owner of Cotton Claudius
E. I to be identified with certainty. The majority of Prise's collection derived from the monasteries of Wales and the border shires
of England, although he is not known to have possessed any other
manuscripts with a medieval provenance in Tewkesbury.[28] Part
of Prise's collection found its way to Hereford and part to Jesus
College, Oxford. Claudius E. I ended up in Jesus College and from
there it entered Cotton's collection, apparently by exchange.[29]

Vatican City, BAV Ottob. lat. 173 – W²

s. xiii²/²; parchment; 705 numbered columns; 250 × 180 (190 × 125) mm;
40 lines in two columns

Contents

cols. 1–131	Robert de Braci?, *De similitudinibus* (*PL* 159, cols. 605–708)
cols. 132–163	Anselm, *De ueritate*
cols. 163–185	Anselm, *De libertate arbitrii*
cols. 185–245	Anselm, *De casu diaboli*
cols. 246–286	Anselm, *Epistola de incarnatione Verbi*
cols. 287–413	Anselm, *Cur Deus homo*
cols. 414–463	Anselm, *De conceptu uirginali et de originali peccato*
cols. 464–465	blank
cols. 466–588	Anselm, *Monologion*
cols. 588–609	Anselm, *Proslogion*
cols. 610–657	missing (probably one quire)
cols. 658–687	Anselm, *Epistolae* (W², begins abruptly in *AEp.* 2: [multi et non] tam numero)
cols. 688–705	Anselm, *De processione Spiritus Sancti* (ends abruptly: sunt si uterque de [nullo est penitus])

[27] N. R. KER, 'Sir John Prise', *The Library*, 5th series, 10 (1955), pp. 14, 19, note J. 33. KNOWLES *et al.*, *Heads*, 2001, pp. 34, 73, 256. DUGGAN, *Thomas Becket*, 1980, p. 87 *et passim*.

[28] See e.g. fol. 186r: 'Gregory pryse esquier one of the Iustices of the pece'. The annotation was made by Prise's oldest son Gregory. KER, 'Sir John Prise', 1955, pp. 12–17.

[29] The manuscript appears in the list of books and manuscripts donated by Prise, which was compiled in 1621 or 1622: KER, 'Sir John Prise', 1955, pp. 12, 14. On Cotton see *ibid.*, pp. 6, 19, note J. 32. See also C. TITE, *The Early Records of Sir Robert Cotton's Library. Formation, Cataloguing, Use*, London, 2003, p. 128.

The manuscript is from the thirteenth century, apparently from its second half.[30] The main text is in a single hand, which represents a textualis of average quality. This manuscript had an avid late medieval reader as is indicated by several inscriptions in margins; there are no entries referring to the letters, however. The manuscript has been in Italy since the beginning of the seventeenth century at the latest, when it occurred in the collection of Giovanni Angelo, duke of Altemps (†1625).[31] Ten folios, probably comprising a quire, are missing. These bore the parts now lost from the text of *Proslogion*, the first letter of the collection (*AEp.* 65), and a part of the second (*AEp.* 2).

Paris, BNF lat. 15694 – W[3]

s. xiv[1/2]; (?)Paris; parchment; ii + 376 + i'[32]; I–XIII[8] XIV[4] XV–XL[8] XLI[4] XLII–XLVIII[8]; 295 × 220 (210 × 150) mm; 49 lines in two columns

Contents

fols. 2r–108r	Hugh of Saint-Victor, *De sacramentis christianae fidei*
fols. 108v–109v	blank
fols. 110r–134v	Richard of Saint-Victor, *De trinitate*
fols. 135r–141v	Anselm, *De processione Spiritus Sancti*
fols. 142r–147v	Anselm, *De conceptu uirginali et de originali peccato*
fols. 147r–159v	Anselm, *Monologion*
fols. 159v–163r	Anselm, *Proslogion*
fols. 163r–164r	Gaunilo, *Liber pro insipiente*
fols. 164r–165v	Anselm, *Responsio Anselmi contra Gaunilonem*
fols. 165v–176v	Anselm, Orationes and *Meditationes* (*Or.* 2, 5, 6, 7, 8, 9, 11, 12, 13, 15, 16, 17, 18, 19, *Med.* 1, 2, *Or.* 14)
fols. 176v–181r	Anselm, *Epistolae* (W[3])
fols. 181r–194v	Anselm, *Cur Deus homo*
fols. 194v–202r	'Postilla super Nahum prophetam'[33]
fols. 202r–205v	'Christiani a Christo nomen acceperunt' (possibly Victorine sentences)[34]
fols. 206r–321v	William Brito, *Expositiones uocabulorum Bibliae*
fols. 322r–377v	William Brito, *Expositio in prologos Bibliae* (unprinted)

---

[30] Cf. Schmitt in *SAO*, vol. 3: 's. XII.–XIII.'

[31] Fol. ii[r]: 'Ex codicibus Joannis Angeli Ducis ab Altaemps'.

[32] The foliation starts at ii and thus ends at 378. Flyleaves i and i' are paper.

[33] Possibly extracted from Julian of Toledo, *Commentarius super Nahum prophetam*, *PL* 96, cols. 706–758.

[34] Cf. *PL* 177, col. 859 *sq.* and *PL* 184, col. 1141 *sq.*

The manuscript is from the first half of the fourteenth (or the late thirteenth) century and probably from Paris. There are several hands, all professional and difficult to distinguish from one another. The manuscript comprises four units (fols. 2–109; 110–205; 206–321; 322–377), of which the last ends abruptly. The units may have been designed as a single book from the beginning, since the written area is uniform throughout, and on fol. ii^v there is a table of contents covering the whole manuscript. The list is in a cursive hand, which is contemporaneous or near-contemporaneous with the text.[35] Indeed, the whole manuscript may have been produced for one man. Above the table, an inscription states 'isti libri sunt Jacobi de padua professoris parisiensis in theologia medicina et artibus'. The next piece of evidence places the manuscript at the Sorbonne.[36]

Brussels, Bibliothèque Royale de Belgique 2004–10 – W⁴

s. xii$^{2/4}$; France; parchment; i + 132 + i'; 265 × 175 mm; prickings; 30 (long) lines

Contents

fol. 1r	Table of contents
fols. 2r–20r	Anselm, *De processione Spiritus Sancti*
fols. 20r–36r	Anselm, *De conceptu uirginali et de originali peccato*
fols. 36r–75r	Anselm, *Monologion*
fols. 75r–94v	Anselm, *Proslogion*
fols. 94v–122v	Anselm, *Orationes* and *Meditationes* (*Or.* 2, 5, 6, 7, 8[?],[37] 9, 11, 12, 13, 15, 16, 17, 18, 19, *Med.* 1, 2, *Or.* 14)

---

[35] Originally the table (fol. ii^v) read as follows: 'in hoc uolumine continentur isti libri per ordinem / primo liber de sacramentorum / secundo liber richardi de sancto uictore de trinitate / tertio liber de conceptu uirginali / quarto liber monologion / quinto liber proslogion / sexto liber cur deus homo / septimo liber summa britonis / octauo liber expositio super [?] et prologos biblie'. Another hand added 'Item processione spiritus sancti' (after 'de trinitate'), Item epistola ad lanfrancum (after 'de conceptu uirginali'), 'Item orationes et meditationes et epistole' (after 'Proslogion'), and 'item super Nahum prophetam postilla' (after 'cur deus homo'). There are, moreover, two layers of corrections. The earlier hand corrected the ordinal numbers in front of each original title from ablative to nominative. The later hand renumbered the works, taking the added titles into account, and made some minor corrections to titles.

[36] Fol. 2r: 'Sorb. 334.'

[37] According to the catalogue, the manuscript, which I have not studied in autopsy, has pseudo-Anselmian prayer lxii of the *PL* edition. It is nevertheless likely that the number should be lxiii, which is Anselmian *Or.* 8 in Schmitt.

fols. 122v–132v Anselm, *Epistolae* (*W⁴*)

Brussels 2004–10 or *W⁴* has not survived in full: at the end of the final folio, the text breaks off in the middle of *AEp.* 208. The letters might have been followed by *Cur Deus homo*, on the grounds that the work closes the otherwise identical Anselmian section in the previous manuscript, BNF lat. 15694, which ultimately derived its letter collection from the same source as *W⁴*. The palaeographical evidence places the manuscript in France, roughly in the second quarter of the twelfth century, a date and location supported by our information on the manuscript's provenance and place in the tradition. The annotations on fols. iᵛ and 1r reveal that Henricus de Zoemeren († 1472), secretary to Cardinal Bessarion († 1472), bought the book from Paschalis Bonhomme on the Pont Saint-Michel in November 1455, and that later he donated the manuscript to the monastery of St Martin at Louvain.[38] During the last quarter of the seventeenth century, the manuscript was probably used as a source by Gabriel Gerberon, as we shall see in chapter V.2. The book was subsequently taken back to Paris, as fols. 2r and 132v bear the red stamp of the Bibliothèque nationale, Paris. The present binding, with Leopold I's monogram, provides the earliest indication of the manuscript's return to Belgium once more. *W⁴* has a significant position in the transmission of *Wilmart 14*, as it is the parent to an extensive sub-branch. The earliest descendants are from French Cistercian monasteries; later the branch also made its way into Italy and England.

Troyes, Médiathèque 513 — W⁵

s. xii²ᐟ³; (?)Clairvaux (OCist); parchment; i + 238 + i'; catchwords in I–VI; 320 × 225 (225 × 180) mm; 33 lines in two columns

Contents

fols. 1r–26r   Anselm, *Monologion*
fols. 26r–33v   Anselm, *Proslogion*

The Paris manuscript lat. 15694, having an otherwise identical selection of prayers and meditations, gives *Or.* 8 where the Brussels catalogue places lxii.

[38] Fol. 1r: 'Pertinet autem iste liber magistro henrico de zoemeren quem emit a pascasio libraio in ponte Sancti Michaelis Parisius commorante Anno domini 1455'. Fol. iᵛ: 'Iste liber pertinet magistro Henrico de Zoemeren teste signo suo manuali hic apposito H. de Zoemeren quem dono dedit monasterio diui Martini in Louanio'. Zoemeren was professor of theology in Louvain. Folio iⁱᵛ has 'nonnus bernodus faber' in a faint hand that is hard to date.

fols. 38v–45v   Anselm, *Epistolae* (*W⁵*)
fols. 45v–102v   Hildebert of Lavardin, *Epistolae*[39]
fols. 102v–238v   Valerius Maximus, *Memorabilia*

Troyes 513 or *W⁵* appears in the Clairvaux catalogues of 1472 and *c.* 1521.[40] The palaeographical dating is xii²ᐟ³. While the hand bears no identifiable Cistercian features, the general impression is French rather than English. *W⁵* derives from a lost source that was certainly continental and probably Cistercian in origin: two other French Cistercian witnesses descend from the same source and the origin of *W⁴*, the forefather of *W⁵*, is continental. The manuscript, therefore, probably comes from a continental Cistercian community, the prime candidate being Clairvaux. The texts following the Anselmiana are in a new hand.

Paris, BNF lat. 4878 – W⁶

s. xii^{med–3/4}; ?Preuilly (OCist); parchment; i (paper) + 152 + i' (paper); I–X⁸ XI⁶ XII⁸ XIII⁶ XIV⁴ XV–XX⁸; 325 × 230 (260 × 170) mm; 36 lines in two columns

Contents

fols. 1r–104v   Orosius, *Historia aduersus paganos*
fols. 105r–131v   Anselm, *Monologion*
fols. 131v–144r   Anselm, *Proslogion*
fols. 144r–152v   Anselm, *Epistolae* (*W⁶*)
fol. 152v   Hugh of Saint-Victor, two extracts from *Didascalicon*[41]

There are three main hands in BNF lat. 4878, which all are Cistercian *Praegothica* of the mid twelfth century.[42] The first hand copied Orosius, the second Anselm, and the third two extracts

---

[39] Fol. 52r–v: Hildebert's letters to Anselm, *AEp.* 239, 240 (=*Z'*).

[40] VERNET, *La bibliothèque de Clairvaux*, 1979, item 664 in Pierre de Virey, 1472; and item 375 in Pierre de Virey, 1472.

[41] Hugh of Saint-Victor, *Didascalicon de studio legendi*, ed. C. H. BUTTIMER, *Studies in Medieval and Renaissance Latin*, 10, Washington, 1939: 'Tribus modis res subsistere – ad actum rerum', pp. 134–135; 'Multi sunt quos – affluere et torpere ocio', pp. 1–2.

[42] Fol. 1r: '[Regiae] 464', '3788'. The former number refers to the 1645 catalogue and the latter to the catalogue of 1682; H. OMONT, *Concordances des numéros anciens et des numéros actuels des manuscrits latins de la Bibliothèque nationale*, Paris, 1903, pp. 8, 151.

from the *Didascalicon* of Hugh of Saint-Victor.[43] The *Didascalicon* extracts were clearly added to vacant space on the last folio.[44] Orosius (quires I–XIV) appears to have originally constituted a separate book, since the quiring, in Roman numerals, commences only at quire XIV with the beginning of the Anselmiana. In addition, a rubric on fol. 1r states that 'In hoc uolumine continentur pauli orosii presbiteri hystoriarum libri .vii. contra paganos'. The layout of these two parts is, however, almost indistinguishable, reflecting the dynamics of Cistercian book production. The *Didascalicon* extracts occur in the witnesses that are below W^6 in the stemma. According to the 1721 printing of Gerberon's edition, the manuscript is from Preuilly.[45]

Paris, Bibliothèque de l'Arsenal 984 – W^7

s. xii$^{med–3/4}$; Fontenay (OCist); parchment; ii (paper) + 152 + ii (paper); I–XVIII^8; 350 × 255 (265 × 190) mm; 36 lines in two columns

Contents

fols. 1r–107v   Orosius, *Historia aduersus paganos*
fols. 107v–132v   Anselm, *Monologion*
fols. 132v–144v   Anselm, *Proslogion*
fols. 144v–152r   Anselm, *Epistolae* (W^7)
fol. 152r–v   Hugh of Saint-Victor, two extracts from *Didascalicon*

The palaeographical evidence identifies Arsenal 984 as a Cistercian manuscript of the mid or later twelfth century. The manuscript is from Fontenay, as the annotation on fol. 152v says.[46] Around 1778–80, it entered the collection of Baron d'Heiss, who acquired thirty-eight Fontenay manuscripts from a book dealer called François de Los Rios. In 1781, d'Heiss sold his manuscripts to the Marquis of Paulmy, Antoine-René d'Argenson, whose collection was to provide the basis for the Arsenal library.[47]

---

[43] On fol. 150r, an informal hand amended the rubric of *AEp.* 1 (lanfr[ancum] *corr. from* radulfum). The initials in Orosius and those in Anselm were made by two different men.

[44] Hugh of Saint-Victor, *Didascalicon*, pp. 134–135: 'Tribus modis res subsistere – ad actum rerum'; pp. 1–2: 'Multi sunt quos – affluere et torpere ocio'.

[45] See chapter V.2.

[46] 'Liber Sancte Marie de Fonteneto. D 20.'

[47] A. Bondéelle-Souchier, *Bibliothèques cisterciennes dans la France médiévale. Répertoire des abbayes d'hommes*, Paris, 1991, pp. 105, 108; H. Martin,

The contents of Arsenal 984 and the previous manuscript, BNF lat. 4878, are identical. The layout of the text and even the placing of the (rather simply) decorated initials are also almost identical, and furthermore my collations indicate an astonishingly small number of differences between W^7 and W^6. It is important to note that these two manuscripts give the prefatory letter to *Monologion* in its correct place, i.e. before the work. The three English witnesses, $W^9W^{10}W^{11}$, which place themselves beneath W^6 in the stemma, present the prefatory letter within the letter collection.

Oxford, Bodleian Library Canon. Pat. Lat. 204 – W^8

s. xiii²/²; (?)Montello, Treviso (OCarth); parchment, i + 99 + i'; I–III¹²–?⁴⁸; 310 × 220 (225 × 155) mm; 50 lines in two columns

Contents

fols. 1r–14v	Anselm, *Monologion*
fols. 14v–18v	Anselm, *Proslogion*
fols. 18v–19v	Gaunilo, *Liber pro insipiente*
fols. 19v–21r	Anselm, *Responsio Anselmi contra Gaunilonem*
fols. 21r–26r	Anselm, *Epistola de incarnatione Verbi*
fols. 26r–39v	Anselm, *Cur Deus homo*
fols. 39v–45v	Anselm, *De conceptu uirginali et de originali peccato*
fols. 45v–52v	Anselm, *De processione Spiritus Sancti*
fols. 52v–57r	Anselm, *De ueritate*
fols. 57r–60v	Anselm, *De libertate arbitrii*
fols. 60v–67v	Anselm, *De casu diaboli*
fols. 67v–74v	Anselm, *De concordia praescientiae et praedestinationis*
fols. 74v–79r	Anselm, *Epistolae* (W^8)
fol. 79r	Hugh of Saint-Victor, two extracts from *Didascalicon*
fols. 79r–80v	Anselm, *Epistola de sacrificio azymi et fermentati*
fols. 80v–81r	Anselm, *Epistola de sacramentis ecclesiae*
fol. 81r	Pseudo-Anselm, De corpore et sanguine Domini (Ep. IV,107 in *PL* 159, cols. 255–259)
fols. 81r–99v	Alexander of Canterbury, *Similitudines Anselmi*[?]

The medieval provenance and possibly the origin of this manuscript is the Carthusian monastery of Montello in Treviso.[49] While

---

Histoire de la bibliothèque de l'Arsenal. Catalogue des manuscrits de la bibliothèque de l'Arsenal, vol. 9, Paris, 1899, pp. 242–243.

[48] The modern binding is too tight to determine the collation. The first three quires have catchwords.

[49] Fol. 1r: 'Est monasterii montelli ordini cartusiensis dyocesis trauisine Y. 3.' The library signum is on an erasure.

the main hand shows certain elements, such as the 'box a', typical of Northern textualis, the rubrics represent Italian Rotunda more clearly. The date is roughly *s.* xiii[2/2].

Cambridge, Peterhouse 246 – W[9]

s. xiv[(in?)]; England; parchment; i + 333 (153 + 180) + i; a[12] b[14] c–k[12] (wants 8) –M[12] N? (wants 8 and all after) / A[12] B[12] C[4] (4 cancelled) D–I[12] K[10] L–Q[12] (12 blank);[50] the unit A: 325 × 200 (230 × 145) mm; 56 lines in two columns

Contents

Unit A

fols. 1r–5r	Anselm, *Monologion*
fols. 5r–12r	Anselm, *Proslogion*
fols. 12r–16v	Anselm, *De ueritate*
fols. 16v–20v	Anselm, *De libertate arbitrii*
fols. 20v–28v	Anselm, *De casu diaboli*
fols. 28v–33v	Anselm, *Epistola de incarnatione Verbi*
fols. 33v–49v	Anselm, *Cur Deus homo*
fols. 49v–56r	Anselm, *De conceptu uirginali et de originali peccato*
fols. 56r–64v	Anselm, *De processione Spiritus Sancti*
fols. 64v–68v	Anselm, *De grammatico*
fols. 68v–89r	Robert de Braci?, *De similitudinibus* (*PL* 159, cols. 605–708)
fols. 89r–96v	Anselm, *De concordia praescientiae et praedestinationis*
fols. 96v–101v	'Questiones Anselmi archiepiscopi', unidentified, 'Ligacio flagellacio ubi – facienda esse dicunt'
fols. 101v–104v	Anselm?, *Disputatio inter christianum et gentilem* (in MEWS, 'St Anselm and Roscelin', 1992, pp. 86–98)
fols. 104v–107v	Alexander of Canterbury, *Dicta Anselmi* (extract: cap. 5, *De XIV partibus beatitudinis*, *Memorials*, pp. 127–141)
fols. 107v–111r	'De beata uita et felicitate iustorum', unidentified, 'Respondeatur illis quod scriptum – deferuntur inuitos deferunt.'
fol. 111r–v	Anselm?, *De custodia interioris hominis* (*Memorials*, pp. 355–360)
fols. 112r–113r	Ralph d'Escures, *Homilia de assumptione Mariae* (*PL* 95, cols. 1505–1506; *PL* 158, cols. 644–649)
fols. 113r–117r	Eadmer, *De conceptione sanctae Mariae* (*PL* 159, cols. 301–318)

[50] Collation from M. R. JAMES, *A Descriptive Catalogue of the Manuscripts in the Library of Peterhouse*, Cambridge, 1899, p. 299.

fols. 117r–122r   Eadmer?, *De excellentia uirginis Mariae* (*PL* 159, cols. 557–580)
fols. 122r–123r   Pseudo-Anselm, *De antichristo* (*PL* 40, cols. 1131–1134)
fol. 123r   Anselm, *AEp.* 204 ('De diuersitate persone')
fol. 123r–v   Pseudo-Anselm, *De corpore et sanguine Domini* (*Ep.* IV,107 in *PL* 159, cols. 255–259)
fols. 123v–125v   Anselm, *Epistola de sacrificio azymi et fermentati*
fol. 125r–v   Anselm, *Epistola de sacramentis ecclesiae*
fols. 125v–130v   Anselm, *Epistolae* (W⁹)
fols. 130v–145v   Anselm, *Orationes* and *Meditationes*
fols. 146r–149v   Pseudo-Anselm, *Meditatio* XV (*PL* 158, cols. 785–792)
fols. 149v–150v   Ralph d'Escures, *Homilia de assumptione Mariae* (*PL* 95, cols. 1505–1506; *PL* 158, cols. 644–649)
fol. 150v   Pseudo-Basil of Caesarea, *Monita Basilii* (ends imperfectly: Et quando te p...', P. LEHMANN, *Erforschung des Mittelalters*, 6 (1962), pp. 200–245)

Peterhouse 246 consists of two originally separate units, of which the first contains an extensive collection of Anselm's works and other mainly Anselmian texts. The hands represent fourteenth-century *Anglicana*. The letter collection in W⁹ includes the prefatory letter to *Monologion* addressed to Lanfranc and is followed by extracts from *Didascalicon* by Hugo of Saint-Victor. The arrangement of letters has been slightly altered.[51] The manuscript appears in the catalogue of Peterhouse from 1418.

Worcester Cathedral F. 41 – W¹⁰

s. xiv^in; ?Oxford; parchment; iv + 229, A⁴ I–XI¹² XII¹⁰ XIII¹⁴ XIV–XV¹² XVI¹²(+1 before 1) XVII–XIX¹²; catchwords; a quire missing after XI; 290 × 180 (210 × 130) mm; 48 lines in two columns[52]

Contents

fols. 1r–10r   Anselm, *De casu diaboli*
fols. 10r–18r   Anselm, *De conceptu uirginali et de originali peccato*
fols. 18r–36v   Anselm, *Monologion*
fols. 36v–42r   Anselm, *Proslogion*

[51] W⁸: 41, 65, 8, *Monologion Ep.*, 2, 37, 4, 5, 45, 13, 1, 3, 183, 208, 337, *Didascalicon.*

[52] R. THOMSON & M. GULLICK, *A Descriptive Catalogue of the Medieval Manuscripts in Worcester Cathedral Library*, Woodbridge, 2001, pp. 26–27.

fols. 42r–46r   Anselm and Gaunilo, *Sumptum ex eodem libello, Liber pro insipiente, Responsio Anselmi contra Gaunilonem*

fols. 46r–67v   Anselm, *Cur Deus homo*

fols. 67v–78r   Anselm, *De concordia praescientiae et praedestinationis*

fols. 78r–83v   Anselm, *De libertate arbitrii*

fols. 83v–90v   Anselm, *Epistola de incarnatione Verbi*

fols. 90v–97r   Anselm, *De ueritate*

fols. 97r–108r   Anselm, *De processione Spiritus Sancti*

fols. 108r–136r   Robert de Braci?, *De similitudinibus* (*PL* 159, cols. 605–708)

fols. 136r–142r   Anselm, *De grammatico*

fols. 142r–150r   'Questiones Anselmi', unidentified, 'Ligacio flagellacio ubi coronatus fuit – Vt sacramentis assit donatio mentis.'

fols. 150r–155v   Anselm?, *Disputatio inter christianum et gentilem* (in Mews, 'St Anselm and Roscelin', 1992, pp. 86–98)

fols. 156v–160r   Alexander of Canterbury, *Dicta Anselmi* (extract: cap. 5 of *De XIV partibus beatitudinis, Memorials*, pp. 127–141)

fols. 160r–165r   'De beata uita et felicitate iustorum', unidentified, 'Respondetur illis quod scriptum – non deferuntur inuitos deferunt.'

fols. 165r–167r   Anselm?, *De custodia interioris hominis* (*Memorials*, pp. 355–360)

fol. 167r–v   Ralph d'Escures, *Homilia de assumptione Mariae* (*PL* 95, cols. 1505–1506; *PL* 158, cols. 644–649)

fols. 167v–174r   Eadmer, *De conceptione sanctae Mariae*

fols. 174v–181v   Eadmer?, *De excellentia uirginis Mariae*

fols. 182r–189r   Anselm, *Epistolae* (W^{10})

fols. 189r–213v   Anselm, *Orationes* and *Meditationes* (*Or. prol.*, 2, 5–17; two Pseudo-Anselmian prayers *PL* 158, cols. 876–877 and cols. 1035–1036; *Med.* 1–3)

fols. 213v–214v   Pseudo-Anselm, *De antichristo* (*PL* 40, cols. 1131–1134)

fols. 214v–215v   Pseudo-Anselm, *De corpore et sanguine Domini* (*Ep.* IV,107 in *PL* 159, cols. 255–259)

fols. 215v–217v   Anselm, *Epistola de sacrificio azymi et fermentati*

fols. 217v–218r and 218r–219r   Anselm, *Epistola de sacramentis ecclesiae* (given twice)

fols. 219r–225r   Pseudo-Anselm, *Meditatio XV* (*PL 159*, cols. 785–792)

fol. 225r–v   Anselm, *AEp.* 97:22–91 ('De malo')

fols. 225v–229v   Anonymous, 'Quaestiones' (in the same hand as fol. iii)

Worcester F. 41 or W^{10} is from the beginning of the fourteenth century. The text is in a fine *anglicana formata*, possibly written by an Oxford professional scribe. It appears as if the manuscript soon afterwards made its way to Worcester to serve as a source for yet another manuscript for the cathedral.[53] The contents are largely the same as those of W^9, Peterhouse 246. The arrangement of the letters in W^{10} is a little further away from the original *Wilmart 14* than is the case in W^9. Furthermore, W^{10} includes *AEp.* 204, which is not found at the earlier stages of the *Wilmart 14* tradition. The letter addressed to Lanfranc prefacing *Monologion* is included in the collection, as are the *Didascalicon* extracts.[54]

Worcester Cathedral F. 132 – W^{11}

s. xiv[in] and xiv; (?)Worcester cathedral priory (OSB); parchment; i + 224, A^4 I–XVIII[12] IX[6(lacks 4)]; catchwords; 330 × 215 (225 × 140) mm; 43 lines in two columns[55]

Contents

fols. 1r–29r	Robert de Braci?, *De similitudinibus* (*PL* 159, cols. 605–708)
fols. 29r–47r	Anselm, *Orationes* and *Meditationes* (*Or.* prol., 2, 5–19; *Med.* 1–3; *Or.* 1, 3, 4)
fols. 47r–51v	Anselm, *Proslogion*
fols. 51v–53v	Anselm, *Meditatio 2 de redemptione humana*
fols. 54r–59v	Anselm, *De ueritate*
fols. 60r–64v	Anselm, *De libertate arbitrii*
fols. 65r–74v	Anselm, *De casu diaboli*
fols. 74v–83r	Anselm, *De conceptu uirginali et de originali peccato*
fols. 83r–93v	Anselm, *De processione Spiritus Sancti*
fols. 93v–104r	Anselm, *De concordia praescientiae et praedestinationis*
fols. 104r–110v	Anselm, *Epistola de incarnatione Verbi*
fols. 110v–116r	Anselm, *De grammatico*
fols. 116r–117v	Anselm, *Epistola de sacrificio azymi et fermentati*
fols. 117v–118r	Anselm, *Epistola de sacramentis ecclesiae*
fols. 118r–119v	Ralph d'Escures, *Homilia de assumptione Mariae* (*PL* 95, cols. 1505–1506; *PL* 158, cols. 644–649)

[53] First flyleaf: 'Liber sancte Marie Wygorn' (*s.* xiv).

[54] W^{10}: 65, 204, 41, 8, *Monologion Ep.*, 2, 37, 4, 5, 45, 13, 1, 3, 183, 208, 337, *Didascalicon*.

[55] THOMSON & GULLICK, *Medieval Manuscripts in Worcester Cathedral*, 2001, pp. 93–94.

The text is in two hands; the second hand begins on fol. 112r, in the middle of *De grammatico*. Both hands wrote Gothic textualis, *semi-quadrata* to be more precise. The first flyleaf has an annotation mentioning that the book was the property of 'magistri T. Wych'. We know that there was a monk named Thomas Wych in Worcester in 1274, who was still living in 1296.[56] The contents of Worcester F. 132, and the preceding manuscript, F. 41, are almost identical. They have the same selection of letters (predominantly from *Wilmart 14*), but their arrangement differs slightly.[57]

---

[56] *BRUO*, vol. 3, 2101; THOMSON & GULLICK, *Medieval Manuscripts in Worcester Cathedral*, 2001, p. 27.

[57] *W^{11}*: 2, 37, 4, 5, 45, 13, 1, 3, 183, 208, 337, *Didascalicon*, 65, 204, 41, 8, *Monologion Ep.*

Stemmatic structure of Wilmart 14

Where the agreement of W^1W^2 differs from the text of the family's other members, it is stronger. W^1 and W^2 are independent of each other, both having isolated weak readings. Such weaknesses in neither W^1 nor W^2 agree with the other members of the family — excluding the few anomalies reported at the end of the footnote.[58] We must conclude that W^1W^2 derive (directly or indirectly) from the same manuscript; that they must be closer to the archetype of the family *Wilmart 14* than any other survivor; and that no known manuscript derives from them. The archetype of *Wilmart 14* is φ.

W^3W^4 represent the next stemmatic step. They share certain weak readings against W^1W^2.[59] In addition, each includes its own

---

[58]   (1) W^1 weaker than W^2 (*AEp.* 1–4, 37, 41). 1:4 fidei et sapientiae] fidei sapientieque W^1; 1:8 Anglis] angelis W^1; 3:14–15 prosint] prosit W^1; 3:34 quantum in deo] quanto in deum W^1; 3:38 uobis] nobis W^1; 4:13 patrem meum] meum patrem W^1; 4:21 de inuicem] ad inuicem W^1; 4:38 retribuam tibi] retribuas mihi W^1; 37:21 Ingressus es karissime] Ingressus karissime es W^1; 37:30 illi persuadet] persuadet illi W^1; 37:56 maioribus] minoribus W^1; 37:80 quod] quia W^1.
(2) W^2 weaker than W^1 (1–4, 37, 41). 1:1 multum] *om.* W^2; 2:73 allocutionis in memoriam] allocucionis memoriam W^2; 3:5 inertiae] inertio W^2; 3:12 lentum] talentum W^2; 3:31 delectabilius] delectabilis W^2; 4:6 id est] idem W^2; 4:17–18 meam conscientiam] meam con scientiam W^2; 4:21 sumus conscientiarum] sumus cum scientiarum W^2; 4:24 mecum] meum W^2; 37:29 imprudentemque] imprudentem W^2; 37:29 uersutiis] uersutus $W^2(S^1)$; 37:40 nusquam] numquam W^2; 37:42 distescit] ditescat W^2; 37:50 inutiles] utiles W^2; 37:68 qualemcumque] qualecumque W^2; 38:82 moneam] meneam W^2; 37:86 circumspicere] conspicere $W^1W^3W^4W^5W^6$ cumspicere W^2; 37:88 pertingere] *om.* W^2; 37:91 studuerit] studierit W^2; 37:94 apparuerit] appruerit W^2; 37:94 et ego] ego W^2; 41:11 meae dilectionis] dilectionis mee $W^1W^3W^4W^5W^6$; dilectionis tue W^2. 3) Anomalies 1:1 Suo domino et suo patri W^5W^6] Suo et domino suo patri W^1 Suo et domino et suo patri W^2W^4; 3:12 praestolata lentum W^1] prestolata talentum W^2W^3 prestolata tam lentum W^4; 3:32 fragrat] fraglat W^1W^6 flagrat $W^2W^3W^4$; 4:1 domno Gundulfo] domino Gundulfo W^1W^6; 4:41 Domno] Domino W^1W^2.
[59]   (1) The agreement of W^3W^4 against W^1W^2 (*AEp.* 1–4, 37, 41). 1:17 carissimi] karissimo $W^3W^4W^5W^6$; 2:57 quia] *om.* $W^3W^4W^5W^6$; 2:66 letius] leuius $W^3W^4W^5W^6$; 2:appendix quippe opus] quoque opus $W^3W^4W^5W^6$; 2:appendix ergo] uero $W^3W^4W^5W^6$; 3:19 certus] *om.* $W^3W^4W^5W^6$; 4:9 desiderium meum] desiderium me $W^3W^4W^5W^6$; 37:7 distineat] distinguat $W^3W^4W^5W^6$; 37:9 sese] *om.* $W^3W^4W^5W^6$; 37:12 annuente] adiuuante $W^3W^4W^5W^6$; 37:16 in hac epistola] *om.* W^3; 37:66 misericordiam] misericordia $W^3W^4W^5W^6$. See also 3:6–7 possit

weak readings (those of W^4 also appear in its derivatives).[60] We may conclude that W^3W^4 descend from a shared source. This is called χ. In $W^1W^2\chi$, no two witnesses share the same weak reading against a strong one in the third. Thus $W^1W^2\chi$ descend from the same source independently of one another. This source is φ. Since χ's descendants are French, it was itself probably either French or brought to France from England. χ's earliest witness, W^4, is from s. xii[2/4]. I shall return below to the origin of φ.

The Cistercian manuscripts $W^5W^6W^7$ descend from W^4. Certain corrections to the text of W^4, generating new readings that appear in the Cistercian manuscripts, provide clear proof of this descent.[61]

compensari] compensari ualeam W^3 ualeat compensari $W^4W^5W^6$; 3:36 Babylonia] babilonica $W^1W^2W^3$ *from* babilonica W^4; 37:27 monachicum] monacho W^3 monachi $W^4W^5W^6$; 37:91 peruiderit] prouiderit *from* peruiderit[?] W^3 preuiderit[?] $W^4W^5W^6$; 65:44 quibus debent] opera W^3 operibus debent *del.* W^4.

(2) Anomalies (1–4, 37, 41). 1:19 quo modo W^3] quoquo modo $W^4W^5W^6(S^1S^2)$; 3:16 mihi prosint et tibi W^3] mihi prosint ut et tibi $W^1W^2W^4W^5W^6$; 3:30–31 Cuius bonus odor W^5W^6] Cum bonus odor W^3 Cui bonus odor W^4.

[60] (1) W^3 weaker than W^4 (*AEp.* 1–4, 37, 41) 1:19 minus] *om.* W^3; 2:10 reuerenda] referendo W^3; 2:18 emolumento] emolumenta W^3; 2:19 sibi] *om.* W^3; 2:21 feruorem multis] feruorem et multis W^3; 2:42–43 uitam suam] uitam W^3; 2:51 quasi] *om.* W^3; 2:58 diutius] diu W^3; 2:80 irrideatis] rideatis W^3; 2:84 ille] illam W^3; 2: appendix uirtute patientiae] paciencie W^3; 3:2 inter – numerus] *om.* W^3; 4:4 incertus] incertum W^3; 4:41 alteram epistolam] hanc epistolam W^3; 37:29 multimodis] multismodis W^3; 37:20 cessat] cesset W^3; 37:38 ariditatem] *om.* W^3; 37:38–39 prouenit] peruenit W^3; 37:44 inde se] mens se W^3 (*from* inse W^4); 37:45 odium eorum] eorum odium W^3; 37:69 in portus tranquillitatem] in tranquillitatem portus W^3; 37:77 quam] *om.* W^3; 37:81 aliquam admonitionem] aliqua ammonitione W^3; 37:84 consulit] confidit W^3; 41:8 deest] deesse W^3; 41:12 me] *om.* W^3.

(2) W^4 weaker than W^3 (*AEp.* 1–4, 37, 41, (45)). 3:1 Domino] Domno $W^4W^5W^6$; 3:8 9 amicum tuum] amicus tuus *corr. from* amicu tuu W^4 amicus tuus W^5W^6; 3:12 lentum] tam lentum *corr. from* talentum W^4 tam lentum W^5W^6; 5:20 confrui] perfrui *corr. from* confrui W^4 perfrui W^5W^6; 37:11 patria] patriam $W^4W^5W^6$; 37:26 in qua est] *om.* W^5W^6 in qua *del.* W^4 est *om.* W^4; 37:71 sollicitudini] sollicitudine *from* sollicitudinis W^4; 41:4 meus] is *corr. from* nis W^4 is W^5W^6; 41:5 indicemus] indagemus *corr. from* indigemus W^4 indagemus W^5W^6; 45:12 intimatum] intimandum W^4; 45:26 et] et *del.* ut *inserts* W^4 ut W^5W^6.

[61] For the sake of convenience, this footnote deals with W^8, the next stemmatic step as well. 3:2 tantum numerus] tantos numeros *from* tantum numero W^4 tantos numeros $W^5W^6W^7(W^8)$; 3:7–8 possit compensari] possit *om.* ualeat *inserts in marg.* compensari *corr. from* conpresensari W^4 ualeat compensari

The Cistercian group subdivides into two independent branches, W^5 and W^6W^7.[62] Since the agreement of branches W^5 and W^6W^7 is weaker than W^4, at least one lost manuscript must have stood between $W^5W^6W^7$ and W^4.[63] This lost witness is called ψ. W^6 is the source of W^7, a conclusion that is based on limited but unequivocal evidence.[64]

$W^5W^6W^7(W^8)$; 3:8–9 amicum tuum] amicus tuus *corr. from* amicu tuu W^4 amicus tuus $W^5W^6W^7(W^8)$; 3:12 lentum] tam lentum *corr. from* talentum W^4 tam lentum $W^5W^6W^7(W^8)$ talentum W^{10}; 4:33 Osberno] osberto *corr. from* osberno W^4 osberto $W^5W^6W^7(W^8)$; 4:35 Osbernus] osbertus *corr. from* osbernus W^4 osbertus $W^5W^6W^7(W^8)$; 5:7 unam] unum *corr. from* unam W^4 unum $W^5W^6W^7(W^8)$; 5:20 confrui] perfrui *corr. from* confrui W^4 perfrui $W^5W^6W^7(W^8)$; 37:26 in qua est] *om.* $W^5W^6W^7(W^8)$ est *om.* in qua *del.* W^4; 37:71 sollicitudini et amoris delectationi] sollicitudine et amoris delectationi *from* sollicitudinis et amaris dilectioni W^4 sollicitudine et amoris delectatione $W^5W^6W^7(W^8)$; 37:85 dilectus dilector] dilectus et dilector $W^5W^6W^7(W^8)$; et *inserts in marg.* W^4; 41:4 meus (W^8)] is *corr. from* nis W^4 is W^5W^6 his W^7; 41:5 indicemus] indagemus *corr. from* indigemus W^4 indagemus $W^5W^6W^7(W^8)$; 45:26 et] et *del.* ut *inserts* W^4 ut $W^5W^6W^7(W^8)$. In at least one case, W^4 restored a previously corrupted reading to the original. 45:10 per caritatis communionem] per caritatem communionem $W^1W^2W^3(S^1S^2)$ per caritatis communionem *corr. from* per caritate communionem W^4 per caritatis communionem $W^5W^6W^7(W^8)$.

[62] This footnote, likewise, also deals with W^8.
(1) W^5 against the agreement of $W^4W^6W^7(W^8)$ 2:appendix potuisset $W^4W^6W^7(W^8)$] posset W^5; 3:22 scito $W^4W^6W^7(W^8)$] scio W^5; 3:31–32 animae meae $W^4W^6W^7(W^8)$] animae nostrae W^5; 37:85 mentis $W^4W^6W^7(W^8)$] menti W^5. (2) The agreement of W^4W^5 against the agreement of W^6W^7: rubric to *AEp.* 1 (to Lanfanc): Epistola anselmi ad Lanfrancum $W^5(W^8)$; Epistola anselmi ad ~~radulfum~~ *in marg. in another hand* lanfr[ancum] W^6; Epistola anselmi ad radulfum W^7; 2:3 percipere] recipere $W^6W^7(W^8)$; 2:appendix conualeat] conualescat $W^6W^7(W^8)$; 4:1 domno] domino $W^6W^7(W^8)$; 5:18 rationabili] racionali $W^6W^7(W^8)$; 5:22 quo] quod $W^6W^7(W^8)$; 37:18 nostro amico] amico nostro $W^6W^7(W^8)$; 37:19 possim] possum $W^6W^7(W^8)$. Such agreements do not appear as $W^5W^6 \neq W^4W^7$; $W^5W^7 \neq W^4W^6$.
[63] 3:39 abire] ambire $W^5W^6W^7(W^8)$; 5:24 indeficienter] indesinenter $W^5W^6W^7$ (indesignenter W^8) 37:26 in qua est] *om.* $W^5W^6W^7(W^8)$ in qua W^4; 37:71 sollicitudini...delectationi] sollicitudine...dilectatione *from* sollicitudinis...dilectioni W^4 sollicitudine...delectatione $W^5W^6W^7(W^8)$. Anomalies are: 1:1 Suo domino et suo] Suo et domino et suo $W^4(W^1W^2)$; 8:5 dulcedo] ducedo W^4; 45:12 intimatum] intimandum W^4. Each of the preceding readings could be amended without access to another source.
[64] In W^6, the explicit rubric to *Proslogion* and the incipit rubric to the following *AEp.* 65 stand separately: Explicit. [*a new line*] Epistola anselmi archi-

W^8 bears the idiosyncrasies of W^4, found in $W^5W^6W^7$ too.[65] Furthermore, like W^6W^7, it gives the *Didascalicon* extracts after the letters. Since it does not exhibit the weak readings of W^7 (or those of the English subgroup discussed next), W^8 must derive from W^6. At the beginning of the fourteenth century at the latest, the transmission of *Wilmart 14* came to life again in England, with three witnesses, $W^9W^{10}W^{11}$, known from this period. My analysis of the English branch is based on a limited sampling of the evidence but the results, especially those concerning the relationship of the English group to the Cistercian group, appear relatively strong. In contrast, the conclusions regarding the relationship between W^9 and W^{10} are somewhat less certain. Like W^6W^7, manuscripts $W^9W^{10}W^{11}$ give two extracts from *Didascalicon*. $W^9W^{10}W^{11}$ also reproduce the weak readings of W^6W^7, while contributing more of their own.[66]

---

episcopi. Ad Willelmum abbatem W^6; W^7 joins the two rubrics together as Explicit epistola anselmi ar [*a new line*] chiepiscopi ad willelmum aabbatem W^7. The error in W^7 may be due to the layout in W^6. 3:31 multos $W^6(W^8)$] multas W^7; 41:4–5 quia ego et tu $W^6(W^8)$] quia et ego et tu W^7; 65:43 De lapsis] *division sign in* $W^4W^5W^6$. Cf. also 41:4 meus] is *corr. from* nis W^4 is W^5W^6 his W^7. The numbering of the quires also supports the idea of W^6 influencing W^7. In lat. 4878 (W^6), the quiring does not take into account the opening text, Paulus Orosius, whereas in Arsenal 984 (W^7) the quires containing Orosius's work are also included in the numbering. In other words, Arsenal 984 seem to have been copied from a manuscript that already included both Orosius and Anselm, while there were probably two manuscripts behind lat. 4878.

[65] However, at 41:4, W^8 corrects an error originally caused by W^4: meus W^8] is $W^4W^5W^6$ *corr. from* nis W^4 his W^7. This could have happened without recourse to another source, because the context makes the correct reading more or less obvious: 'Et meus [is W^{4-6}] Gondulfus et tuus Anselmus est testis'. Previous footnotes dealt with the case of W^8.

[66] $W^9W^{10}W^{11}$ share a significant number of weak readings against the other manuscripts; the following includes only those gleaned from *AEp*. 41. 41:4 Et meus] Et idem $W^9W^{10}W^{11}$; 41:5 affectus] effectus $W^9W^{10}W^{11}$; 41:6 ab inuicem] ad inuicem $W^9W^{10}W^{11}$; 41:10 archa?] archa. $W^9W^{10}W^{11}$; 41:10 Quid] Quod $W^9W^{10}W^{11}$; 41:11 te?] te. $W^9W^{10}W^{11}$. Note that W^9W^{10} give a fuller rubric for *AEp*. 65 than W^6 or its known Cistercian relatives. W^9W^{10}: Incipit epistola uenerabilis anselmi ad dominum abbatem Willelmum fiscanensem. $W^4W^5W^6W^7$ do not mention Fécamp. Furthermore, $W^9W^{10}W^{11}$ include the prefatory letter to *Monologion* addressed to Lanfranc, while in general, the manuscripts largely contain the same works, including many pseudo-Anselmian texts not present in the other manuscripts in the family *Wilmart 14*.

The English group thus descends from W^6; this did not apparently happen through W^7.[67]

On the basis of my collation of *AEp*. 41, W^9 is never weaker than $W^{10}W^{11}$. In addition, the two Worcester manuscripts share certain distinctive features, which distinguish them from W^9.[68] Finally, W^{10}'s weak readings are repeated in W^{11}, which also includes some isolated weak readings.[69] Thus W^9 is W^{10}'s (fore)father, which in turn is W^{11}'s (fore)father. The Worcester provenance naturally suggests that W^{11} was a direct copy of W^{10}. The arrangement of the letters in $W^9W^{10}W^{11}$ also reflects this pedigree. While none of the three follows the basic arrangement in *Wilmart 14*, W^9 comes closest to it and W^{11} is furthest from it, with W^{10} falling in between the two.[70]

[67] 3:31 multos $W^9W^{10}W^{11}$] multas W^7; 41:4–5 quia ego et tu W^9] et tuo *om.* $W^{10}W^{11}$ quia et ego et tu W^7.

[68] $W^{10}W^{11}$ weaker than W^9: 41:1 Domno] Domino $W^{10}W^{11}$; 41:4–5 et tu] *om.* $W^{10}W^{11}$; 41:8 quia] de *add.* $W^{10}W^{11}$; 41:9 nobis] *om.* $W^{10}W^{11}$; 41:12 me] ne $W^{10}W^{11}$. Manuscripts $W^{10}W^{11}$ include *AEp*. 204, which does not otherwise appear in *Wilmart 14*. A possible anomaly is: 41:10 assidue serues] serues assidue $W^{10}W^{11}$ serues assiduo[?] W^9. From the microfilm, it is unclear whether the reading in W^9 is *assiduo* or *assidue*. At all events, the context would allow assiduo to be corrected to an adverb.

[69] Problems in reading W^{10}'s Anglicana hand were clearly responsible for some of the errors in W^{11}: *AEp*. 2:50 electione W^{10}] *corr. from* electionis W^{11}; the former results from the cursive final e, which resembled a rounded s. 2:56 nutriunt W^{10}] nutriuit W^{11}; in W^{10}, the abbreviation for a nasal is too far to the right (as is typical in rapid cursives). *AEp*. 2, '*In ipsa quippe*': languescat W^{10}] sanguescat W^{11}. In Anglicana, the letter l has a loop to the right, making it resemble a straight letter s. See also 41:15 Vale.] Valete W^{11}.

[70] *Wilmart 14*: 65, 2, 37, 4, 5, 41, 45, 8, 13, 1, 3, 183, 208, 337. W^8: 41, 65, 8, *Monologion Ep.*, 2, 37, 4, 5, 45, 13, 1, 3, 183, 208, 337, *Didascalicon*. W^{10}: 65, 204, 41, 8, *Monologion Ep.*, 2, 37, 4, 5, 45, 13, 1, 3, 183, 208, 337, *Didascalicon*. W^{11}: 2, 37, 4, 5, 45, 13, 1, 3, 183, 208, 337, *Didascalicon*, 65, 204, 41, 8, *Monologion Ep.*

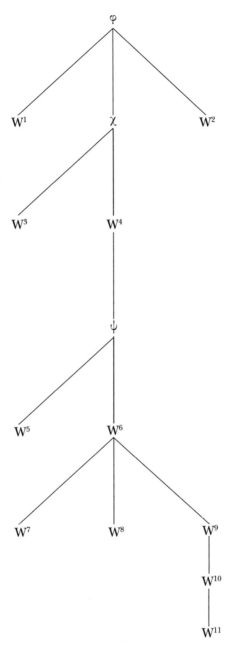

Figure 10: The manuscript tradition of *Wilmart 14*

The origins of Wilmart 14

Certain conclusions may be drawn regarding φ, the parent of the family *Wilmart 14*. φ seems to have joined together two or three originally distinct units or groups of letters. These were:

(1a) *AEp.* 65, 2 (adds '*In ipsa quippe*'), 37
(1b) *AEp.* 4, 5, 41, 45, 8, 13, 1, 3
(2) *AEp.* 183, 208, 337

The letters in divisions 1a and 1b are from Anselm's time as prior, and those in division 2 from his period as archbishop. The material in 1a and 1b is largely identical to that in *Schmitt 15*, which includes all the letters apart from *AEp.* 65. While *AEp.* 65, therefore, appears to have been added to an earlier body of material, there is other evidence suggesting that *Wilmart 14* might have taken the following two letters — *AEp.* 2 and 37 — from the same source. This evidence, distinguishing divisions 1a and 1b, derives from other collections (and we do not have, for example, an attached non-Anselmian text which would mirror a break like the one between 2a and 2b in *Schmitt 15*). First, manuscript *H*'s original letter section is identical to division 1a. Second, the arrangement of letters in *Schmitt 15* and *Sharpe 5* suggests that they too received *AEp.* 2 and 37 from a source that did not provide them with their other letters, as will be discussed later.

Each of the letters in division 2 is connected with the nunnery of Shaftesbury: *AEp.* 183 and 337 were addressed to the convent's Abbess Eulalia and her nuns; *AEp.* 208 was to Archdeacon Hugo, whom Anselm asked to convey his greetings and blessing to the abbesses and nuns of Shaftesbury, Winchester, and Wilton. Furthermore the contents of the letters in division 2 differ from the other material in *Wilmart 14*. In the first eleven letters, Anselm considers fundamental themes of monastic life at a relatively general level. In contrast, the letters in division 2 — *AEp.* 208 in particular — primarily relate to a specific historical context through their addressees, and thus give the impression of being later additions to an earlier body. Finally, *AEp.* 337 reveals clearly that Anselm's letters were of particular importance to the Shaftesbury nuns; they had asked him to write to them.[71] The conclusion is

---

[71] *AEp.* 337: '...petiit dilectio uestra...nostris litteris salutari...Scio quia abundantia uerae et religiosae dilectionis hoc facit, ut litteras meas libenter

that *Wilmart 14* was born in a scriptorium within Shaftesbury's
sphere of influence, possibly at Shaftesbury itself. Salisbury near
Shaftesbury would be a strong candidate, were it not for the fact
that it is known to have produced manuscript *S¹*, which is possibly
the archetype of *Schmitt 15* and of which *Wilmart 14* is independent.

AEp. 337 supplies the *a quo* for *Wilmart 14*. The letter was sent
from Lyon, where Anselm resided between December 1103 and
May 1104. The *ad quem* is supplied by the date of the earliest witness, *W⁴*, which is *s.* xii²/⁴. The collection saw the light probably
closer to the *a quo* than the *ad quem*.

3. SHARPE 5

Contents
AEp. 37, 2 (adds '*In ipsa quippe*'), 183, 160, 161

Before Richard Sharpe's investigations into the main witness
to the family *Sharpe 5*, scholarly interest in this group had been
fitful at best. Five manuscripts are known to survive, but their
widespread circulation — two exemplars are now in the Vatican —
suggests that more may emerge.

London, BL Harley 203 – R¹

s. xii¹/⁴ (unit B); (?)Normandy; parchment; ii (paper) + (28 +)24 + (48 +)
iv' (paper); 205 × 140 (130 × 90) mm; 31 (long) lines

Contents

Unit A	
fols. 1r–26r	Lothar of Segni (Innocent III), '*De sacro altaris mys-terio*' (extracted from *De missarum mysteriis*, PL 217, cols. 773–916)
fols. 26r 27v	'Expositio symboli apostolorum', unidentified, 'Credo in deum patrem omnipotentem. apostoli consiliando'
fols. 27v–28v	Vincent of Beauvais, *Expositio orationis dominicae*

uidere uelitis...Vt cum meam praesentiam, quam religioso affectu desideratis,
secundum uoluntatem uestram habere non potestis, saltem per epistolam meam
aliquatenus illam uobis exhibeatis, et forsitan ut in me memoriam uestri, quasi
ne obdormiat, excitetis.'

| fol. 28v | 'Quaestio an licitum sit statim comedere post sumptionem corporis et sanguinis Christi', an unidentified later addition |
| fol. 28v | 'De excommunicatione', an unidentified latter addition |

Unit B

fols. 29r–40r	Anselm, *Epistola de incarnatione Verbi*
fols. 40r–47v	Anselm, *Proslogion* (entitled first: 'Fides querens intellectum', then 'i. Proslogion')
fols. 47v–52v	Anselm, *Epistolae* (R^1)
fol. 52v	'Adnotatio de modo cogendi mulieres domi remanere', an unidentified addition from *s*. xiv

Unit C

fols. 53r–60r	Anselm, *De conceptu uirginali et de originali peccato*
fols. 60r–65r	Anselm, *De libertate arbitrii*
fols. 65r–75r	Anselm, *De casu diaboli*
fols. 75r–94r	Anselm, *Cur Deus homo*
fols. 94r–98v	Anselm, *De ueritate*
fols. 98v–102r	Later additions including a table of the works in the manuscript
fol. 102v	blank

The second codicological unit of Harley 203 is a booklet of uneven quality. The hand is Norman and may be dated to the beginning of the twelfth century. The initial on fol. 40r suggests an origin in Normandy rather than in England.[72] Interestingly, the booklet has an early text of *Proslogion*, bearing the work's original title 'Fides querens intellectum', subsequently replaced with the present title.[73] Despite the potential Norman origin, the rubricator was acquainted with ecclesiastical circles in southern England. In the rubric to *AEp*. 37, he anachronistically referred to its addressee Lanzo, who was still a novice when the letter was written, as prior. Lanzo held that office at the Cluniac priory of Lewes in 1077–1107. The first and third units are later, *s*. xii[4/4]. By the turn of the thirteenth and fourteenth centuries, the three units had been bound together, as is evidenced by the table of contents at the end. In a fifteenth-century book list from the abbey of St Mary's, York, there appears an identical or near-identical item to the last two booklets; this will shortly be discussed. Since the selection of

---

[72] SHARPE, 'Anselm as author', 2009, p. 24, note 62.

[73] *SAO*, vol. 1, p. 97.

Anselmiana in Harley 203 would only emerge once the two book-lets were bound together, the manuscript may, indeed, embody the item in the list. If so, its medieval provenance was York.

Oxford, Merton College 19 – R²

s. xiv; England; parchment; iv (iv counted in foliation) + 46 + 31 + 170 + ii'; unit 1 and 2: 360 × 230 (280 × 170) mm; 77 lines in two columns

Contents

Unit A

fols. 2r–4r	Anselm, *De ueritate*
fols. 4r–5v	Anselm, *De libertate arbitrii*
fols. 5v–9v	Anselm, *De casu diaboli*
fols. 9v–12v	Anselm, *De conceptu uirginali et de originali peccato*
fols. 12v–20r	Anselm, *Cur Deus homo*
fols. 20r–22v	Anselm, *Epistola de incarnatione Verbi*
fols. 23r–29v	Anselm, *Monologion*
fols. 29v–31r	Anselm, *Proslogion*
fols. 31r–35r	Anselm, *De processione Spiritus Sancti*
fols. 35r–36r	Anselm, *De sacrificio azymi et fermentati*
fol. 36r	Anselm, *Epistola de sacramentis ecclesiae*
fols. 36r–40r	Anselm, *De concordia praescientiae et praedestinationis*
fols. 40r–41v	Anselm, *Epistolae (R²)*
fols. 41v–43r	'De caritate,' unidentified, 'Cogit me instancia tue caritatis monachorum'
fols. 43r–46r	'De corpore Christi', unidentified, 'Primum quidem quid hoc sacrificii corpus appelletis'
fol. 46r–v	Pseudo-Anselm, *De corpore et sanguine Domini (Ep.* IV,107 in *PL* 159, cols. 255–259)
Unit B	
fols. 47r–58v	Robert de Braci?, *De similitudinibus (PL* 159, cols. 605–708)
fols. 58v–60v	Anselm, *De grammatico*
fols. 60v–65v	Eadmer, *De conceptione sanctae Mariae*
fols. 65v–67r	Anselm or/ and Gaunilo?, 'Contra insipientem'
fols. 67r–77v	Anselm, *Meditationes* and *Orationes*
Unit C	A collection of works of Augustine[74]

The manuscript has a long history at Merton College. In exchange for another manuscript, William Rede (bishop of Chichester 1369–85) acquired the present Merton College 19 from William

---

[74] See H. O. Coxe, *Catalogus codicum mss. qui in collegis aulisque oxoniensibus hodie adseruantur*, vol. 1, Oxford, 1852, p. 17.

de Lynham († 1361), a fellow of Merton from 1330 until 1349.[75] In 1374, Rede donated the manuscript to the College.[76]

Vatican City, BAV Vat. lat. 310 – R[3]

s. xiii[2]; Northern Textualis; parchment, ii (paper) + ix (parchment) + 162 + ii (paper); I–IX[12] X[6] XI–XIV[12]; quire IX (fols. 97–108) originally from another manuscript; 300 × 210 (215 × 240) mm; 46–58 lines in two columns

Contents

fol. 1r	John of Damascus, *De fide orthodoxa*, libri I–V (*PL* 94, cols. 790–1227)
fol. 25r	John Chrysostom, *Homilies* (see *PL* 52, cols. 459–480)
fol. 30v	Anselm, *De ueritate*
fol. 35v	Anselm, *De libertate arbitrii*,
fol. 40r	Anselm, *De casu diaboli*
fol. 49r	Anselm, *De conceptu uirginali et de originali peccato*
fol. 55r	Anselm, *Cur Deus homo*
fol. 72r	Anselm, *De processione Spiritus Sancti*
fol. 80r	Anselm, *Epistola de sacrificio azymi et fermentati*
fol. 81r	Anselm, *Epistola de sacramentis ecclesiae*
fol. 82r	Anselm, *De concordia praescientiae et praedestinationis*
fol. 89r	Anselm, *Epistola de incarnatione Verbi*
fol. 93v	Anselm, *Proslogion* (ends abruptly: 'quelibet non immunda' *Pros.*, c. xxv, *SAO*, vol. 1, p. 119, l. 2)
Unit B1	
fol. 97r	Anselm, *Proslogion* (entitled, 'fides querens intellectum')
fols. 100r–108v	Anselm, *Monologion* (ends: 'essentiam et sapientiam et' *Mon.* c. xliv, *SAO*, vol 1, p. 61, l. 4)
Unit B2	
fol. 109r	Anselm, *Monologion* (begins: et uitam in semetipso, *Mon.*, c. xliv, *SAO*, vol. 1, p. 61, l. 4)
fols. 114r–116v	Anselm, *Epistolae* (R[3])
fol. 116v	Robert de Braci?, *De similitudinibus* (*PL* 159, cols. 605–708)
fol. 145r	Gaunilo, *Liber pro insipiente*
fol. 146r	Anselm, *Responsio Anselmi contra Gaunilonem*

---

[75] Fol. 1v: 'Liber M. Willelmi Red prepositi Wynghammensis quem habuit per escambium pro alio libro cum M [...] Willelmi lynham quondam socij domus de Merton. Oretis igitur pro utroque.' *BRUO*, vol. 2, 1193.

[76] Fol. 1v: 'Liber domus scholarium de Merton in Oxon, in communi libraria eiusdem et ad usum communem sociorum ibidem studentium cathenandus Ex dono uenerabilis patris domini Willelmi, tercii Episcopi Ciscestrie Oretis igitur pro eodem et benefactoribus eiusdem ac fidelium animabus a purgatoris liberandis. Walter Roberti.'

fol. 148r	'Bonus homo de omnibus' (an adaption of Similitudines Anselmi clxii, PL 159, col. 691; also in Cambridge, University Library Dd. 9. 5 above)
fols. 148v–149r	Anselm, AEp. 109
fol. 149r	Anselm, Meditatio 3 de redemptione humana
fol. 151r	Bernard of Clairvaux?, Meditationes[?] (cf. PL 184, cols. 485–508)
fol. 155v	Ambrose, De bono mortis

To judge from its palaeographical evidence, Vat. lat. 310 is from the north of the Alps, from the second half of the thirteenth century. The provenance is otherwise unknown. While units B1 and B2 differ from each other in codicological terms, they come from the same book. Where the former ends, the latter continues Monologion without interruption. This manuscript too includes the early version of Proslogion, entitled 'Fides querens intellectum'.

Vatican City, BAV Vat. lat. 10611 – R[4]

s. xiii; parchment; 239 fols.; 193 + 22 + 24; 280 × 195 (185–205 × 130–140) mm; 40–50 lines in two columns

Contents

Unit A

fols. 1r–48v	John of Damascus, De fide orthodoxa, libri I–IV (PL 95, cols. 790–1227)
fols. 49r–72r	Anselm, Cur Deus homo
fols. 72v–80v	Anselm, De conceptu uirginali et de originali peccato
fols. 80v–86v	Anselm, Proslogion
fols. 87r–107r	Anselm, Monologion
fols. 107r–113r	Anselm, De ueritate
fols. 113r–118r	Anselm, De libertate arbitrii
fols. 118r–129r	Anselm, De casu diaboli
fols. 129r–139r	Anselm, De concordia praescientiae et praedestinationis
fols. 139r–141r	Anselm, De sacrificio azymi et fermentati
fol. 141r–v	Anselm, Epistola de sacramentis ecclesiae
fols. 141v–152v	Anselm, De processione Spiritus Sancti
fols. 152v–156v	Gaunilo, Liber pro insipiente (may include Anselm's reply)
fols. 156v–163r	Anselm, Epistola de incarnatione Verbi
fols. 163v–192r	Robert de Braci?, De similitudinibus (PL 159, cols. 605–708)
fol. 193v	blank
Unit B	
fols. 194r–199r	Eadmer, De beatitudine perennis uitae (Memorials, pp. 271–291)
fols. 199r–201r	Anselm, Meditationes 1–3

fols. 201v–203v *Prophetia Sibyllae*[?] (see *PL* 90, cols. 1181–1186)
fols. 203v–208r Eadmer, *De conceptione sanctae Mariae*
fols. 208r–210r Anselm, *Epistolae* (*R⁴*)
fols. 210v–215r Honorius Augustodunensis, *Sigillum sanctae Marie* (*PL* 172, cols. 495–518)
fol. 215v   blank
  Unit C
(*s.* xiv, Gothic cursive)
fols. 216r–237v 'Tabula super dicta Anselmi'
fols. 238r–239v blank

Vat. lat. 10611 has three codicological units, of which the second is ours. There are at least two thirteenth-century hands in this booklet. The first copied the texts by Anselm and Eadmer on fols. 194r–210r, the second *Sigillum beate Marie*.

Paris, BNF lat. 14502 – R⁵

s. xiii²ᐟ³; ?Saint-Victor, Paris (OSA); parchment; I + 178 (+ 124 + I')⁷⁷; I¹² II¹²⁻¹ III¹²–XIV¹² XV¹²⁻¹; 280 × 210 (185 × 130) mm; 36 lines in two columns

Contents

fols. 1r–22v   Anselm, *Monologion*
fols. 22v–28v   Anselm, *Proslogion*
fols. 28v–54r   Anselm, *Cur Deus homo*
fols. 54r–62v   Anselm, *Epistola de incarnatione Verbi*
fols. 62v–73v   Anselm, *De conceptu uirginali et de originali peccato*
fols. 73v–87v   Anselm, *De processione Spiritus Sancti*
fols. 87v–100r   Anselm, *De concordia praescientiae et praedestinationis*
fols. 100r–107v   Anselm, *De ueritate*
fols. 107v–104v   Anselm, *De libertate arbitrii* ('De libero arbitrio')
fols. 104v–126v   Anselm, *De casu diaboli*
fols. 126v–132v   Anselm, *De grammatico*
fols. 132v–135r   Anselm, *Epistola de sacrificio azymi et fermentati*
fol. 135r–v   Anselm, *Epistola de sacramentis ecclesiae*
fols. 135v–136v   *AEp.* 2 (originally without title; 'Epistola ad odonem et lanzonem' added in *s.* xiii/xiv)
fols. 136v–171v   Robert de Braci?, *De similitudinibus* (*PL* 159, cols. 605–708)
fols. 171v–173r   Gaunilo, *Liber pro insipiente*
fols. 173r–175v   Anselm, *Responsio Anselmi contra Gaunilonem*

---

⁷⁷ The foliation skips cxiij and cxlj and thus ends with clxxx. The list of contents below follows the foliation. I have not analyzed the second unit codicologically.

fols. 175v–178v Anselm, *Epistolae* (R^5)
fol. 178v   List of contents covering both units
fols. 179r–180v blank
  Unit B
fols. 181r–303v Petrus Poquetus?, 'Orationarium de uita Christi et de
                  suffragiis sanctorum'[78]
fol. 304r–v   blank

BNF lat. 14502 comprises two originally separate manuscripts. The first, which concerns this study, is roughly from the second third of the thirteenth century. There may be more than one hand in the main text. The manuscript is probably French and from Saint-Victor. André Hausselet, the great Victorine librarian in the late fifteenth century, entered a list of contents on fol. 178v. He also foliated the second unit, beginning from fol. 181. Under Hausselet's foliation, an older one is occasionally visible, showing that the units had previously been separate. The manuscript has a broad selection of Anselm's tracts, *Similitudines*, and the five letters of *Sharpe 5*. The letters do not follow the collection's standard arrangement. They come in two sequences separated by *Similitudines* and the discussion between Anselm and Gaunilo. The first sequence consists of *AEp.* 2 and the latter of *AEp.* 161, 183, 37 and 160.

olim *York BVM, A 7*

    Anselm, *Epistola de incarnatione Verbi*
    Anselm, *Proslogion*
    Anselm, *De conceptu uirginali et de originali peccato*
    Anselm, *De libertate arbitrii*
    Anselm, *De casu diaboli*
    Anselm, *Cur Deus homo*
    Anselm, *De ueritate*
    Anselm, *Epistolae (Sharpe 5)*

A fifteenth-century book list from the Abbey of St Mary's, York, attests to a manuscript bearing an assortment of Anselmiana under shelf mark A 7.[79] The book list covers only a selec-

---

[78] Fol. 181r: 'Sepe rogatus sum ut quo simplex Religiosus debeat potissime quantum ad interiorem hominem se habere'. Ouy attributes the work to Petrus Poquetus.

[79] SHARPE *et al.*, York: Index catalogue of selected authors, 15th cent., *Benedictine Libraries*, 1996, B120.358–362 and A 7.

tion of the texts in the library. It itemizes individual works, instead of individual manuscripts, providing the shelf mark(s) of the manuscript(s) including the work in question. The list does not necessarily mention all items in a given manuscript, and the works mentioned do not necessarily follow the arrangement in which they occurred in the actual manuscripts. The texts in item A 7 are the same as in units B and C of Harley 203, and with one exception, they are listed identically to the arrangement in the manuscript. In the list, the letters (itemized one by one) are placed after the tracts, whereas in Harley 203 they occur between *Proslogion* and *De conceptu uirginali*. Whether the list rearranges the contents to draw a distinction between treatises and letters cannot be known, but this is a possibility. If so, Harley 203 either embodies the York manuscript or served as its (ultimate) source.

Date and structure

AEp. 183 places the *a quo* for *Sharpe 5* in around 1094, and manuscript R^1 provides the *ad quem*, which is loosely s. xii$^{1/4}$. Since Harley 203 is apparently of Norman origin, the family may have been established there. R^1's witness is superior to that of the other manuscripts, which must, therefore, derive from it.[80] Between R^1 and its four derivatives there was a lost intermediary, σ.[81] The four are likely to be independent of each other since the weaknesses in

---

[80]   *AEp.* 2 and 161 were collated from $R^1R^2R^3$, and *AEp.* 37, one of Anselm's longest letters, from $R^1R^2R^3R^4R^5$. As for *AEp.* 2 and 161, R^4 and R^5 were checked where $R^1R^2R^3$ disagree with other manuscripts or one another. In general, R^1 provides the best readings. Where it disagrees with other families, the other manuscripts in *Sharpe 5* follow it. A very few anomalies emerged: 2:84 posteriora $R^2R^3R^4R^5$] posteria R^1; 161:13 petens $R^2R^3R^4$] petes R^1 om. R^5; 161:48 hoc episcopus rapiat $R^2R^3R^4R^5$] hoc christus rapiat R^1 (*an absurd reading which could have been corrected on the basis of the preceding sentence*). See also: 161:6 debet R^2R^5] debuerat R^3 deberet R^1R^4; 161:52 prudentia uestra R^3] prudentia $R^1R^2R^4R^5$

[81]   161:17 loquor R^1] quod *add* $R^2R^3R^4R^5$; 161:37 ergo dicere contra dominum R^1] ergo contra dominum dicere $R^2R^3R^4R^5$; 161:40 os dei sicut R^1] os sicut $R^2R^3R^4R^5$; 161:42 adhaerentem post deum R^1] adherentem deum R^2R^3 adherentem de non R^4 adherentem consilio deum R^5 (*in R^3R^4 empty space follows* adherentem); 161:51–52 sed quia desidero ut R^1] sed desidero $R^3R^4R^5$ sed ut R^2.

them are either isolated or shared by all four with certain exceptions that appear accidental.[82]

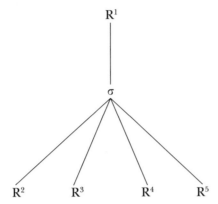

Figure 11: The manuscript tradition of *Sharpe 5*

4. Hereford Cathedral P. I. 3 – *H*

s. xii[in]; St Peter's abbey, Gloucester (OSB); ii + 101 + i; I–II[8] III[4] / IV–XIII[8]; 250 × 170 (175 × 90) mm, 28 (long) lines

Contents

[82] (1) *R²*: 2:78–79 eius irrideatis – lugente *R¹R³R⁴R⁵*] ei arrideatis *R²*. (2) *R³*: 37:85 ut totis uiribus *R¹R⁴*] om. *R³*. (3) *R⁴*: 37:35 structuram – superedificare *R¹R³*] sucurrere homine uite sunt edificare *R⁴*. (4) *R⁵* rearranges the letters, and no manuscript follows its sequence. (5) Anomalies are 37:18 nostro *R¹R²R³*] om. *R⁴R⁵* (*eras. in R⁵*); 37:27 monachicum *R³R⁵*] monachi cum *R¹R²R⁴*; 37:63 ulli *R¹R³R⁴*] illi *R²R⁵*; 37:72 delectationem *R¹R³R⁵ corr. from* sollicitudinem *R⁵*] dilectationem *R²R⁴*; 37:85 quieti mentis *R¹R⁴R⁵ corr. from* quiete mentis *R²R³*].

fol. 101r   Anselm, *Epistolae* (*AEp*. 471, 472, 401 added in *s*. xii)[83]

Hereford Cathedral P. I. 3 is from St Peter's abbey, Gloucester, at the very beginning of the twelfth century. Thomson has
identified the first hand in the manuscript, that of fols. 1r–17v, in
several Gloucester manuscripts (plate 11).[84] At first the manuscript
covered only three letters, *AEp*. 65, 2, and 37. The last letter is
followed by three empty lines, which end the folio. The next folio
(101r) has three further letters, *AEp*. 471, 472, and 401; these are
slightly later additions and I shall omit them from discussion. The
letters on fols. 93v–100v have several hands, none of which is apparently encountered in the previous texts. *H* might have originated
with Lanzo, to whom *AEp*. 2 and 37 were addressed. Lanzo surely
preserved these two letters, which he had asked Anselm to write
to him, and he could have been one of the 'dociles discipuli' who
kept and circulated Anselm's letters according to Orderic Vitalis.[85]

5. THE STRUCTURE OF THE GROUP OF THE MINOR COLLECTIONS

The families *Schmitt 15*, *Wilmart 14*, and *Sharpe 5*, together with
manuscript *H*, make up a stemmatic group that drew on sources
independent of the major collections of Christ Church and Bec.[86]

---

[83] R. M. THOMSON, M. GULLICK & R. A. B. MYNORS, *Catalogue of the Manuscripts of Hereford Cathedral Library*, Woodbridge, 1993, p. 66.

[84] THOMSON, 'Books at Gloucester', 1997, p. 8. The scribe appears in Cambridge, University Library Kk. 3. 28, fols. 98v, l. 20–100r; Hereford Cathedral
O. III. 1, fols. 1r–64v; and possibly BL Royal 5 A. XI, fols. 47–92.

[85] Orderic Vitalis, *Historia ecclesiastica*, vol. 2, p. 296: 'Dociles discipuli epistolas tipicosque sermones eius scripto retinuerunt, quibus affatim debriati non
solum sibi sed et aliis multis non mediocriter profecerunt.'

[86] (1) The shared letters in *S* (= *Schmitt 15*), *W* (= *Wilmart 14*) and *R*
(= *Sharpe 5*) and *H* (*AEp*. 2 and 37). 2:8 aut obsequiis] obsequiis *SWRH*;
2:17 debita *NMCVESWRH*] dilecta *LF on eras. P*; 2:20 domine mi
NMFCVESWRH] mi domine mi *LP*; 2:26 paginis *FEPMDSWRH corr.
from* paginibus *EP*] paginibus *NCVL*; 2:75 quod] que *SWRHMD (*quod *R⁵);
2:82 huius] *om. SWRH*; 2:85 ualete.] '*In ipsa quippe*' (*Moralia 35.14.43–44*)
add. SWRH; 37:15 dei dispositioni *NECVGBSWRH*] dispositioni dei *LPF*;
37:19 Urso *NMECVBSWRH*] Ursione *LPFG* Ursione *corr. from* Urso *R⁵*
(*Schmitt's apparatus is in error as to E*); 37:24 eum] cum *SWRH*; 37:28 professus *FNMCVEGBSWRH*] proffessus *LP*; 37:41 utile] *om. SWRH insert in
marg. R³R⁵*; 37:58 qua] quia *SWRH*; 37:64 iudicem iustum] iustum iudicem
SWRH; 37:75 illaqueet] illaqueat *SWRH corr. from* illaqueat *R³*; 37:81 Ursus

I shall consider the character of these sources, assessing first briefly the Canterbury letters and then in more detail the Bec letters.

The Canterbury correspondence

Of the group of minor collections, only *Wilmart 14* and *Sharpe 5* include any Canterbury correspondence. Of the three Canterbury letters in *Wilmart 14*, only one is found in the witnesses to the major collections. This is *AEp.* 337, which occurs in *M* by William of Malmesbury. As we have seen, *M* also covers other material outside the scope of the family, and we may conjecture that *AEp.* 337 was obtained from a source that was not a major collection. The Canterbury correspondence in *Wilmart 14* is independent of the major collections.

In the case of *Sharpe 5*, there is a real possibility of a connection with the Canterbury and Bec branches of the tradition, since *AEp.* 160 and 161 in *Sharpe 5* appear in the major collections as well. In the case of *AEp.* 160, *Sharpe 5* clearly always disagrees with the Bec tradition δ^a.[87] The collation of *AEp.* 161 adds to the evidence: *Sharpe 5* did not descend from *L* but from at least one step in the transmission above it, since the collection agrees with ω's other

---

NCVESWRH corr. from urso *R⁵*] ursio *LPFG lacuna in B*; 37:85 dilectus dilector] dilector dilectus *SWRH* dilector et dilectus (et *in marg.* W^4) $W^5W^6W^7$. See also 2:49 si iam W^1H] suam *SW (not W^1)*; 2:83 constituetur *FNCVSWRH (not W^{3-7})*] constituitur $LPEW^3W^4W^5W^6W^7$. An anomaly: 2:54 amatissime *NCVEPSR (not R^3) corr. from* amatissime *P*] amantissime *LFMWR³H*. (2) The shared letters in *SW*: 4:17 accipias *NECV*] uideas *LPSW (in marg. S^1 om. S^2*); 4:26–32 Saluta – fratrem nostrum. *om. SW*; 5:15 in nostra *NCVS* (inostra S^1) *W*] nostra *LPE from* in nostra *E*; 5:18 delectatione *NECVSW*] dilectione *L* dilectioni *P*; 5:25–28 Commendo – breuitate.] *om. SW*; 8:3 sapore *ECV*] a sapore *LPFSW*; 8:20 numquam ueracius *NECVSW*] numquam sic ueraciter *LPF*; 8:26 ponat *NCVSW*] ponet *LPFE from* ponat *E*; 13:5 domnum *NVFESW*] donnum *C* dominum *LP*; 13:9 domino *NECVSW*] domno *LPF*; 13:10 fratri *NCV*] suo *add. ELPFSW*; 13:27 archiepiscopo Lanfranco cum de Anglia uenerit] archiepiscopo cum uenerit *SW*; 41:1–3 Suo – felicitate *NECV*] Domino – Anselmus *LPSW*; 41:14 deus tibi *NECSW*] dominus tibi *V* tibi deus *LP*. See also: 1:14 interiorem $NCVSW^1W^2$] interiore $LPEW^4W^5W^6W^7$ *from* interiorem W^4 interiori *MD (W^4 explains $W^{5,6,7}$)*; 45:20 et carissima *NECVS (et inserts S^2) W (not W^1)*] et *om. LPW¹*.

[87] *Sharpe 5* is here *R*. 160:20 diligit minus C^aV^a] minus diligit $RLPEOC^b$ V^bG; 160:26 Delectat C^aV^a] me *add* $RLPEOC^bV^bG$; 160:36 securius uos C^aV^a] uos securius $RLPEOC^bV^bG$ (securius uos R^5) 160:52 siue episcopatum $RLPEO$-C^aV^aG] *om.* OC^bV^b; 160:64 si mea me $RLEOC^bV^bG$] me *om.* C^aV^a.

witnesses whenever these unanimously disagree with L.[88] Since all
the other material in the minor collections is independent of the
major collections, $AEp.$ 160 and 161 are unlikely to have derived
from ω. Rather they come from some earlier stage, perhaps from
the single-sheet letters, released for circulation either by Anselm or
some other party.

The Bec correspondence

I open the discussion with its conclusion: the minor collections
appear to be independent of one another and to have built on
smaller units consisting of not many letters. On account of the historical background of *Schmitt 15* and *Wilmart 14* and their near
identical selections of letters, such a conclusion may at first appear
implausible: our earliest witness to *Schmitt 15*, Trinity College
B. 1. 37 or S^1, is a Salisbury manuscript, while *Wilmart 14* was
probably put together within the same diocese; with the exception of $AEp.$ 65, all Bec letters in *Wilmart 14* are found in *Schmitt 15*. Under these circumstances, an obvious conclusion would
be that *Wilmart 14* derives from *Schmitt 15*. None the less, the
pedigree of the collections is probably more complicated than what
is hinted at by their origin and contents. S^1 has errors that are
not encountered in *Wilmart 14*. A good example is an omission of
eleven words from $AEp.$ 45.[89] S^1 did not father the other families
in the group either, and insofar as it is possible to derive from textual and manuscript evidence, *Schmitt 15*, *Wilmart 14*, *Sharpe 5*,
and H are independent of one another.[90] If, however, *Wilmart 14*

---

[88] 161:11 dominus $LPEOC^bV^b$] domnus RC^aV^aFMDGB (do⁹ R^5) 161:17 sapientiori $RC^aV^aOC^bV^bFMDGB$] sipientiori LPE; 161:20 qui $RC^aV^aOC^bV^bEFM-
DGB$] quid LP; 161:22–23 cum illo in iudicio RFC^aV^aGB cum illo *om.* R^5] in
iudicio cum illo $LPEOC^bV^b$; 161:34 clericos $RLEPFC^aV^aMDGB$] clericis OC^bV^b;
161:44 contra RFC^aV^aGB] aduersum $LPEOC^bV^b$. See also 161:45 eligit $RLPE-
FMC^bV^b$ *(not* R^2*)*] elegit $C^aV^aOGR^2$ *lacuna in* B.

[89] *Schmitt 15 =* S; *Wilmart 14 =* W. 41:15 Vale. $WNCVELP$] Vinculum
coniugale – una caro. *adds* S; 45:3–6 uitae – Postquam $WNCVELP$] *om.* S.
See also: 45:9 Ut] et S; 45:10 possem $WNCVELP$] possum; 45:10 caritatis
$WNCVELP$] caritatem S (*Schmitt erroneously reports this reading for* W^2 *as
well*); 45:28 possint $WNCVELP$] possim S; 45:36 domina $WNCVELP$] *om.* S.

[90] (1) S weaker than the other collections: 2:1 Dominis] Karissimis S
(KARISSIMIS S^1 [Karissi]mis S^2); 3:9 patriae supernae] supernae patriae S;
3:15 quas tuas] quas tua S; 3:23 efficacius] scias *adds* S; 4:10 Et tu] Et tuis
S; 5:6 desiderari] desiderare S; 5:12 Et sic exhibeamus] Vt sic exhibeamus S;

and *Sharpe 5* do derive from *Schmitt 15*, and *H* from *Wilmart 14*, textual evidence necessitates more hypothetical manuscripts to be established: a lost archetype of *Schmitt 15* would have provided the basis for *Wilmart 14* and *Sharpe 5*, and since the agreement of W^1 and W^2 at times produces inferior text to *H*, an additional lost manuscript, beside φ, would also be needed. While this scheme must remain a possibility, there is another solution, which has much to recommend it. The following table shows the letters in the minor collections in their actual order.

H	65, 2 (adds '*In ipsa quippe*'), 37
Wilmart 14	65, 2 (adds '*In ipsa quippe*'), 37, 4, 5, 41, 45, 8, 13, 1, 3, 183, 208, 337
Schmitt 15	136, 1, 3, 11, 13, 4, 5, 6, 38, 8, 45, 61, 41 (adds '*Vinculum coniugale*'), 37, 2 (adds '*In ipsa quippe*')
Sharpe 5	37, 2 (adds '*In ipsa quippe*'), 183, 161, 160

The table immediately reveals certain structural elements that are repeated. As already noted, in *Schmitt 15* there is a split between *AEp.* 41 and *AEp.* 37, marked by notes extracted from Ernulf's *De incestis coniugiis*; a gap filled with foreign text suggests a change of sources. The letters that follow the split in *Schmitt 15* — *AEp.* 37 and 2 (adds '*In ipsa quippe*') — are the only Bec letters to appear in *Sharpe 5*, which arranges them likewise. Since *Sharpe 5* is independent of *Schmitt 15* (or at least of its surviving witnesses), the suggestion is that both collections drew on the same source for these two letters. In contrast, *Wilmart 14* and

37:8 fit ut] *om.* S ut *interlinear* H; 37:14 quoniam] si *adds* S; 37:16 cum] *om.* S; 37:17 admonitionis] admonitiones S; 37:31 in eo] *om.* S; 37:42 ad bonum] ab omni S; 37:51 ubi] *om.* S; 37:58 agat] agit S; 37:59 etiam] *om.* S; 37:78 breuis] *om.* S; 41:15 Vale.] Vinculum coniugale – una caro *adds* S
(2) W weaker than the other collections: 2:12 caritatis amplexu] amplexu caritatis W; 2:29 ex eiusdem] eiusdem W; 2:44 timeat] inueniat W; 2:45 Quippe quoniam] Quoniam quippe W; 37:86 circumspicere] conspicere W (cumspicere W^2).
(3) As for *Sharpe 5* and manuscript *H*, the whole problem is irrelevant: their limited coverage (two Bec letters in *Sharpe 5* and three in *H*) suggests that they played no role in the tradition of *Schmitt 15* and *Wilmart 14*. *Sharpe 5* weaker than the other collections: 2:6 amorem] amore R; 2:34 perdat (*sic* S^2)] prodat RS^1; 2:38 ad quae] atque R *corr. in* R^3 (*likewise in* S^1); 2:46 si iam] suam R *corr. in* R^3 (*likewise in* S^1 *and possibly in* S^2). H weaker than the other collections: 65:4 eius concepi] concepi H; 65:94 oboedientiae] *om.* H.

H reverse the arrangement of the two letters and insert *AEp.* 65
— absent from the other two families — before them.[91] Since *H* is
independent of *Wilmart 14* (or at least the agreement of its surviving witnesses is sometimes weaker than *H*), the suggestion is that
H and *Wilmart 14* drew on the same source for these three letters.
The hypothetical source for *AEp.* 2 and 37 and potentially behind
Schmitt 15 and *Sharpe 5* may be called *η*, and that for *AEp.* 65,
37, and 2 and potentially behind *Wilmart 14* and *H* may be called
θ. If these two hypothetical sources existed, *η* was likely to have
served as a source for *θ*.

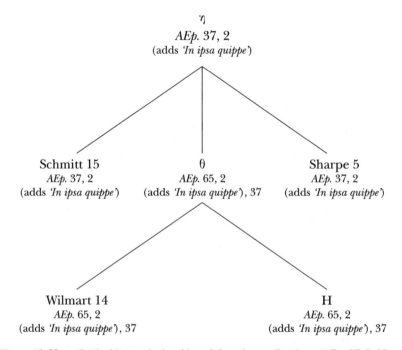

Figure 12: Hypothetical interrelationships of the minor collections: *AEp.* 37, 2, 65

The following table presents the contents of the families
Schmitt 15 and *Wilmart 14* stripped both of the '*ηθ* material'

---

[91] *Wilmart 14* and *H* also agree against the other collections at: 37:41–42
bonorum operum] operum bonorum *WH*; 37:51 se iam tandem] iam se tandem
WH (tandem se iam *R³*). See also 2:54 amatissime *NCVEPSR (not R³) corr.
from* amantissime *P*] amantissime *WHLFMR³*.

(*AEp.* 2, 37, 65) presently considered and of the letters postdating Anselm's period as prior of Bec, which are almost certainly later additions to earlier bodies.[92]

Schmitt 15	*AEp.* 1, 3, 11, 13, 4, 5, 6, 38, 8, 45, 61, 41 (adds '*Vinculum coniugale*')
Wilmart 14	*AEp.* 4, 5, 41, 45, 8, 13, 1, 3[93]

Twelve letters remain in *Schmitt 15* and eight in *Wilmart 14*. All letters that appear in *Wilmart 14* are included in *Schmitt 15*. While these two clutches of letters — or at least their surviving witnesses — are independent of each other, they must share their source. I call this hypothetical source *ι*. Although the arrangement of the *ι* material in *Schmitt 15* and *Wilmart 14* differs from each other, there are certain points of correspondence: *AEp.* 1 and 3 as well as 4 and 5 occur in the identical order in both collections. This might reflect the codicological character of the hypothetical *ι* source; it was perhaps made up of small separate units, e.g. bifolia. How could such small units accumulate into *Schmitt 15* and *Wilmart 14* in the region of Salisbury and Shaftesbury, in other words outside Canterbury? One explanation is that Bishop Osmund of Salisbury obtained — perhaps from Anselm — the letters and the treatises found in Trinity College B. 1. 37 in small units, such as booklets, quires, and folia. After the production of the surviving Salisbury booklets, the originals, at least for the letters, would have remained and circulated in the diocese. Later these small entities would have served as sources for *Wilmart 14*.

Since the *ι* letters belong to the early years of Anselm's public career, he may have published them when prior of Bec. Equally, some of our hypothetical sources could easily have been compiled outside Bec and Canterbury, perhaps by an addressee or a pupil. The testimony of Orderic Vitalis that Anselm's pupils circulated

---

[92] The Canterbury correspondence (*AEp.* 183, 208, 337) has been removed from *Wilmart 14*, and the only letter from Anselm's time as abbot (*AEp.* 136) has been removed from *Schmitt 15*. In each case, both the date and the placing of the letter within the collections suggest a pedigree that is not dependent of that of the letters included in the table.

[93] The '*Vinculum coniugale*' is absent from *Wilmart 14*.

his letters would support this view.[94] For example, Lanzo, a novice and monk of Cluny, ultimately prior of Lewes, could have been behind η, comprising *AEp.* 37 and 2, both of which were addressed to him.

Since where argumentation is speculative, any conclusion must remain tentative, this discussion closes with a caveat. We cannot yet, if ever, see what existed behind the minor collections. No editor of Anselm's correspondence should risk reaching for the text of any of the hypothetical collections outlined here.

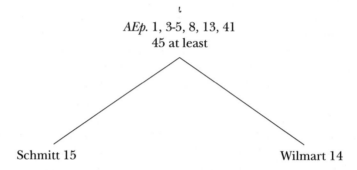

Figure 13: The hypothetical source behind the main sequence of *Schmitt 15* and *Wilmart 14*

[94] Orderic Vitalis, *Historia ecclesiastica*, vol. 2, p. 296: 'Dociles discipuli epistolas tipicosque sermones eius scripto retinuerunt, quibus affatim debriati non solum sibi sed et aliis multis non mediocriter profecerunt.'

V. THE PRINTED EDITIONS

Preliminary remarks

Anselm's letters were published in print for the first time during the period of the incunabula. The number of letters available in print remained modest until the early seventeenth century when certain monastic scholars in France took a fresh interest in Anselm. New manuscripts were found, and new editions were published, often absorbing texts from earlier ones. The process of digesting previous editorial work culminated in the *Patrologia Latina*, where the reader encounters an almost indigestible mess, characterized by duplication and misattribution. What follows serves as a textual history of the editions up to and including the *Patrologia Latina*.

1. Incunabula

*Editio princeps: Petrus Danhauser 1491 – a (*GW 2032*)*

On 27 March 1491, fourteen letters of Anselm's were published in print as part of the *Opera et tractatus beati Anselmi archiepiscopi cantuariensis ordinis sancti Benedicti*.[1] This *editio princeps* is *a*. The project was initiated and funded by the editor, Peter Danhauser († *c*. 1515). His other publications included works by both medieval and contemporary humanist authors.[2] The Anselm

---

[1] For this study I have used Helsinki, National Library Ink. k. 93 and Stockholm, KB Inkunabel 64. *Cur Deus homo* had twice previously been published in print, in 1474 at the latest (*GW* 2035) and in around 1485 (*GW* 2036). Texts misattributed to Anselm were printed before and after 1491: *GW* 2037–2045, of which the last three were in Low German. For a wider discussion of the publication of Anselm's texts, see *Prolegomena*, pp. 9–34 and *Histoire littéraire de la France*, par des réligieux Bénédictins de la Congrégation de Saint-Maur, Paris 1733–, vol. 9, pp. 460–465.

[2] *Repertorium auctoritatum Aristotelis et aliorum philosophorum*, Peter Wagner, Nuremberg 1490 (*GW* 3757). – Hermolaus Barbarus, *Oratio ad Fridericum III. imperatorem et Maximilianum I. regem Romanorum* (Brügge 1486), Nuremberg: Peter Wagner, after 2.4.1490 (*GW* 3346). – Thomas à Kempis, *Opera*, Nuremberg: Kaspar Hochfeder, 1494 (*HC* 9769). – Dionysius Carthusiensis/Jacobus de Gruytrode, *Specula omnis status uitae humanae*, Nuremberg: Peter Wagner, 1495 (*GW* 8419), including a dedication letter to Georg Pirckheimer. – Guillermus Alvernus episcopus Parisiensis, *Opera*, Nuremberg: Georg

edition was printed in Nuremberg by Caspar Hochfeder. Later
in 1494 Hochfeder collaborated with Danhauser in editing the
Opera of Thomas à Kempis.[3] Danhauser's publication includes all
Anselm's most important treatises (bar *De grammatico*), a handful
of his prayers and meditations,[4] and only fourteen of the letters.[5]
A number of works misattributed to Anselm in the Middle Ages
were also included in the edition.[6] I have noted above that Danhauser's source was a lost manuscript that had probably also been
G's exemplar.[7]

Danhauser's work has been heavily criticized.[8] The biography
of Anselm that Danhauser compiled is in particular riddled with
mistakes, casting a shadow of doubt over the entire work. Nevertheless, the edition shaped scholarship for almost five hundred

Stuchs, after 31.3.1496 (*GW* 11862). – Danhauser participated in the Nuremberg edition of Fidelis Cassandra's *Oratio pro Bertucio Lamberto* (*GW* 9889),
which *inter alia* includes a letter of his; the dating of the letter, 22.11.1489, is
the edition's *a quo*. Danhauser's projects also included the incomplete *Arche-
typus Triumphantis Romae*, for which he commissioned allegorical illustrations
from Michael Wolgemut, Dürer's teacher.

[3] *BMC* II, 473.

[4] *Med.* 2 and 11; *Or.* L and LI in part.

[5] *AEp.* 101, 112, 417 (*Epistola de sacramentis ecclesiae*), 121, 168, 258, 231,
37, 65, 160, 161, 188, 281, 285.

[6] On these, see the *Prolegomena*, p. 11.

[7] See subsection III.2.18.

[8] *Prolegomena*, pp. 9–10. This criticism has in part been unfair, however.
Schmitt reported that Danhauser had ranked Anselm beneath Jerome as a
writer and that the well-known German humanist Loeffelholtz († 1509), to whom
Danhauser dedicated the edition and from whom he had sought an evaluation
of Anselm's literary merit, reprimanded the editor for this. Schmitt's perception was mistaken and derived from a typographical error in the Basel edition
he used (descended from the Nuremberg one). According to the Basel text,
Danhauser wrote: 'Vt uidere mihi uideor eum [Anselmum] diuo Hieronimo qui
tamen multarum rerum peritia et eloquentia summa calluit, mirabili quadam
ingenii acrimonia, *pene* parem atque comparandum [my emphasis]'. In the original edition, however, the word 'piene' replaces 'pene', which is self-evidently a
misprint: Danhauser's original reading must have been *plene*. This is also supported by Loeffelholtz. In the letter appended to the work, he wrote 'Ipsoque
[Anselmo] adeo delectaris, ut uel beati Hyeronimi sanctissimi, ac elegantissimi
doctoris eloquio parem existimare ausis'. Thus the substance of Loeffelholtz's
criticism was rather different from Schmitt's understanding of it. In writing
'nemo iudicare qui ignoret' Loeffelholtz was not defending Anselm, but indicating that great men should not be compared in the first place.

years, and Danhauser's influence is detectable in every subsequent publication of Anselm's collected works, including Schmitt's edition.[9]

The later printings of Danhauser's edition – a² *(GW 2034)*, a³ *(GW 2033)*

Before 1500, Danhauser's work was apparently reprinted with slight alterations at least three times. The earliest of these reprints, and a somewhat uncertain case, was perhaps made in Nuremberg in 1494, though at present this is known only from a later reference.[10] Two reprints have been identified with certainty. According to the *Gesamtkatalog der Wiegendrücke*, the earlier was printed in Strasbourg by Georg Husner apparently after 1496 (although we perhaps should take this year as our initial terminus),[11] and the later in Basel, in or before 1497, by Johann Amerbach, one of the most famous book printers of his day. I shall call the former a^2 and the latter a^3.[12] a^2 was a^3's source.[13]

The most significant innovations in the Strasbourg edition were the omissions of Danhauser's and Loeffelholtz's letters to each other and of Danhauser's biography of Anselm, the transfer of certain texts to the end of the work,[14] the addition of the tool *annotatio principalium sententiarum* at the beginning of the work, and the removal of *AEp.* 417, that is the *De sacramentis*, from the letter collection, which appeared both among treatises and letters in the *editio princeps*.[15] a^3, which adopted a^2's novelties, further amended the arrangement of the works, presenting *Monologion* and *Proslogion* in chronological order.

---

[9] *Prolegomena*, p. 12.

[10] *Histoire littéraire de la France*, vol 9, p. 460.

[11] I have consulted BAV Inc. III. 231 (*olim* Arm. 367. 1151). Georg Husner also produced the earliest printing of the *Cur Deus homo*, GW 2035, cited above.

[12] I have consulted Stockholm, KB Inkunabel 65.

[13] Schmitt (*Prolegomena*, p. 13, note 10) noted the annotation 'Nicolaus Pol Doctor 1494' in a a^3 in the collections of the Innichen Stiftsbibliothek. '1494' always follows Nicholas Pol's name in his inscriptions, however, and it does not indicate the year of the inscription.

[14] 'Inuocatio matris uirginis simul et filij in oratione ad sanctam Mariam' and 'Ex gestis Anselmi colliguntur forma et mores beate Marie'.

[15] On the other alterations, see *Prolegomena*, p. 13.

The edition of Anselm's collected works by Anton Demochar ès constitutes an epilogue to the incunabula. The edition, which appeared in Paris in 1544, derived the letters from Danhauser via the Strasbourg printing, i.e. a^2. Demochar ès's edition is here referred to as a^4. Although Demochar ès added no new letters to the corpus in print, his contribution was not insignificant: it was apparently his publication that transmitted Danhauser's work to subsequent editors.[16]

2. EDITIONS PRIOR TO THE PATROLOGIA LATINA

In 1612 Jean Picard, an Augustinian monk of Saint-Victor, Paris, enlarged the correspondence in print to include 289 letters in total.[17] I shall refer to Picard's edition as b. Manuscript V, i.e. BNF lat. 14762, which was then still part of the library of Saint-Victor, served as Picard's source, except for letters III,157–159; the numbering is of his edition and, thus, of the *Patrologia*. Picard retained the arrangement of his source and divided the collection into three books, mirroring the development of Anselm's career: the first book comprises his letters as prior, the second those as abbot, and the third his correspondence as archbishop. This was a natural, solid solution, but when later editors, especially Gabriel Gerberon, expanded the collection by adding in new letters, the final arrangement became awkward and misleading, as can be seen from the *Patrologia Latina*.[18] Of the letters published by Danhauser, only *AEp.* 168 was missing from his source, and Picard

---

[16] A. DEMOCHARÈS (ed.), *Omnia diui Anselmi Cantuariensis archiepiscopi theologorum omnium sui temporis facile principis opuscula*, Paris, 1544, fols. 112r–117r. A further *opera omnia* with the letters originally from Danhauser is *Diui Anselmi Cantuariensis archiepiscopi...omnia quae reperiri potuerunt opera*, 3 vols., Cologne, 1573, published under the auspices of Maternus Cholinus. The letters are in volume 3, pp. 278–289. See *Prolegomena*, pp. 14–20, 151

[17] J. PICARD (ed.), *Diui Anselmi archiepiscopi Cantuariensis opera omnia quattuor tomis comprehensa*, Cologne, 1612. Picard knew that Archbishop Parker had stated that 367 of Anselm's letters were known. Parker based this figure on *E*, which formed part of his own collection (Cambridge, Corpus Christi College 135), and which contained 367 letters according to its erroneous numbering.

[18] b's material was taken into the *Patrologia Latina*, where its content is divided between volumes 158 and 159. The *Patrologia*'s *libri epistolarum* i and ii, and letters 1–159 of the third are taken from b and follow its arrangement. The *liber epistolarum* iv includes the material added by subsequent editors.

placed it after the material he had edited from *V* as III,157. He
also published two further letters, of which the first was misattributed (III,158) and the second (III,159) may belong to Anselm,[19]
and which were to remain attached to Anselm's letter collection
until Schmitt removed them from the corpus. In 1630, Théophile
Raynaud SJ reproduced Picard's editions of the letters in his *opera
omnia* of Anselm.[20]

The Maurist Luc d'Achery († 1685) published the prefatory letter to *Monologion*, addressed to Lanfranc, in the third volume of
his *Spicilegium*, which drew on the manuscripts of French Benedictine monasteries, and then eight of Anselm's letters in the ninth
volume of the series. D'Achery's editions in volume nine will be
referred to as *c*.[21] These letters were absent from Picard's edition
and his source *V*. Textual criticism indicates that *c*'s source was
Troyes 1614, *O* in this study: the letters are arranged identically
and with a few exceptions, *c* repeats *O*'s textual idiosyncrasies;[22] the

---

[19] On III,158 ('*Gratulor admodum*') see SCHMITT, 'Die echten und unechten
Stücke', 1955, pp. 223–224. On III,159 ('*Quando respondi*') see *Memorials*,
pp. 320–322 (for a discussion and an edition of the text from Hereford O. I. 6,
fol. 43r–v; Picard's exemplar is unknown). Schmitt misattributes the publication of these two to Gerberon.

[20] T. RAYNAUD, *Sancti Anselmi archiepiscopi Cantuariensis opera omnia*,
Lyon, 1630, pp. 1–110.

[21] D'ACHERY, *Spicilegium*, vol. 9, 1669, pp. 111–125. *AEp.* 196, 230, 232,
245, 254, 328, 194, 198. d'Achery's great work was republished as *Spicilegium
siue collectio ueterum aliquot scriptorum qui in Galliae bibliothecis delituerant.
Noua editio*, 3 vols., (eds.) É. BALUZE & E. MARTÈNE, 1723, Paris.

[22] E.g. *AEp.* 194:1 reuerendo] *om. Oc*; 194:6 loquendo] *om. Oc*; 194:10 mei
memor] memor mei *Oc*; 194:11 illum] illam *Oc*; 198:2 seniori] *om. Oc*; 198:14
non rogando] *om. Oc*; 198:16 quod gerebatur displiceret] displiceret quod gerebatur *Oc*; 198:18 metropolitani Rotomagensis] Rotomagensis episcopi *Oc*; 198:25
ut mea interat] *om. Oc*; 198:30 me cosidero] considero me *Oc*; 198:35 pacem
uobis] nobis pacem *Oc corr.* nobis *from* uobis *O*; 198:40–41 dei uoluntatem] uoluntatem dei *Oc*; 198:44 definiri] diffiniri *Oc*; 198:45 nostram proferri] nostram
deferri *c* uestram deferri *O*; 232:13 enim] *om. Oc*; 232:15 suos] *om. Oc*; 232:17
in mente] in corde *Oc*; 232:34 mauis] maius *Oc*; 232:35 melius] *om. Oc*; 232:35
quia] quod *Oc*; 232:37 tuis] *om. Oc*. See also 196:20 tolerare nequit] nequit tolerare nequit *O* nequit tolerare *c*. According to Schmitt, d'Achery's source may
have been *P* (*Prolegomena*, p. 153). *P*'s characteristic readings do not, however, appear in *c*: 198:32 ditione] detione *P* 198:35 orate] orare *P etc.* Note that
Schmitt's critical apparatus mistakenly presents the readings of d'Achery's edition as manuscript *C*'s readings. The following weak readings attributed to *C*

exceptions are such that d'Achery could have improved the reading without access to another source.[23] Later d'Achery's material was published in the *Patrologia Latina* as a consecutive sequence (IV,109–116).[24]

In 1675 the Maurist Gabriel Gerberon († 1711), a well-known Jansenist, further expanded Anselm's printed letter collection.[25] He published Anselm's *opera*, largely on the basis of Picard's work, but he collated a number of letters with some new manuscripts and added in some new material as well.[26] I shall refer to the letters he added to the collection as *d*. He placed some of the letters he edited after Picard's book III and the remainder as their own book IV. This solution undermined the logic of Picard's arrangement. In general, Gerberon's work has been considered poor.[27]

d's first two letters (III,160, 161 in the edition and the *Patrologia*; *AEp*. 239, 240) come from Hildebert of Lavardin's let-

---

do not in fact appear there, but derive from d'Achery: *AEp*. 230:7 sprituali] spiritali; 230:11–12 proficere] perficere; 232:15 suos] *om*.; 232:17 in mente] in corde; 232:34 mauis] maius (maius *from* mauis *C*); 232:34 melius] *om*.; 232:35 quia] quod; 232:37 tuis] *om*. Note also 230:26 dixit], where Schmitt attributes the reading dicit, which he adjudged the weaker, to *FM*. In fact, all the manuscripts (*LPECFM*) that Schmitt reports he collated have the reading dicit, as do d'Achery and the *Patrologia latina*. Dixit is possibly Schmitt's own reading. There are several cases where *c* is stronger than *C*: *AEp*. 230:16 quia *c*] *om*. *C*; 232:11 monachicum *c*] monachum *C*; 232:17 igitur *c*] ergo *C*; 328:7 ab *c*] *inserts in another hand C*; 328:30 Interim *c*] Iterum *C*.

[23] 194:7 sub *c*] *bis O*; 196:5, 18 contristare *c*] contristari *O*; 198:39–40 si quid contra ecclesiasticam doctrinam *c*] si quid contra ecclesiasticam doctrinam si quid *O*; 198:25 coercere *c*] cohortari *et inter lineas* uel ercere *O*; 198:45 nostram proferri *c*] nostram deferri *c* uestram deferri *O*; 232:4, 5 gratuleris…contristeris *c*] gratularis…contristaris *O*; 232:12–13 si numquam culpam tuam aut celare aut defendere *c*] si numquam aut culpam aut celare aut defendere *O*; 232:13–14 uulpes foueas habent ubi latenter catulos pariunt *c*] uulpes foueas habent si latenter catulos pariunt *O*; 245:5 qui sincera dilectone te suscepi *c*] qui sunt[?] sincera dilectione te suscepi *O*.

[24] Compare WILMART, 'La tradition', 1931, p. 39, note 1, stating that d'Achery's material extended up to letter IV,117.

[25] G. GERBERON (ed.), *Sancti Anselmi ex Beccensi abbate Cantuariensis archiepiscopi opera omnia nec non Eadmeri monachi Cantuariensis Historia nouorum et alia opuscula*, Paris, 1675.

[26] The collated manuscripts are reported in the 1675 printing, pp. 668–683; his additions are in *ibid.*, pp. 427–454.

[27] See especially WILMART, 'La tradition', 1931, p. 39, note 1.

ter collection; Gerberon's source is unknown. He misattributed the next two letters in *d* (III,162, 163) to Anselm.[28] The end of book III (III,164–188) consisted of an incomplete selection of the material in Eadmer's *Historia nouorum*, drawn from Selden's edition. Letters 1–101 in book IV were published from the transcript Gerberon had commissioned of manuscript BL Cotton Claudius A. xi, i.e. *C*.[29] The transcription, from 1673, survives, and is BNF lat. 13415. Gerberon published a further seven letters he had found in other manuscripts; in the *Patrologia*, these are letters IV,102–108. This group included only two letters which form a natural part of Anselm's correspondence, however; these are IV,104 and 105 or *AEp.* 204 and 183.[30] *AEp.* 204 is known only from manuscripts *MD* and BNF lat. 17400, which appears to have served as Gerberon's source.[31] It is hard to identify the source for *AEp.* 183. Gerberon's text seems to have been a member of family *Sharpe 5*, rather than of family *Wilmart 14*, which would have been extensively available in France however.[32] Gerberon did not completely manage to avoid republishing material which was already in print: his additions to the third letter book already included some repetition of material in Picard's edition, and in the fourth book he repeated his own work as well.[33]

---

[28] SCHMITT, 'Die echten und unechten Stücke', 1955, p. 225.

[29] Cf. SOUTHERN, *A Portrait*, 1990, p. 480.

[30] SCHMITT, 'Die echten und unechten Stücke', 1955, pp. 221–222, 225–226. Apart from IV,103 the letters are misattributions. IV,103 is the dedicatory letter introducing *Monologion*, which started circulating in conjunction with Anselm's letters only in the late medieval period, as in Worcester, F. 41; F. 132; and Cambridge, Peterhouse 246, all members of the family *Wilmart 14*.

[31] BNF lat. 17400 = A^5; 204:9 est] esse A^5d. On the other hand, 204:34 filius *d*] flius A^5; 204:44 qua *d*] quam A^5; both of which could easily have been amended without a correct text.

[32] 183:13–14 nec solum R^1d] non solum $W^5W^6W^7$; 183:24–25 Tam male – uiuere] *om.* R^1d

[33] I,23 = IV,1 (*AEp.* 31); III,53 = III,161 (*AEp.* 240); III,74 = III,168 (*AEp.* 281); III,106 = IV,53 (*AEp.* 345); III,111 = III,174 (*AEp.* 368); III,186 = IV,88 (*AEp.* 445); IV,105 = IV,129 (*AEp.* 344). Wilmart ('La tradition', 1931, p. 39, note 3) also includes among the duplicates letter I,19, published by Picard, and IV,122, published by Baluze. I,19 is from *V*, and like its source, it amalgamates the beginning of *AEp.* 25 (lines 1–22) and the end of *AEp.* 23 (lines 14–30) into a single letter. IV,122 is from *P* and gives the complete text of *AEp.* 23.

The first printing of Gerberon's edition has a partial manuscript copy; this is BL Lansdowne 984.[34] The manuscript includes 50 items, among them a group of short extracts from Anselm's letters. The manuscript belonged to Bishop White Kennett of Peterborough, a famous man of letters (†1728), who may also have made the compilation.

Étienne Baluze (†1718) was the next to extend the selection of letters in print. The fourth volume of his famous *Miscellanea* includes seven letters sent by Anselm and two received by him.[35] The list of contents reveals that the letters originated 'ex codice 4195 eiusdem bibliothecae [Colberti]'. Colbert 4195 today is BNF lat. 2478 or *P*, as the readings too confirm.[36] Baluze's compilation may be named *e*. Of Baluze's editions, the *Patrologia* took only the letters sent by Anselm, which form IV,120–126. Although I have not found IV,127, i.e. *AEp*. 447, in Baluze's publications, the edition is probably his work, as the source behind the letter was clearly *P*.[37]

Baluze also published the letter collection of Lambert, bishop of Arras (†1115), which includes his correspondence with Anselm. Here, the source was 'an old manuscript of the church of Arras'. Since the letters do not appear in our medieval witnesses to Anselm's letters, it is reasonable to conclude that Baluze's source was a collection of Lambert's correspondence.[38] The seventh volume

---

[34] 'Excerpta quaedam ex Epistolis Anselmi Cant. Archiepiscopi in Operum ejus columine Parisiis impresso, 1675.' The list of contents appended here, and the other information given, is taken from the catalogue. *AEp*. 53, 78, 80, 98, 106, 117, 130, 148, 170, 179, 156 or 157 or 164, 212, 222, 236, 257, 276 or 286, 364, 374, 384, 427 or 435, 404, 443, 451, 445, 467.

[35] É. BALUZE, *Miscellaneorum collectio ueterum*, Paris, 1678–1715, vol. 4 (1683), pp. 471–478: *AEp*. 9, 10, 23, 24, 107, 108, 265 (*PL Ep. lib*. IV,120–126) and *AEp*. 19, 128. Mansi's edition of Baluze's work, *Miscellanea nouo ordine digesta*, Lucca, 1761, vol. 2, p. 174, also included *AEp*. 20, Anselm's reply to *AEp*. 19.

[36] OMONT, *Concordances*, 1903, p. 68. See e.g. *AEp*. 24:15 et uestris *N*] et a uestris *LPe*; 107:5–6 ubicumque se *N*] om. *LPe*; quondam *N*] quia *LPe*; 108:9 ad eiusdem *N*] et eiusdem *LPe*. 23:8 Iob mihi *NL*] om. *Pe*; 108:3 iterum *NL*] iterum *Pe*.

[37] *P* and this text share the same omission against the other witnesses: 447:7–8 prudentiam et prudentem religionem.

[38] Lambert of Arras, *Ep*. 37, 92, and 93; *AEp*. 437–439. BALUZE, *Miscellaneorum collectio ueterum*, vol. 5, 1700, pp. 306, 342–343; and in Mansi's *Mis-*

in the series also includes *AEp.* 281 from Paschal II to Anselm.[39] The list of contents reports this was 'ex codice Lamberti Episcopi Attrebatensis'; we may presume that the same manuscript was in question in both cases.

A new printing of Gerberon's edition of Anselm's *Opera* was made in 1721, to which two *Supplementum* sections were appended. A number of letters appear twice in the work, adding still further to the collection's confusion. The first *Supplementum* consists of the letters published by d'Achery,[40] along with two letters apparently transcribed by Gerberon himself: *AEp.* 208 and 337, the former appearing as IV,117 in the *Patrologia*. These two letters were said to be from 'ms. 464 Bibl. Regiae', the present BNF lat. 4878, and manuscript *W*[6] within this work.[41] The second *supplementum*, which is *nouum*, includes 14 letters. The first two of these are the letters from Anselm to Lambert, bishop of Arras, edited by Baluze and discussed above.[42] These are followed by the first seven letters Baluze edited from manuscript *P*.[43] The next letter, *AEp.* 447, is also from *P*, and, as noted before, it too may have been taken from Baluze, although I have not encountered it within the *Miscellanea*. A group of four letters, *AEp.* 208, 337, 183, and 219, concludes the section, of which the first three were probably edited by Gerberon and the fourth taken from the series *Anglia sacra*, as the 1744 Venetian reprint of the *Opera* reveals. This printing of the *Opera* also stated which manuscripts had served as the sources for the three preceding letters. The first two letters, *AEp.* 208 and

cellanea novo ordine digesta, vol. 2, pp. 142, 150. *PL* only includes the letters Anselm sent (IV,118, 119).

[39] Baluze, *Miscellaneorum collectio ueterum*, vol. 7, Paris, 1715, pp. 135–137.

[40] *d* (the 1721 edition, fols. Eeee ij[r]–iij[v]): *AEp.* 196, 230, 232, 245, 254, 328, 194, 198. In conjunction with the first letter, the reference 'octo priores epistolae ex tom. 9. Spicileg.' appears.

[41] The signum is that in the first catalogue of 1645, where it is number 464; this became number 3788 in the 1682 catalogue, which in turn is number 4878 today. Omont, *Concordances*, 1903, pp. 8, 151.

[42] *d* (the 1721 edition, *Novum supplementum* [no foliation]): *AEp.* 437 and 439 (IV,118 and 119). Lambert's letter to Anselm (*AEp.* 438), published by Baluze in conjunction with the other letters previously discussed, was not included, accounting for its omission from the *Patrologia* too.

[43] *d* (the 1721 edition, *Novum supplementum*): *AEp.* 9, 10, 23, 24, 107, 108, 265; IV,120–126.

337, now published for the second time, were both 'ex Ms. Codicibus Ecclesie Turonensis et Monasterii Pruliacensis', and the following letter, *AEp*. 183, was 'ex ms. Pruliacensis monasterii Ordinis Cisterciensis'. The Tours manuscript is unknown; three Cistercian manuscripts survive. Textual criticism of *AEp*. 337 confirms the contamination indicated by the fact that the readings in the text follow both the Cistercian and the non-Cistercian French branches of the family *Wilmart 14*. We must thus trust the edition's announcement: Gerberon had had two manuscripts, one from the Cathedral of Tours and the second from the Cistercian monastery of Preuilly.[44] As for *AEp*. 183, collation clearly demonstrates that it was from a Cistercian source, although textual criticism does not indicate clearly which of manuscripts $W^5W^6W^7$ (if any) the publication followed. These three manuscripts diverge only once, and at this point the edition rejects W^5 and follows the reading in W^6W^7.[45] (Where the edition diverges from W^6W^7, it is always weaker than them, nor is it supported by other known manuscripts.) Of the manuscripts, W^6 is the strongest candidate to be the source for the publication, however. For W^7 is known to be from Fontenay (and not from Preuilly), and Gerberon is known to have already used W^6 as a source for *AEp*. 208 and 337 in the first *Supplementum*, as noted above. The implication is that W^6 comes from Preuilly.

3. The *Patrologia Latina*, contaminated Letters, and their Sources

Migne founded his publication of Anselm's writings on Gerberon's edition.[46] As a consequence, the *Patrologia*'s text, in volumes 158 and 159, is made up of successive strata of editorial work, including traces of all editions from Danhauser onwards. The following table presents the editor of each letter, and his principal source.

---

[44] The Cistercian manuscripts: $W^5W^6W^7$; the non-Cistercian French manuscript is W^3. 337:4 Per W^3d] Propter $W^5W^6W^7$. 337:26 ad iudicem deum W^3] ad inuicem deum $W^5W^6W^7d$. The letter is otherwise known only from the family descended from M, which has unique readings not appearing in the edition.

[45] 183:21 ascendetis] ascendatis W^5.

[46] *PL* 159: 'labore ac studio D. Gabrielis Gerberon'.

Table 4: The editors and sources in the *Patrologia Latina*

Patrologia	*Editor*	*Source*
I–III,156	Picard	V
III,157	Danhauser	ζ
III,158	Picard	(misattributed)
III,159	Picard	? (possibly misattributed)
III,160, 161	Gerberon	Hildebert of Lavardin
III,162, 163	Gerberon	(misattributed)
III,164–188	Gerberon	Selden's *Historia nouorum*
IV,1–101	Gerberon	C through BNF lat. 13415
IV,102	Gerberon	(misattributed)
IV,103	Gerberon	Prefatory letter to *Monologion*
IV,104	Gerberon	BNF lat. 17400?
IV,105	Gerberon	*Sharpe 5*?
IV,106–108	Gerberon	(misattributed)
IV,109–116	D'Achery	O
IV,117	Gerberon	W^6
IV,118–119	Baluze	Lambert of Arras
IV,120–127	Baluze	P
IV,128	Gerberon	ms. Turonensis ecclesiae and W^6
IV,129	Gerberon	probably W^6

The *Castigationes* in Gerberon's edition, which the gloss of the *Patrologia* edition reproduces (at least in part) and enhances, reveals that a number of letters are contaminated. Here I analyze only the cases that may provide new information regarding the manuscript tradition. In other words, I have not taken into account the easily identifiable manuscripts. The following table presents the letters that were contaminated thereby.[47]

---

[47] As for *Ep.* 123 (II,53), the 1675 printing of Gerberon's edition states: 'Collata cum duobus Mss. Victorinis'. This is almost certainly an error: the letter is only know from V, which is a Victorine manuscript, and from C of the Cotton's library, and from C's derivatives, of which Gerberon's transcript, BNF, lat. 13415, is one.

Table 5: The sources of contamination

The sources of contamination	Patrologia	Schmitt
MS Lovaniensis, probably Brussels, Bibliothèque Royale 2004–10 (W^4)	I,1–3, 8, 29, 33, 37, 56	1–3, 8, 37, 41, 45, 65
MS Vict. Bd 18 ('al. EE. 13') = BNF lat. 14502 (R^5)	I,2, 29; III,11, 12	2, 37, 160, 161
MS S. Ebrulphi = Alençon, Bibliothèque municipale 16	I,56; II,8	65, 97
MS Corb. 160; MS Thuanus 267; MS S. Bened. Floriacensis	I,20	28
MS S. Audoeni Rothomagensis	III,53	240

The readings from the Louvain manuscript are likely to have been collected for Gerberon by the 'dominus' of Nonancourt (situated relatively close to Bec however). According to Gerberon, the Louvain manuscript comprised 13 letters, of which nine are identified.[48] In addition, the collations take into account two further letters in the manuscript. This information indicates that the Louvain manuscript included letters 1, 2, 3, 5, 8, 13, 37, 41, 45, 65, and 208 at least. The Louvain manuscript clearly belongs to the family *Wilmart 14*, which included every single one of these letters in its selection, plus a further three, *AEp.* 4, 183, and 337. The family includes a manuscript, Brussels, Bibliothèque Royale 2004–10, which is known to have been in Louvain and now has thirteen letters, since losing its final folios. All the readings mentioned for the Louvain manuscript do not correspond to those in this manuscript, W^4, however.[49] Moreover, the manuscript does not include the tract *De pace et concordia*, which Gerberon also published from the Louvain manuscript, according to his own marginal note.[50] I should be inclined to believe that Gerberon's Louvain was our manuscript, nevertheless. Gerberon had also had other manuscripts of this family at his disposal, which may explain the sepa-

[48] *PL* 158, col. 1059 note to *Ep.* 1, 1: 'Collata cum ms. Vict. Ef. 20. et Lovan. qui prae caeteris tredecim habet Anselmi epistolas, 1, 5, 8, 11, 29, 33, 37 et 56 lib. I et 104, lib. IV. Ex eodem ms. etiam transumptus est libellus de pace et concordia. Haec ad nos nobilitate et scientia spectatissimus transmisit dominus de Nonancourt.'

[49] 37:71 sollicitudini *Louvain*] sollicitudine *from* sollicitudinis W^4.

[50] GERBERON 1675, pp. 704–706; *PL* 158, cols. 1015–1020.

rative variants; the sources for the variants given in the notes were perhaps muddled up at the some point in the transmission, and it should also be noted that his references to sources are sometimes incorrect in details.

MS Vict. Bd 18, the second item in the list, is now BNF lat. 14502, R^5 of *Sharpe 5*. The third item, MS S. Ebrulphi, is almost certainly Aleçnon, Bibliothèque municipale 16, a collection of patristic and monastic texts, which has long been associated with Saint-Evroult. The old departmental catalogue mentions only one letter (*AEp.* 97), whereas the edition refers to two (*AEp.* 65 and 97).[51] The latter information is likely to be correct.[52] One can infer from the edition that the manuscript probably gave the two letters separately, not in association with each other, and that *AEp.* 65 had been reduced into a short polemic against clerical marriage; the letter had lost the two key epistolary elements, the salutation and valediction, and it had also been given a title, 'tractatus de presbyteris concubinariis'.[53] The catalogue dates the manuscript to *s.* xii, whereas its Victorine texts indicate the mid century as the *a quo*.

Gerberon's collation of *Ep.* 28 from three manuscripts is of particular interest since the letter is not known to have been transmitted outside the major collections. As for 'Corb. 160', my best guess is that this was a lost Corbie manuscript known from the monastery's book list, or, more precisely, the item 154 entitled 'omelie ejusdem [Anselmi] cum cuibusdam libellis ejus'. The manuscript has been dated 'vers 1200?'.[54] 'MS Thuanus 267' and 'MS S. Bened. Floriacensis' remain completely unidentified, and we know but that the former once belonged to Jacques-Auguste de Thou (1553–1617), a historian, book collector, and statesman, and the latter to the abbey of Fleury. The reported readings indicate

---

[51] *Catalogue général des manuscrits des Bibliothèques publiques de France. Départements*, vol. 2, Paris, 1888, pp. 492–493.

[52] *AEp.* 65 and 97 are known to have been transmitted alone. *AEp.* 65: Eton College 120; Rome, Biblioteca Casanatense 499. *AEp.* 97: Munich, Bayerische Staatsbibliothek Clm 19136 and 22291.

[53] 65:32–76 De presbyteris – confessionem compellit. The 1675 print of *d*, p. 671; *PL* 158, cols. 555, 1125.

[54] L. DELISLE, *Recherches sur l'ancienne bibliothèque de Corbie*, Paris, 1861, p. 66. Items 151–153 also include Anselm's works.

that the Corbie and the Thuanus manuscripts gave the same version of *AEp*. 28 as *LP* in contrast to that in *NECV*, while some of their readings do not match *LP*. The Fleury manuscript presented the version found in *NECV*.[55]

[55] GERBERON 1675, p. 669: 'Mss. *160 & 267*. Suo suus, amico amicus, fratri frater, Gondulpho Anselmus, pro amore foelicitatis (*In* ms. *160. omitt.* pro amore) perseuerantiam in sanctitate, pro praemio sanctitatis aeternitatem in foelicitate.' The other reported variants of interest are: 'Numquam in me mutatus *Ms. I.* nunquam mutatus…Sum imitatus *Mss. Vict. & Flor.* sum imitatus *Mss. 160. & 267.* sum incitatus…Ita longae *Mss. 160. & 267. & Flor.* tam longae sint / Magnitudinem *Ms. 267.* Longitudinem / Eas ipsas orationes *Ms. I.* ipsas orationes / Incipire. *Mss. & editio Picardi,* incidere. *Ms. 267.* intercidere.'

VI. CONCLUSION

Schmitt's critical edition represents the current orthodoxy in the textual tradition of Anselm's letter collection. His work has been criticized repeatedly in this study, but it must be noted in his defence that the first critical editor of any text faces far harder challenges than any subsequent critical scholar working on the same text. The value of Schmitt's edition is nevertheless seriously undermined by the fact that his selection of manuscripts for collation was determined without his ever having properly established the structure of the tradition. Ultimately, it is impossible to undertake systematic textual research on the letters on the basis of Schmitt's edition. In short, the edition does not and cannot serve the critical reader. What, then, are the desiderata for a new edition?

To begin with, the manuscript tradition is obviously too large for each surviving witness to be reported in the apparatus to each letter. Two principles should govern the selection of witnesses. First, the selection must include all the witnesses that are independent of other surviving manuscripts. The derivatives of any surviving manuscripts can be excluded. Second, only those manuscripts that reflect editorial and scribal individuality in circles under Anselmian influence should be revived from the group of manuscripts rejected on the grounds of the first principle. The terminus should be set at the 1130s, by the end of which the generation of Anselm's known disciples had mostly passed away or become inactive. In practice, this means reviving P, the Canterbury section of E, and those parts of M that derive from F (and therefore the three manuscripts in question should be collated in full). Furthermore, because the relationships *between* the sub-branches of the minor collections are difficult to establish and because they are at least partially independent of each other, the apparatus should present each sub-branch. The manuscripts for the apparatus should be selected from these groups according to the two aforementioned principles. As a result, the apparatus for the Bec correspondence should report $ECVNMLPFJBGa$ of the major collections and $S^1W^1W^2W^3W^4R^1H$ of the minor collections, while the apparatus for the Canterbury

correspondence should report *LPEFJCVOMBGa* and $S^1W^1W^2W^3$-W^4R^1.[1]

Next, the reader should be aware of what he or she is reading. The simplest way to ensure this is to choose one manuscript as a base manuscript for the editorial text. This would mean that the editorial text would not in the main reflect the editor's personal judgement (as is currently the case), but rather the historical context to which the manuscript belongs. The situation is complicated by the fact that no authorial manuscript survives, and that no surviving manuscript is a pure witness to an authorial collection. There is not even a manuscript including all the letters. Nevertheless, I would suggest that one manuscript should be chosen as 'the number one' witness, on which the editorial text would be built. There are three requisites for such a manuscript. (One.) A base manuscript has to have a broad selection of letters. This rules out the minor collections, and those witnesses to the major collections that include only a reduced selection of the letters, i.e. manuscripts *NMFGB*. (Two.) The manuscript itself has to be linked to the Anselmian sphere of influence as closely as possible. Therefore we can eliminate manuscripts *CV*, the former of which comes from England or France and dates from *s.* xiii$^{2/2}$, and the latter from Paris, Saint-Victor of *s.* xii$^{3/4}$. (Three.) The manuscript has to be stemmatically as close as possible to the collection which it witnesses. Thus manuscript *P* and the Canterbury section of manuscript *E* must be removed from the list of candidates, since *L* fathered both: it is closer to ω than they are. As a result, we are left with two candidates for the Bec correspondence, *E* and *L*, and only one candidate for the Canterbury correspondence, *L*.

For the Bec correspondence, my choice would be *E*. First, the textual evidence shows that *E* derives, possibly without any intermediary, from the Christ Church exemplar of collection β, that is β^2. *L* descends from the same manuscript, but through (at least) one intermediary, ω, which added variant readings to the letters and remodelled their arrangement. As a result, *L*'s witness to the authorial β-stage is significantly more distorted than that of *E*. Second, manuscript *E* seems to come from the inner circle

---

[1] Few pieces of the Canterbury correspondence survive outside these manuscripts, for example in Eadmer's *Historia nouorum*. These letters should naturally be edited from the manuscripts in question.

of Anselm's pupils since his nephew and protégé, Anselm, abbot of Bury St Edmunds, may have commissioned it. Third, the medieval transmission of the Bec letters was originally independent of the transmission of the Canterbury letters. In other words, there exists no obvious reason why a single base manuscript should prevail throughout both the Bec and the Canterbury correspondence. Since no manuscript covers all letters, this would of course be impossible.

For the Canterbury correspondence, my choice as the main witness must be manuscript L, as already stated. L is clearly a Christ Church product from the 1120s, and Eadmer may have been behind it. The manuscript is textually the purest of our witnesses to the Canterbury correspondence because it either fathered our other large witnesses (PE) or contaminates them through a lost intermediary (CVO). F is independent of L, but it covers only a narrow selection of letters, which are, moreover, heavily abridged. The editorial text of the letters absent from the two main witnesses should likewise build on one manuscript. In selecting the 'best' manuscript, the three principles given above should be applied.

The editorial application of the base manuscripts should not be too rigorous. After all, Anselm's modern readers are likely to benefit more from an edition than a transcript. The editorial text should, naturally, correct the mistakes of the base manuscripts with the aid of our other witnesses. Where possible and relevant, the text should target Anselm's authorial intention. It is virtually inevitable, I think, that the edition of the Bec correspondence should aim to establish β in its editorial text, for the surviving evidence allows the reconstruction of β's text — to which our base manuscript E witnesses — with a high degree of certainty. While reaching for authorial intention, the edition would stand on solid ground by being based on E. For example, the edition should follow β's arrangement as witnessed by ECV. This should apply even to the letters that E lacks due to the absence of one quire from β^2, its source. These letters should be presented as they are placed in the witnesses to β^1, that is manuscripts CV. A headnote would easily alert the reader of the edition to such a restoration. β included 128 of the 147 surviving pieces of Anselm's Bec correspondence. The letters preserved in the other collections could perhaps follow the E material in two sets, the first set following E's pre-abbatial ones, the second following its abbatial letters. The principal arrangement

would then be identical to that of Picard's edition (1612), which was based on manuscript *V*. But it would differ considerably from Schmitt's arrangement, which derives partly from earlier editions and partly from his own relative chronology — something that cannot be established in any absolute terms.

As for the Canterbury correspondence, our solution is more straightforward because the transmission is more complicated. The hypothetical collection *ω* cannot be viewed in full through our manuscripts, and Anselm's authorial intention is for the most part, then, beyond our perception. The editor should preserve *L*'s arrangement of the letters, and give the letters absent from the manuscript after the material derived from it. However, the advice given in the manuscript's margins as to where 'to place' (*ponere*) the additional letters on the manuscript's last leaves could be followed. In other words, these letters might be inserted in their 'correct' places amongst the material from *L*. The marginalia clearly reflect the informed judgement of the anonymous early twelfth-century annotator from Christ Church, whose instructions were followed by subsequent medieval copyists.

Since the editorial status changes from letter to letter, the edition should express the status of each letter in a few words. A headnote, being easy to observe, would be preferable to a footnote or a mention in the apparatus. Headnotes would keep the readers, even those not engaged in textual criticism, alert to problems emerging from transmission. The headnotes should be concise and uniform, stating, for example, 'collection *β* through *ECV NM LP*, controlled by independent transmission in S^1W^{1-4}'.

Only letters sent by, or addressed to, Anselm should be included in the edition, except where our manuscript witnesses include such non-Anselmian letters among his own correspondence. The material of this kind in Eadmer's *Historia nouorum*, which also contains correspondence between parties other than Anselm, cannot qualify for inclusion in the edition because the *Historia* is not a letter collection but a historical work.

Finally, in our proposed edition built on these principles, the *apparatus criticus* would have a two-fold function. First, it would report the textual variants that may reflect different authorial versions or represent editorial and scribal individuality up to the 1130s. Where a letter exists in two distinct versions, however, both should be presented by way of the editorial text. Second, the

apparatus would support the editorial text where a reading from the base manuscript is rejected, by demonstrating the manuscript evidence for the correction. As a general rule, the apparatus should report errors only from the base manuscript. If in the process of editing, errors — or any other evidence — emerge that uncover stemmatic qualities undetected by this sample-based study, these will be listed and discussed in the introduction to the edition, already under construction.

APPENDICES

1. Manuscripts and Works excluded from the Study

The appendix examines compilations of various texts that include more than two of Anselm's letters. Since analyses are based on limited textual and manuscript evidence, the results are only preliminary.

Eadmer's Historia nouorum *and papal letter collections*

Eadmer's *Historia nouorum* contains letters from and to Anselm, and also correspondence neither sent nor received by him. Seven of the letters in the former category are not known from the main tradition of our text, though several are included in manuscript *M* and *D*, its derivative.[1] *M* obtained these letters from *Historia nouorum*. Likewise, certain letters included also in *ω* appear to have come to the *Historia* from Anselm's archives.[2] Finally, *Historia nouorum* incorporates papal correspondence from (a) source(s) other than *ω*, a conclusion that derives from previous research into the sources used by Eadmer and by William of Malmesbury in his *Liber Pontificalis*, and which is briefly discussed below. The relationship between the letters found in both *ω* and the *Historia* awaits clarification, and I hope to return to this in a future study.[3]

– *London, BL Cotton Cleopatra E. i and Claudius E. v*

  Cleopatra E. i, fols. 17–38, 40–57; c. 1120–21; Christ Church

Contents

papal letters to English kings and bishops; *AEp.* 222, 303 (both from Paschal II to Anselm), 283 (from Paschal II to Gerard of York), 471

---

[1] *AEp.* 442 (to Bp Ranulf of Durham, also in *MD*); *AEp.* 282 (from Paschal II, also in *MD*); 301 (from Prior Ernulf?), 365 (from anonymous); 367 (from Henry I, also in *MD*); 456 (from Thomas of York); 470 (from Henry I, also in *MD*).

[2] *r* = *Historia nouorum*. *AEp.* 171:5–11 Nouit – defendant *r*] *om. LPEC*[b]; 201:19–20 a uestra paternitate *r*] *om. LEPC*[b].

[3] See M. Brett, 'A note on the *Historia nouorum* of Eadmer', *Scriptorium*, 33 (1979), pp. 56–58.

(from Anselm to the English bishops); and *AEp.* 472 (from Anselm to Archbishop-elect Thomas of York)

Claudius E. v, fols. 233–256; after 1119 × 22; Christ Church
Contents
privileges for Canterbury, papal letters to Lanfranc, Anselm, Henry I, Gerard of York and Ralph d'Escures concerning the Canterbury primacy; from Paschal II: *AEp.* 222, 303, 283 (to Gerald of York), 224 (to Henry I), 216 (to Henry I), 305 (to Henry I), 281, 397

The collections of papal letters in manuscripts Cleopatra E. ɪ and Claudius E. v are from Christ Church. They used a lost source, and an intermediate copy stands between this lost source and Cotton Claudius E. v. The lost intermediary probably served as Eadmer's source for *Historia nouorum* as well. William of Malmesbury used either Eadmer's source or the *Historia* for his *Liber pontificalis.*[4]

– *London, British Library Cotton Appendix 56, fols. 1–4, and Cotton Vespasian E. ɪv, fols. 203–210*

s. xii$^{1/2}$; Worcester; 4 + 8 fols.; 220 × 155 (185 × 110) mm; 29 (long) lines
Contents
Augustine, letters of Lanfranc, Thomas of York, Anselm and Paschal II; *AEp.* 223 (from Paschal II), 226 (from Paschal II to Osbern of Exeter), 304 (from Paschal II), 254 (to Herbert of Thetford), 430 (to Paschal II), 398 (from Paschal II to Bishop William of Rouen), 397 (from Paschal II)

Cotton Appendix 56, fols. 1–4 and Cotton Vespasian E. ɪv, fols. 203–210 originally belonged together: the first leaves of Appendix 56 contain the beginning of Augustine's *De doctrina christiana*, while the last folios of the Vespasian manuscript have the end of this work and a selection of letters mainly relating to Canterbury's primacy dispute. The last letters, copied in a new hand, belong to Anselm's correspondence. The manuscript is from Worcester, dating from the first half of the twelfth century. The group of Anselm's letters is apparently independent of the main tradition of our text, at least in part. The textual criticism of *AEp.* 397, which appears both in *LPEC^{b}V^b* and *Historia nouorum*, indicates independence from the major collections. It should be noted, however,

---

[4] THOMSON, *William of Malmesbury*, 2003, p. 133.

that the manuscript sometimes agrees with F, another derivative of ω, in a way that might be potentially significant.[5] Nevertheless, the source for these letters could have been the papal letter collection closely related to *Historia nouorum*.

– London, British Library Add. 32091
Various codicological units dating between *s.* xii[1/2] and the year 1575; our unit: fols. 1–13 *s.* xii[1/2]; 320 × 205 (250 × 175) mm (trimmed); 41 lines in two columns

Contents

Papal correspondence to England including: *AEp.* 206, 210, 214, 213, 216, 219, 220, 222, 223, 224, 226, 284, 227, 280, 281, 305, 348, 351, 352, 354, 397, 422, 423

This is a compilation of papal correspondence to England, in which letters not by or to Anselm are interspersed with his correspondence. In his edition, Schmitt associated this material with Anselm's letter collection — an unobvious decision.[6] Again the papal letter collection related to *Historia nouorum* possibly lies behind Add. 32091.[7] In this study, Add. 32091, referred to as A^2, has been deployed to assist in determining C's stemmatic position.[8]

The letter collection of Ivo of Chartres

At least four manuscript witnesses to the letter collection of Bishop Ivo of Chartres († 1116) include a small number of Anselm's letters in association with one another. The precise selection and/ or arrangement vary slightly from manuscript to manuscript.[9] All the letters are papal correspondence and relate to the investiture dispute: *AEp.* 218 and 280 are from Anselm to Paschal II; *AEp.*

---

[5] A^1 refers to the letters in Cotton Vespasian E. IV. 397:2 apostolicam benedictionem A^1FMr] apostolicam *om. LPEVC*; 397:40 tantum A^1Mr] *om. LPEVC.*

[6] *AEp.* 216, 224, 305, 348, 351, 352, 354. The letters in italics also appear in Eadmer's *Historia nouorum*.

[7] See e.g. *AEp.* 213:24 industriam.] Dat. VI. Kal. Mart. *Add. 32091.* Manuscripts *LPEVC* do not include the date.

[8] See III.2.13.

[9] Not all manuscripts with Ivo's letter collection include these letters of Anselm; see e.g. Paris, BNF lat. 2887A (*s.* xii), lat. 2888 (*s.* xii); lat. 2889 (*s.* xii–xiii); lat. 2890 (*s.* xiii); lat. 2891 (*s.* xii); lat. 2892 (*s.* xii); lat. 2892A (*s.* xii); lat. 2893 (*s.* xii). Ivo's collection normally includes his letter to Anselm, *AEp.* 181, which Schmitt edited from BNF. lat. 2887 and 16713.

222 and 281 from Paschal II to Anselm; and *AEp.* 284 is from Cardinal John to Anselm. The section appears at a slightly different point in each manuscript, but is always placed near other letters dealing with the issue of ecclesiastical investiture by laymen.[10] On the basis of this narrow sampling, it appears that Ivo's letter collection drew on existing units containing a few letters each.

My analysis is based on the testimony of manuscripts $Y^1 Y^2$ (see below) and upon Schmitt's apparatus. Since the main tradition of Anselm's letters does not cover *AEp.* 284, the Anselmian group in Ivo's collections is at least in part independent of it. As for the other letters, Schmitt's apparatus suggests that in a few cases the text of Ivo's collection may be slightly stronger than that of Anselm's.[11] Furthermore in *AEp.* 222, $Y^1 Y^2$ and D tend to agree with each other, although the evidence for this is both limited and weak.[12] The impression is that the Anselmian section within Ivo's letter collection derives from an unknown collection of papal correspondence.

A *very* preliminary list of the manuscripts of the letter collection of Ivo of Chartres including the Anselm section follows. Schmitt's collations of the letters given in italics take into account the manuscripts in question.

- Paris, BNF lat. 2887 (fols. 94r–96v = Y^1) – s. xii; *AEp. 218, 222, 280, 281*
- Vienna, Nationalbibliothek 533 (fols. 75v–78v = Y^2) – s. xii; *AEp. 222, 280, 281, 284*

- Paris, BNF lat. 2894 (fols. 122r–123v) – s. xii; *AEp.* 218, 222, 280, 281, 284,

---

[10] In manuscript Berlin, Staatsbibliothek Phill. 1694, Anselm's letters are preceded by Ivo, *Ep.* 95, 102, 287, of which the first two relate to the investiture dispute. In BNF lat. 2887 and 2894 Anselm's letters are preceded by Ivo, *Ep.* 95. In lat. 2887, Anselm's correspondence is followed by Ivo, *Ep.* 102 and 287, whereas lat. 2894 on the other hand continues Ivo's collection from a different point, Ivo, *Ep.* 251. I have only been able to consult the catalogue entry for the Vienna manuscript.

[11] E.g. 280:1 Domino et patri reuerendo $Y^1 Y^2$] patri *om. LPEVCM*; 280:48 expostulo.] Valete *add.* $Y^1 Y^2$; 281:41 inuocarunt $Y^1 Y^2$] commutauerunt *LPEVCF.* $Y^1 Y^2$ are in any case independent of *L*: 281:15 hoc immane $Y^1 Y^2 (FGC^b V^b D)$] hoc in immane *LP corr. from* hoc in immane *E*.

[12] *AEp.* 222:12 agas] peragas $D Y^1 Y^2 r$; 222:12 loquaris] perloquaris $D Y^1 Y^2 r$. Comparing the readings reported by Schmitt's apparatus for manuscripts $Y^1 Y^2$ and *D* in *AEp.* 281 did not indicate any significant agreement between these.

– Berlin, Staatsbibliothek Phill. 1694 (fols. 26r–27v, 29v) – *s*. xii/
xiii; *AEp*. *218*, 222, 280, 281, *284*, and 240

The letter collection of Hildebert of Lavardin

The letter collection of Hildebert of Lavardin († 1133) includes
the two letters we know he sent to Anselm, *AEp*. 239 and 240.
The second of these is also found in the key derivatives of ω. In
contrast *AEp*. 239 only appears in three of the manuscripts with
Anselm's letters, *DUA³*, none of which are from Christ Church. Of
these manuscripts, *DU* are related to each other (as shown earlier)
and *A³*, Oxford, Laud. Misc. 344, will be discussed next. There is
no critical edition of Hildebert's letters, but von Moos has drawn
up an extensive list of the manuscripts, which classifies them into
groups.[13] Some 120 manuscripts survive, and like Schmitt, I have
consulted only two, Troyes, Médiathèque 513 (*Z¹*) and BAV, Vat.
lat. 6024 (*Z²*),[14] as well as the edition in the *Patrologia Latina* 171.
(These manuscripts have already been referred to in section III.1.4.)
Here we need only note that both *AEp*. 239 and 240 entered Hildebert's collection from his own archive.

– *Oxford, Bodleian Library Laud. misc. 344*

s. xii^ex; Durham; parchment; vi + 59 + 91 + ii'; codicological unit I:
210 × 155 (150 × 115) mm; 24 (long) lines

Contents

Victorine texts and *AEp*. 468, 65, 169, 281, 240 (fols. 36v–39r)

Laud. Misc. 344, to which I have already referred as *A³*, is a
compilation of several identified and unidentified texts, among
which there occur five of Anselm's letters. *AEp*. 169 is known
from nowhere else than *A³*. Furthermore, *AEp*. 240 is clearly more
closely related to the letter collection of Hildebert of Lavardin
than to Anselm's collection. Of the manuscript witnesses to Hilde-

---

[13] P. von Moos, *Hildebert von Lavardin 1056–1133: Humanitas an der
Schwelle des höfischen Zeitalters*, Stuttgart, 1965, pp. 360–365.

[14] This manuscript also includes *AEp*. 216 and a letter misattributed
to Anselm (*PL* III,162), rejected by Schmitt on apparently good grounds
(fols. 156r–157r). Troyes, Médiathèque 513 includes the *Wilmart 14* collection
as well, the siglum W⁵ denoting its witness. In order to avoid confusion, I have
chosen to refer to the two sets of letters in the manuscript by two different
sigla.

bert's collection studied here, BAV Vat. lat. 6024 (Z^2) and Troyes 513 (Z^1), A^3 seems to be closer to the latter, Z^1, which belongs to Type A in von Moos's classification.[15] Similarly in AEp. 468, A^3 is nearer to the manuscript Durham cathedral B. IV. 24 — dated to *s*. xi/xii, as well as *s*. xii^{in}, and referred to as Q by Schmitt, but here as A^4— than to Anselm's collections.[16] This is not surprising since both manuscripts are from Durham. (The Durham cathedral manuscript includes AEp. 313 and 468 as later additions.)

A^3 is the only manuscript to state that Willelmus, the recipient of AEp. 65, was 'abbas salmurensis', i.e. the abbot of Saint-Florent, Saumur.[17] I have not been able to conduct a proper textual comparison of this letter otherwise. It is likewise hard to determine the position of the final letter included in A^3, AEp. 281. A^3 does not share the distinctive readings reported by Schmitt for $Y^1 Y^2 A^6$;[18] $Y^1 Y^2$ represent the collection of Ivo's letters and were discussed above, while A^6 is London, BL Stowe 31, which includes an assortment of texts, by and large all related to the investiture dispute. A negative result of this kind does not necessarily mean that A^3 would have drawn on ω. A^3 is either mainly or entirely independent of the main Christ Church tradition.

---

[15] 240:6 domino] *om.* $Z^1 A^3$; 240:16 ex adytis] ex abditis Z^1 ex additis A^3; 240:18–20 et miratus – confiteor] *om.* $Z^1 A^3$; 240:22–24 Vale – apud te] Vicem mihi, pater sancte, rependes, si tuarum participem me feceris orationum $Z^1 A^3$. Z^2 is included in Schmitt's critical apparatus, but it is possible that it agrees with $Z^1 A^3$ in the last readings cited too, although the apparatus does not indicate this. See also von Moos, *Hildebert von Lavardin*, 1965, pp. 326–327.

[16] 468:1 reuerendo] *om.* $A^3 A^4$; 468:3 uultis audire] audire uultis $A^3 A^4$; 468:6 apud] *om.* $A^3 A^4$; 468:10 ad tempus] *om.* $A^3 A^4$; 468:12 quod faciunt communiter fratres] quod alii faciunt conmuniter $A^3 A^4$.

[17] According to William of Malmesbury (a marginal note, M fol. 132r), the William of this letter was abbot of Fécamp. This was William de Rots, who held the office *c*. 1078–1105; see Orderic Vitalis, *Historia ecclesiastica*, vol. 2, pp. 151, 293; Fröhlich, 'Introduction', 1990, p. 186. Eton College 120 supports this view: fol. 173r: 'Epistola uenerabilis Anselmi ad dompnum Willelmum abbatem fiscan.' I have not seen the Eton manuscript, which does not include any other letters of Anselm's correspondence. However, the incipit given by Ker (*Medieval Manuscripts in British Libraries*, vol. 2, Oxford, 1977, p. 735) suggests that Eton was independent of M: 65:3 Ex quo uestra probitas mihi] Ex quo michi uestra probitas M Ex quo uestra probietas...*Eton*. Southern (Review: The Letters of St Anselm, vols. i–iii, ed. Walter Fröhlich, *EHR*, 112 (1997), p. 161) considered A^3's information to be the most reliable.

[18] E.g. 281:52 Datae – Beneuentum] Valete $Y^1 Y^2 A^6$ Amen *LPEVCA*^{3}.

2. A preliminary List of Manuscripts
including fewer than three successive Anselmian Letters

Alençon, Bibliothèque municipale 16 – s. xii$^{2/2}$, *olim* Saint-Evroult; *AEp.* 97, fol. 209v; *AEp.* 65 (shortened)

Brussels, Bibliothèque Royale de Belgique 2772–89 – s. xiii, *olim* Rouge-Cloître (Brussels); *AEp.* 37, fols. 146r–147v

Brussels, Bibliothèque Royale de Belgique 12014–41 – s. xiv; Liège; *AEp.* 239, 240 (both from Hildebert to Anselm), fols. 254r, 261r.

Brussels, Bibliothèque Royale de Belgique II. 994 – s. xiii; Saint-Ghislain; *AEp.* 28

Cambrai, Bibliothèque municipale 249 – s. xii; Cambrai, Saint-Sépulcre; *AEp.* 288, fol. 83r

Cambrai, Bibliothèque municipale 263 – s. xiv; *AEp.* 37, fol. 188v

Cambridge, Corpus Christi College 117 – s. xiv, Bury St Edmunds, *AEp.* 255, 256, fol. 166r–v; on fol. 166v: 'Ex libro manuscripto quondam monasterij S. Edmundi martyris', refers to manuscript *E* (see Wilmart, 'La tradition', 1931, p. 45)

Cambridge, Corpus Christi College 316 – s. xiii^{in}; Dominicans of London; *AEp.* 112 and a letter to prior Baldric fol. 214r–v

Cambridge, Jesus College QG 5 – s. xi/xii; *AEp.* 284 (from Cardinal John)

Cambridge, Peterhouse 74 – s. xii$^{1/3}$; layers of papal and royal letters; *AEp.* 224 (not Anselmian), 222, 319; s. xii$^{2/3}$: *AEp.* 303 (from Paschal II), 283

Cambridge, University Library Dd. 9. 52 – s. xiv; *AEp.* 37, 414, fols. 131r–134v, *AEp.* 332, fols. 135v–137v

Cambridge, University Library Dd. 11. 5 – *AEp.* 410

Cambridge, University Library Hh. 4. 3 – s. xv; *AEp.* 414 (om. lines 1–18), fols. 50–52v

Cambridge, University Library Ii. 3. 33 – 1079–1101 and s. xii^{in} additions; Christ Church; *AEp.* 216 (Paschal to Henry I), 353, 364, fols. 194v–195v

Cologne, Stadtarchiv GB 4° 106 – s. xv; Cologne; *AEp.* 37, fol. 1r–2v

Douai, Bibliothèque municipale 201 – s. xii; Abbey of Anchin; *AEp.* 37:21– (Ingressus es –; probably from *Vita Anselmi*, c. 20), fol. 10v–

Douai, Bibliothèque municipale 279 – s. xii, Abbey of Marchiennes; Augustine, Jerome, *AEp.* 37:21– Ingressus es (probably from *Vita Anselmi*, c. 20), fol. 224v–

Douai, Bibliothèque municipale 352 – s. xii, Abbey of Anchin; *AEp.* 233[19]; includes a copy of *Vita Anselmi*

Durham Cathedral B. IV. 24 – s. xi/xii and additions s. xi/xii–xii[med]; *AEp.* 313, 468, fol. 96r (*Q* in Schmitt)

Eton College 120 – s. xiv[med]; *AEp.* 65:1–113; fol. 173r–v

Hamburg, Staats- und Universitätsbibliothek Cod. Theol. 2176 – s. xv, *AEp.* 112, fols. 141r–143v

Hereford Cathedral O. I. 6 – s. xii[1]; St Peter's Abbey, Gloucester; letter to Abbot William, possibly from Anselm, not known from other manuscripts (*Memorials*, pp. 320–322), fol. 43r–v; Picard published this letter from a lost manuscript

Hereford Cathedral P. II. 15 – s. xii[1]; Cirencester?; *AEp.* 434, 436; and Lanfranc, *Ep.* 55, 56, 59, fols. 161r–162v

Lincoln Cathedral Chapter Library 188 (B. 4. 1) – s. xv[med]; *AEp.* 133, fol. 162v

Lincoln Cathedral Chapter Library 210 (B. 5. 8) – s. xv[1]; *AEp.* 414, fols. 127v–128r

Lincoln Cathedral Chapter Library 239 (A. 7. 10) – s. xii[ex]; *AEp.* 414, an extract amongst other extracts from various authors on fols. 100v–106r

London, BL Arundel 507 – s. xiv (and xiii); *AEp.* 2, 414, fol. 78r–v

London, BL Cotton Claudius A. iii – s. xii; *AEp.* 303 (from Paschal II)

London, BL Cotton Faustina B. vi – *AEp.* 303, fol. 96

London, BL Cotton Tiberius A. vi – s. xii[2]; *AEp.* 458

London, BL Stowe 31 – s. xii, *AEp.* 280, 281, fols. 2r–5r

London, Society of Antiquaries of London 7 – s. xii[1]; Durham; *AEp.* 10:13–19 (s. xiv addition), fol. 1v

Munich, Bayerische Staatsbibliothek Clm 19136 – s. xiv; Tegernsee? (Teg. 1136); *AEp.* 97, fol. 12r–v (includes an early version of the *De concordia praescientiae et praedestinationis*; see SCHMITT, 'Eine fruehe Rezension', 1936, pp. 43–44 *et passim*)

Munich, Bayerische Staatsbibliothek Clm 22291 – s. xii, Windberg; *AEp.* 97, fols. 105r–106r (includes an early version of the *De concordia praescientiae et praedestinationis*; see SCHMITT, 'Eine fruehe Rezension', 1936, pp. 43–44 *et passim*)

Oxford, Bodleian Library Bodley 630[?] – s. xv; *AEp.* 414, fol. 279

Oxford, Bodleian Library Laud. Misc. 117 – s. xii; Augustine; *AEp.* 284[20] (an addition), fols. 131v–133v

---

[19] This and Douai, BM 827 (s. xv) include a letter of Ivo mistattributed to Anselm, see SCHMITT, 'Die echten und unechten Stücke', 1955, p. 225.

[20] See WILMART, 'Une lettre adressée', 1928, pp. 263–265.

Oxford, Bodleian Library Laud. Misc. 264 – *s.* xiv; *AEp.* 65, 204, fols. 106v–108r

Oxford, Bodleian Library Tanner 383 – *s.* xvi; *AEp.* 284

Oxford, Jesus College 37 – *s.* xii^{in}; Hereford; *AEp.* 436 and 434, *s.* xii$^{1/2}$ additions, fols. 156v–157r

Oxford, Jesus College 51 – *s.* xii; *AEp.* 401, fol. 104r

Paris, BNF lat. 14647 – *s.* xii^{ex}; at Saint-Victor from *s.* xiii; various authors including a letter of Anselm, fol. 162r

Paris, BNF lat. 15040 – *s.* xiii, Exposition of Regula of St Augustine attributed to Hugo of Saint-Victor, *AEp.* 37[?]

Paris, BNF lat. 16713 – *s.* xii, collection of Ivo of Chartres, *AEp.* 181 (from Ivo)

Paris, BNF lat. 17400 – *s.* xii; *AEp.* 204, fol. 30r–v

Rome, Biblioteca Casanatense 499 (A. VI. 41) – *s.* xv; works of Anselm, *AEp.* 65, fols. 21r–22v

Trier, Bibliothek des Priesterseminars? – *AEp.* 37, fol. 62, *AEp.* 2[?]; see *In Principio*, which gives *Trierisches Archiv*, Ergänzungsheft 13 (1912) as a reference

Vatican City, BAV Pal. lat. 314 – *s.* xiv, *AEp.* 37:21–, fols. 259v–260v

Verdun Bibliothèque municipale 7 – *s.* xv, *AEp.*?, fols. 17r–18v

3. Collated Letters and Witnesses

	N	CV	C⁶Vᵇ	V²	V³	LPE	F	J	GB	MD	O	S	W	R	H
1	✓	✓	n/a	✓	n/a	✓	n/a	n/a	n/a	✓	n/a	✓	W^{1-8}	n/a	n/a
2	✓	✓	n/a	✓	✓	✓	✓	✓	n/a	✓	n/a	✓	$W^{1-8,10,11}$	R^{1-3}	✓
3	✓	✓	n/a	✓	n/a	✓	n/a	n/a	n/a	✓	n/a	✓	W^{1-8}	n/a	n/a
4	✓	✓	n/a	✓	n/a	✓	n/a	n/a	n/a	n/a	n/a	✓	W^{1-8}	n/a	n/a
5	✓	✓	n/a	✓	✓	✓	n/a	n/a	n/a	n/a	n/a	✓	W^{1-8}	n/a	n/a
8	✓	✓	n/a	✓	✓	✓	✓	n/a	n/a	✓	n/a	✓	W^{1-8}	n/a	n/a
13	✓	✓	n/a	✓	✓	✓	✓	n/a	n/a	M	n/a	✓	W^{1-8}	n/a	n/a
37	✓	✓	n/a	✓	✗	✓	✓	n/a	✓	✓	n/a	✓	W^{1-8}	✓	✓
41	✓	✓	n/a	n/a	n/a	✓	n/a	n/a	n/a	n/a	n/a	✓	✓	n/a	n/a
45	✓	✓	n/a	✓	n/a	✓	n/a	n/a	n/a	n/a	n/a	✓	W^{1-8}	n/a	n/a
65	✓	✓	n/a	✓	✗	n/a	n/a	n/a	✓	✓	n/a	S^1	$W^{4,5,7}$	n/a	✓
161	n/a	✓	✓	n/a	✓	✓	✓	n/a	✓	✓	✓	n/a	n/a	R^{1-3}	n/a
162	n/a	✓	✓	n/a	n/a	✓	✓	n/a	✓	✓	✓	n/a	n/a	n/a	n/a

Where manuscripts in a given group remain uncollated, the table reports the collated manuscripts. In group *GB*, *AEp*. 65 is witnessed only by *G*, and *AEp*. 162 only by *B*.

✓ = collated
✗ = not collated

4. The Arrangement of Letters in *NMFLPEVCO* and *Historia novorum*[1]

SAO	N	HN	M	F	L	P	E	V	C	O
1	N1		M18		L1	P1	E1	V1	C1	
2	N40		M25	F1	L3	P3	E2	V2	C2	
3	N2		M19		L2	P2	E3	V3	C3	
4	N3				L5	P5	E4	V4	C4	
5	N4				L6	P6	E5	V5	E5	
6	N5, 30		M20	F2	L7	P7	E6	V6	C6	
7	N6		M22		L8	P8	E7	V7	C7	
8	N7		M21	F3	L9	P9	E8	V8	C8	
9			M4	F4	L10	P10				
10					L11	P11				
11	N14				L12	P12	E9	V9	C9	
12	N12				L4	P4	E10	V10	C10	
13	N13		M23	F5	L13	P13	E11	V11	C11	
14	N10				L14	P14	E12	V12	C12	
15	N11				L15	P15	E13	V13	C13	
16	N8				L16	P16	E14	V14	C14	
17	N15		M24	F6	L17	P17	E15	V15	C15	
18	N16									
19					L18	P18				
20	N17				L19	P19	E16	V16	C16	
21	N18				L20	P20	E17	V17	C17	
22	N19				L21	P21	E18	V18	C18	
23	N21				L22	P22	(E19)	(V19)	(C19)	
24	N24				L23	P23				
25	N22				L24	P24	E19	V19	C19	
26	N46									
27	N48									
28	N23				L25	P25	E20	V20	C20	
29	N20		M5	F7	L26	P26	E21	V21	C21	
30					L27	P27	E22	V22	C22	
31			M13	F8	L28	P28	E23	V23	C23	
32	N25				L29	P29	E24	V24	C24	
33	N26				L30	P30	E25	V25	C25	
34	N27				L31	P31	E26	V26	C26	
35	N29				L32	P32	E27	V27	C27	

[1] The table was begun by Prof. Richard Sharpe. I am grateful to him for allowing me to use and insert new materials in his table.

SAO	N	HN	M	F	L	P	E	V	C	O
36	N28				L33	P33	E28	V28	C28	
37	N58		M26	F9	L34	P34	E29	V29	C29	
38	N9, 36			F10	L35	P35	E30	V30	C30	
39	N37				L36	P36	E31	V31	C31	
40	N35				L37	P37	E32	V32	C32	
41	N34				L38	P38	E33	V33	C33	
42					L39	P39	E34	V34	C34	
43					L40	P40	E35	V35	C35	
44	N33				L42	P42	E36	V36	C36	
45	N39				L43	P43	E37	V37	C37	
46	N45				L44	P44	E38	V38	C38	
47					L45	P45	E39	V39	C39	
48	N49				L46	P46	E40	V40	C40	
49	N42		M7	F12	L47	P47	E41	V41	C41	
50	N32				L48	P48	E42	V42	C42	
51	N31				L49	P49	E43	V43	C43	
52					L306	P305	E289	V252	C333	O30
53	N60		M27	F13	L52	P52	E44	V44	C44	
54	N50				L54	P54	E45	V45	C45	
55	N51				L62	P62	E46	V46	C46	
56	N52				L63	P63	E47	V47	C47	
57	N54		M71		L64	P64	E48	V48	C48	
58	N43				L50	P50		V49	C49	
59	N47				L57	P57		V50	C50	
60					L53	P53		V51	C51	
61	N41		M6	F11	L41	P41		V52	C52	
62	N56		M8	F14	L61	P61		V53	C53	
63								V54	C54	
64								V55	C55	
65	N67		M31					V56	C56	
66	N38				L55	P55		V57	C57	
67	N57				L56	P56		V58	C58	
68	N44				L51	P51		V59	C59	
69					L58	P58		V60	C60	
70					L59	P59		V61	C61	
71	N53				L60	P60		V62	C62	
72					L65	P65	E49	V63	C63	
73			M9	F15	L66	P66	E50	V64	C64	
74					L67	P67	E51	V65	C65	
75					L68	P68	E52	V66	C66	
76	N55				L69	P69	E53	V67	C67	
77					L70	P70	E54	V68	C68	
78	N59		M28	F16	L71	P71	E55	V69	C69	
79					L72	P72	E56	V70	C70	

SAO	N	HN	M	F	L	P	E	V	C	O
80	N61		M29	F17	L73	P73	E57	V71	C71	
81	N62		M30	F18	L74	P74	E58	V72	C72	
82	N63		M45		L75	P75	E59	V73	C73	
83	N64		M69		L76	P76	E60	V74	C74	
84	N65		M39		L77	P77	E61	V75	C75	
85	N66		M59	F19	L78	P78	E62	V76	C76	
86	N68		M60		L79	P79	E63	V77	C77	
87	N69		M61		L309	P308	E292		C336	
88			M62							
89	N70		M32		L80	P80	E64	V78	C78	
90	N71		M63		L81	P81	E65	V79	C79	
91	N72		M65	F20	L82	P82	E66	V80	C80	
92	N73		M64		L83	P83	E67	V81	C81	
93	N74		M66		L84	P84	E68	V82	C82	
94	N75		M67		L85	P85	E69	V83	C83	
95	N76		M70		L308	P307	E291	V253	C335	O31
96			M68	F21	L86	P86	E70	V84	C84	
97				F22	L87	P87	E71	V85	C85	
97*	N80		M35							
98	N90		M49		L88	P88	E72	V86	C86	
99	N78		M34		L89	P89	E73	V87	C87	
100	N81		M36		L90	P90	E74	V88	C88	
101	N79		M2	F23	L91	P91	E75	V89	C89	
102			M1		L110	P110	E94	V108	C108	
103	N82		M37		L92	P92	E76	V90	C90	
104	N91		M43		L93	P93	E77	V91	C91	
105	N87		M42		L94	P94	E78	V92	C92	
106	N83		M38		L95	P95	E79	V93	C93	
107	N93				L130	P130				
108	N84				L131	P131				
109	N96		M53		L96	P96	E80	V94	C94	
110	N85		M40		L99	P99	E83	V97	C97	
111	N86		M41		L100	P100	E84	V98	C98	
112			M17	F25	L101	P101	E85	V99	C99	
113			M10	F26	L102	P102	E86	V100	C100	
114	N88		M44		L103	P103	E87	V101	C101	
115	N89		M48		L104	P104	E88	V102	C102	
116	N92		M50		L97	P97	E81	V95	C95	
117	N77		M33	F24	L98	P98	E82	V96	C96	
118	N94		M51		L105	P105	E89	V103	C103	
119	N95		M52	F27	L106	P106	E90	V104	C104	
120			M76	F28	L107	P107	E91	V105	C105	
121			M11	F29	L108	P108	E92	V106	C106	
122	N97		M54	F30	L109	P109	E93	N107	C107	

SAO	N	HN	M	F	L	P	E	V	C	O
123								V157	C158	
124								V158	C159	
125					L111	P111	E95	V109	C109	
126							E96	V110	C110	
127							E97	V111	C111	
128					L112	P112				
129					L113	P113	E98	V112	C112	
130			M47		L114	P114	E99	V113	C113	
131			M46		L115	P115	E100	V114	C114	
132			M57	F31	L116	P116	E101	V115	C115	
133	N98		M55		L117	P117	E102	V116	C116	
134			M56	F32	L118	P118	E103	V117	C117	
135			M58		L307	P307	E290		C334	
136			M12	F33	L119	P119	E104	V118	C118	
137			M14	F34	L120	P120	E105	V119	C119	
138					L121	P121	E106	V120	C120	
139					L122	P122	E107	V121	C121	
140			M15	F35	L123	P123	E108	V122	C122	
141					L124	P124	E109	V123	C123	
142					L125	P125	E110	V124	C124	
143					L126	P126	E111	V125	C125	
144			M16	F36	L127	P127	E112	V126	C126	
145										
146			M72		L128	P128	E113	V127	C127	
147			M73		L129	P129	E114	V128	C128	
148			M75					V129	C129	
149					L132	P132		V130	C130	
150								V131	C131	
151								V132	C132	
152								V133	C133	
153					L133 Scribe C					
154		HN3 (i, p. 48)			L134 Scribe C					
155								V134	C134	
156			M74	F37	L135	P133	E115	V135, 159	C135, 160	O1
157					L136	P134	E116	V136, 160	C136, 161	O50
158					L137	P135	E117	V137, 161	C137, 162	O51
159								V138	C138	
160					L138	P136	E118	V139, 162	C139, 163	O52

[2] Between *AEp.* 164 and 165, *C* includes the *Epistola de incarnatione Verbi,* counted here as *C144.*

SAO	N	HN	M	F	L	P	E	V	C	O
161			M108	F38	L139	P137	E119	V140, 163	C140, 164	O2
162			M109	F39	L140	P140	E120	V141, 164	C141, 165	O3
163								V142	C142	
164								V143	C143[2]	
165								V144	C145	
166								V145	C146	
167								V146	C147	
168										
169										
170					L163	P161	E145	V147	C148, 189	
171		HN4 (i, pp. 46–7)			L164	P162	E146		C190	
172								V148	C149	
173								V149	C150	
174								V150	C151	
175								V151	C152	
176								V152	C153	
177										
178								V154	C155	
179								V155	C156	
180					L141	P139	E121	V156, 165	C157, 166	O53
181										
182					L142	P140		V166	C167	O4
183										
184										
185			M110	F40	L143	P141	E123	V167	C168	O5
186			M111	F41	L144	P142	E124	V168	C169	O54
187					L145	P143	E125	V169	C170	O55
188			M112	F42	L146	P144	E126	V170	C171	O56
189					L147	P145	E127	V171	C172	O6
190										
191					L148	P146	E128	V172	C173	O57
192			M123	F53	L149	P147	E129	V173	C174	O58
193					L388 Hand C		E130	V174	C175	O59
194					L150	P148	E131		C176	O60
195										
196			M113	F43	L151	P149	E132		C177	O7
197			M114	F44	L152	P150	E133	V175	C178	O8
198					L153	P151	E134		C179	O61
199			M115	F45	L154	P152	E135	V176	C180	O9

SAO	N	HN	M	F	L	P	E	V	C	O
200					L394 Hand C					
201		HN5 (ii, pp. 76–7)			L200	P198	E182		C226	
202					L393 Hand C					
203			M124	F54	L182	P180	E164	V191	C208	O14
204			M78							
205								V293	C417	
206		HN6 (ii, pp. 91–3)			L155	P153	E136		C181, 418	O62
207					L396 Hand C					
208										
209									C154	
210					L156	P154	E137	V177	C182	O63
211					L158	P156	E140	V180	C184	
212					L391 Hand C		E138	V178	C416	
213					L157	P155	E139	V179	C183	
214					L159	P157	E141		C185	
215										
216		HN7 (iii, pp. 128-31)								
217					L165	P163	E147		C191	
218					L166	P164	E148	V184	C192	
219					L168	P166	E150		C194	
220					L169	P167	E151	V185	C195	
221										
222		HN9 (iii, pp. 135–6)	M148	F154	L160	P158	E142	V181	C186	
223			M149	F155	L161	P159	E143	V182	C187	
224		HN8 (iii, pp. 134–5)								
225										
226		HN10 (iii, 136–7)								
227					L162	P160		V183	C188	
228					L167	P165	E149		C193	
229					L170	P168	E152		C196	
230			M116		L171	P169	E153		C197	O10
231			M117	F47	L172	P170	E154	V186	C198	O11
232			M118	F48	L173	P171	E155		C199	O12
233			M119	F49	L174	P172	E156	V187	C200	O13
234					L175	P173	E157		C201	
235			M120	F50	L176	P174	E158		C202	

SAO	N	HN	M	F	L	P	E	V	C	O
236					177	P175	E159	V188	C203	
237					L178	P176	E160		C204	
238					L179	P177	E161	V189	C205	
239										
240			M121	F52	L180	P178	E162	V190	C206	
241			M122	F51	L181	P179	E163		C207	
242					L183	P181	E165	V192	C209	
243					L185	P183	E167	V194	C211	
244					L184	P182	E166	V193	C210	
245					L186	P184	E168		C212	O15
246					L187	P185	E169		C213	
247			M125	F55	L188	P186	E170	V195	C214	
248			M126	F56	L189	P187	E171		C215	
249			M127	F57	L190	P188	E172	V196	C216	
250					L191	P189	E173	V197	C217	
251			M128	F58	L192	P190	E174		C218	
252			M129	F59	L193	P191	E175	V198	C219	
253					L194	P192	E176		C220	
254			M130	F60	L195	P193	E177		C221	O16
255					L392 Hand C					
256					L196	P194	E178		C222	
257					L197	P195	E179	V199	C223	
258					L198	P196	E180	V200	C224	
259			M131	F61	L199	P197	E181		C225	
260					L201	P199	E183	V201	C226	
261					L202	P200	E184		C228	
262			M132	F62	L203	P201	E185	V202	C229	
263					L204	P202	E186		C230	
264			M133	F63	L205	P203	E187	V203	C231	
265			M134	F64	L206	P204	E188		C232	
266			M135	F65	L207	P205	E189		C233	
267			M136	F66	L208	P206	E190		C234	
268					L209	P207	E191	V204	C235	
269					L210	P208	E192		V236	
270					L211	P209	E193		C237	
271					L212	P210	E194	V205	C238	
272			M138	F69	L213	P211	E195	V206	C239	
273					L214	P212	E196		C240	
274					L215	P213	E197		C241	
275					L216	P214	E198		C242	
276					L217	P215	E199	V207	C243	
277					L218	P216	E200		C244	
278			M170	F70	L220	P218	E202	V209	C246	
279					L221	P219	E203		C247	

SAO	N	HN	M	F	L	P	E	V	C	O
280			M139	F71	L222	P220	E204	V210	C248	
281		HN12 (iii, pp. 149–51)	M140	F72	L223	P221	E205	V281	C249	
282		HN11 (iii, p. 139)	M80							
283		HN44 (iv, p. 216)	M142	F139	L336	P335	E320	V268	C364	
284										
285			M204	F73	L224	P222	E206	V212	C250	O17
286			M173	F74	L225	P223	E207	V213	C251	O18
287					L226	P224	E208		C252	
288			M153	F75	L227	P225	E209		C253	
289			M174	F76	L228	P226	E210	V214	C254	O19
290					L229	P227	E211		C255	
291			M177	F80	L235	P233	E217	V213	C261	
292			M175	F77	L230	P228	E212		C256	
293			M176	F78	L231	P229	E213	V215	C257	
294			M152	F79	L232	P230	E214	V216	C258	
295					L233	P231	E215	V217	C259	
296					L234	P232	E216	V218	C260	
297					L236	P234	E218	V220	C262	
298			M205	F81	L237	P236	E219	V221	C263	
299			M178	F82	L238	P237	E220	V222	C264	
300					L239	P238	E221		C265	
301					L240	P239	E222	V223	C266	
302			M202	F83	L241	P240	E223	V224	C267	O20
303		HN13 (iii, pp. 154–5)	M145	F100	L264	P263	E246		C290	
304										
305		HN14 (iii, pp. 155–7)								
306					L242	P241	E224		C268	
307					L263	P262	E245		C289	
308		HN15 (iii, pp. 157–8)	M81	F84	L243	P242	E225	V225	C269	
309					L244	P243	E226		C270	
310		HN16 (iv, pp. 160–2)								
311			M180	F86	L246	P245	E228	V227	C272	
312			M179	F85	L245	P244	E227	V226	C271	O21
313			M181	F87	L247	P246	E229	V228	C273	O22
314			M182	F88	L248	P247	E230	V229	C274	
315					L272	P271	E255		C299	
316			M183	F89	L249	P248	E231		C275	
317			M154	F90	L250	P249	E232	V230	C276	
318					L251	P250	E233	V231	C277	

SAO	N	HN	M	F	L	P	E	V	C	O
319			M151	F101	L252	P251	E234	V232	C278	
320			M155	F91	L253	P252	E235	V233	C279	
321			M156	F102	L254	P253	E236	V234	C280	
322			M169	F92	L255	P254	E237	V235	C281	
323					L256	P255	E238	V236	C282	
324			M164	F93	L257	P256	E239		C283	
325			M166	F94	L258	P257	E240		C284	
326			M143	F96	L260	P259	E242		C286	
327			M184	F97	L261	P260	E243	V237	C287	
328			M186	F98	L262	P261	E244		C288	O23
329			M157	F103	L266	P265	E249		C293	
330			M172	F68	L270	P269	E253		C297	
331					L390 Hand C	P235	E247		C291	
332			M187	F104	L267	P266	E250	V238	C294	O24
333			M188	F105	L268	P267	E251	V239	C295	O25
334					L265	P264	E248		C292	
335			M203	F67	L269	P268	E253	V240	C296	O26
336			M185	F107	L271	P270	E254		C298	
337			M82						C300	
338					L273	P72	E256		C301	
339					L274	P273	E257		C302	
340					L275	P274	E258		C303	
341					L276	P275	E259		C304	
342					L277	P276	E260		C305	
343			M201	F106	L278	P277	E261	V241	C306	
344					L279	P278	E262	V242	C307	
345			M200	F108	L280	P279	E263	V243	C308	O27
346			M158	F109	L281	P280	E264		C309	
347			M159	F110	L282	P281	E265	V244		
348									C310	
349			M189	F111	L283	P282	E266		C311	
350			M165	F112	L284	P283	E267			
351										
352										
353		HN17 (iv, pp. 163)	M83	F113	L285	P284	E268		C312	
354			M141				E241		C285	
355			M190	F114	L286	P285	E269	V245	C313	O28
356			M191	F115	L287	P286	E270		C314	
357			M192	F116	L288	P287	E271		C315	
358					L289	P288	E272		C316	
359					L291	P290	E274		C318	
360					L290	P289	E273		C317	
361			M146	F117	L292	P291			C319	

314 APPENDICES

SAO	N	HN	M	F	L	P	E	V	C	O
362										
363										
364			M193	F119	L295	P294	E278	V247	C322	
365		HN18 (iv, pp. 167–8)								
366										
367		HN19 (iv, p. 169)	M84							
368		HN20 (iv, pp. 169–70)	M85	F123	L296	P295	E279	V248	C323	
369		HN21 (iv, pp. 170–71)	M86		L297	P296	E280		C324	
370					L298	P297	E281		C325	
371					L299	P298	E282		C326	
372			M144	F120	L300	P299	E283		C327	
373										
374			M194	F121	L301	P300	E284	V249	C328	
375			M206	F122	L302	P301	E285	V250	C329	O29
376					L303	P302	E286		C330	
377					L304	P303	E287		C331	
378					L305	P304	E288	V251	C332	
379					L310	P309	E293		C337	
380			M195	F124	L311	P310	E294	V254	C338	
381					L312	P311	E295		C339	
382			M137	F126	L314	P313	E297	V255	C340	O32
383			M207	F125	L313	P312	E296		C341	
384			M160	F127	L315	P314	E298	V256	C342	
385			M161	F128	L316	P315	E299	V257	C343	
386		HN22 (iv, pp. 173–4)	M87	F99	L317	P316	E300	V258	C344	
387		HN23 (iv, pp. 174–5)	M88	F129	L318	P317	E301	V259	C345	
388			M147	F130	L319	P318	E302		C346	
389			M167	F131	L320	P319	E303	V260	C347	
390			M168	F132	L321	P320	E304	V261	C348	
391		HN24 (iv, pp. 175–6)	M89	F118	L293	P292	E276	V246	C320	
392		HN25 (iv, p. 176)	M90		L294	P293	E277		C321	
393		HN26 (iv, pp. 176–7)	M91		L324	P323	E304		C351	
394		HN27 (iv, p. 177)	M92		L323	P322	E306		C350	
395					L322	P321	E305		C349	
396					L327	P326	E310		C354	

SAO	N	HN	M	F	L	P	E	V	C	O
397		HN29 (iv, pp. 178–9)	M94	F147	L350	P349	E334	V277	C378	
398		HN28 (iv, pp. 177–8)	M93							
399					L325	P324	E308		C352	
400					L326	P325	E309		C353	
401		HN30 (iv, p. 184)	M95		L338	P337	E322		C366	
402					L339	P338	E323		C367	
403			M211	F133	L328	P327	E311	V262	C355	O33
404			M150	F134	L329	P328	E312	V263	C356	
405			M212	F135	L330	P329	E313	V264	C357	O34
406			M162	F136	L331	P330	E314	V265	C358	
407			M199	F137	L332	P331	E315	V266	C359	
408					L333	P332	E316		C360	
409					L334	P333	E317		C361	
410			M210	F138	L335	P334	E318	V267	C362	O35
411					L389 Hand C		E319		C363	
412					L337	P336	E321		C365	
413			M163	F140	L340	P339	E324	V269	C368	
414			M213	F141	L341	P340	E325	V270	C369	O36
415			M215	F160	L342	P341	E326	V271	C370	O37
416				F161	L343	P342	E327	V272	C371	O38
417			M216	F162	L344	P343	E328	V273	C372	O39
418			M209	F142	L345	P344	E329	V274	C373	O40
419			M171	F143	L346	P345	E330		C374	
420			M214	F144	L347	P346	E331	V275	C375	O41
421			M198	F145	L348	P347	E332	V276	C376	O42
422		HN31 (iv, pp. 185–6)	M96	F148	L351	P350	E335		C379	
423					L352	P351	E336		C380	
424					L353	P352	E337		C381	
425			M77	F149	L354	P353	E338	V278	C382	O43
426					L355	P354	E339		C383	
427					L356	P355	E340	V279	C384	
428					L357	P356	E341		C385	
429					L358	P357	E342	V280	C386	
430		HN32 (iv, p. 191)	M97	F146	L349	P348	E330		C377	
431			M196	F150	L359	P358	E343	V281	C387	O44
432					L360	P359	E344		C388	
433					L361	P360	E345	V282	C389	
434			M208	F151	L362	P361	E346	V283	C390	O45
435					L363	P362		V284	C391	
436			M79		L364	P363		V285	C392	O46

SAO	N	HN	M	F	L	P	E	V	C	O
437										
438										
439										
440					L395 Hand C					
441		HN33 (iv, pp. 195–6)	M98		L368	P367	E352		C396	
442		HN34 (iv, pp. 198–9)	M99							
443		HN35 (iv, p. 199)	M100	F152	L365	P364	E349	V286	C393	
444		HN36 (iv, pp. 199–200)	M101		L366	P365	E350		C394	
445		HN37 (iv, pp. 200–201)	M102	F153	L367	P366	E351		C395	
446					L369	P368	E353	V287	C397	O47
447					L370	P369	E354		C398	
448					L371	P370	E355		C399	
449					L372	P371	E356		C400	
450					L373	P372	E357	V288	C401	O48
451		HN38 (iv, pp. 201–2)	M103		L375	P374	E351	V289	C403	
452		HN39 (iv, pp. 202–3)	M104		L376	P375	E352	V290	C404	
453										
454					L374	P373				
455		HN40 (iv, pp. 203–4)	M105				E358		C402	
456		HN41 (iv, p. 204)								
457										
458										
459										
460										
461					L377	P376	E361		C405	
462					L378	P377	E362		C406	
463					L389	P388	E363		C407	
464					L380	P379	E364		C408	
465					L381	P380	E365		C409	
466					L382	P381	E366		C410	
467				F156	L383	P382	E367		C411	
468			M197	F157	L384	P383	E368	V291	C412	
469					L385 & L399	P384	E369		C413	

SAO	N	HN	M	F	L	P	E	V	C	O
470		HN42 (iv, p. 205)	M106							
471				F158	L386 & L397	P385	E370		C414	
472		HN43 (iv, p. 206)	M107	F159	L387 & L398	P386	E371		C415	

BIBLIOGRAPHY

Main Publications of Anselm's Correspondence in Print

Petrus Danhauser   *Opera et tractatus beati Anselmi archiepiscopi cantuariensis ordinis sancti Benedicti*, Nuremberg: Caspar Hochfeder, 27 March 1491 (*GW* 2032).
repr. 1496×97, Strasbourg (*GW* 2034); 1496×97, Basel (*GW* 2033); Anton Democharès (ed.), *Omnia diui Anselmi Cantuariensis archiepiscopi theologorum omnium sui temporis facile principis opuscula*, Paris, 1544; *Diui Anselmi Cantuariensis archiepiscopi...omnia quae reperiri potuerunt opera*, Cologne, 1573.

Jean Picard   *Diui Anselmi archiepiscopi Cantuariensis opera omnia quattuor tomis comprehensa*, Cologne, 1612.
repr. Théophile Raynaud (ed.), *Sancti Anselmi archiepiscopi Cantuariensis opera omnia*, Lyon, 1630.

Luc d'Achery   *Veterum aliquot scriptorum qui in Galliae Bibliothecis maxime Benedictorum latuerant Spicilegium*, 13 vols., Paris, 1657–1677 [vol. 9, 1669].
repr. *Spicilegium siue collectio ueterum...Noua editio*, with corrections by É. Baluze & E. Martène, Paris, 1723.

Gabriel Gerberon   *Sancti Anselmi ex Beccensi abbate Cantuariensis archiepiscopi opera omnia nec non Eadmeri monachi Cantuariensis Historia nouorum et alia opuscula*, Paris, 1675.
repr. with corrections and additions: *Sancti Anselmi...opera omnia. Secunda editio*, Paris, 1721; *Sancti Anselmi...opera omnia. Prima editio Veneta*, Venice, 1744; *Pat. Lat.* 158 and 159, Paris, 1853 and 1854.

Étienne Baluze   *Miscellaneorum collectio ueterum*, Paris, 1678–1715 [vol 4, 1683; vol. 5, 1700].
repr. *Miscellanea nouo ordine digesta*, 4 vols., with corrections and additions by G. Mansi, Lucca, 1761 [vol 2].

André Wilmart   'La tradition des lettres de S. Anselme. Lettres inédites de S. Anselme et de ses correspondants', *Revue Bénédictine*, 43 (1931), pp. 38–54.

see also Wilmart's two 1928 articles in the bibliography.

F. S. Schmitt   'Zur Ueberlieferung der Korrespondenz Anselms von Canterbury. Neue Briefe', *Revue Bénédictine*, 43 (1931), pp. 224–238.

F. S. Schmitt   *Sancti Anselmi Opera Omnia*, 6 vols., Seckau, Rome, Edinburgh, 1938–61 [vols 3–5].
repr. with *Prolegomena*, Stuttgart – Bad Cannstatt, 1968 and 1984.

PRINTED SOURCES

ADALBERTUS SAMARITANUS, *Praecepta dictaminum*, ed. Franz-Josef SCHMALE, *MGH, Quellen zur Geistesgeschichte des Mittelalters*, 3, Weimar, 1961.

ALBERIC OF MONTECASSINO, *De dictamine*, in ROCKINGER, *Briefsteller*, 1863, pp. 29–46.

ANONYMOUS OF BOLOGNA, *Rationes dictandi*, in ROCKINGER, *Briefsteller*, 1863, pp. 9–28.

ANONYMOUS OF ROCHESTER, *The Life of Gundulf, Bishop of Rochester*, ed. Rodney M. THOMSON, *Toronto Medieval Latin Texts*, Toronto, 1977.

ANSELM OF CANTERBURY, *Anselmo d'Aosta: Lettere*, vol. 1, eds. I. BIFFI & C. MARABELLI, Milan, 1988.

ANSELM OF CANTERBURY, *L'œuvre de S. Anselme de Cantorbéry*, ed. Michel CORBIN, vol 6, *Lettres 1 à 147*, Paris, 2005.

ARNULF OF LISIEUX, *The Letters of Arnulf of Lisieux*, ed. Frank BARLOW, *Camden Third Series*, 61, London, 1939.

BATES, David, (ed.), *The Acta of William I, Regesta Regum Anglo-Normannorum*, Oxford, 1998.

BERNARD OF CLAIRVAUX, *Epistolae*, in *Sancti Bernardi Opera*, vols. 7 and 8, eds. J. LECLERCQ & H. ROCHAIS, Rome, 1974–1977.

BERNARD OF CLAIRVAUX, *De praecepto et dispensatione*, in *Sancti Bernardi Opera*, vol. 3, eds. J. LECLERCQ & H. ROCHAIS, Rome, 1963, pp. 241–294.

BRETT, Martin, & Joseph A. GRIBBIN (eds.), *English Episcopal Acta*, 28, *Canterbury 1070–1136*, Oxford, 2004.

COLKER, Marvin L., (ed.), 'Epistolae ad amicum', in *Three Medieval Latin Texts in the Library of Trinity College, Analecta Dublinensia*, Cambridge (Mass.), 1975, pp. 91–160.

DELISLE, Léopold, (ed.), *Rouleau mortuaire de B. Vital, abbé de Savigny*, Paris, 1909.

EADMER OF CANTERBURY, *Historia Nouorum in Anglia*, ed. Martin RULE, *RS*, London, 1884.

EADMER OF CANTERBURY, *Vita Anselmi*, ed. Richard SOUTHERN, *OMT*, 2nd ed., Oxford, 1972 [1962].

FULBERT OF CHARTRES, *The Letters and Poems of Fulbert of Chartres*, ed. Frederick BEHRENDS, *OMT*, Oxford, 1976.

GERVASE OF CANTERBURY, *The Historical Works of Gervase of Canterbury*, ed. W. STUBBS, 2 vols., *RS*, London, 1879–1880.

GERVASE OF PRÉMONTRÉ, *Epistolae*, in *Sacrae Antiquitatis Monumenta*, vol. 1, ed. C. L. HUGO, Étival, 1725, pp. 1–124.

GILBERT CRISPIN, *Disputatio iudaei et christiani*, in *The Works of Gilbert Crispin*, eds. Anna Saphir ABULAFIA & G. R. EVANS, Oxford, 1986.

GREGORY VII, *Das Register Gregors VII*, 2 vols., ed. E. CASPAR, *MGH, Epistolae Selectae*, Munich, 1920–1923.

GREGORY VII, *The* Epistolae Vagantes *of Pope Gregory VII*, ed. H. E. J. COWDREY, *OMT*, Oxford, 1972.

GREGORY THE GREAT, *Moralia in Iob*, ed. M. ADRIAEN, *CCSL* 143, Turnhout, 1985.

GUIDO OF BAZOCHES, *Liber epistularum Guidonis de Basochis*, ed. Herbert ADOLFSSON, *Studia Latina Stockholmiensia*, 18, Stockholm, 1969.

HENRY DE KIRKESTEDE, *Catalogus of Henry de Kirkestede*, eds. Richard H. ROUSE & Mary A. ROUSE, *Corpus of British Medieval Library Catalogues*, vol. 11, London, 2004.

HERBERT LOSINGA, *Epistolae*, in *The Life, Letters and Sermons of Bishop Herbert de Losinga*, eds. E. M. GOULBURN & H. SYMONDS, Oxford, 1878, pp. 1–107.

HUGH OF SAINT-VICTOR, *Didascalicon de studio legendi*, ed. Charles Henry BUTTIMER, *Studies in Medieval and Renaissance Latin*, 10, Washington, 1939.

HUMPHREYS, K. W., (ed.), *The Friars' Libraries, Corpus of British Medieval Library Catalogues*, vol. 1, London, 1990.

JOHN OF SALISBURY, *The Letters of John of Salisbury*, 2 vols., eds. W. J. MILLOR, H. E. BUTLER & C. N. L. BROOKE, *NMT* (vol 1) and *OMT* (vol 2), London & Oxford, 1955–1979.

JOHNSON, Charles, & H. A. CRONNE (eds.), *Regesta Henrici Primi, Regesta Regum Anglo-Normannorum*, 2, Oxford, 1956.

LAMBERT OF ARRAS, *Epistolae*, ed. É. BALUZE, in *Miscellaneorum collectio ueterum*, vol. 5, Paris, 1700, pp. 283–376.

LANFRANC OF CANTERBURY, *The Monastic Constitutions of Lanfranc,* ed. David KNOWLES, *NMT*, London, 1951.

LANFRANC OF CANTERBURY, *The Letters of Lanfranc Archbishop of Canterbury*, eds. Helen CLOVER & Margaret GIBSON, *OMT*, Oxford, 1979.

MAGNUS OF REICHERSBERG, *Chronica collecta*, ed. Wilhelm WATTENBACH, *Monumenta Germaniae Historica, Scriptores*, 17, Hannover, 1861, pp. 476–523.

NICHOLAS OF CLAIRVAUX, *Epistolae*, ed. J. PICARD, *PL* 196, Paris, 1855, cols. 1593–1654.

ODO OF CANTERBURY, *The Latin Sermons of Odo of Canterbury*, eds. Charles DE CLERCQ & Raymond MACKEN, *Verhandelingen van de Koninklijke Academie voor Wetenschappen, Letteren en Schone Kunsten van België, Klasse der letteren*, 105, Brussels, 1983.

OMONT, Henri, (ed.), *Tituli librorum Beccensis almarii*, in *Catalogue général des manuscrits des bibliothèques publiques de France*, vol. 2, Paris, 1888, pp. 385–398.

ORDERIC VITALIS, *The Ecclesiastical History of Orderic Vitalis*, 6 vols., ed. Marjorie CHIBNALL, *OMT*, Oxford, 1968–1980.

PETER OF BLOIS, *Epistolae*, ed. I. A. GILES, *PL* 207, Paris, 1855, cols. 1–560.

PETER OF CELLE, *The Letters of Peter of Celle*, ed. Julian HASELDINE, *OMT*, Oxford, 2001.

PETER OF ST JOHN, 'The Letter from Peter of St John to Hato of Troyes', ed. Giles CONSTABLE, *Studia Anselmiana*, 40 (1956), pp. 38–52.

PETER THE VENERABLE, *The Letters of Peter the Venerable*, 2 vols., ed. Giles CONSTABLE, Cambridge (Mass.), 1967.

ROUSE, Richard H., Mary A. ROUSE & R. A. B. MYNORS (eds.), *Registrum Anglie de libris doctorum et auctorum ueterum, Corpus of British Medieval Library Catalogues*, vol. 2, London, 1991.

SHARPE, Richard, James P. CARLEY, Rodney M. THOMSON & Andrew G. WATSON (eds.), *English Benedictine Libraries: The Shorter Catalogues, Corpus of British Medieval Library Catalogues*, vol. 4, London, 1996.

VERNET, André, (ed.), *La bibliothèque de l'abbaye de Clairvaux du XIIe au XVIIIe siècle*, vol. 1, Paris, 1979.

WEBBER, Teresa, & Andrew G. WATSON (eds.), *The Libraries of the Augustinian Canons, Corpus of British Medieval Library Catalogues*, vol. 6, London, 1998.

WILLIAM OF MALMESBURY, *Gesta Pontificum Anglorum*, ed. M. WINTERBOTTOM, *OMT*, Oxford, 2007.

SECONDARY SOURCES

BARLOW, Frank, *The English Church 1066–1154: A Constitutional History*, London, 1979.

BESTUL, Thomas H., 'The Collection of Private Prayers in the *'Portiforium'* of Wulfstan of Worcester and the *'Orationes sive Meditationes'* of Anselm of Canterbury', in *Les mutations socio-culturelles au tournant des XIe-XIIe siècles*, ed. Raymonde FOREVILLE, Paris, 1984, pp. 355–364.

BISCHOFF, Bernard, *Latin Palaeography. Antiquity and the Middle Ages*, trans. by Dáibhí Ó CRÓINÍN & David GANZ, Cambridge, 1990.

BISHOP, T. A. M., 'Notes on Cambridge Manuscripts. Part I', *Transactions of the Cambridge Bibliographical Society*, 1 (1953), pp. 432–441.

—, *English Caroline Minuscule*, Oxford Palaeographical Handbooks, Oxford, 1971.

BONDÉELLE-SOUCHIER, A., *Bibliothèques cisterciennes dans la France médiévale. Répertoire des abbayes d'hommes*, Paris, 1991.

BRETT, Martin, 'A note on the *Historia nouorum* of Eadmer', *Scriptorium*, 33 (1979), pp. 56–58.

—, 'John of Worcester and his contemporaries', in *The writing of history in the Middle Ages. Essays presented to Richard William Southern*, eds. R. H. C. DAVIS & J. M. WALLACE-HADRILL, Oxford, 1981, pp. 101–126.

BROWN, Michelle P., *A Guide to Western Historical Scripts from Antiquity to 1600*, Toronto & Buffalo, 1999.

CAMARGO, Martin, *Ars dictaminis. Ars dictandi, Typologie des sources du moyen âge occidental*, 60, Turnhout, 1991.

—, 'Introduction', in *Medieval Rhetorics of Prose Composition. Five English Artes Dictandi and Their Tradition, Medieval & Renaissance texts & studies*, 115, Binghampton & New York, 1995.

CANTOR, Norman F., *Church, Kingship, and Lay Investiture in England 1089–1135*, Princeton, 1958.

—, *Inventing the Middle Ages. The Lives, Works, and Ideas of the Great Medievalists of the Twentieth Century*, New York, 1991.

—, *Inventing Norman Cantor: Confessions of a Medievalist*, Tempe Arizona, 2002.

CAPPUYNS, M., 'S. Anselmi Cantuariensis Archiep. Opera omnia... Vol. IV', *Bulletin de théologie ancienne et médiévale*, 6 (1950–1953), pp. 322–323.

—, 'S. Anselmi Cantuariensis Archiep. Opera omnia. T. V', *Bulletin de théologie ancienne et médiévale*, 7 (1954–1957), p. 424.

—, 'S. Anselmi Cantuariensis Archiepiscopi Opera omnia. T. VI', *Bulletin de théologie ancienne et médiévale*, 9 (1962–1965), pp. 91–92.

CASTAN, A., 'La bibliothèque de l'abbaye de Saint-Claude du Jura. Esquisse de son histoire', *Bibliothèque de l'École des chartes*, 50 (1889), pp. 301–354.

CARERI, Maria, *et al.*, *Album de manuscrits français du XIIIe siècle. Mise en page et mise en texte*, Rome, 2001.

CHENEY, C. R., 'Gervase, Abbot of Prémontré: A Medieval Letter-Writer', *Bulletin of the John Rylands Library*, 33 (1950–51), pp. 25–56.

CLANCHY, M. T., *From Memory to Written Record: England 1066–1307*, 2nd edn., Oxford, 1993 [1979].

CONSTABLE, Giles, *Letters and Letter-Collections, Typologie des sources du moyen âge occidental*, 17, Turnhout, 1976.

—, *The Reformation of the Twelfth Century*, Cambridge, 1996.

COWDREY, H. E. J., *The Register of Pope Gregory VII (1073–1085)*, Oxford, 2002.

—, *Lanfranc: Scholar, Monk and Archbishop*, Oxford, 2003.

COXE, H. O., *Catalogus codicum mss qui in collegis aulisque oxoniensibus hodie adseruantur*, vol. 1, Oxford, 1852.

CRAMER, Peter, 'Ernulf of Rochester and Early Anglo-Norman Canon Law', *Journal of Ecclesiastical History*, 40 (1989), pp. 483–510.

DE HAMEL, Christopher, 'The Dispersal of the Library of Christ Church, Canterbury, from the Fourteenth to the Sixteenth Century', in *Books and Collectors 1200–1700: Essays presented to Andrew Watson*, eds. James P. CARLEY & Colin G. C. TITE, London, 1997, pp. 263–279.

DELISLE, Léopold, *Recherches sur l'ancienne bibliothèque de Corbie*, Paris, 1861.

DEROLEZ, Albert, *The Palaeography of Gothic Manuscript Books from the Twelfth to the Early Sixteenth Century*, Cambridge, 2003.

DODWELL, C. R., *The Canterbury School of Illumination 1066–1200*, Cambridge, 1954.

DU BOULAY, F. R. H., *The Lordship of Canterbury. An Essay on Medieval Society*, London, 1966.

DUCHET-SUCHAUX, Monique, 'Introduction', in *Bernard de Clairvaux, Lettres*, vol. 1, *Sources chrétiennes*, 425, Paris, 1997.

DUGGAN, Anne, *Thomas Becket. A Textual History of his Letters*, Oxford, 1980.

DUMVILLE, David, 'Introduction' in *The Annals of St Neots with Vita Prima Sancti Neoti*, Anglo-Saxon Chronicle, vol. 17, Suffolk, 1985.

ERDMANN, Carl, *Studien zur Briefliteratur Deutschlands im elften Jahrhundert*, MGH, Schriften des Reichsinstituts für ältere deutsche Geschichtskunde, 1, Stuttgart, 1938.

ERNOUT, A., 'Dictare "Dicter" allem. *Dichten*', *Revue des études latines*, 29 (1951), pp. 155–161.

FASSLER, E. Margot, 'The Office of the Cantor in Early Western Monastic Rules and Customaries: A Preliminary Investigation', *Early Music History*, 5 (1985), pp. 29–51.

FISKE, A., 'Saint Anselm and Friendship', *Studia Monastica*, 3 (1961), pp. 259–290.

FRÖHLICH, Walter, *Die bischöflichen Kollegen Erzbischof Anselms von Canterbury*, [PhD diss., unpublished] Munich, 1971.

—, 'Die Entstehung der Briefsammlung Anselms von Canterbury', *Historisches Jahrbuch*, 100 (1980), pp. 457–466.

—, 'The Genesis of the Collections of St. Anselm's Letters', *American Benedictine Review*, 35 (1984), pp. 249–266.

—, *The Letters of Saint Anselm of Canterbury*, 3 vols., trans. & annotated by Fröhlich, *Cistercian Studies Series*, 96, 97, 142, Kalamazoo, 1990–1994.

GAMESON, Richard, 'English Manuscript Art in the Late Eleventh

Century: Canterbury and its Context', in *Canterbury and the Norman Conquest: Churches, Saints and Scholars 1066–1109*, eds. Richard EALES & Richard SHARPE, London, 1995, pp. 95–144.

—, *The Manuscripts of Early Norman England (c. 1066–1130)*, Oxford, 1999.

—, *The Scribe Speaks? Colophons in early English manuscripts*, Cambridge, 2002.

GARRISON, Mary, 'The emergence of Carolingian Latin literature and the court of Charlemagne (780–814)', in *Carolingian culture: emulation and innovation*, ed. Rosamond MCKITTERICK, Cambridge, 1994, pp. 111–140.

GASPARRI, Françoise, 'Le 'scribe G', archiviste et bibliothécaire de l'abbaye de Saint-Victor de Paris au XIIᵉ siècle', *Scriptorium*, 37 (1983), pp. 92–98.

—, 'Ex-libris et mentions anciennes portés sur les manuscrits du XIIᵉ siècle de l'abbaye Saint-Victor de Paris', *Scriptorium*, 44 (1990), pp. 69–79.

DE GHELLINCK, Joseph, *Patristique et moyen âge. Études d'histoire littéraire et doctrinale*, vol. 2, *Museum Lessianum, Section historique*, 7, Paris, 1947.

GOULLET, Monique, & Charles VULLIEZ, 'Étude littéraire de la correspondance', in *La correspondance d'un évêque carolingien. Frothaire de Toul (ca 813–847)*, *Textes et documents d'histoire médiévale*, 2, Paris, 1998, pp. 41–55.

GRAHAM, Timothy, & Andrew WATSON, *The Recovery of the Past in Early Elizabethan England: Documents by John Bale and John Joscelyn from the Circle of Matthew Parker*, *Cambridge Bibliographical Society Monograph*, 13, Cambridge, 1998.

GRANATA, Aldo, 'Anselmo d'Aosta: maestro di stile epistolare', *Anselmo d'Aosta Figura Europea, Atti del Convengo di studi, Aosta 1° e 2° marzo 1988*, eds. Inos BIFFI & Costante MARABELLI, Milano, 1989, pp. 247–268.

GREATREX, Joan, *Biographical register of the English cathedral priories of the province of Canterbury c. 1066–1540*, Oxford, 1997.

GROSJEAN, P., 'Franciscus Salesius Schmitt, O.S.B. Sancti Anselmi Cantuariensis archiepiscopi Opera omnia. T. I–III', *Analecta Bollandiana*, 65 (1947), p. 304.

GULLICK, Michael, 'Professional Scribes in Eleventh- and Twelfth-Century England', *English Manuscript Studies 1100–1700*, 7 (1998), pp. 1–24.

—, & Richard W. PFAFF, 'The Dublin pontifical (TCD 98 [B.3.6]): St Anselm's?', *Scriptorium*, 55 (2001), pp. 284–294.

—, 'Manuscrits et copistes normands en Angleterre (XIᵉ–XIIᵉ siècles)', in *Manuscrits et enluminures dans le monde normand (Xᵉ–XVᵉ siècles)*, 2nd edn., Caen, 2005 [1999], pp. 83–91.

HASELDINE, Julian, 'The Creation of a Literary Memorial: The Letter Collection of Peter of Celle', *Sacris erudiri*, 37 (1997), pp. 333–379.

HEALY, Patrick, 'A Supposed Letter of Archbishop Lanfranc: Concepts of the Universal Church in the Investiture Contest', *EHR*, 121 (2006), pp. 1385–1407.

HESLOP, T. A., 'The Canterbury calendars and the Norman conquest', in *Canterbury and the Norman Conquest: Churches, Saints and Scholars, 1066–1109*, eds. R. EALES & R. SHARPE, London, 1995, pp. 53–85.

HOFFMANN, Richard C., 'Fishing for Sport in Medieval Europe: New Evidence', *Speculum*, 60 (1985), pp. 877–902.

HOWE, John, 'The alleged use of *cursus* by Bishop Arbeo of Freising', *Archiuum latinitatis medii aeui*, 42 (1982), pp. 129–131.

JAMES, Montague Rhodes, *A Descriptive Catalogue of the Manuscripts in the Library of Peterhouse*, Cambridge, 1899.

—, *The Western Manuscripts in the Library of Trinity College, Cambridge: A Descriptive Catalogue*, 2 vols., Cambridge, 1900–1902.

—, *The Ancient Libraries of Canterbury and Dover*, Cambridge, 1903.

—, *A Descriptive Catalogue of the Manuscripts in the Library of Lambeth Palace. The Mediaeval Manuscript*, Cambridge, 1932.

JANSON, Tore, *Prose Rhythm in Medieval Latin from the 9th to the 13th Century*, Studia Latina Stockholmiensia, 20, Stockholm, 1975.

JOHNSON, C., & H. JENKINSON, *English Court Hand, A.D. 1066 to 1500*, Oxford, 1915.

KER, Neil Ripley, 'Sir John Prise', *The Library*, 5th series, 10 (1955), pp. 1–24.

—, *Catalogue of Manuscripts Containing Anglo-Saxon*, Oxford, 1957.

—, *English Manuscripts in the Century after the Norman Conquest*, Oxford, 1960.

—, 'Archbishop Sancroft's rearrangement of the manuscripts of Lambeth Palace', in *A Catalogue of Manuscripts in Lambeth Palace Library. MSS. 1222–1860*, ed. E. G. W. BILL, Oxford, 1972, pp. 1–51.

—, *Medieval Manuscripts in British Libraries*, vol. 2, Oxford, 1977.

KIENZLER, Klaus (with assistance of Eduardo BRINACESCO, Walter FRÖHLICH, Helmut KOHLENBERGER, Fredrick VAN FLETEREN, Coloman VIOLA), *International Bibliography: Anselm of Canterbury*, Anselm Studies, 4, Lewiston, Queenston, Lampeter, 1999.

KNOWLES, David, Review: *SAO* I–III, *EHR*, 64 (1949), pp. 363–364.

—, Review: *SAO* IV, *EHR*, 67 (1952), pp. 110–111.

—, Review: *SAO* V, *EHR*, 68 (1953), p. 304.

—, C. N. L. BROOKE & Vera C. M. LONDON, *The Heads of Religious Houses: England & Wales, I. 940–1216*, 2nd edn., Cambridge, 2001 [1972].

KRISTELLER, Paul Oskar, *Renaissance Philosophy and the Mediaeval Tradition*, Latrobe, 1966.

KRÜGER, Thomas Michael, *Persönlichkeitsausdruck und Persönlichkeits-wahrnehmung im Zeitalter der Investiturkonflikte: Studien zu den Briefsammlungen des Anselm von Canterbury, Spolia Berolinensia,* 22, Hildesheim, 2002.

LADD, C. A., 'The 'Rubens' Manuscript and Archbishop Ælfric's Vocabulary', *Review of English Studies,* New Series, 11/44 (1960), pp. 353–364.

LECLERCQ, Jean, 'Introduction' in *Yves de Chartres: Correspondance,* vol. 1, Paris, 1949.

—, 'Lettres de S. Bernard: Histoire ou literature?', *Studi Medievali,* 12 (1971), pp. 1–74.

LEVISON, Wilhelm, 'Aus Englischen Bibliotheken. II', *Neues Archiv der Gesellschaft für deutsche Geschichtskunde,* 35 (1910), pp. 331–431.

LOGAN, Ian, 'Ms. Bodley 271: Establishing the Anselmian Canon?', *Saint Anselm Journal,* 2 (2004), pp. 67–80.

—, 'Anselm and Thidricus: Revisiting MS Bodley 271', in *Anselm and Abelard. Investigations and Juxtapositions,* eds. G. E. M. GASPER & H. KOHLENBERGER, Toronto, 2006, pp. 67–86.

LOUGHLIN, J., *Saint Anselm as a Letter Writer,* [Ph.D. diss., unpublished] Washington, 1968.

MARTIN, Henry, *Histoire de la bibliothèque de l'Arsenal. Catalogue des manuscrits de la bibliothèque de l'Arsenal,* vol. 9, Paris, 1899.

MARTIN, Janet, 'Classicism and Style in Latin Literature', in *Renaissance and Renewal in the Twelfth Century,* eds. Robert L. BENSON & Giles CONSTABLE with Carol LANHAM, Cambridge (Mass.), 1982.

McBRIDE, Deborah C., *Benevolent letters: Ecclesiastical epistles to nobles in the early twelfth century,* [Ph.D. diss., unpublished] Santa Barbara, 1998.

McCUSKER, Honor, 'Books and Manuscripts Formerly in the Possession of John Bale', *The Library,* 4th series, 16 (1935), pp. 144–165.

McGUIRE, Brian Patrick, *Friendship and Community. The Monastic Experience 350–1250, Cistercian Studies Series,* 95, Kalamazoo, 1988.

McLACHLAN, Elizabeth Parker, 'The scriptorium of Bury St. Edmunds in the third and fourth decades of the twelfth century: books in three related hands and their decoration', *Mediaeval Studies,* 40 (1978), pp. 328–348.

—, *The Scriptorium of Bury St. Edmunds in the Twelfth Century,* New York & London, 1986.

MEWS, Constant J., 'St Anselm and Roscelin: some new texts and their implications', *Archives d'histoire doctrinale et littéraire du moyen âge,* 66 (1992), pp. 55–81.

VON MOOS, Peter, *Hildebert von Lavardin 1056–1133: Humanitas an der Schwelle des höfischen Zeitalters,* Stuttgart, 1965.

Morey, Adrian, & C. N. L. Brooke, *Gilbert Foliot and His Letters*, Cambridge Studies in Medieval Life and Thought, New Series, 11, Cambridge, 1965.

Morin, D. G., 'Lettre inédite d'A[nselme] à G[odefroy de Bouillon]?', *Revue Bénédictine*, 34 (1922), pp. 135–146.

Morris, Colin, *The Discovery of the Individual 1050–1200*, London, 1972.

Murray, Alexander, 'Pope Gregory VII and his Letters', *Traditio*, 22 (1966), pp. 149–201.

Norberg, Dag, *Critical and Exegetical Notes on the Letters of St. Gregory the Great*, Filologiskt arkiv, 27, Stockholm, 1982.

Omont, Henri, *Concordances des numéros anciens et des numéros actuels des manuscrits latins de la Bibliothèque nationale*, Paris, 1903.

Ohler, Norbert, 'Reisen, Reisenbeschreibungen: Westen', *LexMA*, vol. 7, Munich, 1995, cols. 672–675.

Ortenberg, Veronica, 'Archbishop Sigeric's Journey to Rome in 990', *Anglo-Saxon England*, 19 (1990), pp. 197–246.

Österley, Hermann, *Wegweiser durch die Literatur der Urkunden Sammlungen*, Berlin, 1885.

Ouy, Gilbert, *Les manuscrits de l'abbaye de Saint-Victor, Catalogue établi sur la base du répertoire de Claude de Grandrue (1514)*, 2 vols., *Bibliotheca Victorina*, 10, Turnhout, 1999.

Page, R. I., *Matthew Parker and his books*, Sandars Lectures in Bibliography, Western Michigan University, 1993.

Parkes, M. B., 'Tachygraphy in the Middle Ages: writing techniques employed for *reportationes* of lectures and sermons', *Medievo e rinascimento*, 3 (1989), pp. 159–169.

—, *Their Hands before Our Eyes: A Closer Look at Scribes*, Aldershot, 2008.

Patt, William D., 'The early *'ars dictaminis'* as response to a changing society', *Viator*, 9 (1978), pp. 133–155.

Petzold, Andreas, '*De coloribus et mixtionibus*: The Earliest Manuscripts of a Romanesque Illuminator's Handbook', in *Making the Medieval Book: Techniques of Production*, ed. Linda L. Brownrigg, Los Altos Hills & London, 1995, pp. 59–65.

Pranger, Burcht, 'Anselm's *Brevitas*', *Anselm Studies*, 2, *Proceedings of the Fifth International Saint Anselm Conference*, eds. Joseph C. Schnaubelt, Thomas A. Losoncy, Fredric Van Fleteren & Jill A. Frederick, New York, 1988, pp. 447–458.

Queller, Donald E., 'Thirteenth-century diplomatic envoys: *Nuncii* and *procuratores*', *Speculum*, 35 (1960), pp. 196–213.

Robinson, P. R., *Catalogue of Dated and Datable Manuscripts c. 888–1600 in London Libraries*, 2 vols., London, 2003.

Rockinger, Ludwig, *Briefsteller und Formelbücher des elften bis vierzehnten Jahrhunderts*, vol. 1, *Quellen und Erörterungen zur Bayerischen und*

Deutschen Geschichte, ix/1, 1863; repr. *Burt Franklin research & source works series*, 10, New York, 1961.

Roos, Teemu, Tuomas Heikkilä & Petri Myllymäki, 'A compression-based method for stemmatic analysis', *Proceedings of the 17th European Conference on Artificial Intelligence*, Amsterdam, 2006, pp. 805–806.

Roos, Teemu, & Tuomas Heikkilä, 'Evaluating methods for computer-assisted stemmatology using artificial benchmark data sets', *Literary & Linguistic Computing*, 24 (2009), pp. 417–433.

Rouse, Richard H., 'Bostonus Buriensis and the author of the *Catalogus Scriptorium Ecclesiae*', *Speculum*, 41 (1966), pp. 471–499.

Schaller, H. M., '*Ars dictaminis, ars dictandi*', *LexMA*, vol. 1, Munich, 1980, cols. 1034–1039.

Schmale, Franz-Josef, 'Brief, Briefliteratur, Briefsammlungen: IV. Lateinisches Mittelalter', *LexMA*, vol. 2, Munich, 1983, cols. 652–659.

Schmeidler, Bernhard, 'Die Briefsammlung Froumunds von Tegernsee. Bemerkungen zur Beschaffenheit frühmittelalterlicher Briefsammlungen überhaupt', *Historisches Jahrbuch*, 62–69 (1942–49), cols. 220–238.

Schmitt, F. S., 'Zur Ueberlieferung der Korrespondenz Anselms von Canterbury. Neue Briefe', *Revue Bénédictine*, 43 (1931), pp. 224–238.

—, 'Zur Entstehungsgeschichte der Handschriftlichen Sammlungen der Briefe des hl. Anselm von Canterbury', *Revue Bénédictine*, 48 (1936), pp. 300–317 [*Prolegomena*, pp. 154–171].

—, *Ein neues unvollendetes Werk des hl. Anselm von Canterbury, Beiträge zur Geschichte der Philosophie und Theologie des Mittelalters, Texte und Untersuchungen*, 33, Münster, 1936.

—, 'Eine fruehe Rezension des Werkes De concordia des Hl. Anselm von Canterbury', *Revue Bénédictine*, 48 (1936), pp. 41–70 [*Prolegomena*, pp. 100–131].

—, 'Cinq recensions de l'epistola de incarnatione verbi de S. Anselme de Cantorbéry', *Revue Bénédictine*, 51 (1939), pp. 275–287.

—, 'Die Chronologie der Briefe des hl. Anselm von Canterbury', *Revue Bénédictine*, 64 (1954), pp. 176–207 [*Prolegomena*, pp. 172–203].

—, 'Die unter Anselm veranstaltete Ausgabe seiner Werke und Briefe, die Codices Bodley 271 und Lambeth 59', *Scriptorium*, 9 (1955), pp. 64–75 [*Prolegomena*, pp. 226–239].

—, 'Die echten und unechten Stücke der Korrespondenz des hl. Anselm von Canterbury', *Revue Bénédictine*, 65 (1955), pp. 218–227 [*Prolegomena*, pp. 204–212].

—, 'Intorno all'Opera omnia di S. Anselmo d'Aosta', *Sophia*, 27 (1959), pp. 220–231.

—, 'Verzeichnis der benutzten Handschriften', in *Prolegomena*, pp. 213–225.

SELWYN, David G., 'Cranmer and the Dispersal of Medieval Libraries. The provenance of some of his medieval manuscripts and printed books', in *Books and Collectors 1200–1700: Essays presented to Andrew Watson*, eds. James P. CARLEY & Colin G. C. TITE, London, 1997, pp. 281–294.

SHARPE, Richard, 'Two contemporary poems on Saint Anselm attributed to William of Chester', *Revue Bénédictine*, 95 (1985), pp. 266–279.

—, *Titulus. Identifying medieval Latin texts: an evidence-based approach*, Turnhout, 2003.

—, 'The medieval librarian', in *The Cambridge History of Libraries in Britain and Ireland*, vol. 1, eds. E. LEEDHAM-GREEN & T. WEBBER, Cambridge, 2006, pp. 218–241.

—, 'King Harold's daughter', *Haskins Society Journal*, 19 (2008), pp. 1–27.

—, 'Anselm as author. Publishing in the eleventh century', *Journal of Medieval Latin*, 19 (2009), pp. 1–87.

—, 'Early Manuscripts of Anselm: A discussion with five manuscripts', *Gazette du livre médiéval*, 54 (2009), pp. 49–52.

—, & Teresa WEBBER, 'Four early booklets of Anselm's works from Salisbury cathedral', *Scriptorium*, 63 (2009), pp. 58–72.

SOUTHERN, Richard, 'St. Anselm and Gilbert Crispin, Abbot of Westminster', *Mediaeval and Renaissance Studies*, 3 (1954), pp. 78–115.

—, Review: *The Letters of John of Salisbury*. Edited by W. J. MILLOR; H. E. BUTLER; C. N. L. BROOKE. *Vol. i: The Early Letters (1133–1161)*, *EHR*, 72 (1957), pp. 493–497.

—, 'The Canterbury forgeries', *EHR*, 73 (1958), pp. 193–226.

—, *Saint Anselm and his Biographer. A Study of Monastic Life and Thought 1059–c.1130*, Cambridge, 1963.

—, 'Sally Vaughn's Anselm: An Examination of the Foundations', *Albion*, 20 (1988), pp. 181–204.

—, 'Verso una storia della corrispondenza di Anselmo', in *Anselmo d'Aosta Figura Europea, Atti del Convengo di studi, Aosta 1° e 2° marzo 1988*, eds. Inos BIFFI & Costante MARABELLI, Milano, 1989, pp. 269–289.

—, *Saint Anselm. A Portrait in a Landscape*, Cambridge, 1990.

—, 'Towards an Edition of Peter of Blois's Letter-Collection', *EHR*, 110 (1995), pp. 925–937.

—, Review: The Letters of St Anselm, vols. i–iii, ed. Walter Fröhlich, *EHR*, 112 (1997), pp. 160–161.

STEELE, M. W., *A Study of the Books Owned or Used by John Grandisson, Bishop of Exeter (1327–1369)*, [PhD diss., unpublished] Oxford, 1994.

THOMSON, Rodney, 'The Library of Bury St Edmunds Abbey in the Eleventh and Twelfth Centuries', *Speculum*, 47 (1972), pp. 617–645.

—, Michael Gullick & R. A. B. Mynors, *Catalogue of the Manuscripts of Hereford Cathedral Library*, Woodbridge, 1993.

—, 'Books and Learning at Gloucester Abbey in the Twelfth and Thirteenth Centuries', in *Books and Collectors 1200–1700: Essays presented to Andrew Watson*, eds. James P. Carley & Colin G. C. Tite, London, 1997.

—, *William of Malmesbury*, 2nd edn., Woodbridge, 2003 [1987].

Thomson, Rodney, & Michael Gullick, *A Descriptive Catalogue of the Medieval Manuscripts in Worcester Cathedral Library*, Woodbridge, 2001.

Tite, Colin G. C., *The Early Records of Sir Robert Cotton's Library. Formation, Cataloguing, Use*, London, 2003.

Tóth, Petrus, *Catalogus Codicum Latinorum Medii Aeui Bibliothecae Vniversitatis Budapestinensis*, Budapest, 2006. [www.manuscripta-mediaevalia.de/hs/kataloge/Budapest_07_04.pdf]

Turner, Andrew J., & Bernard J. Muir, 'Introduction' in Eadmer of Canterbury, *Lives and Miracles of Saints Oda, Dunstan, and Oswald*, *OMT*, Oxford, 2006.

Vaughn, Sally N., *Anselm of Bec and Robert of Meulan. The Innocence of the Dove and the Wisdom of the Serpent*, Berkley, 1987.

—, 'Anselm: saint and statesman', *Albion*, 20 (1988), pp. 205–220.

—, *St Anselm and the Handmaidens of God. A Study of Anselm's Correspondence with Women*, Utrecht Studies in Medieval Literacy, 7, Turnhout, 2002.

Viola, Coloman Étienne, 'Une réimpression des œuvres complètes de Saint Anselme', *Gregorianum*, 52 (1971), pp. 555–561.

Wagner, M. Monica, 'A Chapter in Byzantine Epistolography: The Letters of Theodoret of Cyrus', *Dumbarton Oaks Papers*, 4 (1948), pp. 119–181.

Wahlgren, Lena, *The Letter Collections of Peter of Blois: Studies in the Manuscript Tradition*, Studia Graeca et Latina Gothoburgensia, 58, Gothenburg, 1993.

Wahlgren-Smith, Lena, ' "*Ambrosianum illud*" in the Letters of Herbert Losinga', *Classica et mediaevalia*, 50 (1999), pp. 207–209.

—, 'On the composition of Herbert Losinga's letter collection', *Classica et mediaevalia*, 55 (2004), pp. 229–246.

Warner, G. F., & H. J. Ellis, *Facsimiles of Royal and Other Charters in the British Museum*, vol. 1, London, 1903.

—, & J. P. Gilson, *Catalogue of Western Manuscripts in the Old Royal and King's Collection*, 4 vols., London, 1921.

Warner, Kathryn, *Medieval & Early Modern Women. Part 1: Manuscripts from British Library, London*, Marlborough, 2000.

Wilmart, André, 'La destinaire de la lettre de S. Anselme sur l'état et les vœux de religion', *Revue Bénédictine*, 38 (1926), pp. 331–334.

—, 'Une lettre adressée de Rome à Saint Anselme en 1102', *Revue Bénédictine*, 40 (1928), pp. 262–266.

—, 'Une lettre inédite de S. Anselme à une moniale inconstante', *Revue Bénédictine*, 40 (1928), pp. 319–332.

—, 'Les prières envoyées par S. Anselme à la comtesse Mathilde en 1104', *Revue Bénédictine*, 41 (1929), pp. 35–45.

—, 'La tradition des lettres de S. Anselme. Lettres inédites de S. Anselme et de ses correspondants', *Revue Bénédictine*, 43 (1931), pp. 38–54.

—, *Auteurs spirituels et textes dévots du moyen âge latin. Études d'histoire littéraire*, Paris, 1932.

—, 'Deux lettres concernant Raoul le Verd, l'ami de saint Bruno', *Revue Bénédictine*, 51 (1939), pp. 257–274.

INDICES

MANUSCRIPTS CITED

GENERAL INDEX

Abbot, George, archbishop of Canterbury: 125

d'Achery, Luc: 171–2, 279–80, 283, 285

Adalbertus Samaritanus: 49n

Adela of Blois, daughter of William I: 54n

Alain de Lille: 49n

Alan, prior of Christ Church, abbot of Tewkesbury: 49n, 239–40

Alberic, monk of Monte Cassino, cardinal: 49n

Alcuin of York: 156

Alexander, monk of Christ Church: 218, *see* Anselm, *Dicta Anselmi*

Amerbach, Johan: 277

Anglia sacra: 283

Anonymous of Bologna: 49–50n

Anselm, abbot of Saint Saba and Bury St Edmunds: 123, 132, 291

Anselm, prior and abbot of Bec, archbishop of Canterbury:
archives of —: 19, 64, 84n, 86n, 91, 93, 113–4, 167, 171, 179, 186, 196–200, 205–14, 217, 295; *see* drafts of his letters
exiles of —: 58, 84n, 108, 162, 207–14, 259
letter writer: 21, 42, 44–57, 66n
reputation:
modern: 35–38
posthumous: 221–2, 224–5
sanctification of —: 35–36, 140
seal of —: 60
social hierarchy as expressed by salutations in his letters: 51–4
use of messengers: 59
visits to England as abbot of Bec: 71, 80, 90, 93n, 177, 201n, 203, 213–4

letters:
hypothetical major collections of —:
α: 19, 24, 73–4, 81, 83–4, 86n, 92–5, 97, 99–100, 109–10, 177–8, 181, 196n, 199n, 200–6, 213–4
β: 20, 24, 73, 93–4, 99, 110–11, 167, 170, 177–86, 189, 195–6, 198–206, 209, 213–4, 290–2
ω: 24, 73, 93–4, 100n, 110–1, 150–1, 180–1, 183, 185–91, 195, 196–7n, 198–215, 220, 269–70, 290, 292, 295, 297, 299–300
minor collections of —:
Schmitt 15: 24–5, 92–3, 196n, 227–38, 258–9, 268–74
Sharpe 5: 24–5, 227–8, 258–72, 281, 285, 287
Wilmart 14: 24–5, 100–1, 196n, 227–8, 238–59, 268–74, 281, 284, 286, 299n
collected by him or at his request: 21, 24, 29, 33–8, 71, 73–4, 90–3, 110, 121, 177–85 *passim*, 200–20 *passim*, 227; *see* Maurice, Ernulf, Thidricus, α, β, ω
collected by his followers at Bec: 176–7, 183–5
collected posthumously by his disciples at Christ Church: 119, 140–1, *see* Eadmer, (Thidricus), *L*, *P*, (ω)
collected by his (near-)contemporaries outside Bec and Canterbury: 79, 89, 132, 228, 230–1, 237–8, 258–60, 273–4; *see* William of Malmesbury, Anselm of Bury St Edmunds, Lan-

PLATES

sic transire p bona teporalia. ut habiter m aeternis.

Vtilis ei patna uia celsitudo. p suo fideli osberno de
functo. ma frib; nris misit. humili oboediencia &
oboediencie humilitate suscepim? Nichil eni peticioni
uře decreuim? denegare. s; in qb;cunq; dilectissimo
dno & dulcissimo patri oboediendu? uel honui &
statui nro obtēp are. Ca eni uos hoc merui? se dilectio
nis & beneficie? p eio cognoscam? nimis uos arguen
dos ostendim? si nos oboedient subicere uoluntati
uře recusam? In qb; littis illud qde gratissimu acce
p ga ibi certitudine de mutua dilectione uře & ma
gnitudinis & mee paruitatis legi. Na quus é scien
tia p pa & ex p iuto ia duct? hinc n pos si dubitare.
dulcis tam honor & honorabili? dulcedo michi est.
cum tantus tantillo hoc dignatur mandare;

Hactenus continentur epłe domyi
 divseloi Abbatis quas fecit donec por
Beccensis fuit; Que uo ia deinceps equunt'
egit post qm abbatis nom & officiu suscepit;

pit;

gutturis mei inundantes agemitu
cordis mei obturantes & interrupendo
tardantes scriptori uerba oris mei.
Quam uis sint quedam ut atioro qui autem
sint ds scit. q aut fingunt malicia
aut suspicantur erroe aut cogunt
dicere indiscreto dolore quos magis
trahar ad archiepopatu uitiosa cupidi
tate quam cogar religiosa necessitate.
Quib; nescio qum possim psuadere
que sit inhac reconscientia mea sillis
n satis facit uita & conuersatio mea
Sic eni uixi ia ptriginta ores annos
inhabitu monachico tribz scilicet sine
platione aut dominatione, cotidieq;
inabbatia annis sue omnes boni me
diligerent qui me nouere n mea industa
sed gra dei faciente & magis illi q me
interi & familiari nouere nec aliqs
in me uideret aliquod op unde me
platione delectare cognosceret. Quid
g facia Quom ppulsabo & exeon
tingua hanc falsa & odibilem suspi
cione ne animab; eor noceat q me
ppt deum diligebant caritate illis
minuendo aut eor quib; qualecuq;
consilium aut exemplu mex paruitas
pdesse poterat me peiore qua sim
illis psuadendo aut etia hor & alior
qui me n nouere & hoc audient malu
illis exemplu pponendo Ds tu q omnia
scis non me iustifico sedm ueram
districti iudicii tui quia ille magn
aptz tuus q dicere potuit nichil in
consci su cu hoc dixisset subdidit
sed non inhoc iustificat sum qui
aute iudicat me dns & uir ille
semplex & rectus timens dm & recedens
amalo cui te ipso teste n erat simil
incra dixit uehebar omia opa mea

sed sedm quod anima mea cophendit
conscientia sua coram te dico eam
ut omnes q hanc mea eplam legent
aut audient sub tuo testimonio sciant
& credant eam. Tu domine uides
& tu esto testis meus qa nescio sicut
mea in escientia dicit qo me rapiat
aut alliget ad consensu archiepac
ad quem subito rapt trahor amor
alicui rei qua seruus tuus conteptor
mundi debeat contepnere & qsi
in licere seruata obedientia & caritate
quas ppt te quantu dedisti uolo custo
dire pocius eligerem sub plato sicut
monachus seruire & obedire & ab illo
consilio anime mex & necesaria
corporis mei accipere qua aliis homi
nibz dnari aut p ee siue ad anima
ru gubernatione siue ad corporale
sustentatione aut terrenas diuitias
possidere. Tu uides & tu esto testis
meus qa sicut mea in conscientia dic
nescio quom me sine peccato possim
euoluere ab hac me eligentium
intentione & qa timor tuus & caritas
& obedientia quas tibi & eccle tue
debeo me cogunt me ligant ut n
audeam religiosis pcib; eor & magno
no sicut in ostendunt desiderio pu
naat contra dicere Dne si fallit me
conscientia mea ostende in me
ipsu & corrige me & dirige in con
spectu tuo uia meam. Et siue e
placeat ut quod inceptu e ab homi
nib; de hac mea electione fiat siue
pocius ut non fiat deduc me in uia
tua & ingrediar inuertate tua
Dne tu uides sic dixi conscientiam
mea cu esto in testis ad eos q aliter
de me suspicantur & ostende illis

Plate 2: London, Lambeth Palace 224, fol. 145v
(slightly reduced)

ur triſtando. Ia nc repeto omnibus
medullis optando. q̄d p̄miſſ ſalu
ando. exaurſ dn̄i raca receſ conſ
inſ ag. ur dn̄i recta conſtita danda
ualeaſ p̄mereri. dn̄e ſctiſſime. ſapi
entiſſime. & ſup omſ anı̄o dul
ciſſime.

℟OBERTVS dux norman
noꝛ. ANSELMO vene
rabili Abbat3. uñꝗ p̄nniꝶ frui
collegio. Legatione firiſime re
gnſ anglor̄ ſuſcepienſ. ꝗ uoſ arꝑi
epiſcopatuꝗ cantuarienſiſ eccłꝫ
fficere mandauit. taꝙꝙ uꝛ no
lenſ petioni reſiſtere. uiꝗ tam pl
rui. ſaenſ p̄culdubio uoſ uniuer

multaꝗ; p̄tetaui. & amicoꝛ meoꝛ &
uꝛoꝛ ſup hoc c̄ſiliū queſiui. Rurꝛ uꝛuꝗ;
uoluiſleta ſi poſſible fuiſſet. & curam
ſcp̄ uꝛolim habere pfentia. dn̄ifacere
unde offenderent uoluntate etiumida.
Sed ꝗa idhoc reſ ueniꝛe uꝛ uꝛuꝗ; ī
plꝛī nequeat. ſic dı̄gnū c̄ etiumiduo
tuuaꝛe uoluntate mꝛ ꝓponim. &
uram uoluntate etiumq ſubyeciū. atꝙ
exparte dı̄ & ſci petri omnuꝗ. amico
rumeoꝛu ac uꝛoꝛ ꝗ ſcdm dn̄i uos
Aligut. iubeo. uꝛ paſtoralē curam
cantuarienſiſ eccłꝫ. & eccłaſtico mo
re benedictione epałē ſuſapiatſ.
omnuꝗ. atumarru uob uꝛ erectī dī
māꝛc cō mıſſatrū ſalutē ſtēnſcepī in
unglꝛterſ. Valeꝛe.

Plate 3: London, Lambeth Palace 59, fol. 63r
(slightly reduced)

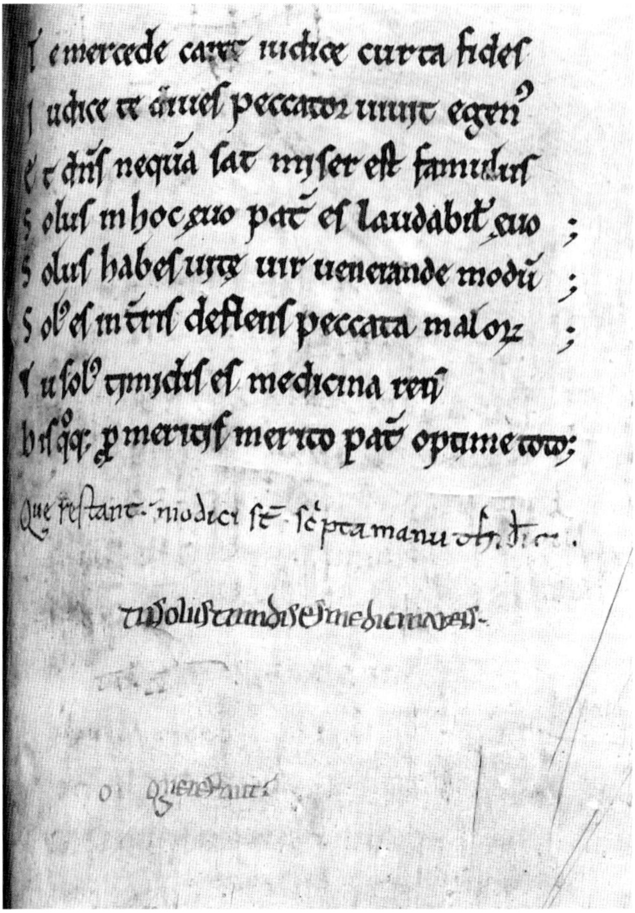

Plate 4: London, Lambeth Palace 59, fol. 190r

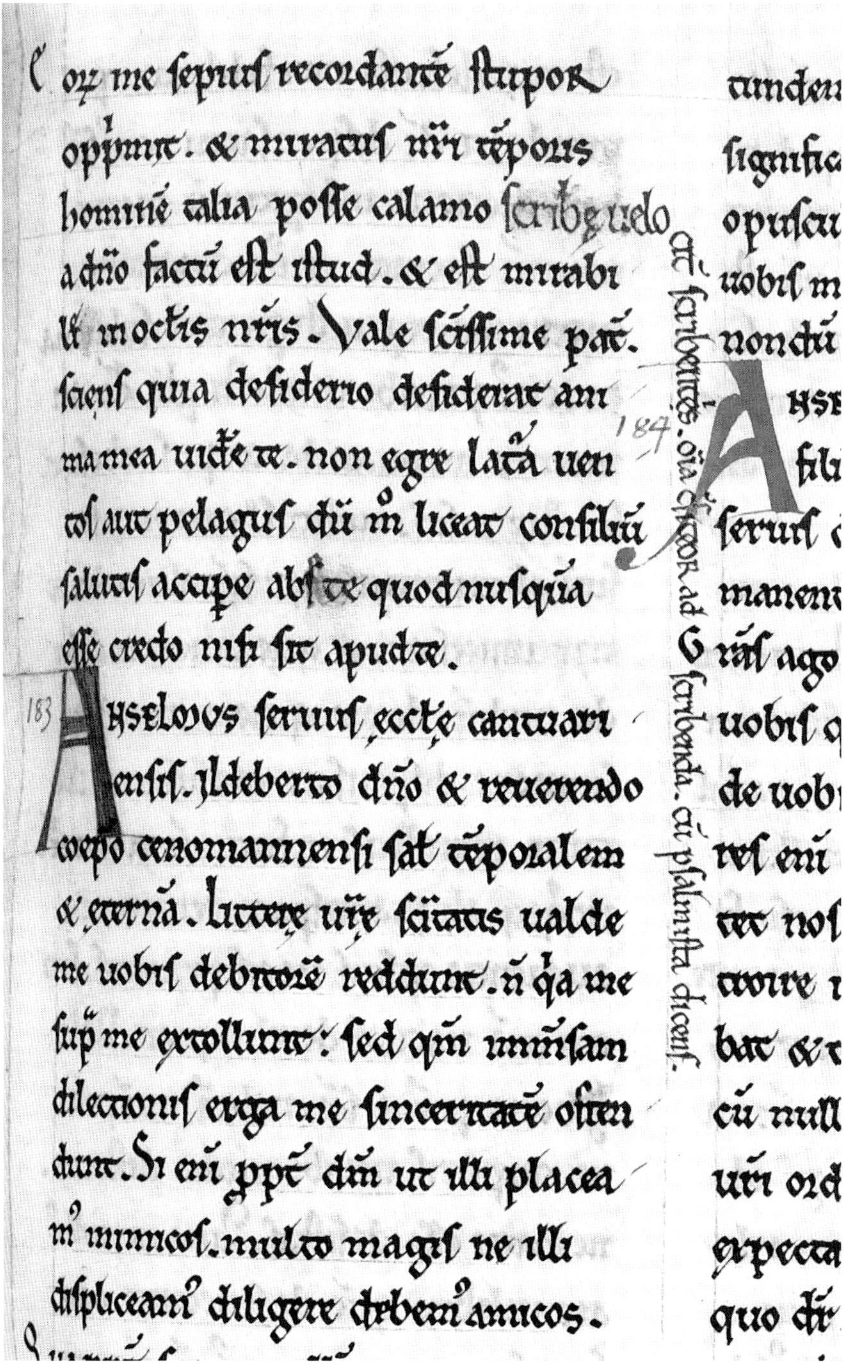

Cor me sepius recordante stupor
oppimit. & miratus nir tpous
hominé talia posse calamo scribe uelo
a dno factu est istud. & est mirabi
le in oculis nris. Vale scissime pat.
sciens quia desiderio desiderat ani
ma mea uide te. non egre lata uen
tos aut pelagus du in liceat consiliu
salutis accipe abs te quod nusquia
esse credo nisi sit apud te.

184

Anselmus seruus ecce cantuari
ensis. ildeberto dno & reuerendo
cepo cenomannensi sat tporalem
& eterna. litere ure scitatis ualde
me uobis debitorie redduit. n qa me
sup me extollunt: sed qin immsam
dilectionis erga me sinceritate osten
dunt. Si eni ppt dnm ut illi placea
in inimicos. multo magis ne illi
displiceam diligere debem amicos.

183

tunden
significa
opuscu
uobis m
non du
hsr
fili
seruis
manen
rias ago
uobis q
de uob
res eni
ter nos
couire
bat &
cu null
uri ord
expecta
quo dr

dr farberes. oia cpeor ad scribenda. cu psalmista dicens.

Plate 5: London, Lambeth Palace 59, fol. 89r

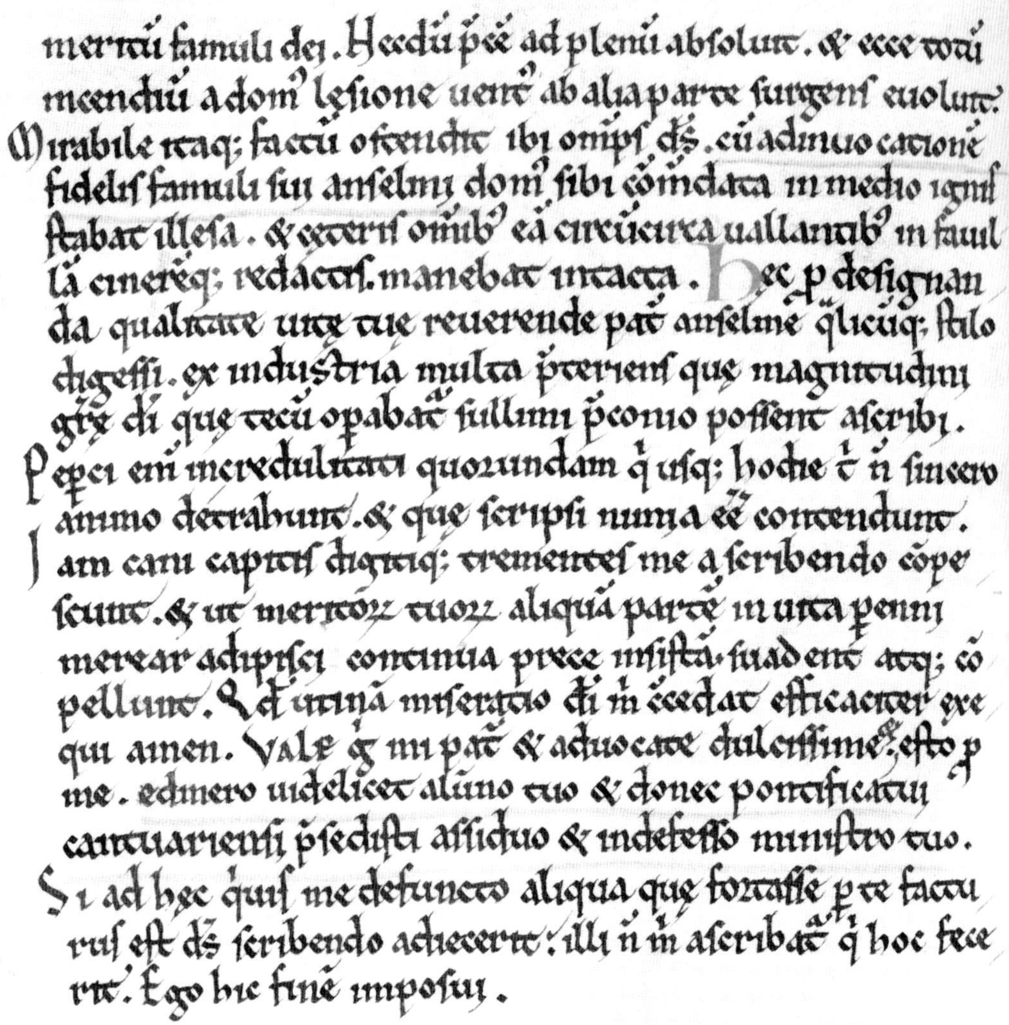

mertui famuli dei. Hec dum pre ad plenu absolute. & ecce totu
incendiu a dom' lesione uent ab alia parte surgens euolute.
Mirabile itaq; factu ostendit ibi omips dis. cu admiuo catione
fidelis famuli sui anselmi dom' sibi comendata in medio ignis
stabat illesa. & ceteris omnib' ea circuitca uallantib' in fauil
la cinereq; redactis. manebat intacta. Hec p designan
da qualitate uite tue reuerende pat anselme qlicuq; stilo
digessi. ex industria multa preteriens que magnitudini
gre di que tecu opabat sullimi pconio possent ascribi.
Peper eni incredulitati quorundam q usq; hodie t in sincero
animo detrahunt. & que scripsi numia ee contendunt.
Iam catu capteis digniq; crementes me a scribendo cope
scunt. & ut meritor tuor aliqua parte in uita penni
merear adipisci continua prece insista. suadent atq; co
pellunt. Et utinam miseratio di in cedat efficaciter exe
qui amen. Vale g mi pat & aduocate dulcissime esto p
me. edmero uidelicet alumno tuo & donec pontificatui
cantuariensi pdista assiduo & indefesso ministro tuo.
Si ad hec quis me defuncto aliqua que fortasse p te factu
rus est dis scribendo adiecerit: illi n in ascribat q hoc fece
rit. Ego hic fine imposui.

Plate 6: Cambridge, Corpus Christi College 371, fol. 195v
(slightly reduced)

nich adintegritatē doctrine. Beatū sane petr̄. qd̄ uirtutū conuenē
reuerendū sibi penetrale consecrauit. Inde uelut exactis diuina ꝑde
uit oracula. nichq; aluid sacra uerba ꝑstituēt. quā celestis intꝑete
uoluntatis. Cor me sepi recordante stupor oppriuit. ⁊ mutat̄ nr̄i
tēporis homine talia posse calamo scriber̄ uelo adiꝰ factū est illud.
⁊ est mirabile moctis nr̄is. Vale scissime pat. sciens qa desiderio desi
derat anima mea uidr̄ te. non egre lata uentos aut pelaḡ dū in liceat
ēsilū salutis accipe abste qd̄ nuq̄n esse credo n̄ sit apudte.

A nselas serū eccl̄e cantuariensis. ildebr̄ dn̄o ⁊reuerendo coeps
acenomannensi sat tēporalē egnā. Littere ur̄e sc̄itatis ualde me uob
debitorē reddunt. n̄ qa me sup̄ me extollunt. sed qin uniūsī dilectionī
ergame sinceritatē ostendunt. Si enī ꝓpt̄ dn̄m ut illi placeam inimicos.
multo magis ne illi displiceam diligere debeī amicos. Iua ꝓpter si
aut nullā aut minorē dilectionē uob retribuo. in uestrī minea ēstien
tia me iudico. Sic ⁊ hanc uolo uitare iniustiā. sic uestrā amplecti desi
dero amicitiā. fateor etiā qa si mi esset possibile. uos adduplū ꝗn me
diligatis deberē diligere. qa uos me ꝓueniustis amore qd̄ ꝑbastis
munere. Illa qin immeritū dilexistis n̄ mrī debeo rependere. ⁊ sicut
datis exemplū tantundē gratis debeo impendere. In significastis
uob placere hoc qd̄ de opusculis nr̄is uidistis. ꝑsumam uob mittere
quedā que ut puto. non dū uidistis.

A nselm̄ gr̄a dī ar̄eps. fr̄ib; ⁊ filiis kr̄is. dn̄o ꝑort ⁊aliis seruus
dī inmonasterio sc̄i albani manentib;. salutē ⁊benē. Gr̄as ago dō
aq̄ est om̄e bonū. ⁊uob q̄ seruatis ei donū. qa de auidio om̄e bonū.
Amores eiū uos eē monstratis. qa oportet nos ꝑmultas tribulationē
intrare inreḡu dī. ⁊qa tēptatio ꝓbat ⁊ceptat iustū si diligat
dn̄m. eiū nulla uos aduersitas ⁊ctodia uestri ordinis ꝓhibere potest. Sic
eiū expectare secure potestis ꝑmiū de q̄ dr̄. Beat̄ uir q̄ sustīet tem
ptationē. qin cū ꝓbat̄ fuerit accipiet coronā uite. Riuo ⁊ uos studi
osi adseruandū monachicū ordinē insistere cognosco. tanto securi
uos patria monitione ex ordem. q̄ui inbono ꝓposito ⁊ inhoc ad qd̄
uos dī puex̄t ꝑseueretis. ⁊ sep̄ admeliora inspe diuini auxilii
ꝑficere ⁊iniquā deficere tēptatis. Id efficacie poteritis efficere.
si nulla minima uestri ordinis uolueritis ⁊tēnere. qin q̄ modica spnt̄.
paulati decidit. D̄s uidet qd̄ uos expectat. Si morā fecerit uos conso
landi. expectate eiū qa n̄ tardabit. Ipse enī est adiutor inopportu
nitatib; intribulatione. Om̄ips d̄s corda uestra inseruitio suo cor

viiii Leo. nonus. q̄ uocat̄ bruno añ. v. m̄. ii. d̄. xvi. Anni d̄ñi. oī. xlviii. añn. i. dñiꝯpone. iii.

.i. Victor. q̄ uocat̄ gebeardus. añn. ii. ō. ii. dieſ. xvii.

xiiii Stephan. q̄ uocat̄ fredericuſ. m̄ſeſ. vii. dieſ. xxviii.

.x. Benedict. ut renuit belluitenensis epſ. m̄ſeſ. viii. dieſ. xxvii

.ii. Nicolauſ. q̄ uoca e ᵹerarduſ añn. ii. m̄. vi. dieſ. i. 7 ceſſñ. ep. iii. ii. dieſ. viii.

.ii. Alexander. q̄ uocat̄ anſelm̄. añn. xii. m̄ſet. vi. dieſ. xiv.

.vii Gregoꝝ. q̄ uocat̄ Ildebranduſ. monach. añn. xii. m̄. i. d̄. iii. 7 ceſſef ep añn. ii.
     añn. d̄ñj. ott. Lxx. iii. Indictione. xvi.

.ii. Victor. q̄ 7 deſideriuſ cenobij caſſineñſis abbaſ m̄. iii. dieſ. vii. 7 ceſſī ep. vi. d̄. xxxvi.

.ii. Vrbanuſ ſedit añn. xi. m̄ſeſ. v. dieſ. xviii.

.ii. Paſchaliſ. ii. ſed añn. xviii. ō. v. dieſ. vii. 7 ceſſām epad. ii. dieſ.

.ii. Gelaſiuſ. ii. nat campan ſedit ann. i. 7 dieſ. v. 7 ceſſām epad. iiii. dieſ.

.ii. Calixtuſ. ii. nat galluſ. ſedit añn. v. m̄. x. dieſ. xvi. 7 ceſſāuepac. dieſ. v.

.ii. Honoriuſ 2

q̄ 2 11 dñ͡e

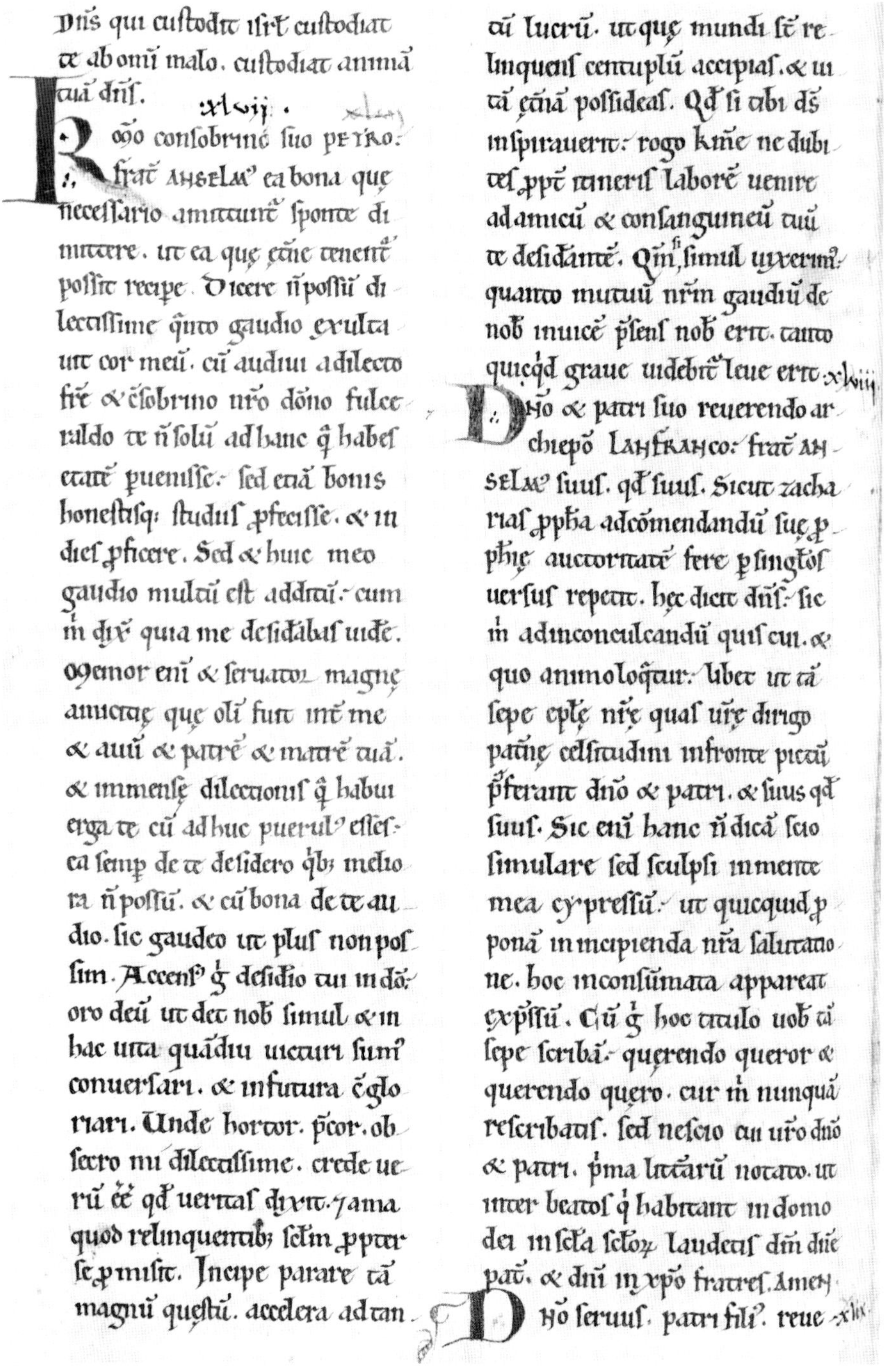

Left column

Dñs qui custodit isrł custodiat
te ab omni malo. custodiat animã
tuã dñs.   xlvij .

Rogo consobrino suo petro:
frat anselm' ea bona que
necessario amittunt' sponte dimittere. ut ea que ęterna tenent'
possit recipe. Dicere si possim dilectissime quanto gaudio exulta-
uit cor meu. cu audiui a dilecto
fře & consobrino nřo dono fulce-
raldo te ñ solu ad hanc q habes
etate puenisse. sed etiã bonis
honestisq; studiis pfecisse. & in
dies pficere. Sed & huic meo
gaudio multu est additu. cum
in dix quia me desidabis uide.
ogenor eni & seruator magne
amicitie que oli fuit int me
& auu & patre & matre tua.
& immense dilectionis q habui
erga te cu adhuc puerul' esses.
ea semp de te desidero qb; meliora ñ possu. & cu bona de te audio. sic gaudeo ut plus non possim. Accens' g desidio tui in do-
oro deu ut det nob simul & in
hac uita quãdiu uicturi sum'
conuersari. & in futura c̃ glo-
riari. Unde hortor. pcor. obsecro mi dilectissime. crede ue-
ru ee qd ueritas dixit. 7 ama
quod relinquentab; setm ppter
se p misit. Incipe parare tã
magnu questu. accelera ad tan..

Right column

cu lucru. utque mundi se re-
linquens centuplu accipias. & ui-
tã ęterna possideas. Qd si tibi ds
inspirauerit: rogo kme ne dubi-
tes ppt itineris labore uenire
ad amicu & consanguineu tuu
te desiderãte. Qñ simul uixerim'
quanto mutuu nřm gaudiu de
nob inuice plens nob ert. tanto
quicqd graue uidebit leue ert. xlviij

Dño & patri suo reuerendo ar-
chiepo lanfranco: frat anselm' suus. qd suus. Sicut zacha-
rias ppha ad comendandu sue p-
phie auctoritate fere p singłos
uersus repetit. hęc dicit dñs. sic
in ad inconculcandu quis cui. &
quo animo loq̃tur. libet ut tã
sepe epłe nře quas uře dirigo
patie celsitudini in fronte picta
pferant dño & patri. & suus qd
suus. Sic eni hanc ñ dicã scio
simulare sed sculpsi in mente
mea express̃u. ut quicquid p
ponã in incipienda nřa salutatione. hoc inconsumata appareat
expss̃u. Cu g hoc titulo uob tã
sepe scribi. querendo queror &
querendo quero. cur in nunquã
rescribatis. sed nescio an uřo dño
& patri. pma litterãru notato. ut
inter beatos q habitant in domo
dei in secła sctox laudetis dñm diie
patris. & dñi in xpo fratres. Amen

Dño seruus. patri fili'. reue xlix

Plate 9: Cambridge, Corpus Christi College 135, fol. 20v
(slightly reduced)

exceptis his que fragilitas humane nature ad su_
a exigit sustentatioe: ut ura cuersatio sep i celis
sit. anglica in omib; considate & imitamini con
uersatione. hec teplatio sit magistra ura. he sida
tio sit regla ura. Que uite anglice ccordat secta
mini. que ab illa discordat execramini. Anglos
uros sic dicit dns. angli eor sep uidet facie prii
mei. semp uob psentes. & acce & cogitat uros e
sidantes cogitate. & ita uelut si eos uisibilit i spi
ceretis sep uiuere curate. Ompc ds nuqua pmit
tat uos ab hoc ad qd puenistis deficere. s; semp
faciat uos ad meliora pficere. aoIE I———o———I;

A HS arepc frib; & filiis suis k mis. oro. orate p
me. monachis i cestrensi cenobio scq uuerbur
ge conmanentib;. sal & bndictioe dic & sua. Gras
ago do p gra sua qua ostendit i uob. & oro ut sic ea
de gra uos puenire dignac e. ita idesinent subse
quat: quatui nunq, uos de hoc ad qd uos puexit
pmittat deficere. s; semp ad meliora donec pfice
re. Qd pcerto ipse faciet. si n negligentes fueritis
bona ad gra puenistis seruare. Cu eni di sit sua
gra sep nos puenire: nrm e qd accepimi ei auxi
lio studiose custodire. Na quauis nec habe nec ser
uare possim aliqd n p illu: pde tu & deficere n
e nex nra negligentia. Q ue sepissime icipit a mi
nimis. i qb; nos callid hostis solet decipe. e nob p
suadet ea n magnipende. Inde naq; segr illud
danu execrabile qd legr. quia q despic paulati

dent pcauendo. maioris ū criminis auctor ēē uidet
ad qd multos impellit etiā si n uolendo. tam inor-
dinate plus qd mini quā qd maius erat ūindo.
Sed manifestū ÷ qa illi qui humili ūritaone su-
pbā uerecundā ūculcando. semet ipsos iudicantes.
indicenta cessaaone sponte ūsenaunt. multo cu-
aus ministrant pmissi seu etiā iussi. quā illi que-
recundia humana int dm & se iuste iudicare re-
fugiunt. licet is cui confitent ualde piculosius pro-
hibeat istos inuitos ut supdictū ÷ quā illos sponta-
neos. Et cū utrisq; necessariū sit ut ad tp abst-
nere. puto qa illi q non libent cessant. ad qd n bene
pparant sunt tantū relaxandi. ii ū q sponte absti-
nent. ad qd bene n psumunt etiā reuocandi. Nā
in illis si reuocent obedientie tegmine psūpao pal-
liatur. in istis ū humilitas robore adiuuat. Que
reuocaao n indifferent sed magna plaa ūfessione
suscipientas discreaone facienda est. Sepe nanq;
ūangit. ut qs n pimmisū criminis horroie & pui
humilitaas. humanā uerecundiā supet: sed per
stulaae tenebras & impudente duriaā. feditate
sceleris & pudore nsenaat. & p negligenaā officiū suū n appetat. Qui aute hui modi est. nunqm
ad sacrū officiū aut uocandus aut reuocandus est.
Sed cū pipso penitente supplicat humilitas. fug-
gent ūraao. inūedit uite mutaao. ū nimirū si
plat n ūa de meritis aliqb; quā de magna misericordia & de multaudine miseraaonū di illū

Plate 11: Hereford Cathedral P. I. 3, fol. 95v